Quiz Master

Quiz Master

Over 5,000 general knowledge questions

Collins

First published in 2006 by Collins
an imprint of
HarperCollins Publishers
77–85 Fulham Palace Road
London
w6 8jb

www.collins.co.uk

© 2006 HarperCollins

12 11 10
4

A cip catalogue record for this book
is available from the British Library

isbn 978-0-00-724256-6

Typset by Davidson Pre-Press, Glasgow
Printed and bound in Great Britain by
Clays Ltd, St Ives, plc

Mixed Sources
Product group from well-managed
forests and other controlled sources
www.fsc.org Cert no. SW-COC-1806
© 1996 Forest Stewardship Council

FSC is a non-profit international organisation established to promote the
responsible management of the world's forests. Products carrying the FSC
label are independently certified to assure consumers that they come
from forests that are managed to meet the social, economic and
ecological needs of present and future generations.

Find out more about HarperCollins and the environment at
www.harpercollins.co.uk/green

CONTENTS

Books
and
literature

The Classics

● ●

QUIZ 1
PART 1 – *Can you name the authors of these classic novels?*
1   Middlemarch
2   Jude The Obscure
3   Les Miserables
4   The Age of Innocence
5   Heart of Darkness
6   Wuthering Heights
7   Barchester Towers
8   Anna Karenina
9   Dracula
10 Tristram Shandy
11 Portrait of the Artist as a Young Man
12 Sons and Lovers
13 Germinal
14 The Bostonians
15 The Great Gatsby

Books and literature - The Classics

PART 2

1. Which Victorian writer wrote the popular *Barsetshire Chronicles*?
2. Which great English novel is narrated by Lockwood, resident of Thrushcross Grange?
3. Who are Alyosha, Dmitri, Ivan and Smolykov?
4. What is the name of the principal character in Jane Austen's *Mansfield Park*?
5. Who rode a horse called Rosinante and had a companion called Sancho Panza?
6. Who wrote the seminal work of science fiction, *2001: A Space Odyssey*?
7. Who lived at Thornfield Hall?
8. What was John Cleland's Victorian erotic classic?
9. James Hilton's *The Lost Horizon* is set in which fictitious Tibetan retreat?
10. Who wrote the swashbuckling adventure, *The Three Musketeers*?
11. What is George and Weedon Grossmith's only major work?
12. *Rebecca* and *Jamaica Inn* are sophisticated thrillers by which twentieth-century writer?
13. What served as balls in the mad croquet game in *Alice In Wonderland*?
14. Mark Twain's *The Adventures of Huckleberry Finn* was a follow-up, by popular demand, of which successful novel?
15. What was the name of the Giant who threatens to waylay the Pilgrim in *Pilgrim's Progress*?

? Tie-breaker

Who is the villainous Italian aristocrat in Wilkie Collins' The Woman In White, and who is The Woman?

Words

● ●

QUIZ 2
PART 1

1 What is the study of the origin of words?
2 Where would you be if you were up in front of the beak?
3 Who was the man who devised shorthand writing in 1837?
4 'Hissed all my mystery lectures' instead of 'missed all my history lectures' is an example of what?
5 By what name is an analgesic more commonly known?
6 What word indicates something accepted as correct and therefore suitable as the basis for a logical proposition?
7 A prelate is a member of what?
8 What is the opposite of cacophony?
9 And, on the same theme, what is the opposite of dissonance?
10 What comes in avoirdupois, troy or apothecaries?
11 In Spain it is Jerez; what do we call it?
12 What is the fear-inducing word spoken by a cult band of Knights in *Monty Python and the Holy Grail*?
13 What name is given to rule by the wealthy?
14 Boondocks, originally meaning a remote, rural area, metamorphosed in US slang into a general word for what?
15 How many letters are in the Hebrew alphabet: 12, 22 or 30?

Did you know?

Cockney rhyming slang is great fun, but very imprecise. Many of the phrases quoted on the Internet or in plays or books are simply invented by the writer. Amongst the genuine East and South London words or phrases are 'Would you Adam and Eve it, I went to get my barnet cut and fell down the apples and pears.' Or, 'Would you believe it, I went for a haircut and fell down the stairs.'

PART 2

1 LATENT: (a) fluid and milky (b) having potential (c) full and ripe, as a tree with fruit
2 SIDEWINDER: (a) a type of locking mechanism (b) a tropical rainstorm (c) a North American rattlesnake
3 IGNOMINY: (a) lack of knowledge (b) low or humble upbringing (c) public shame or humiliation
4 CONCORDANT: (a) in agreement (b) able to fly (c) tied together
5 LISSOM: (a) languid and easy-going (b) supple and lithe (c) not subject to a country's laws
6 FASCICULE: (a) monocellular marine life-form (b) an instalment (c) a rift between to glaciers
7 WINSOME: (a) determined and competitive (b) always at the ready (c) charming or engaging
8 THEISM: (a) study of pronouns (b) belief in God (c) belief in the rule of the masses
9 GLORIOLE: (a) a startling religious experience or epiphany (b) a flowering plant of northern Europe (c) a halo or small glory
10 PEREGRINATE: (a) to wander from place to place (b) to sleep in the day (c) to harbour vengeful thoughts

? Tie-breaker
If you were bashing out a ding-dong on the joanna in the East End, what would you be doing?

Books (non-fiction)

● ●

QUIZ 3
PART 1

1   What is the subject matter of Halliwell's guide, updated every year?
2   What was Alex Haley's account of the fight against the slave trade amongst black Americans in the south, later made into a major TV series?
3   Which humorous writer and performer wrote *Stately As A Galleon*?
4   *Our Kate* is the autobiography of which bestselling English novelist?
5   Who was the subject of James Boswell's groundbreaking and celebrated biography from 1791?
6   Who wrote the account of beatnik life in the 1950s in *On the Road*?
7   And what was Robert Pirsig's bestselling account of the 1960s?
8   *A Child Called It* is whose best-selling account of his difficult childhood?
9   Whose book, *Fever Pitch*, put football on the literary map?
10 Who had a bestseller with her account of the life of her husband, Billy Connolly?
11 What is the annual cricket publication whose Players of the Year awards are the game's most coveted accolade?
12 Who wrote the key feminist tract, *The Female Eunuch*, in 1970, aged 31?
13 *I Know Why The Caged Bird Sings* is the first of a cycle of autobiographical books by which African-American author?
14 *It Shouldn't Happen To A Vet* was the first in whose comic and moving accounts of life as a country vet after the war?
15 According to John Gray's bestseller, where are men and women from?

Did you know?

Publius Vergilius Maro (Virgil) was a poet and writer working during the revolutionary period in Rome. His first major work was the *Eclogues*, a philosophical reflection of rural life and the nature of love, mainly homosexual. His masterwork was a commission for Octavian, who wanted a celebration of Rome to mark his new status as Emperor. So was conceived the epic poem, *The Aeneid*.

Books and literature - Books (non-fiction)

PART 2 – *Match the biography/autobiography to the celebrity.*

1   *Memoirs Of An Unfit Mother*
2   *Addicted*
3   *Hitting Across The Line*
4   *Blessings In Disguise*
5   *Unreliable Memoirs*
6   *Grand Inquisitor*
7   *Long Walk To Freedom*
8   *Boy*
9   *Summoned By Bells*
10 *Bring On The Empty Horses*

A   John Betjeman
B   Roald Dahl
C   Robin Day
D   David Niven
E   Anne Robinson
F   Alec Guinness
G   Clive James
H   Tony Adams
I   Viv Richards
J   Nelson Mandela

? Tie-breaker

What was the subject matter of Virgil's The Georgics?

Shakespeare

● ●

QUIZ 4
PART 1

1 Which "green-eyed monster" does the scheming Iago use to bring down Othello and stir him to murder his innocent wife?

2 Who is Prospero's spirit-helper in *The Tempest*?

3 Who is married to the Duke of Cornwall in *King Lear*?

4 Who has a wife called Virgilia and a mother called Volumnia?

5 "Now is the winter of our discontent/Made glorious summer...". To which play are these the opening lines?

6 *The Merry Wives of Windsor* was written as a vehicle for which popular character from the history plays?

7 With whom is Henry Bolingbroke, later Henry IV, about to fight a duel at the start of *Richard II*?

8 Who is the lover of the goddess Venus, in a long poem by Shakespeare?

9 How many poems are in Shakespeare's Sonnet cycle: 24, 90 or 154?

10 In which play is a character tricked into eating her own children, in revenge for the rape and mutilation of another character's daughter?

11 What shocking task does Beatrice give Benedick to prove his love in *Much Ado About Nothing*?

12 At which famous battle does the King give the famous "Once more unto the breach..." speech in *Henry V*?

13 By what name is Robin Goodfellow referred to in *A Midsummer Night's Dream*?

14 "Dost thou think because thou art virtuous there shall be no more cakes and ale?" To which hypocrite does Sir Toby Belch bellow this line in *Twelfth Night*?

15 By what name are Proteus and Valentine known in the title of a Shakespeare play?

PART 2

1. Laertes, Polonius, Ophelia, Horatio, Gertrude: which of these is left standing at the end of *Hamlet*?
2. In which two cities are the two sets of twins living in *Comedy of Errors*?
3. In which play does a Count fall in love with a woman who falls in love with a page boy who is really a woman in love with the Count?
4. Which character delivers the famous "Friends, Romans, countrymen ..." speech from *Julius Caesar*?
5. Who delivers the famous "This sceptred isle" speech in *Richard II*?
6. Which late play concerns the arrogance and then comeuppance and reconciliation of King Leontes?
7. What must come to Dunsinane before Macbeth can fall?
8. In which play does Petruchio put an unruly Kate in her place?
9. Who is Angelo ordered to marry in the denouement to *Measure For Measure*?
10. Which Tom Stoppard play revolves around the off-stage antics and deliberations of two minor characters from *Hamlet*?
11. Which unfortunate character has his eyes put out in *King Lear*?
12. In which play does Jaques, a disillusioned courtier, deliver the famous 'Seven Ages of Man speech'?
13. What is the name of Juliet's cousin, slain by Romeo?
14. In *Cymbeline*, Imogen wakes next to the headless corpse of which villain?
15. Four lovers woo four ladies under the cynical eye of a courtier called Dumain: what is the play?

? *Tie-breaker*

What is the first name of Bottom in A Midsummer Night's Dream, what is his occupation, and what part does he play in the entertainment the rustics devise for the King and Queen?

Words and language

● ●

QUIZ 5
PART 1

1   What do Americans call jam?
2   Epistemology is the study of what, essentially?
3   What word is given to a listing of a rock band's output?
4   Which popular character in Sheridan's play, *The Rivals*, has given her name to the misuse of words?
5   Seismology is the study of what natural phenomena?
6   Which term, derived from the parcelling of official documents, is used to describe unnecessary bureaucracy?
7   What expression is used when an addict comes off drugs without any placebos or substitutes?
8   What is the name given to the hottest days of the summer, derived from the rising of the star, Sirius?
9   What would you employ a chippy for?
10 Where would you find a gunwale?
11 Which Latin word is used when there is a need for something to be repeated 'word for word'?
12 What does the word subcutaneous mean?
13 Yiddish, the Jewish language, is based on which North European language?
14 What is the Latin term for the voting mass or common people?
15 What is the third letter of the Greek alphabet?

PART 2 – *Identify these common text message abbreviations.*

1   BY
2   F2T
3   XLNT
4   M8
5   GMTA
6   G2G
7   SIT
8   TY
9   BBS
10 HAND
11 L8R
12 PCM
13 NE
14 B4N
15 FWD

? **Tie-breaker**

What word is given to a disease that spreads rapidly across the qlobe?

Children's books

●●●●●●●●●●●●●●●●●●●●●●●●●●

QUIZ 6
PART 1

1   Who are Meg, Jo, Beth and Amy?
2   In which city do Lyra's adventures begin in Philip Pullman's *Northern Lights*?
3   Who created Alex Rider, the teenage spy?
4   Which book features Hazel and Fiver amongst its animal heroes?
5   Who is the heroine of *It's Alright, I'm Wearing Really Big Knickers*, and *Knocked out By My Nunga-Nungas*, by Louise Rennison?
6   For what is the Kate Greenaway award handed out every year?
7   Who wrote the perennial Christmas favourite, *The Snowman*?
8   What is the surname of Charlie in Roald Dahl's *Charlie and the Chocolate Factory*?
9   In *Eragon*, what does the hero of the title find in the forest, looking like a polished blue stone?
10   Which character is No 1 in the series of Mr Men books?
11   What was the name of Captain Nemo's submarine in Jules Verne's *Twenty Thousand Leagues Under The Sea*?
12   The Disney movie, *The Little Mermaid*, is based on a fairy story by which author?
13   Who created the schoolgirl heroine, Tracy Beaker?
14   When was *Black Beauty* first published: 1877, 1907 or 1927?
15   What is the setting for Colin Dann's series of tales about the English countryside?

Books and literature - Children's books

PART 2

1 Writer Paul Stewart and illustrator Chris Riddell combine in which best-selling fantasy series?
2 What is Eric Carle's classic board book, first published in 1969, and still selling thousands of copies every year?
3 In Jonathon Stroud's *Bartimaeus Trilogy*, what is Bartimaeus?
4 In *The Lion, The Witch and The Wardrobe*, what kind of creature is The White Witch's lieutenant, Maugrim?
5 What is the name of the Hedgehog-housewife in Beatrix Potter's tales?
6 Who is the elf-captain trying to thwart Artemis Fowl in Eoin Colfer's books?
7 Which famous illustrator collaborated with Roald Dahl on most of his stories for younger children?
8 What is the occupation of Danny's father in *Danny The Champion of The World*?
9 Who writes about the mishaps that plague the Baudelaire children after they are orphaned?
10 What kind of creature is Tarka in Henry Williamson's classic nature story?
11 Who wrote the classic adventure story of Roman Britain, *The Eagle of the Ninth*?
12 Smuggler's Cove, Hangman's Tree and Death Creek are all geographical features in which children's novel?
13 What is the name of Hook's boat in *Peter Pan*?
14 Who wrote about Malory Towers and The Faraway Tree?
15 Who is the badly-behaved character at the centre of Francesca Simon's successful series for young readers?

? Tie-breaker
Who are the four children who break through into Narnia in The Lion, The Witch and The Wardrobe, and what is their surname?

Bestsellers

● ●

QUIZ 7
PART 1

1   Who wrote the bestselling romantic novel, *The Shell Seekers*?
2   Who is known for his bestselling legal thrillers, including *The Firm*, *Testament* and *The Last Juror*?
3   Who wrote the original books on which *The Forsyte Saga*, TV's first epic costume drama, were based?
4   *Light A Penny Candle* was the debut success for which multi-million selling Irish author?
5   Whose TV show has become a forum for promoting well-written but easily digestible novels?
6   *The French Lieutenant's Woman* was a cerebral seventies mystery by which author?
7   Who had an international hit with *Perfume*?
8   What was James Clavell 1975 novel, later a major TV series, which popularized Japanese history and culture?
9   *The Beach* was a psychological teaser from which admired young author?
10 What was the debut novel of writer, actor and comedian, Stephen Fry?
11 What was Sarah Waters's debut novel, later dramatized by the BBC, a historical novel with a Sapphic slant?
12 *House of Cards* was a witty and cynical novel of political high-jinks by which author, himself a political animal?
13 *Gridlock* and *Stark* are well-received novels by which articulate stand-up comic?
14 Who wrote the still-popular account of Martian invasion, *The War of the Worlds*, published in 1898?
15 *The Name of the Rose*, part murder mystery, part philosophy, was a major work by which Italian author?

Books and literature - Bestsellers

PART 2 - *Match the author to the book that helped launch their career.*

1 Margaret Atwood
2 Jeanette Winterson
3 Monica Ali
4 Martin Amis
5 Boris Starling
6 Iain Banks
7 Bruce Chatwin
8 Zadie Smith
9 Tony Parsons
10 Joanne Harris
11 Mary Wesley
12 William Golding
13 Paul Scott
14 Louis De Bernieres
15 Nick Hornby

A *The Camomile Lawn*
B *The Jewel In The Crown*
C *Messiah*
D *Man and Boy*
E *White Teeth*
F *Brick Lane*
G *The Rachel Papers*
H *Chocolat*
I *Lord of the Flies*
J *High Fidelity*
K *Oranges Are Not The Only Fruit*
L *Captain Corelli's Mandolin*
M *On The Black Hill*
N *A Handmaid's Tale*
P *The Wasp Factory*

? *Tie-breaker*
Who wrote Fatherland, the frightening "what if ..." account of a Britain under a Nazi regime after Hitler won the war?

Plays and drama

● ●

QUIZ 8
PART 1

1 Who sits in the wings with the text of the play in case an actor forgets their lines?
2 What is the New York equivalent of a fringe or non-West End production?
3 What are RADA, Guildhall and Rose Bruford?
4 *The National Health* and *A Day In The Death of Joe Egg* are among a number of biting satires by which modern playwright?
5 *Habeas Corpus* is an early dramatic work by which popular English writer?
6 Who wrote *The Mousetrap*, London's longest-running play?
7 Which famous play concerns Jack Worthing's "Bunbury-ing" activities?
8 Works like *Alcestis*, *Medea* and *Electra* showed which Greek dramatist more at home with strong female characters than his predecessors and contemporaries?
9 *Dancing at Lughnasa* is an award-winning play by which modern Irish dramatist?
10 And which earlier Irish playwright wrote *Juno and the Paycock* and *The Plough and The Stars*?
11 Which Greek tragedian wrote the trilogy known as the *Oresteia*: Sophocles or Aeschylus?
12 The Swan and The Other Place are satellites of which major theatre?
13 *Sergeant Musgrave's Dance* was an important sixties work by which dramatist?
14 Which great actor-manager was the star of The Lord Chamberlain's Men, who premiered many of Shakespeare's great plays, with him in the lead?
15 And to which theatre did they shift their performances when the Blackfriars Theatre was closed down?

PART 2 - *Match the playwright to the work.*
1 Samuel Beckett
2 Caryl Churchill
3 Bertholt Brecht
4 David Mamet
5 Harold Pinter
6 Anton Chekhov
7 Moliere
8 Tomberlake Wertenbakker
9 Ben Jonson
10 Edmond De Rostand
11 William Shakespeare
12 Tom Stoppard
13 Richard Brinsley Sheridan
14 August Strindberg
15 Terry Johnson

A *Night and Day*
B *The Homecoming*
C *Volpone*
D *Hitchcock Blonde*
E *Serious Money*
F *The Cherry Orchard*
G *Miss Julie*
H *Mother Courage*
I *Glengarry Glen Ross*
J *Waiting for Godot*
K *School for Scandal*
L *Cyrano De Bergerac*
M *The Misanthrope*
N *Our Country's Good*
O *Coriolanus*

? *Tie-breaker*
Which Shakespeare play about mistaken identity borrows plot lines from the Roman dramatist, Plautus? And which later Italian farce, by Carlo Goldoni, borrows heavily from both Plautus and Shakespeare?

Crime fiction

● ●

QUIZ 9
PART 1

1 Which mystery was the bestselling book of both 2004 and 2005?
2 What is the first name of Agatha Christie's Miss Marple?
3 *The Ice House* was the startling 1992 debut of which writer of psychological mysteries?
4 Which city is the main habitat for Ian Rankin's crime fiction?
5 What is the name of Kathy Reich's forensic scientist heroine in her bestselling novels?
6 Herman McNeile, writing as Sapper, created which popular fictional crime-solver between the wars?
7 What is the title held by Elizabeth George's aristocratic Inspector Lynley?
8 Lincoln Rhyme, hero of Jeffrey Deaver's murder mysteries, is hindered by what unusual factor?
9 *The Big Sleep*, immortalized as a movie starring Humphrey Bogart, was written by which American writer and features which hard-nosed private eye?
10 Who wrote the murder mysteries *Cover Her Face*, *Devices and Desires* and *Innocent Blood*?
11 Which contemporary author created the ex-Special Services LA private eye, Elvis Cole?
12 American crime writer Donna Leon sets her mysteries in which European city?
13 Who wrote *The Clerkenwell Tales*, a witty "retelling" of Chaucer's *Canterbury Tales* with a mystery woven in?
14 Who wrote the classic thriller, *The Thirty-Nine Steps*?
15 Which evil genius was the scourge of Sherlock Holmes, and plunged with him to his death off the Reichenbach Falls?

Did you know?

Ellis Peters' first Cadfael mystery was written in 1977, when she was sixty-four years old. The monk's passion for herbs and lore reveal the author's own interests. She had previously been a successful author of historical and contemporary romances under her real name, Edith Pargetter, but it was Cadfael who assured her international stardom.

PART 2 – *Match the writer and the sleuth.*

1   Agatha Christie
2   Patricia Cornwell
3   Dashiell Hammett
4   Janet Evanovich
5   Dorothy L Sayers
6   Ian Rankin
7   James Patterson
8   Colin Dexter
9   Michael Dibdin
10 Georges Simenon

A   Lord Peter Wimsey
B   Sam Spade
C   Stephanie Plum
D   Aurelio Zen
E   Inspector Morse
F   Hercule Poirot
G   John Rebus
H   Inspector Maigret
I   Kay Scarpetta
J   Alex Cross

? **Tie-breaker**
In which town were Ellis Peters' mediaeval Cadfael mysteries set, and who played the monk-sleuth on TV?

Harry Potter

● ●

QUIZ 10
PART 1

1   What do wizards call 'ordinary' humans?
2   And what is a wizard without any magical ability called?
3   What kind of creature is Dumbledore's pet, Fawkes?
4   Who was born as Tom Riddle?
5   Which student character dies at the end of *Goblet of Fire*?
6   What are the names of Harry's parents?
7   Who is the Defence Against The Dark Arts teacher in *Harry Potter and The Chamber of Secrets*?
8   What are the initials on the note Harry finds inside the fake Horcrux he and Dumbledore retrieve?
9   To which house does Draco Malfoy belong?
10 What is Tonks' first name, which she hates?
11 What is Ginny short for, as in Ginny Weasley?
12 What subject does Snape teach at Hogwarts in Books 1-5?
13 Who curses and kills Sirius at the end of *Order of the Phoenix*?
14 Who plays Mrs Weasley in the Harry Potter movies?
15 What is the name of the badly-behaved Hogwarts poltergeist?

PART 2

1   Where does Harry do most of his shopping before the start of term?
2   Who is the Hogwarts caretaker?
3   Who reveals himself as The Half-Blood Prince?
4   What is the name of the hippogriff saved from execution by Hagrid and the children?
5   Who does Ron start dating in revenge for Hermione telling him she kissed Viktor Krum?
6   Who is sacked as Minister For Magic and replaced by Scrimgeour in *The Half-Blood Prince*?
7   What is the name of the wizarding hospital?
8   What sort of creatures are Bane, Ronan and Firenze?
9   Which character's personality does Barty Crouch Jnr adopt to fool Harry in *Goblet of Fire*?
10 Who does Harry take to the Yule Ball in *Goblet of Fire*?
11 Who is the landlady of The Three Broomsticks in Hogsmeade?
12 Who is the Beauxbatons Champion in *Goblet of Fire*?
13 Which member of the Gryffindor Quidditch team is cursed in *The Half-Blood Prince*, but returns in time to help them win the cup?
14 Who plays Madame Hooch, the flying teacher and Quidditch referee, in the movies?
15 What is the name of Neville Longbottom's toad?

? **Tie-breaker**
Who is head of Ravenclaw House, and what does he teach?

The Bible

● ●

QUIZ 11
PART 1

1 Who was Abraham's first-born son, born when Abraham was 86-years-old, and who was his second-born, born when Abraham was 100?
2 After Jesus rose from the dead, how long did he remain on earth before ascending to heaven?
3 Where did the miracle of the loaves and fishes take place?
4 The books of Tobit, Sirach, Maccabees, etc., are known as what?
5 The Bible books of Matthew, Mark, Luke and John are known as the gospels (meaning "good news") of Jesus Christ. Which of the four books was the first one written, and which two tell the story of Jesus' birth?
6 How old was Noah when the flood began?
7 Who was the father of James and John, two of Jesus' Apostles?
8 Jacob had 12 sons: name them. What was the name of his only daughter?
9 Which prophet secretly anointed David as king?
10 Where was Jesus crucified?
11 How many books are in the New Testament?
12 In Jesus' parable of the Good Samaritan, a Jewish man had been beaten by robbers and left beside the road to die. Who passed by but did not stop to help the injured man?
13 After Paul (the first and most influential interpreter of Jesus' message and teachings) began teaching about Jesus in Damascus, some of his former allies conspired to kill him. How did he escape from the city?
14 Which young man sank into a deep sleep and fell out a third-story window while listening to Paul preach?
15 Where did God give Moses the Ten Commandments, and in what form?

PART 2

1   What were Sodom and Gomorrah?

2   The books of Genesis, Exodus, Leviticus, Numbers and Deuteronomy are known as what?

3   Who were Solomon's father and mother?

4   Of the books of the New Testament, which was the first to be written?

5   How many books are in the Protestant version of the Old Testament, and how many are in the Catholic version?

6   After King Saul died, David was elected king of Judah. After a bloody civil war, David emerged as king of all Israel. How long did David's reign over all of Israel last?

7   The Vulgate was the standard Bible of Christianity for many centuries. In what language was it written?

8   Which disciple said he would not believe Jesus had risen "... unless I see the nail marks in his hands and put my finger where the nails were, and put my hand into his side"?

9   After his misadventure at sea, God sent Jonah to the great Assyrian capital city of Nineveh. What was the message Jonah gave to the Ninevites?

10   Complete the following quotation from the book of Psalms: "Thou preparest a table before me in the presence of mine enemies: thou anointest my head with oil; _____ "

11   Which Jewish holiday commemorates Esther's heroic acts?

12   The first English translation of the Bible dates from 1290, 1332 or 1384?

13   How many languages has the Bible been translated into?

14   What was the name of the first Bible printed on a printing press, and in what year was it published?

15   The King James Version of the Bible was published in what year: 1585, 1603 or 1611?

❓ *Tie-breaker*

Noah had three sons. Which one of these was NOT one of his sons: Enos, Japheth, Ham or Shem?

Books – Prize winners

● ●

QUIZ 12
PART 1

1   Which British playwright, once seen as an experimentalist, but now a respected figure, won the Nobel Prize for Literature in 2005?
2   The Hugo and Nebula awards are given for books in which genre?
3   Richard Holmes won the 1989 Whitbread award for his acclaimed biography of which poet?
4   In 2001, Peter Carey won the Booker Prize for the second time with *True History of the Kelly Gang*. What was his first winner, in 1988?
5   What would you have to write to win a Smarties prize?
6   What was unusual about the 2003 award of the Whitbread novel (*Spies*) and biography (*Samuel Pepys*) prizes to Michael Frayn and Clare Tomalin?
7   Who has twice won the Pulitzer Prize for his 'Rabbit' sequence of novels?
8   For what is the annual Gold Dagger award presented?
9   In 2003, which debut novel won both the Whitbread first novel and the Booker prize?
10 Which novelist and champion of black African women was the last American to win the Nobel Prize for Literature in 1993?
11 Who won the Booker Prize for her novel, *The God of Small Things*?
12 Which Irish author won the Booker Prize for *Paddy Clarke Ha Ha Ha*?
13 William Hill sponsors an annual prize for the best book in which field?
14 Who are eligible for the Orange Prize for fiction?
15 In which year was the Booker Prize first awarded: 1955, 1969 or 1977?

Did you know?

The Whitbread Award is given each year in five categories: Novel, First Novel, Biography, Poetry and Children's Book. An overall winner is then chosen from the five category winners. Only once has the best children's book been overall book of the year, in 2001 when Philip Pullman's The Amber Spyglass won Book of the Year.

Books and literature – Books – Prize winners

PART 2 – *Match the author to their prize-winning novel.*

1 Matthew Kneale
2 Graham Swift
3 Ian McEwan
4 Anita Brookner
5 Kate Atkinson
6 Andrea Levy
7 Alan Hollinghurst
8 Jane Smiley
9 Carol Shields
10 Peter Ackroyd

A *The Stone Diaries*, Pulitzer, 1995
B *Behind The Scenes At The Museum*, Whitbread, 1995
C *Small Island*, Whitbread, 2004
D *The Line of Beauty*, Booker, 2004
E *Hotel Du Lac*, Booker, 1984
F *Hawksmoor*, Whitbread, 1985
G *English Passengers*, Whitbread, 2000
H *Last Orders*, Booker, 1996
I *A Thousand Acres*, Pulitzer, 1992
J *Amsterdam*, Booker, 1998

? **Tie-breaker**

Who is the only writer to have won the Whitbread novel award three times, with Children of Dynmouth (1976), Fools of Fortune (1983) and Felicia's Journey (1994)? Where is the author from?

Classics

● ●

QUIZ 13
PART 1

1   *The Modern Prometheus* is an alternative title to which famous 1818 Gothic horror story?
2   Which of Thomas Hardy's novels concerns the love of Clym Yeobright for Eustacia Vye?
3   Which was the only Dickens' novel to have a female narrator?
4   *Dangerous Liaisons* is based on Laclos' 1782 epistolary novel *Les Liaisons Dangereuses*. What is an epistolary novel?
5   Bruce Springsteen's album, *The Ghost of Tom Joad*, takes its name from a character in which US twentieth-century classic?
6   Whose novel, *The Glass Bead Game*, was published in 1943, twelve years after he began writing it?
7   Which novel features lands called Lilliput and Brobdingnag?
8   Whose collection of humorous poems, *Old Possum's Book of Practical Cats* became Andrew Lloyd-Webber's musical, *Cats*?
9   The Vietnam film, *Apocalypse Now*, has a plot loosely based on which work by Joseph Conrad?
10 *La Comedie Humaine* is a title given to the large body of work by which great French novelist?
11 In which American novel does Ishmael relate events aboard the *Pequod*?
12 Whose wife and lover are Tania Gromyko and Lara Antipova?
13 Alexandre Dumas fils' romantic novel, *La Dame Aux Camelias*, was turned into which famous opera?
14 Which 1928 novel by D.H. Lawrence was not officially published in Britain until 1960?
15 Which early English novel was loosely based on the story of Alexander Selkirk, a shipwrecked sailor?

PART 2 – *Match the character to the novel.*

1 Becky Sharp
2 David Balfour
3 Inspector Petrovic
4 Molly Bloom
5 Adela Quested
6 Michael Henchard
7 Maggie Tulliver
8 Catherine Earnshaw
9 Hester Prynne
10 Holden Caulfield
11 Paul Pennyfeather
12 Emma Roualt
13 Prince Andrei Bolkonsky
14 Lydia Bennett
15 Ursula Brangwen

A *Kidnapped* (Robert Louis Stevenson)
B *A Passage To India* (EM Forster)
C *The Mayor of Casterbridge* (Thomas Hardy)
D *War and Peace* (Leo Tolstoy)
E *The Catcher In The Rye* (JD Salinger)
F *Madame Bovary* (Gustave Flaubert)
G *Wuthering Heights* (Emily Bronte)
H *The Rainbow* (DH Lawrence)
I *Ulysses* (James Joyce)
J *Vanity Fair* (WM Thackeray)
K *Pride and Prejudice* (Jane Austen)
L *Decline and Fall* (Evelyn Waugh)
M *Crime and Punishment* (Fyodr Dostoevsky)
N *The Scarlet Letter* (Nathaniel Hawthorne)
P *The Mill On The Floss* (George Eliot)

? ## *Tie-breaker*
The Gothic romance is asserted by many critics to have begun with The Castle of Otranto, written by which son of a statesman?

Words

• •

QUIZ 14

PART 1 – *What do these foreign words or phrases mean in English?*

1   angst
2   billets-doux
3   mot juste
4   bona-fide
5   prêt-a-porter
6   parvenu
7   jihad
8   mal de mer
9   in flagrante delicto
10 au pair
11 magnum opus
12 dramatis personae
13 hoi polloi
14 hors de combat
15 carpe diem

PART 2 – *Here we give you two very different meanings of a word; you have to identify the word.*

1 Carriage; waste paper.
2 Improvement on investment; close attention.
3 Postal aid; Rooney's aberration.
4 Governmental body; bathroom furniture.
5 A prostitute; a rugby pack-forward.
6 Playing surface; tar.
7 Solid precipitation; cocaine.
8 Articulate; rapid.
9 Contemporary; the pull of a river.
10 Irritate; pointed object.
11 Garden creature; shot of booze.
12 Flatfish; glide over ice.
13 Crush; racquet game.
14 Tenacity; submittance.
15 Hold back; second string.

? *Tie-breaker*

What might you wear at work, but could also be an embracing whole?

What the Dickens

● ●

QUIZ 15

PART 1 – *Identify the Dickens novel from the characters listed.*

1 Sarah Pocket, Joe Gargery, Jaggers, Abel Magwitch
2 Frank Cheeryble, Newman Noggs, Sir Mulberry Hawk, Wackford Squeers
3 Tom Pinch, Sarah Gamp, Montague Tigg, Seth Pecksniff
4 Louisa Gradgrind, Sissy Jupe, Stephen Blackpool, Josiah Bounderby
5 Emily Wardle, Alfred Jingle, Sergeant Buzfuz, Sam Weller
6 Harriet Carker, Edith Granger, Susan Nipper, Captain Cuttle
7 Richard Carstone, Inspector Bucket, Tulkinghorn, Esther Summerson
8 Noah Claypole, Nancy, Mr Brownlow, Bill Sikes
9 Bradley Headstone, Mortimer Lightwood, Noddy Boffin, Silas Wegg
10 Barkis, Betsey Trotwood, Wilkins Micawber, Uriah Heep

PART 2

1   What was Dickens's first published novel?
2   In which city was the writer born?
3   What was the name of Dickens's wife?
4   Which Dickens novel was turned into an Oscar-winning musical film directed by Carol Reed?
5   What is Dombey's family firm's business in *Dombey and Son*?
6   Which up-and-coming actress played Lizzie Hexham in the adaptation of *Our Mutual Friend*?
7   The death of Little Nell was a major talking point in its day, but has often been ridiculed by critics as over-sentimental. In which novel does it happen?
8   Who directed the masterly 1946 film of *Great Expectations*?
9   Which central family in a Dickens novel lose their fortune in the Merdle banking scam?
10 *A Tale of Two Cities* is set during which historical period?
11 What is the school in *Nicholas Nickleby* where Nicholas teaches and takes Smike into his care?
12 What was Dickens's fifteenth novel, left unpublished at his death?
13 Who scripted the BBC's brilliant 2006 adaptation of *Bleak House*?
14 And which American actress earned plaudits for her portrayal of Lady Dedlock in that adaptation?
15 An early, almost equally good adaptation, in 1985, saw which Dame of the Empire playing the same part?

? *Tie-breaker*
What are the names of David Copperfield's two wives?

Plays and drama

● ●

QUIZ 16
PART 1

1 Which theatre is playwright Alan Ayckbourn indelibly linked, preferring to premiere many of his works there rather than in London?
2 Which seventeenth-century masterpiece revolves around the society love affair of Mirabell and Mrs Millamant?
3 Which writer, better known as a poet, wrote the dramas, *The Cocktail Party* and *The Family Reunion*?
4 *Romanoff and Juliet* is a play by which actor and wit?
5 Who are Masha, Irina and Olga?
6 If a French theatre audience cry "bis", what do they want?
7 The National Theatre complex comprises the Olivier, The Lyttelton and which other stage?
8 Who is Irish literary icon, Christie Mahon?
9 *Private Lives* and *Hayfever* were social dramas by which famous twentieth-century wit?
10 *The Rover* was the work of which pioneering seventeenth-century female playwright, a sometime pirate and adventurer?
11 What is the expression given to making a theatre appear full by giving away free tickets?
12 What is Tom Stoppard's play featuring "behind the scenes" interplay between minor characters from Shakespeare's *Hamlet*?
13 Which groundbreaking "kitchen-sink drama" told the story of the frustrations of Jimmy Porter and his put-upon wife, Alison, in the 1950s?
14 What is Dublin's famous theatre?
15 Which playwright, an admirer of and successor to Shakespeare, wrote the brutal melodramas, *The White Devil* and *The Duchess of Malfi*?

Books and literature - Plays and drama

PART 2 - *Identify the play from the dramatis personae.*
1 Wagner, Mephistopheles, Helen of Troy
2 Henry Higgins, Colonel Pickering, Freddy Eynsford-Hill
3 Sir Robert Chiltern, Mrs Marchmont, Viscount Goring
4 Alithea, Sparkish, Margery Pinchwife
5 George Hastings, Kate Hardcastle, Tony Lumpkin
6 Petey, Stanley, Lulu, Goldberg
7 Shelley Levene, George Aaronow, Richard Roma
8 Madame Ranevskaya, Lopakhin, Trofimov
9 Launcelot Gobbo, Bassanio, Jessica
10 Simon Shashava, The Fat Prince, Azdak

? Tie-breaker
Which Russian drama teacher is the founding father of method acting?

Did you know?

Method acting is the process whereby a performer totally immerses himself in his subject, trying to think like the protagonist he is playing in order to make the portrayal as realistic as possible. This method undoubtedly takes more out of the actor, and is difficult to achieve on stage. It has proved popular in modern cinema; Marlon Brando was an early proponent, and Robert De Niro and Daniel Day-Lewis are both avid followers of "method".

Bestsellers

● ●

QUIZ 17
PART 1

1   Who wrote *The Hunt For Red October* (1984), the debut outing for his popular character, Jack Ryan?

2   What was Audrey Niffenegger's surprise word-of-mouth bestseller of 2005?

3   How many mystery or crime novels did Agatha Christie write: 60, 80 or 120?

4   Whose fictionalized account of the US Civil War, *Cold Mountain*, was soon turned into a major Hollywood movie?

5   Whose works include the Tilly Trotter trilogy and the Hamilton series?

6   *The Fourth Protocol* and *The Dogs of War* are thrillers by which popular novelist?

7   What was Dan Brown's earlier work that also featured Robert Langdon, the main character in *The Da Vinci Code*?

8   *Along Came A Spider* (1992) was the chilling debut of which writer?

9   Who created the action hero Jason Bourne?

10 *Clan of the Cave Bear* was the first in a series of bestselling prehistoric tales by which US author?

11 Who wrote *Underworld* (1997), an epic account of the Cold War?

12 *Riders* (1986) cemented the reputation as a popular novelist of which journalist and socialite?

13 *The Other Boleyn Girl* and *The Boleyn Inheritance* are historical novels by which popular author of that genre?

14 *Hollywood Wives* and *Hollywood Husbands* were bestsellers for which celebrity sister?

15 What was the title of Andy McNab's bestselling account of the Falklands War, which led to his subsequent career as a novelist?

PART 2 – *Match the author to the series of sci-fi novels they wrote.*
1 Frank Herbert
2 Raymond E Feist
3 Trudi Canavan
4 Terry Brooks
5 Maggie Furey
6 Stephen King
7 Anne McCaffrey
8 Robert Jordan
9 George R Martin
10 Michael Moorcock
11 Isaac Asimov
12 Stephen Donaldson
13 Piers Anthony
14 Terry Pratchett
15 David Eddings

A *The Foundation Trilogy*
B *The Dragons of Pern* series
C *The Belgariad*
D *The Chronicles of Thomas Covenant, The Unbeliever*
E *Dark Tower* cycle
F *Elric/The Eternal Champion* books
G *Discworld*
H *The Artefacts of Power* series
I *The Dune Cycle*
J *The Shannara* series
K *Xanth* series
L *The Wheel of Time*
M *Riftwar Saga*
N *The Magician's Guild Trilogy*
P *A Song of Ice and Fire*

? **Tie-breaker**
What was the title of Dick Francis' 1957 autobiography, a bestseller that inspired him to start his series of successful racing mysteries?

Children's books

● ●

QUIZ 18
PART 1

1   What is the occupation of Montmorency, hero of Eleanor Updale's popular historical stories?
2   Which two characters, now with a TV series of their own, first appeared in Lauren Child's *I Will Not Ever Never Eat A Tomato* (2001)?
3   What is the sequel to Lewis Carroll's *Alice In Wonderland*?
4   What is the name of the lugubrious donkey in A.A. Milne's *Winnie The Pooh* tales?
5   Who is the little girl with an imaginary friend called Susan, who features in a series of 1920s children's books by Joyce Lancaster Brinsley?
6   Who or what is Darren Shan?
7   Who is the superhero created by George and Harold in Dav Pilkey's recent bestsellers?
8   For which children's character is the Reverend Awdry best known?
9   Martin Jarvis became the definitive voice of which children's book character, created by Richmal Crompton, when he narrated the stories on the radio?
10 Who has "terrible tusks, and terrible claws, and terrible teeth in his terrible jaws"?
11 Who is the dragon-hunter narrator in the bestselling picture book, *Dragonology*?
12 What is Babar, the hero of Jean de Brunhoff's stories, first published in the 1930's in France?
13 R. L. Stine made a fortune after creating which series of best-selling American scary stories?
14 What is Miffy, Dick Bruna's pre-school character?
15 Which writer/illustrator wrote a series of picture books about a young boy called Alfie?

PART 2 – *Match the children's classics to the author who wrote them.*

1 *Secret Garden*
2 *Little House On The Prairie*
3 *The Phantom Tollbooth*
4 *Superfudge*
5 *Peter Pan*
6 *The Wizard of Oz*
7 *The Jungle Book*
8 *Stig of the Dump*
9 *The Railway Children*
10 *The Water Babies*
11 *James and the Giant Peach*
12 *Charlotte's Web*
13 *Kidnapped*
14 *Tom Sawyer*
15 *Carrie's War*

A Judy Blume
B Nina Bawden
C L. Frank Baum
D Roald Dahl
E Norton Juster
F E. Nesbit
G Laura Ingalls Wilder
H Robert Louis Stevenson
I J.M. Barrie
J Charles Kingsley
K Frances Hodgson Burnett
L Mark Twain
M Rudyard Kipling
N Clive King
P E.B. White

? **Tie-breaker**
Name the five members of Enid Blyton's Famous 5.

Lord of the Rings

● ●

QUIZ 19
PART 1

1   Who is the King of Rohan in *Lord of the Rings*?
2   By what name is Aragorn first known to the hobbits when they meet him in Bree?
3   What is the name of Boromir's father?
4   Who rescues the hobbits from a malevolent oak tree in the Old Forest?
5   What was the name of the pony Sam bought from Bill Ferny in Bree?
6   Which of the Fellowship is made a Knight of the Riddermark for his courage during the Battle of Pellennor Fields?
7   What lies in wait for Sam and Frodo on the stairs of Cirith Ungol?
8   After the ring falls from Isildur's finger, who is its first victim when it is rediscovered?
9   In Tolkien's mythology, who is the "big bad" worshipped even by Sauron?
10 Who rescues Frodo and Sam from the slopes of Mount Doom?
11 Looking into which powerful object nearly drives Pippin mad?
12 What is the elvish name for Gandalf?
13 Which of the dwarves who travel with Bilbo in *The Hobbit*, is father to Gimli, one of the Fellowship in *Lord of the Rings*?
14 Osgiliath, the citadel lying as the first port of defence against Mordor, lies on which river?
15 Which elvish warrior comes to Frodo's aid at the Ford of Bruinnen in *The Fellowship of the Ring*?

PART 2

1   Who is the chief amongst the Ents?
2   What is the sustaining elven waybread that the hobbits take into Mordor?
3   What demonic opponent does Gandalf encounter in Moria?
4   Where is Legolas' home?
5   Who is the landlord of The Prancing Pony?
6   What is the name of the horse lent to Gandalf by the Rohirrim?
7   What are Alan Lee and John Howe best known for in the context of Tolkien's work?
8   By what name is Amon Sul known to the hobbits?
9   As Ring-Bearers, where are Frodo and Bilbo allowed to retreat when life becomes too burdensome?
10   What is the name of Tolkiein's son, who continued the work of editing and collating his work after his death?
11   Of what is the surcoat Bilbo gives to Frodo made, which saves his life in Moria?
12   After the main events of *Lord of the Rings* are over, the hobbits re-encounter the evil presence of Saruman in The Shire. Under what pseudonym is he operating??
13   By what name is the Witch-King of Angmar better known?
14   Where is the secret refuge of Henneth Annun?
15   What is the name of Sauron's fortress in Mordor?

❓ Tie-breaker
Who is the love of Aragorn, and who is her powerful father?

Cinema and television

Movies

● ●

QUIZ 20
PART 1

1 Who won both the Oscar and the BAFTA for her portrayal of Sally Bowles in *Cabaret*?
2 Which film festival awards a Palme d'Or to that year's 'Best-In-Show'?
3 Which Disney movie features a cool, jazz-loving tomcat called Thomas O'Malley?
4 'Take My Breath Away' was a No1 hit for Berlin on both sides of the Atlantic; which film propelled it to success?
5 Who played the title role in Shekhar Kapur's 1998 film of the life of Queen Elizabeth I, simply called *Elizabeth*?
6 Which epic Steven Spielberg family movie was released into cinemas on June 11th, 1982?
7 On whose novel (*Schindler's Ark*) was Steven Spielberg's *Schindler's List* based?
8 The 2004 blockbuster *I, Robot* was loosely based on whose sci-fi story?
9 What is Harvey in the movie starring James Stewart?
10 Which two box-office heavyweights teamed up on *Butch Cassidy and the Sundance Kid* (1969) and *The Sting* (1973)?
11 Which film features a mysterious sled called Rosebud?
12 Who died during the shooting of *Something's Got To Give* in 1962?
13 Who provides the voice of the donkey in *Shrek*?
14 Which movie features a weapons think-tank organization called the BLAND Corporation?
15 Which Shakespeare play did Baz Luhrman update with exciting results in 1996?

PART 2

1   What connects Michael Caine in 1966 and Jude Law in 2004?

2   What kind of car was Herbie in the comic caper, *The Love Bug*?

3   Who was the former Olympic swimmer who found a lucrative career as Tarzan on screen?

4   What is the name of Simba's wicked uncle in *The Lion King*?

5   What is odd about Charles Herman, Paul Bettany's character in the Oscar-winning *A Beautiful Mind*?

6   *The Magnificent Seven* is essentially an American-set remake of which Japanese classic?

7   *A Man For All Seasons* was an Oscar-winning historical drama starring Paul Schofield as which figure from English history?

8   What was the London film studio famous for such comedies as *The Lavender Hill Mob* and *The Ladykillers*?

9   Which composer is associated with director Peter Greenaway, having scored all his best movies?

10 Who played Billy's (Jamie Bell) dance tutor in *Billy Elliot*?

11 What was the surprise 1986 box-office smash from Australia starring comic Paul Hogan?

12 What connects Dustin Hoffman in *Tootsie* and Robin Williams in *Mrs Doubtfire*?

13 *sex, lies and videotape* was the thoughtful directorial debut of which major US director?

14 Nicole Kidman won an Oscar in 2003 for her portrayal of which literary figure in *The Hours*?

15 And Philip Seymour Hoffman won in 2006 for his performance in a title role as which other famous writer?

? ***Tie-breaker***
What are the names of the boy-gang and the girl-gang in Grease?

Soap operas

● ●

QUIZ 21
PART 1

1 In *Coronation Street*, which legendary rock band appeared as themselves in 2005?

2 Who reached No. 4 in the charts in 1986 with a vocal version of the theme tune of *Eastenders*, 'Anyone Can Fall In Love'?

3 In *Dallas*, what was the first name of Bobby and Pam's adopted son?

4 What is the name of the shop/cafe owned by Harold and Lou in *Neighbours*?

5 What was the BBC's ill-fated and short-running soap set in a Spanish resort?

6 In *Dynasty*, who did Blake Carrington's youngest daughter, Amanda, marry on the eve of a military revolution in his country?

7 Who played Sandy in *Crossroads*?

8 True or false: *Family Affairs* was the first programme to air on Channel Five in 1997.

9 In which year did *Emmerdale Farm* change its title to *Emmerdale*: 1982, 1989 or 1998?

10 In *Eastenders*, what was Alfie Moon's term of endearment for Peggy Mitchell?

11 In *Brookside*, what was the name of Frank Rogers' wife?

12 In *Hollyoaks*, what instrument does Rhys Ashworth play?

13 In *Coronation Street*, who did Gail describe as "Norman Bates with a briefcase" after he confessed to his wrongdoings?

14 In *Home and Away*, what was the name of the character played by Dannii Minogue, sister of Kylie?

15 What was the name of the local rival family with whom the Ewings had a long-running feud in *Dallas*?

PART 2 – *Match the character to the actor.*
1   Marlon Dingle (*Emmerdale*)
2   Sky Mangel (*Neighbours*)
3   Cliff Barnes (*Dallas*)
4   Liz McDonald (*Coronation Street*)
5   Terry Sullivan (*Brookside*)
6   Hattie Tavernier (*Eastenders*)
7   Sadie King (*Emmerdale*)
8   Alf Stewart (*Home and Away*)
9   Margaret Clemence (*Brookside*)
10 Doris Luke (*Crossroads*)
11 Robbie Jackson (*Eastenders*)
12 Brian Tilsley (*Coronation Street*)
13 Kristin Shepard (*Dallas*)
14 James 'Jambo' Bolton (*Hollyoaks*)
15 Amos Brearly (*Emmerdale*)

A   Brian Regan
B   Ronald Magill
C   Patsy Kensit
D   Christopher Quinten
E   Dean Gaffney
F   Kathy Staff
G   Will Mellor
H   Ray Meagher
I   Beverley Callard
J   Ken Kercheval
K   Michelle Gayle
L   Nicola Stephenson
M   Mark Charnock
N   Mary Crosby
O   Stephanie McIntosh

? *Tie-breaker*

Who did Ken Barlow have an affair with in 1989, resulting in Deirdre throwing him out just as midnight dawned on the New Year in 1990?

TV - Sitcoms

●●●●●●●●●●●●●●●●●●●●●●●●●

QUIZ 22
PART 1

1   What is currently (Aug '06) Britain's longest-running sitcom?
2   What was the surname of the family who featured in *The Cosby Show*?
3   What is the *Friends* theme song?
4   Who played Steptoe and Son in the comedy of the same name?
5   In which city was *I Love Lucy* set?
6   Who played Alf Garnett in *Till Death Us Do Part*?
7   What was the name of the Spanish waiter in *Fawlty Towers*?
8   In which sitcom did Nerys Hughes and Elisabeth Estensen play two flatmates?
9   What was the name of Richard Beckinsale's character in *Porridge*?
10 Who is the owner of the pie shop in *Blackadder II*?
11 In the very first episode of *The Office*, what item of Gareth's did Tim keep setting in jelly?
12 In *Cheers*, what was Sam Malone's former occupation?
13 Who created and wrote *Only Fools and Horses*?
14 What was Mrs Doyle's catchphrase in *Father Ted*?
15 In *Keeping Up Appearances*, what was the name of Hyacinth Bucket's husband?

PART 2

1   What was the name of the department store in *Are You Being Served*?
2   Who is The Cat's uncool alter-ego in *Red Dwarf*?
3   Who had a mother called Endora, played by Agnes Moorehead?
4   Who played Alice Springs Tinker in *The Vicar of Dibley*?
5   Who did Peri Gilpin play in *Frasier*?
6   What is Ben's profession in *My Family*?
7   What is the name of the Minister, later PM, in Antony Jay and Jonathan Lynn's *Yes Minister/Yes Prime Minister*?
8   Who starred as René in the WWII sitcom, *'Allo 'Allo*?
9   Who was Geraldine in *The Good Life*?
10 Which 1990s sitcom was about the goings-on at the Whitbury-Newton Leisure Centre, which was run by a very petty-minded manager?
11 In *Desmonds*, from where does Porkpie get his nickname?
12 In *Bread*, what was the occupation of Aveline's husband Oswald?
13 Who played Jeannie in *I Dream of Jeannie*?
14 After *The Good Life*, what was the sitcom created as an opportunity for Penelope Keith to reprise her aristocratic snob persona?
15 Which sitcom stars Will Mellor and Ralf Little and is set in Runcorn?

? Tie-breaker
Who are the creators, writers and stars of Kath & Kim?

Movies – action stations

● ●

QUIZ 23
PART 1

1   What is the name of Bruce Willis's character in the *Die Hard* movies?
2   Who made his name in the West with action movies like *Enter The Dragon* and *The Big Boss*?
3   Who plays Bill of the title in Tarantino's two-parter, *Kill Bill*?
4   Who plays the assassin playing mind games with Clint Eastwood in *In The Line of Fire*?
5   Comedy-action caper, *Shanghai Noon*, featured which double-act?
6   Who gave a scene-stealing performance as the evil Sheriff of Nottingham in *Robin Hood: Prince of Thieves*?
7   In which movie does Geena Davis turn from housewife Samantha Caine into blonde assassin, Charly Baltimore?
8   In which film would you encounter The Baseball Furies, The Lizzies, The Turnbull ACs and The Gramercy Riffs?
9   *Face/Off* allowed which two stars to enjoy a spot of role reversal?
10 Who plays Indiana Jones' father in *Indiana Jones and the Last Crusade*?
11 Where does the climactic battle at the end of *Lord of the Rings: The Two Towers* take place?
12 Who played Charlie's Angels in the screen version?
13 *First Blood* was the film debut of which action character?
14 Who played Arthur and Guinevere in the 2004 version of the legend?
15 Who plays the wheelchair-bound leader of the X-Men, Professor Charles Xavier?

PART 2 – *Match the action hero to the movie star.*

1 Trinity
2 Our Man Flint
3 Captain Blood
4 Jason Bourne
5 Outlaw Josey Wales
6 Daredevil
7 Casey Ryback
8 Ethan Hunt
9 Domino
10 Sarah Connor
11 Jack Sparrow
12 Spider-Man
13 Xander Cage, xXx
14 Buffy The Vampire Slayer
15 Wolverine

A Johnny Depp
B Tobey Maguire
C Ben Affleck
D Kristy Swanson
E James Coburn
F Keira Knightley
G Errol Flynn
H Steven Seagal
I Clint Eastwood
J Vin Diesel
K Linda Hamilton
L Carrie-Ann Moss
M Tom Cruise
N Matt Damon
P Hugh Jackman

? **Tie-breaker**
Who played Wyatt Earp in the following films: My Darling Clementine, Gunfight At The OK Corral, Wyatt Earp and Tombstone?

The name is Bond

● ●

QUIZ 24

PART 1 – *Name the Bond film.*

1   Bond battles a man with three nipples and a dwarf henchman.
2   A moon buggy chase and a romp with Bambi and Thumper.
3   Bond has to battle Whisper, the Baron and Tee Hee, as well as a big boss with a penchant for aliases.
4   In which the bad guy is a Maxwellian (or is that Murdochian?) media mogul.
5   A Bond girl seeks revenge for her parents' murder and Sheena Easton croons the title song.
6   Bond gets married – but it all ends in tragedy ...
7   Ninja and piranha.
8   Bond goes rogue in Colombia.
9   In which a villainous henchman gets electrocuted with his own hat.
10 Where the villain gives himself away by drinking red wine with fish, and Bond encounters a lady with sharp feet.
11 Bond abseils down a dam in a memorable opening sequence, and then encounters an old friend.
12 Unofficial *Thunderball* remake.
13 A bearded Bond is taken prisoner but comes to terms with his Jinx.
14 In which M is captured and Bond falls for the wrong pretty face.
15 Bond teams up with an unwilling Russian agent.

Did you know?

Ian Fleming, the creator of James Bond whose books were the source of the early movies, envisaged the part being played by the suave David Niven. Pierce Brosnan was undoubtedly the Bond closest to Niven in looks and manner.

PART 2 – *Match the Bond girl to the actress.*
1   Xenia Onotopp in *Goldeneye*
2   Solitaire in *Live and Let Die*
3   Mary Goodnight in *The Man With The Golden Gun*
4   Dr Holly Goodhead in *Moonraker*
5   Natalya Simyonova in *Goldeneye*
6   Kara Milovy in *The Living Daylights*
7   Paris Carver in *Tomorrow Never Dies*
8   Honey Rider in *Dr No*
9   Dr Christmas Jones in *The World Is Not Enough*
10 May Day in *A View To A Kill*

A   Teri Hatcher
B   Denise Richards
C   Britt Ekland
D   Maryan D'Abo
E   Grace Jones
F   Famke Janssen
G   Ursula Andress
H   Lois Chiles
I   Izabella Scorupco
J   Jane Seymour

? *Tie-breaker*
What was the make of Bond's gun for the first eighteen movies?

American telly

● ●

QUIZ 25
PART 1

1 Frasier Crane, of *Frasier*, was originally a character in which other US sitcom?
2 Which US show concerned the lives of the Fisher family and their undertaking business?
3 What is the name of Jennifer Garner's character in the complex spy thriller, *Alias*?
4 Which maverick film director was behind the cult show, *Twin Peaks*?
5 Who played laid-back Private Eye Jim Rockford in the seventies series?
6 Which TV series shot David Soul to stardom in the same decade?
7 Which TV soap launched the career of George Clooney?
8 By what name are Eric McCormack and Debra Messing remembered on US TV?
9 Which actor played Roseanne's husband Dan in *Roseanne*?
10 Which supermodel played Janine, a girlfriend of Joey's in *Friends*?
11 Who is Seinfeld's best buddy in the long-running US sitcom?
12 Liza Minnelli stars as Lucille 2, manipulative rival to one of which series' main characters?
13 Who hosted *The Tonight Show* from 1962 to 1992?
14 Who plays the avaricious former model, Gabrielle, in *Desperate Housewives*?
15 What was the name of Bill Cosby's character in *The Cosby Show*?

Cinema and television – American telly

PART 2 – *Match the actor to the character.*

1   Kojak in *Kojak*
2   Sam Malone in *Cheers*
3   Riley Finn in *Buffy The Vampire Slayer*
4   Samantha Jones in *Sex and the City*
5   Liz Parker in *Roswell*
6   Carmela Soprano in *The Sopranos*
7   Dana Scully in *X-Files*
8   Summer Roberts in *The OC*
9   Dr Elizabeth Corday in *ER*
10   Abigail Bartlet in *West Wing*
11   Dr Elliot Reid in *Scrubs*
12   Emily Waltham in *Friends*
13   Agent Dale Cooper in *Twin Peaks*
14   Brenda Chenoweth in *Six Feet Under*
15   Kim Bauer in *24*

A   Rachel Griffiths
B   Stockard Channing
C   Sarah Chalke
D   Mark Blucas
E   Rachel Bilson
F   Elisha Cuthbert
G   Kyle Maclachlan
H   Shiri Appleby
I   Gillian Anderson
J   Alex Kingston
K   Ted Danson
L   Telly Savalas
M   Helen Baxendale
N   Edie Falco
P   Kim Cattrall

❓ *Tie-breaker*

How many households watched the finale to the last series of M*A*S*H in 1983, the most watched programme of all-time on US TV?

Things that go bump

● ●

QUIZ 26
PART 1

1 What is a lycanthrope?
2 What was Joe Ahearn's six-part 1998 vampire TV series, with more than a nod to the *X-Files*, starring Jack Davenport and Susannah Harker?
3 What is the name of Laurell Hamilton's vampire hunter heroine?
4 *The Raven* and *The Fall of The House of Usher* are works by which early horror writer?
5 What are the shapeshifting foxes of Japanese folklore?
6 How old was Stephen King when his debut novel, *Carrie*, was published: 17, 27 or 43?
7 The 2004 film, *Underworld*, concerns a war between which two races of supernatural creatures?
8 Who wrote a series of novels about a vampire called Lestat?
9 Which creatures in Celtic mythology sing eerie laments after a death in the family?
10 The ghosts of Walter Raleigh and Anne Boleyn are said to haunt which London location?

Did you know?

The real ghost ship the *Marie Celeste* is at the heart of one of history's great unsolved mysteries. The ship was found off the coast of Portugal in 1872, drifting at sea with no-one aboard. She had set off from New York with ten people on board – the captain, his wife and daughter, and seven crew. There was some evidence of conflict, but the vessel was intact and seaworthy.

Cinema and television – Things that go bump

PART 2 – Horror Movies

1   Who played Dracula in Coppola's 1992 version of the tale?
2   And who was hammer Horror's most successful Count?
3   Who wrote the script for Robert Rodriguez' *From Dusk 'Til Dawn*, as well as appearing in the film?
4   In what year was Nosferatu, featuring Max Schreck, first released?
5   Which baroque early horror actor was known as 'The Man Of A Thousand Faces'?
6   What is the name of the razor-fingered killer in the *Nightmare On Elm Street* series?
7   Which actor was buried in his Dracula cape on his death in 1956?
8   Which openly homosexual director and, later, painter made horror movies for Universal in the thirties, including *Bride of Frankenstein*?
9   Whose 1968 debut, *Night of the Living Dead*, turned the horror genre on its head?
10 Which early horror actor made his lead debut in the 1931 version of Frankenstein?
11 Who made *Scream*, an homage to slasher movies, and a damn scary pic itself?
12 In which defining horror movie does Sissy Spacek wreak havoc at the high school prom?
13 What was the 2002 box-office hit starring Naomi Watts, a remake of a Japanese shocker from four years earlier?
14 What was James Wan's low-budget 2004 hit, with an equally nasty 2005 sequel?
15 What was Tobe Hooper's 1974 shocker about the ubiquitous group of teens being chased by Leatherface and his mad family?

? **Tie-breaker**
What is the name of the ghost ship, doomed to sail the seven seas forever?

Eastenders

● ●

QUIZ 27
PART 1

1 In which year did *Eastenders* first transmit: 1978, 1980 or 1985?
2 Soon after her arrival in the Square, and some time before her marriage to Mark Fowler, with whom did Lisa Shaw have a clandestine affair?
3 What was the name of Robbie Jackson's dog, later looked after by Gus?
4 Who played the shrill-voiced Bianca Jackson?
5 Who were Zoe Slater's unconventional parents?
6 What was the name of Sonia's baby, which she was forced to give up for adoption?
7 Who slept with both Tiffany Raymond and her mother, Louise?
8 Why was Jim Branning opposed to his daughter Carol's relationship with Alan Jackson?
9 What is the fictional London Borough of Walford's postcode?
10 Which *Eastenders* actress proved an adept ballroom dancer, winning the 2004 *Strictly Come Dancing* contest with ease?
11 What relation is Tony Hills to Kathy Beale?
12 What were the names of Joe Wicks' mother and father?
13 Which well-respected actor arrived in Walford in early 2006 as Kevin Wicks?
14 What was the occupation of Anthony Trueman, played by Nick Bailey?
15 Which two couples were married in a joint ceremony on New Year's Eve, 1999?

PART 2 – *Match the character to the actor.*

1 Martin Fowler
2 Ian Beale
3 Dot Cotton/Branning
4 Grant Mitchell
5 Sharon Watts/Rickman
6 Kelly Taylor
7 Michelle Fowler
8 Sarah Hills
9 Simon Wicks
10 Nana Moon
11 Laura Beale
12 Frank Butcher
13 Beppe Di Marco
14 Tiffany Mitchell
15 Joe Wicks

A Hilda Braid
B Martine McCutcheon
C Daniela Denby-Ashe
D Laetitia Dean
E James Alexandrou
F Mike Reid
G Hannah Waterman
H June Brown
I Paul Nicholls
J Susan Tully
K Michael Greco
L Ross Kemp
M Brooke Kinsella
N Nick Berry
P Adam Woodyatt

? *Tie-breaker*
Name the four Ferreira siblings; and their half-sibling.

Movies - Oscar winners

● ●

QUIZ 28

PART 1 – *(years given refer to the year the Oscar ceremony took place, unless otherwise stated).*

1   What is the proper title of the Oscar ceremony?

2   Frank Sinatra and Donna Reed won their only acting Oscars for supporting roles in which movie (1954)?

3   Which Shakespearean role won Laurence Olivier his only Best Actor Oscar in 1949?

4   In 1965 *My Fair Lady* scooped the big awards apart from Best Actress, which went to Julie Andrews for *Mary Poppins*. Why was this ironic?

5   Who won a sentimental Best Actor Oscar in 1969 for his portrayal of Rooster J Cogburn, and in which movie?

6   Which movie won Best Picture at the 2006 ceremony, and which other feature was widely expected to carry off the award?

7   Who won four Best Actress Oscars, the first in 1934 and the last nearly fifty years later in 1982?

8   The same actress shared the prize in 1969 with which star of *Funny Girl*?

9   *Sergeant York* and *High Noon* earned which actor a brace of Best Actor Oscars?

10 Which pair won Best Actor and Actress in 1998 for their roles in *As Good As It Gets*?

11 Which rock legend provided the Oscar-winning song 'Streets of Philadelphia' for the movie, *Philadelphia*?

12 Which country singer did Sissy Spacek portray to win her 1981 Best Actress Oscar?

13 Which Henry Mancini song won him an Oscar when used in the film *Breakfast At Tiffany's*?

14 Which movie earned the much-maligned Kim Basinger a thoroughly deserved Best Supporting Actress Oscar?

15 *The Sound of Music* won Best Picture in 1966; which was the next musical to scoop the award?

PART 2 – *All these movies won Best Picture and Best Director. Match the film to the director.*

1 *Lawrence of Arabia*
2 *The Apartment*
3 *The Godfather Part I*
4 *Schindler's List*
5 *Silence of the Lambs*
6 *Unforgiven*
7 *It Happened One Night*
8 *Annie Hall*
9 *Braveheart*
10 *A Beautiful Mind*

A Mel Gibson
B Jonathon Demme
C David Lean
D Ron Howard
E Billy Wilder
F Steven Spielberg
G Francis Ford Coppola
H Clint Eastwood
I Frank Capra
J Woody Allen

? Tie-breaker
Who won the Best Actress Oscar in both 1999 and 2005, and for which movies?

Did you know?

Both George C Scott and Marlon Brando declined to accept the Best Actor Oscar; Scott after winning in 1971 for his portrayal of General Patton, and Brando for Don Corleone in *The Godfather* at the 1973 ceremony.

SFTV

● ●

QUIZ 29
PART 1

1 Of what race was Mr Spock?
2 Who plays Buffy's watcher, Giles?
3 Which popular radio and TV SF show featured characters called Ford Prefect and Zaphod Beeblebrox?
4 Who takes over leadership of the rebels when Blake is killed in *Blake's 7*?
5 In *Red Dwarf*, who or what is Rimmer?
6 Which writer/director created *Buffy The Vampire Slayer*?
7 And what was his popular but mysteriously short-lived series about the crew of the ship 'Serenity'?
8 What is the name of second Slayer who manifests when Buffy briefly loses consciousness at the end of the first series? (The character doesn't appear until S2.)
9 In which series does Kathryn Janeway lead the crew of a stranded starship?
10 *Smallville* concerns the early life of which super-hero?
11 Which Hollywood celeb plays bartender Guinan in *Star Trek, The Next Generation*?
12 Richard Dean Anderson starred in which successful spin-off from a movie, which started a long run in 1997?
13 In *Charmed*, what is a whitelighter?
14 Which early sixties SF series gave Julie Christie an early career boost in the title role?
15 Which children's TV show featured a spoof SF series called *Pigs In Space*?

PART 2

1 Who succeeded William Shatner as the ship's captain in *Star Trek: The Next Generation*?

2 Who was the original creator of *Star Trek*?

3 Who got her big break as lesbian teenager, later lesbian ghost in *Hex*?

4 Who played the fleet's commander in the 2003 revamp of *Battlestar Galactica*?

5 Which SF series features characters called Chiana, Ka D'Argo and Aeryn Sun?

6 What is Lt Worf, first of *Next Generation*, later of *Deep Space Nine*?

7 Which semi-robotic race is the scourge of the crew in *Star Trek: The Next Generation*?

8 Who is the object of Lister's fantasies who joins the *Red Dwarf* team for the last series?

9 What is the name of the Mayor, the big bad in S3 of *Buffy The Vampire Slayer*?

10 Who are Piper, Phoebe and Paige?

11 What is the name of Spike's mad girlfriend in S2 of *Buffy The Vampire Slayer*?

12 What is the name of the shape-shifting member of the crew in *Deep Space Nine*, who lives in a tank because his natural form is a liquid?

13 Which character in *Buffy The Vampire Slayer* becomes a werewolf during the show?

14 What was the eighties series about a group of humans based in Los Angeles resisting an alien invasion?

15 Who was the Federation officer played by Jacqueline Pearce who constantly harassed *Blake's 7*?

? *Tie-breaker*

Which former Buffy character is re-united with Angel at the start of Angel? And which other appears later in Angel, S1 as a self-styled "Rogue Vampire-Hunter"?

Quotes – The movies

● ●

QUIZ 30
PART 1

1   "I would like, if I may, to take you on a strange journey ..." are the narrator's opening lines to which movie?
2   "I shall stay until the wind changes." Whose promise?
3   "Violence in real life is terrible; violence in the movies can be cool. It's just another colour to work with." Whose rationale for the violence in his movies?
4   "I now pronounce you men and wives." The final words to which musical?
5   "You're only supposed to blow the bloody doors off!" From which classic crime movie?
6   "Major Strasser has been shot. Round up the usual suspects." Which earlier movie lent the title to Bryan Singer's 90s thriller?
7   "Forget it Louis. No Civil War picture ever made a nickel." Irving Thalberg advises against taking an option on turning which book into a movie?
8   "We're on a mission from God." Who were?
9   "There's no reason to become alarmed, and we hope you'll enjoy the rest of your flight. By the way, is there anyone on board who knows how to fly a plane?" A stewardess in which movie?
10 "My acting range? Left eyebrow raised, right eyebrow raised." Whose honest appraisal of his limitations?
11 "Mother – what's the phrase? – isn't quite herself today." Who is being weird in what movie?
12 "I don't know how to kiss, or I would kiss you. Where do the noses go?" Ingrid Bergman gets to grips with kissing whom in *For Whom The Bell Tolls*?
13 "Don't torture yourself, Gomez. That's my job." Which adoring wife?
14 "If I made Cinderella, people would be looking for the body in the coach." Who?
15 "It's just a meat parade in front of an international television audience." What is George C. Scott talking about?

PART 2

1   "My name is Maximus Decimus Meridius, Commander of the Armies of the North, General of the Felix Legions, loyal servant to the true emperor, Marcus Aurelius. Father to a murdered son, husband to a murdered wife. And I will have my vengeance, in this life or the next." Which actor is coming over all macho?

2 "I believe God made me for a purpose. But he also made me fast. When I run, I feel His pleasure." From which sport movie?

3 "Listen, strange women lyin' in ponds distributin' swords is no basis for a system of government. Supreme executive power derives from a mandate from the masses, not from some farcical aquatic ceremony." Trenchant political stuff from which movie?

4 "They may torture my body, break my bones, even kill me. Then they will have my dead body, not my obedience." Who's being a bit of a rebel?

5 "Above all things I believe in love! Love is like oxygen. Love is a many-splendoured thing. Love lifts us up where we belong. All you need is love!" From which film is this little pop montage of a quote?

6 "It sort of cools the ankles, doesn't it?" Who, in classic pose?

7 "I'm loud, and I'm vulgar, and I wear the pants in the house because somebody's got to. But I am not a monster." Whose rant from Who's Afraid Of Virginia Woolf?

8 "Man: No man can be friends with a woman that he finds attractive. He always wants to have sex with her. Woman: So you're saying that a man can be friends with a woman he finds unattractive. Man: No. You pretty much want to nail them too." An exchange from which movie?

9 "Forgive me, Majesty. I am a vulgar man! But I assure you, my music is not." Whose disclaimer?

10 "To call you stupid would be an insult to stupid people. I've known sheep that could outwit you; I've worn dresses with higher IQs. But you think you're an intellectual, don't you, ape?" Who is insulting whom in which movie?

11 "I could dance with you 'til the cows come home. On second thought, I'd rather dance with the cows 'til you came home." A gem from which comic actor?

12 "I'm gonna make him an offer he can't refuse." Who in which film?

13 "Greed ... is good! Greed is right! Greed works! Greed clarifies, cuts through, and captures the essence of the evolutionary spirit ... Greed ... will save the USA." An eighties mantra from which definitive movie of that decade?

14 "Life's a bitch. Now so am I." Who, after undergoing a transformation?

15 "Let me see if I've got this straight: in order to be grounded, I've got to be crazy and I must be crazy to keep flying. But if I ask to be grounded, that means I'm not crazy anymore and I have to keep flying." What is being explained here?

? *Tie-breaker*

Han Solo is about to be deep-frozen by Jabba The Hut. Leia cries out, "Han, I love you!" What is Solo's reply?

Dr Who

● ●

QUIZ 31
PART 1

1   Who played Dr Who in the very first episodes?
2   What is the name of the meddling Time Lord, the Doctor's nemesis, who opposed him in many story lines?
3   What is the Doctor's favourite piece of kit, used for opening doors and for substituting various other electronic devices?
4   What is the name of the Daleks' home planet?
5   Who played Madame de Pompadour, who has a romantic liaison with the Doctor in *The Girl In The Fireplace* in 2006?
6   Which former child-star played Mel, companion to Sylvester McCoy?
7   Who is the commanding officer of UNIT, the crack army team who helped Jon Pertwee in many episodes?
8   Who lived on Gallifrey?
9   What was the name of Jon Pertwee's companion played by Katy Manning?
10 Which acclaimed scriptwriter was given the task of bringing Dr Who into the twenty-first century?
11 Who guest-starred as Queen Victoria in *Tooth and Claw* in 2006?
12 John Barrowman played which recurring character in the 2005 series?
13 What is the name of the secret Government covert ops centre that the Doctor visits at the end of the 2006 series?
14 What was the favourite fashion accessory of Patrick Troughton's Doctor?
15 Who created the Daleks during the very first series of Dr Who?

PART 2

1 Who played the ninth Doctor in the triumphant return to the screen in 2005?
2 Who was the Doctor in two made-for-TV movies in the 1960s?
3 What did Mary Tamm and Lalla Ward have in common?
4 What is the name of Rose's mum, and who plays her?
5 Companion Zoe Heriot (Wendy Padbury) had an exceptional degree in what subject?
6 Which Doctor had a penchant for jelly babies?
7 Whose full name was Perpugilliam Brown?
8 What encoded name leads the Doctor and Rose to the secret of the Dalek invasion at the end of the 2005 series?
9 Who connects Dr Who with Blue Peter?
10 Who guest starred as Victor Kennedy (aka The Abzorbaloff) in Dr Who in 2006?
11 Who played a vet in *All Creatures Great and Small* before Dr Who, and a real doctor afterwards in *A Very Peculiar Practice*?
12 Who played the Doctor in the one-off TV movie in 1996?
13 In which UK city was the 2005 episode, *Boom Town*, set?
14 Which monster is controlling events aboard Satellite Five in *The Long Game* (2005)?
15 In which year was Dr Who first transmitted: 1961, 1963 or 1966?

? *Tie-breaker*
Which character, a companion in the 1970s, returned in 2006, and which other favourite accompanied her?

TV - miscellaneous

● ●

QUIZ 32
PART 1

1   Who presented *Bullseye* for nearly 15 years?
2   Who in the 70s and 80s was widely regarded as the king of British chat-show hosts?
3   Who is the only original character left in the long-running series *Casualty*?
4   Which ex-*Neighbours* actor appears in the US drama series *The OC*?
5   *Brideshead Revisited* was adapted from whose novel?
6   Who played Detective Mary Beth Lacey in *Cagney and Lacey*?
7   Name the five toys that appeared with the presenters on *Play School*?
8   In the penultimate episode of *Cold Feet*, which character was killed in a road accident?
9   Which drama series told the harrowing story of women suffering under the cruel regime of their Japanese captors during the Second World War?
10 Which suburban housewife took her own life at the beginning of the first series of *Desperate Housewives*?
11 True or false: Janet Jackson, sister of Michael, appeared in the US TV series *Fame*?
12 Which medical drama series was set in the Peak District?
13 Who played *Dr Quinn, Medicine Woman*?
14 Who was the creator and presenter of *Don't Forget Your Toothbrush*?
15 What was the song sung by Paddy and Tucker at a wedding reception in *Soldier, Soldier*, which the actors later released as a single, reaching No. 1 in the UK charts?

PART 2

1 Who played Filthy, Rich and Catflap in the comedy series of the same name?
2 In *Champion the Wonder Horse*, what was the name of Ricky's dog?
3 What was the name of the pop group created by the talent show Popstars?
4 Where does Homer Simpson work?
5 Who did the wacky voiceovers on the original version of *Celebrity Squares*?
6 What was Colonel Steve Austin, played by Lee Majors, better known as?
7 Who was the first person to win a million pounds on *Who Wants To Be A Millionaire*?
8 What was the name of the chef played by Lenny Henry in the comedy series of the same name?
9 Which popular early evening drama series, set in Cornwall, was based upon the four novels by Winston Graham?
10 Which US long-running serial medical drama was created by Michael Crichton?
11 What is the name of the weekly series that features hymns being sung in various churches and cathedrals around the country?
12 *Bad Girls* was about life inside which fictitious prison?
13 What number do the Kumars live at?
14 Who lived in Ten Acre Field at Scatterbrooke Farm?
15 Which programme took neighbours, friends or relatives and split them into two teams with the challenge of creating a makeover for a room in each other's houses?

? *Tie-breaker*
Who was the leader of the Tooting Popular Front? And who played him?

Movies – gangsters, molls, cops and robbers

● ●

QUIZ 33

PART 1 – *Name the movie*

1 De Niro does Capone, Connery does a barnstorming cop, and Costner does Eliot Ness. Plus David Mamet script and Morricone score. What's not to like?

2 John Travolta excels as Chilli Palmer in this entertainingly foul-mouthed comedy gangster movie.

3 Daniel Day-Lewis chills the blood as old-time gangster, Bill The Butcher.

4 Howard Hawks does Chandler and Bogey woos Bacall.

5 Angelica Huston and Annette Bening as John Cusack's mother and wife in tale of small-time hustlers.

6 Barbara Stanwyck leads Fred McMurray into darkness in the archetypal noir thriller.

7 Gene Hackman as Popeye in pursuit of drug-runners.

8 Jack Nicholson gets a slit nostril and lot of grief from Faye Dunaway.

9 Coen Brothers' debut.

10 James Cagney's Rocky goes to the chair at the end of a career-defining performance.

11 Sydney Greenstreet's delightfully talkative villain, Kasper Gutman, is just one of the treats in John Huston's 1941 debut.

12 De Niro and Scorsese's first visit to their favourite New York milieu.

13 The tale of Mr Barrow and Ms Parker.

14 Tom Hanks running from a suave and almost silent Jude Law.

15 Paul Muni or Al Pacino; take your pick.

74

Cinema and television –
Movies – gangsters, molls, cops and robbers

PART 2

1 Who won an Oscar as a pregnant cop in The Coen Brothers' *Fargo*?
2 Who was Married to The Mob in the gangster-comedy of that name?
3 Who gave a mature and laid-back performance as Raymond Chandler's Private Eye Philip Marlowe in Robert Altman's 1973 version of *The Long Goodbye*?
4 Who played the fatally enmeshed couple in *Body Heat*?
5 Who plays the pivotal role of Danny Ocean in Steven Soderbergh's remake of *Ocean's Eleven*, and who was the original?
6 Who played the moll to Bob Hoskins psychotic gangster in *The Long Good Friday*?
7 Which movie features Orson Welles as the enigmatic and untrustworthy Harry Lime?
8 Who played Breathless Mahoney alongside Warren Beatty in the title role of *Dick Tracy*?
9 Which actress provides the love interest in *The Fast and The Furious*?
10 Which gangster movie veteran played the villainous Rico opposite Bogart in *Key Largo*?
11 Who plays the title role in Tarantino's *Jackie Brown*?
12 *Serpico* and *Dog Day Afternoon* were both collaborations between Sydney Lumet and which lead actor?
13 Who made the hugely successful Brit crime caper, *Lock, Stock & Two Smoking Barrels*?
14 What was the name of the sexy animated moll in *Who Framed Roger Rabbit*?
15 Who played the femme fatale Bridget in John Dahl's underrated 1994 thriller, *The Last Seduction*?

? Tie-breaker

Who stars alongside Dennis Quaid as an assistant DA drawn into a relationship with a crooked cop in The Big Easy? And what is The Big Easy?

TV – children's

●●●●●●●●●●●●●●●●●●●●●●●●●

QUIZ 34
PART 1

1 Who created The Clangers?
2 What colour is Tinky Winky in *Teletubbies*?
3 In *Crackerjack*'s Double or Drop game, what did the contestants get if they answered a question wrongly?
4 On whose books is the TV series *The Story of Tracy Beaker* based?
5 In *Bob the Builder*, what is the name of Farmer Pickles's dog?
6 The sea shanty 'Barnacle Bill' is the theme tune to which long-running children's magazine programme?
7 What did TISWAS stand for?
8 Who was head teacher of Grange Hill from 1981 until 1991?
9 In what does SpongeBob Squarepants live?
10 Which series features Joey Potter and Pacey Witter?
11 Which TV drama features the Society for the Protection of our Lives Against Them (SPLAT)?
12 What was the name of the plasticine character who appeared with Tony Hart on several programmes, including *Take Hart* and *Hart Beat*?
13 In *Chigley*, who lived at Winkstead Hall?
14 Who are Throttle, Modo and Vinnie?
15 In *Jamie and the Magic Torch*, how were Jamie and his dog, Wordsworth, transported to Cuckoo Land?

PART 2

1   Who was the presiding presence on the sofa in *Jim'll Fix It*?
2   Who had a cat called Jess?
3   In *Hey Arnold*, who secretly adores Arnold, despite the fact that she calls him "football head"?
4   Tommy, Chuckie, Philip and Lillian are better known as what?
5   Who was Captain Pugwash's mortal enemy?
6   Who narrated his own story, *The Old Man of Lochnagar*, in Jackanory?
7   What was the name of the all-female team of fighter pilots who help the hero in *Captain Scarlet*?
8   What was the magic incantation that turned Prince Adam into He-Man in *He-Man and the Masters of the Universe*?
9   Which Saturday morning show provided the wrap-around for *The Arabian Nights* cartoon?
10 What was set in the town of Pontypandy?
11 What was the name of the band that appeared in *The Muppets*?
12 What connects *The Goodies* and *Bananaman*?
13 What was the ITV network's long-running, but less successful, rival to *Blue Peter*?
14 Before Emily sang her song to waken Bagpuss, what form did Bagpuss take?
15 What was the name of the drama, starring Julia Sawalha and Dexter Fletcher, in which a group of school pupils ran a newspaper entitled the Junior Gazette?

? *Tie-breaker*

Who are the four Teenage Mutant Ninja Turtles?

Telly cops

● ●

QUIZ 35
PART 1

1   When is *Foyle's War* set?
2   Which influential Steve Bochco police drama first aired in 1981 on NBC, and won eight Emmy awards for its first series?
3   What was the name of Helen Mirren's character in the series of TV films under the *Prime Suspect* banner?
4   And who scripted the first three films in the series?
5   Popular American show, *CSI*, concerns which branch of detective work?
6   Who took over from John Hannah in portraying Ian Rankin's Inspector Rebus on the TV screen in 2006?
7   Which TV detective drives a Bristol 410?
8   Who was the cynical cop-turned-private detective played by Jimmy Nail in a series written by Nail and Ian La Frenais?
9   Who played DCI Red Metcalfe in the chilling *Messiah* and its follow-ups?
10 Who plays DI Jack Frost in the Yorkshire TV series, *A Touch of Frost*?
11 Who made an almost definitive Sherlock Holmes in Granada's exhaustive dramatisation of Conan Doyle's books in the 80s and early 90s?
12 Who played George Cowley, Bodie and Doyle's boss in *The Professionals*?
13 Who played DS Mel Silver, whose brutal death in *Waking The Dead* provoked howls of outrage from the show's fans?
14 Who played Pat Chappel in the hard-hitting police drama, *The Vice*?
15 Who was the star of the spoof police drama *The Thin Blue Line*?

PART 2 - *Match the policeman or sleuth to the actor.*

1   George Carter (*The Sweeney*)
2   DI Peter Pascoe
3   DCS Christopher Foyle
4   Supt Sandra Pullman (*New Tricks*)
5   Sgt Barbara Havers (*Inspector Lynley*)
6   DS Jim Bergerac
7   Dr Sam Ryan (*Silent Witness*)
8   DI Sam Tyler (*Life On Mars*)
9   DS Peter Boyd (*Waking The Dead*)
10 Dr Gil Grissom (*CSI*)
11 Sonny Crockett (*Miami Vice*)
12 DCI Jim Taggart
13 Sgt Lewis (*Morse*)
14 DCS Barlow (*Softly Softly*)
15 DI Wexford

A   Colin Buchanan
B   John Nettles
C   George Baker
D   Mark McManus
E   Don Johnson
F   Dennis Waterman
G   John Simm
H   Amanda Burton
I   Kevin Whateley
J   Sharon Small
K   Stratford Johns
L   William Petersen
M   Michael Kitchen
N   Amanda Redman
P   Trevor Eve

? ***Tie-breaker***
Who played Tom Quinn and Zoë Reynolds in Spooks, and what happened to them during filming?

Movies – funny stuff

• •

QUIZ 36
PART 1

1   Which 1977 movie won Woody Allen his only Best Director Oscar the following year?
2   What exactly is Baby in *Bringing Up Baby*?
3   Who wrote the screenplay for *Four Weddings and A Funeral*?
4   *A Shot In The Dark* was the follow-up to which successful 1963 comedy?
5   *Carry On Cleo* featured which unlikely duo as Caesar and Mark Antony?
6   Who plays the middle-aged man dreading his daughter's wedding in Minnelli's *Father of the Bride* (1950)?
7   Who made the classic silent movie, *The General*, in 1927?
8   What is the joke behind the name of John Cleese's character in *A Fish Called Wanda*, Archie Leach?
9   In teen movie terms, who were Misses Duke, McNamara, Chandler and Sawyer?
10 Who was the original Nutty Professor in 1963, and who starred in the 1996 remake?
11 Simon and Garfunkel had a No1 hit in the US with 'Mrs Robinson', a song written for which movie?
12 Who played the two small-time crooks dressed as nuns in the 1990 comedy, *Nuns On The Run*?
13 True or false: *Sex and the City*'s Kim Cattrall appeared in *Police Academy*?
14 Otis B Driftwood and Rufus T Firefly are both characters played by which comic genius?
15 Who had an Animal House, a Class Reunion and a Loaded Weapon?

PART 2 – *Match the comedy to the star(s).*
1   *Sweet Home Alabama*
2   *Some Like It Hot*
3   *Blazing Saddles*
4   *Ace Ventura, Pet Detective*
5   *The Odd Couple*
6   *Shallow Hal*
7   *It Happened One Night*
8   *Fletch*
9   *The Jerk*
10 *Deuce Bigalow: Male Gigolo*
11 *Meet The Parents*
12 *Trading Places*
13 *Up In Smoke*
14 *Bill and Ted's Excellent Adventure*
15 *Road To Morocco*

A   Dan Aykroyd and Eddie Murphy
B   Clark Gable and Claudette Colbert
C   Chevy Chase
D   Bob Hope and Bing Crosby
E   Steve Martin
F   Ben Stiller and Robert De Niro
G   Jim Carrey
H   Tony Curtis and Marilyn Monroe
I   Reese Witherspoon
J   Gene Wilder
K   Keanu Reeves
L   Gwyneth Paltrow and Jack Black
M   Jack Lemmon and Walter Matthau
N   Rob Schneider
P   Cheech and Chong

? **Tie-breaker**
Who played The Wedding Singer in the film of that name from 1998, and who played his waitress-love-interest?

The Simpsons

● ●

QUIZ 37
PART 1

1   Who is Homer's employer?
2   Who is Marge Simpson's mother?
3   Who provides the voice for Homer Simpson?
4   What is the surname of Bart's best friend, Millhouse?
5   Short versions of the cartoon were originally aired on which comedian's show?
6   What is the name of the school caretaker?
7   What is the series name for the 'scary' episodes shown around Hallowe'en?
8   What was the name of the Grammy-winning barbershop quartet containing Homer, Apu, Skinner and Barney?
9   Which well-known US sitcom actor provides the voice for Sideshow Bob?
10   George Bush Snr disapproves of *The Simpsons*; he once stated that he would rather Americans behaved like which other TV family?
11   What happened to Homer's pet lobster, Pinchy?
12   What religion did Lisa adopt in 'She of Little Faith'?
13   Who, or what, is Santa's Little Helper?
14   Lionel Hutz and which other character were retired in 1998 as a mark of respect after the untimely death of voice actor Phil Hartman?
15   What is the brand of beer brewed in Springfield?

PART 2

1   Who is Mr Burns's sycophantic PA?
2   Roy Snyder and Constance Harm share which occupation in the show?
3   What was the title of the first full-length episode aired?
4   Which British writer is the only celebrity guest to have been given the honour of writing an entire episode?
5   Which of these characters is NOT voiced by the same actor (Hank Azaria): Moe, Principal Skinner, Chief Wiggum, Apu?
6   Who is also known as Diamond Joe?
7   Which gangster character is voiced by movie actor, Joe Mantegna?
8   What is the cartoon "show within a show", a parody on Tom and Jerry and other Toons?
9   Bart briefly owned a pet called Stampy; what animal was Stampy?
10 What sort of products does Ned Flanders' shop sell?
11 What is the name of Apu's wife?
12 What is the name of the Simpson's family doctor?
13 What is the name of the Reverend Lovejoy's errant daughter?
14 Which teacher at the school was once engaged to Principal Skinner?
15 Who voiced Lisa's equally brilliant classmate, Allison Taylor, in the sixth-season episode, 'Lisa's Rival'?

? **Tie-breaker**
What is Krusty The Clown's real first name, and what is his father's occupation?

Reality TV

●●●●●●●●●●●●●●●●●●●●●●●●●●●●●

QUIZ 38
PART 1

1   In *The Apprentice*, what was the popular catchphrase used by Alan Sugar when eliminating a candidate?

2   In the first series of *Hell's Kitchen*, who injured himself on the first night and had to be replaced?

3   "Where is East Angular [sic]? Is it abroad?" Which contestant became renowned for this quotation, and many other startling feats of ignorance, in the third series of *Big Brother*?

4   Who won the second series of *The Farm* in 2005?

5   What was the name of the show in which 10 celebrities competed against each other, by doing Olympic-style events, such as weight lifting, gymnastics and diving?

6   The first series of which reality show was won by Jayne Middlemiss and Fran Cosgrave?

7   Who was the presenter of the companion show *Big Brother's Little Brother*?

8   Which two contestants met on *I'm A Celebrity, Get Me Out Of Here!* and have since married?

9   Which show features the domestic life of a rock and roll singer and his dysfunctional family?

10 Name the show commissioned by the BBC in 2000 that took 36 men, women and children from the British public and placed them on Taransay, a remote Scottish island in the Outer Hebrides, for a year.

11 Who was the comedian and winner of *Celebrity Big Brother* in 2001 who, during the eviction of another housemate, briefly absconded to sneak a quick kiss with his wife?

12 Which show marooned a group of contestants on a desert island and split them into two tribes?

13 What condition does the winner of *Big Brother 7*, Pete Bennett, have?

14 In the fourth series of *Celebrity Fit Club*, who was relieved of their captaincy after declaring, "I'm not going to have a stupid, spotty, pubescent little youth yelling at me!"

15 In which makeover reality show was a room built to accommodate a large collection of teapots, when, overnight, the shelves collapsed, decimating the valuable collection?

Cinema and television – Reality TV

PART 2 – *Match the reality shows to their presenters.*

1 Hell's Kitchen
2 Big Brother
3 Celebrity Love Island
4 Supernanny
5 Celebrity Fit Club
6 Big Brother's Big Mouth
7 The Farm
8 I'm A Celebrity, Get Me Out Of Here!
9 Changing Rooms
10 The Games

A Anthony McPartlin and Declan Donnelly
B Justin Ryan and Colin McAllister
C Kirsty Gallacher
D Laurence Llewelyn-Bowen
E Jo Frost
F Davina McCall
G Dale Winton
H Patrick Kielty
I Russell Brand
J Gordon Ramsay

? *Tie-breaker*

Which series sent two young, wealthy urban socialites to work with people in a variety of jobs and environments?

Did you know?

As of the end of *Big Brother 7* in 2006, 156 housemates have inhabited the house (not including the eight participants in Teen Big Brother). Thirty-three of those were celebrities, including Chantelle Houghton, the non-celebrity contestant in *Celebrity Big Brother 4*.

Cult TV

● ●

QUIZ 39
PART 1

1 Who narrated the children's animation *Bod*?
2 What is the name of the town in the television version of *The League of Gentlemen*?
3 What was the name of the van the Scooby-Doo gang travelled around in?
4 In *The Office*, who played the receptionist Dawn Tinsley?
5 Who first hosted *Blankety Blank*?
6 What was the name of Milly's boyfriend in *This Life*?
7 In *Prisoner: Cell Block H*, what was the nickname given to the unpleasant warder Vera Bennett?
8 What was the No. 1 hit for the *Spitting Image* puppets in 1986?
9 Who played Constable Benton Fraser in *Due South*?
10 What was the anarchic TV programme starring Tim Brooke-Taylor, Graeme Garden and Bill Oddie?
11 Who played Dr David Banner in the 1970s television series *The Incredible Hulk*, and who played the green monster?
12 What is Buffy's full name in the television version of *Buffy the Vampire Slayer*?
13 Which Scottish singer played Crockett's ill-fated love in *Miami Vice*?
14 In the children's animation *Ludwig*, what was Ludwig and what musical instrument did he play?
15 Who plays the PM in the recurring sketch in *Little Britain*?

PART 2

1 Which two actors provided the voices for Dangermouse and his sidekick Penfold?
2 In which century is *Babylon 5* set: 22nd, 23rd or 25th?
3 Who played Max, the loyal, gravel-voiced housekeeper to Jonathan and Jennifer Hart in *Hart to Hart*? What was the name of their dog?
4 Which BBC newsreader narrated *Mary, Mungo and Midge*?
5 Whose murder was being investigated in *Twin Peaks*?
6 Which character did Pamela Anderson play in *Baywatch*?
7 In *The Herbs*, what was the magic word that allowed entry into the magical walled garden?
8 True or false: *Countdown* was the third programme aired on Channel 4.
9 Which kids programme featured Uncle Bulgaria and Orinoco?
10 Who played Sapphire and Steele in the sci-fi series of the same name?
11 Which character did Ralf Little play in *The Royle Family*?
12 What is the name of the hotel in *Neighbours*?
13 In *The Sopranos*, what is the name of Tony Soprano's therapist?
14 In which year was *The Weakest Link* first broadcast: 1999, 2000 or 2002?
15 What is the name of the federal agent played by Kiefer Sutherland in *24*?

? **Tie-breaker**
In *Blake's 7*, what was Blake's first name, and who played him?

Star Wars

● ●

QUIZ 40
PART 1

1 What is the name of Han Solo's spaceship?
2 And who is his extremely hairy co-pilot?
3 On which planet does Obi-Wan Kenobi hide Luke?
4 Which star-in-the-making played Amidala's double, Sabe, in *Phantom Menace*?
5 Which icy planet is the setting for the opening of *The Empire Strikes Back*?
6 Which Senator raises Leia on Alderaan?
7 What is the name of the Ewoks' home planet?
8 What was Luke's call sign in the attack on the Death Star in Episode IV?
9 Who composed the music for all six *Star Wars* movies?
10 Of what race is Jar-Jar Binks?
11 The film originally released as *Star Wars* in 1977 now carries which official title?
12 Who is the leader of the Rebel Alliance fleet in *Return of the Jedi*?
13 What is the Sith name of Senator Palpatine?
14 What is the name of Jabba The Hutt's adviser/interpreter?
15 Who is the separatist commander killed by Obi-Wan on Utapau?

PART 2 – *Match the actor to their part in the Star Wars series.*

1 Harrison Ford
2 Ian McDiarmid
3 James Earl Jones
4 Carrie Fisher
5 Natalie Portman
6 Anthony Daniels
7 Samuel L. Jackson
8 Terence Stamp
9 Denis Lawson
10 Frank Oz
11 Daniel Logan
12 Christopher Lee
13 Keisha Castle-Hughes
14 Billy Dee Williams
15 Hayden Christensen

A C-3PO
B Anakin Skywalker
C Lando Calrissian
D Wedge Antilles
E Princess Leia
F Padme Amidala
G Count Dooku
H The Emperor
I Voice of Darth Vader
J Supreme Chancellor Valorum
K Queen of Naboo
L Voice of Yoda
M Mace Windu
N Boba Fett (Clones)
P Han Solo

? *Tie-breaker*
Who is Obi-Wan's Jedi mentor, and who plays him?

Movies – cult and controversy

● ●

QUIZ 41
PART 1

1   *Up Pompeii* revolves around the unique delivery of which comedian?
2   Who plays various members of an aristocratic family being murdered by Dennis Price in the Ealing comedy, *Kind Hearts and Coronets*?
3   *The Ring*, starring Naomi Watts, was a remake of a horror movie originally made in which country?
4   Summerisle, with Christopher Lee as its secretive Lord, is the setting for which cult mystery?
5   *Barbarella* was a sci-fi comedy starring which heavyweight actress in an uncharacteristic sex-symbol role?
6   Who plays Withnail to Paul McGann's I in *Withnail and I*?
7   Which director of fifties' 'turkeys' was himself the subject of a film by Tim Burton in 1994?
8   Who wrote the script, as well as acting in, the cult vampire shocker, *From Dusk Till Dawn*?
9   Who played Hawkeye in Robert Altman's original film of *M*A*S*H*, and who would make the role his own in the long-running TV series?
10 What is the name of the mysterious master-criminal in Bryan Singer's *The Usual Suspects*?
11 Which early Johnny Depp movie had the star playing the delinquent teenage leader of The Drapes in a rock'n'roll comedy?
12 Who made his name churning out watchable B-movies in the 1950s, including *Little Shop of Horrors* and *The Tomb of Ligeia*?
13 Which reggae star played the lead in the Jamaican-set gangster film, *The Harder They Come* (1972)?
14 *Secrets and Lies* and *Naked* are dramas by which experimental British director?
15 What was unusual about the dialogue in Derek Jarman's 1976 *Sebastiane*?

PART 2

1   What is the setting for Alan Clarke's *Scum* (1979), remade as a movie after the BBC banned it?

2   What was Tobe Hooper's 1974 shocker about a group of youngsters under attack from a family of psychos?

3   *The Cook, The Thief, His Wife and Her Lover* was a controversial offering from which art-house director?

4   Which director made the bad taste specials, *Pink Flamingos* and *Female Trouble*, both starring the transsexual cult heroine, Divine?

5   What was Michael Winterbottom's 2004 movie featuring erotic scenes interspersed with footage from concerts attended by the lead characters?

6   David Fincher's murkily shot epics, *Seven* and *Fight Club*, both starred which physically imposing Hollywood star?

7   "Oh behave," became a playground catchphrase after Mike Myers used it in which comedy role?

8   Which director refused, for many years, to allow a video release of his movie *Clockwork Orange*, so disgusted was he by the censors' treatment of the film when it came out in 1971?

9   Which controversial 1996 David Cronenberg film juxtaposed sexual pleasure with the vicarious viewing of traffic accidents?

10 *Theatre of Blood* features which star as a vengeful actor killing off theatre critics in a variety of Shakespearean ways?

11 Roger Vadim's *And God Created Woman* was basically an opportunity for which actress (Vadim's wife) to lounge around in titillating poses?

12 What was the influential 1969 road movie directed by Dennis Hopper and starring Hopper himself and Peter Fonda?

13 What was John Carpenter's 1974 directorial debut about four lonely astronauts recording video diaries of their space trip?

14 And who got his big break as cynical hero Snake Plissken in the same director's 1981 offering, *Escape From New York*?

15 Who gave a brave and excellent performance as child-abuser-on-parole Walter in the 2004 film, *The Woodsman*?

? *Tie-breaker*

Which city provided the beautiful backdrop for Nicolas Roeg's psychological thriller, Don't Look Now? And who starred as the couple at the heart of the drama?

TV - great TV moments

● ●

QUIZ 42
PART 1

1   What did Basil advise Polly not to mention, and then mention repeatedly himself, in *Fawlty Towers*?
2   Which newsreader shocked the nation, when she revealed she had legs, by dancing with Morecambe and Wise?
3   Who was served with divorce papers on Christmas Day in 1986?
4   Which chat show host did Grace Jones famously attack?
5   Which characters shared a lesbian kiss in *Brookside*?
6   Who interviewed Princess Diana on *Panorama*?
7   On which programme was prime minister Margaret Thatcher confronted by a viewer over the sinking of the *Belgrano*?
8   Who shot J.R.?
9   "Well, I am afraid it will have to wait. Whatever it was, I am sure it was better than my plan to get out of this by pretending to be mad. I mean, who would have noticed another madman around here? Good luck everyone." Which series came to an.end with these final words?
10   Who did the world see released from prison on February 11th, 1990?
11   Which period drama provided a thrill for its audience when Colin Firth emerged from a lake, dripping wet?
12   From which programme do the memorable lines "A pint? That's very nearly an armful!" and "Rhesus? They're monkeys aren't they?" come from?
13   Whose death was greeted with extraordinary public grief, with the funeral at Westminster Abbey drawing an estimated three million mourners in London, as well as worldwide television coverage?
14   Who is Del Boy standing next to when he famously falls through the bar in *Only Fools and Horses*?
15   To whom did Jeremy Paxman keep asking the same question over and over again on *Newsnight*?

PART 2

1   What was the name of the elephant that made a mess of the *Blue Peter* studio?
2   What did football commentator Kenneth Wolstenholme cry as England beat Germany in the 1966 World Cup Final?
3   Why did many people buy their first television set in 1953?
4   What, to the horror of the world, exploded shortly after its launch in 1986?
5   An estimated 750 million people watched who get married in 1981?
6   What "giant leap for mankind" occurred on July 20th, 1969?
7   Who was interviewed by Jeremy Paxman on the 1997 election night prior to the calling of his own seat (which he lost) and was stumped by the question of "Are we seeing the end of the Conservative Party as a credible force in British politics?"
8   Who were the Sex Pistols interviewed by on the *Today* show?
9   What is Ronnie Barker actually asking for when Ronnie Corbett presents him with four candles in the DIY shop sketch?
10 Whose news reports from Ethiopia shocked the nation in 1984?
11 Yosser Hughes demanded "Gissa job!" on which drama series?
12 Who punched Rachel in *This Life*?
13 In Monty Python's dead parrot sketch, what reason does the shopkeeper (Michael Palin) give for the parrot having been nailed to its perch?
14 What did an estimated 1.5 billion viewers, across 100 countries, watch on July 13th, 1985?
15 In *Dad's Army*, what is Captain Mainwaring's foolish response to the German commander's demands to know Pike's name?

? **Tie-breaker**
What was the BBC's long-running watchdog programme led by Esther Rantzen? Who provided light-hearted moments by reading out misprints from periodicals in a lugubrious manner?

History

The 21st century - 2001

●●●●●●●●●●●●●●●●●●●●●●●●●●

QUIZ 43
PART 1

1   What struck El Salvador with a magnitude of 7.6 and 6.6 on January 13th and February 13th, respectively?
2   Which Welsh entertainer and member of the Goons died on April 11th, aged 79?
3   Who won the Nobel Prize for Peace?
4   Which television musical talent show debuted in 2001?
5   In Rhyl, Wales, who punched countryside protester Craig Evans in front of television cameras? Why?
6   Which 2001 film is about a professional thief who, with his former partner in crime and a team of con-artists, plans to rob three Las Vegas casinos?
7   Who resigned from the British cabinet for the second time on January 24th?
8   Which two airlines had their planes hijacked on September 11th?
9   The first film of a trilogy was released in cinemas on December 19th. What was its full title and who directed it?
10   Who won the Ladies' Singles at Wimbledon?
11   What countryside crisis began on February 20th?
12   What was the title of Blue's first album, released in 2001?
13   In which country were two Libyans tried by a Scottish Court after being charged with 270 counts of murder in connection with the bombing of Pan Am Flight 103 over Lockerbie in 1988?
14   Which film debuted in November 2001 and made stars out of its child actors Daniel Radcliffe, Rupert Grint and Emma Watson?
15   On which date was the Labour Party elected for a second term in the General Election: June 7th, June 17th or July 7th?

PART 2

1 Which country won the rugby Six Nations championship?
2 Who became prime minister of Israel on February 6th?
3 Which band reached No. 2 in the UK charts with 'Teenage Dirt Bag'?
4 Who was sent to prison for perjury and perverting the course of justice on July 19th? How long was the sentence?
5 Which two Hollywood A-listers were divorced on August 8th?
6 Which former president of Yugoslavia surrendered to police Special Forces, to be tried on charges of war crimes?
7 Which epic film won Best Picture at the 73rd Academy Awards?
8 What is the name of the man who attempted to set his shoe, filled with explosives, on fire whilst on a flight from Paris to Miami on December 22nd? What is he also known as?
9 Who became the youngest person to conquer Mount Everest, and at what age?
10 Which American musician and singer from a band widely considered as the first punk rock group died of lymphoma on April 15th?
11 Which two countries signed the Treaty of Good Neighbourliness and Friendly Cooperation on July 16th?
12 Who was the comedy sci-fi author who died from a heart attack, aged 49?
13 Which prime minister was elected for a third term in Australia?
14 Where did the 27th G8 summit take place, with massive demonstrations against the meeting by anti-globalization groups?
15 What did Apple Computer release on October 23rd, and what did Microsoft release on October 25th?

? *Tie-breaker*

Which 2001 musical film tells the story of a young poet and writer, Christian, who falls in love with actress and courtesan, Satine?

Name the year

• •

QUIZ 44

PART 1 – *Identify the year these events took place – to make it easier they are in chronological order.*

1   Munich air crash kills most of Manchester United squad, Charles de Gaulle forms Fifth Republic in France, Jailhouse Rock is the year's biggest-selling single.

2   Nelson Mandela sentenced to life imprisonment, Match of the Day is first broadcast, *The Sun* is launched.

3   Charles Manson incarcerated for life, Disney World opens in Orlando, Florida Decimal currency introduced to the UK.

4   First *Star Wars* film released, Spain holds first free election for over 40 years, Steve Biko dies in a South African jail.

5   Unemployment tops 3 million in Britain, Freddie Laker's Airways company collapses, Channel 4 is launched.

6   Corporal punishment is abolished in state schools, a gunman murders 14 people in Hungerford in Berkshire, Van Gogh's 'Irises' sold for £27m.

7   Three IRA members shot dead in Gibraltar, Peter Wright's *Spycatcher* is published, 'Desire' becomes U2's first No1 single.

8   Robert Maxwell is lost at sea, John Major launches Citizens' Charter, John McCarthy is released after five years in captivity.

9   Channel Tunnel opens, Oasis' *Definitely Maybe* hits top of album chart, Start of the first Premier League season.

10 Good Friday agreement reached in Northern Ireland, Cher has year's biggest selling single with 'Believe', France win the World Cup on home soil.

Did you know?

Otto Von Bismarck was a conservative Prussian Minister who succeeded in uniting the German states into one nation, whilst keeping Prussia at the heart of that federation. Bismarck continued to cement Germany's position as a major European power until he fell foul of the new Kaiser and was dismissed.

History - Name the year

PART 2

1. French agents sink the Greenpeace boat *Rainbow Warrior*, Toxteth riots, the *Achille Lauro* is hijacked with 420 passengers on board.
2. Juan Peron elected President of Argentina, Bill Clinton born, Derby County win the FA Cup.
3. Vietnamese overthrow Pol Pot in Cambodia, Jeremy Thorpe acquitted of conspiracy to murder, Pope John Paul II visits Ireland.
4. Tate Modern opens in London, fuel price protests lead to shortages, Concorde crash kills 113 in Paris.
5. Portsmouth v Newcastle is first floodlit Football League match, Khrushchev denounces Stalin, Prince Rainier marries Grace Kelly.
6. Soldiers fire on protestors in Tiananmen Square, the *Marchioness* sinks in the River Thames leaving 51 dead, first TV transmissions from the House of Commons.
7. Clive Sinclair sells his business to Amstrad, Clint Eastwood is elected Mayor of Carmel, Soviets admit a problem at Chernobyl.
8. Rudolf Nureyev defects to the West, work begins on the Berlin Wall, Spurs win the double.
9. British Standard Time was trialled unsuccessfully for three years, The Beatles release *The White Album*, Apollo 8 carries out the first manned lunar orbit.
10. NATO air strikes on Serbia begin, Manchester United wins historic treble, Australians decline to become a Republic in a referendum.

? Tie-breaker

To the nearest year, when was Bismarck dismissed as Chancellor of Prussia (Germany)?

Myths and legends – the Greeks

●●●●●●●●●●●●●●●●●●●●●●●●●

QUIZ 45
PART 1

1   Who is forced to perform 10 tasks (later extended to 12) for Eurystheus to atone for a murder?
2   Who is the virgin hunter goddess, sister of Apollo?
3   Who looked in a pool and fell in love with his own reflection?
4   Which Greek hero appears as the King of Athens in Shakespeare's *A Midsummer Night's Dream*?
5   Jason set out with his Argonauts in search of which mythic item?
6   Who rescued his lady from the Underworld but lost her when he looked back before they re-crossed the River Styx?
7   Who is the wife of Hephaestus, the ugly and crippled smith of the gods?
8   Who was the world's first woman, who opened her box and let out the world's evils?
9   Who wished that everything thing he touched turned to gold, but regretted it soon after?
10 Who was the twin of Polydeuces?
11 Which of the gods is half-man and half-goat in form, and plays upon a set of pipes?
12 Which hero had the fate to kill his father and marry his mother?
13 Who went off to slay the Gorgon, Medusa, in order to assist his mother?
14 And what was the name of the winged horse he was given to help him on this quest?
15 And who is the girl he finds chained to a rock, rescues and subsequently marries?

PART 2

1   Paris's abduction of which Greek beauty triggered the Trojan War?
2   Who was King of Troy at the time of the siege?
3   What were Achilles' warriors called?
4   Which Greek commander is usually credited with devising the Trojan Horse scheme?
5   Which famous archer was tricked into going to the war by Odysseus?
6   Whose wife is Andromache?
7   Which friend of Achilles was slain by Hector whilst wearing Achilles' golden armour?
8   According to Shakespeare, who was the faithless lover of Troilus?
9   Who is the King of Argos and friend of Odysseus who is honour-bound to join the Greek expedition due to an earlier oath?
10 Who played Odysseus in the movie, *Troy*, starring Brad Pitt as Achilles?
11 Who was the Commander of the Trojans' Lycian allies: Aeneas, Jason or Sarpedon?
12 Where does Paris fatally shoot Achilles, his only weak spot?
13 Which giant warrior goes mad and kills himself after Odysseus is awarded Achilles' armour after the hero's death?
14 Who is the cruel son of Achilles, in some versions responsible for many atrocities after the war?
15 Penthesilea, slain by Achilles during the war, is the queen of which warrior race?

? *Tie-breaker*
Who led the Greek army at Troy and what was the name of his wife?

Battles and generals

●●●●●●●●●●●●●●●●●●●●●●●●●●●

QUIZ 46
PART 1

1. How many ships did Nelson's fleet lose at Trafalgar?
2. Which order of knights formed the fanatical bulwark of the Christian forces in the 13th century crusades?
3. The Charge of the Light Brigade took place during which battle?
4. What RAF rank lies between Flight Lieutenant and Wing Commander?
5. Gustavus Adolphus was a famous warrior king of which country?
6. Who commanded the English Navy against the Spanish Armada?
7. Who defeated Pompey's much larger army in a decisive battle in 48BC at Pharsalus?
8. In which battle was a Syrian/Egyptian thrust halted during the Israeli-Arab conflict in October 1973?
9. Where was the decisive Russian victory achieved in the biggest tank battle of the Second World War?
10. Who surrendered to Ulysses Grant after the Battle of Appomattox?
11. Cetewayo led which armies against the British in the nineteenth century?
12. Which legendary US general fell at Little Big Horn?
13. The defeat and death of Richard III at which decisive battle effectively ended the Wars of the Roses?
14. In which country did the Contras battle the Sandinistas?
15. Where did the Duke of Cumberland ruthlessly annihilate the Jacobite rebels on 16 April 1746?

Did you know?

Arthur Wellesley, later Duke of Wellington, was actually born in Ireland. A brilliant and uncompromising soldier, he emulated the Duke of Marlborough, a military hero from the previous century, by entering politics and serving twice as a Tory Prime Minister. Wellington died in 1852 at the ripe old age of 83.

PART 2 – *Match the battle to the wider conflict.*
1 Gettysburg
2 Agincourt
3 Kursk
4 Bunker Hill
5 Passchendaele
6 Port Stanley
7 Marston Moor
8 Marengo
9 Guadalcanal
10 Guadalajara

A First World War
B English Civil War
C Napoleonic Wars
D Spanish Civil War
E WWII – Eastern front
F Hundred Years' War
G WWII – Pacific
H US Civil War
I Falklands War
J US War of Independence

? *Tie-breaker*
Most people know who led the British forces at Waterloo, but who led the Prussian allies under the Iron Duke's overall command?

The 21st century - 2002

●●●●●●●●●●●●●●●●●●●●●●●●●●●●

QUIZ 47
PART 1

1   Where did the 2002 Winter Olympics take place?
2   Who famously choked on a pretzel in January 2002 while watching a National Football League game, briefly losing consciousness?
3   Which member of the Royal Family died on March 30th?
4   What was the title of the second single released from Justin Timberlake's solo debut album, and what was the title of the album?
5   What was the name of the oil tanker that sank off the Galician coast, causing a huge oil spill?
6   Which episode of the *Star Wars* films was released, and what was its title?
7   What was the name of the unmanned spacecraft that found signs of huge ice deposits on the planet Mars?
8   Who was re-elected as prime minister of Sweden?
9   Who arrived in Cuba for a five-day visit with Fidel Castro, becoming the first president of the United States, in or out of office, to visit the island since Castro's 1959 revolution?
10 Who did Brazil beat in the football World Cup final, and what was the score?
11 Which painting was sold to Lord Thomson for £49.5 million at a Sotheby's auction? Who was the artist?
12 Which sports person was sent home from the training camp in Saipan by Manager Mick McCarthy after an argument over training arrangements?
13 The Eurovision Song Contest was held in a former Soviet country for the first time: which one?
14 What was celebrated by 'A Party in the Palace' on June 3rd?
15 Which terrorist attack took place in Bali on October 12th?

PART 2

1 What was the title of Eminem's third solo album, released on May 28th?

2 Which reality television show aired for the first time, and who were its winner and runner-up?

3 The U.S. State Department released a report citing seven state sponsors of terrorism: which countries were cited?

4 Which 2002 film directed by Roman Polanski won the Palme d'Or at the Cannes Film Festival?

5 In New Zealand, which leader of the Labour Party was historically re-elected in a landslide victory over the right wing in the General Election?

6 In July, what opened in London as the headquarters of the Greater London Authority and the Mayor of London?

7 Who escaped an assassination attempt unscathed during Bastille Day celebrations?

8 Name the seven countries that were invited to become North Atlantic Treaty Organization (NATO) members at the NATO summit in Prague.

9 Which Kylie Minogue song reached No. 3 in the UK charts after its release in February 2002? On which album did it feature?

10 Which British pianist, comedian and actor died after a long illness on March 27th?

11 Which film starring Russell Crowe won the Academy Award for Best Picture at the 74th Academy Awards in 2002?

12 Which member of The Who died on June 27th? Which instrument did he play?

13 Which country joined the United Nations on September 10th?

14 Which American television series starring Michael J. Fox as a deputy mayor came to an end due to low ratings?

15 Who won the Nobel Prize for Peace?

? *Tie-breaker*
Who won the World Snooker Championship, and whom did he beat?

The fifties

● ●

QUIZ 48
PART 1

1 In which year did George VI die?
2 Which country won the first Eurovision Song Contest in 1956?
3 What was the name of the first space satellite, launched by the Russians in 1957?
4 In which year did the footballer Stanley Matthews play his final England game: 1954, 1957 or 1958?
5 In which year did Elvis Presley enter the US Army?
6 Who ousted President Batista from Cuba and created a communist state there? In which year did this take place?
7 In which year did legendary tenor Mario Lanza die: 1953, 1956 or 1959?
8 Who originally presented the television programme *Blue Peter*? In which year was it first broadcast?
9 What was established as a communist counterweight to NATO (the North Atlantic Treaty Organization) in 1955?
10 Name two of the three male stars of the 1953 film *From Here To Eternity*.
11 Which 1957 Anglo-American war film was based on the novel by Pierre Boulle?
12 The Fourth Republic in France collapsed in 1958 through the ramifications of which crisis? Who subsequently formed a government, established the Fifth Republic and was elected president?
13 Who first recorded 'Johnny B. Goode' in 1958?
14 In which year did Morocco become an independent kingdom: 1952, 1956 or 1958?
15 In which year was *Lord of the Flies* published? Who was its author?

PART 2

1 Which Soviet leader died in 1953?
2 Which actor won an Academy Award for Best Actor in 1953, and for which film?
3 In which year was Cyprus granted independence: 1952, 1955 or 1959?
4 What is Sir Edmund Hillary's middle name, and what is his nationality? With whom did he reach the summit of Mount Everest in 1953?
5 When did the Korean War begin: 1950, 1952 or 1953?
6 In 1953, who was television's first Robin Hood?
7 Who did Harold Macmillan succeed as prime minister in 1957?
8 Which famous novel by J. D. Salinger was published in the United States in 1951?
9 Roger Bannister is best known as the first man to run one mile in less than four minutes. In which British city did this take place, and in which year?
10 Which long-running, current affairs documentary television series was first broadcast on 11 November 1953? Who was the original presenter?
11 Name the three countries of the alliance pitted against Egypt in the Suez Crisis of 1956.
12 What dish was created for the coronation of Queen Elizabeth II in 1953? Who were the creators?
13 In which year did America develop the H-bomb?
14 What was established by the Treaty of Rome in 1957?
15 Which well-known film starring Cary Grant and Grace Kelly was directed by Alfred Hitchcock in 1955?

? *Tie-breaker*

Which two countries united in 1958 to form the United Arab Republic, which was then dissolved in 1961?

The 21st century - 2003

●●●●●●●●●●●●●●●●●●●●●●●●●●●●●●

QUIZ 49
PART 1

1   Which famous telephone number was consigned to history in August?
2   Which cover version of an eighties song was the surprise Christmas No1?
3   The WHO issued a global health warning after an outbreak of which disease in Asia?
4   Who rode Kris Kin to success in the Epsom Derby?
5   In what role did Mervyn King replace Eddie George?
6   In January, British-born Richard Reid was sentenced to life imprisonment in Boston, Mass. after trying to blow up a jet. What nickname did he go by in the Press?
7   Whose sons, Uday and Qusay, both died on the same day in July?
8   What made its final commercial landing on October 24th?
9   What post did Rowan Williams take up on the 27th February?
10 Who resigned from her ministerial post in protest over the government's approach to the war in Iraq?
11 Why was Grand Master Ruslan Ponomariov disqualified at a chess tournament in October?
12 What did David Hempleman-Adams become the first person to do on his own?
13 Who won Wimbledon for the first time?
14 Who turned 21 on June 20th?
15 And what went on sale the following day, exciting children across the UK?

Did you know?

Three days before Christmas, Pharos, one of the Queen's corgis, was mauled to death by Princess Anne's bull terrier, Dotty. Dotty had already earned the Princess Royal a £500 fine and a warning after frightening two children the previous year.

PART 2

1   What major conflict began on the 20th March?
2   Who was made a saint in October, six years after their death?
3   For what alleged crime, perpetrated in 2001, did Major Charles Ingram enter the dock in March?
4   Which obscure American 'no-hoper' won the 2003 Open Golf Championship?
5   Which two Italian sides contested the Champions League Final at Old Trafford?
6   Which spaceship disintegrated on re-entering the atmosphere, killing all seven crew members?
7   Who was the BBC journalist who had a controversial meeting with Dr David Kelly, leading to Kelly's involvement in a Home Affairs leak inquiry?
8   Which high street entrepreneur was made a dame of the British Empire?
9   Who was the winner of *I'm A Celebrity, Get Me Out Of Here*, in May?
10   What was historic about Mike Fuller's appointment as Chief Constable in Kent?
11   Who paid the price for not paying the price for Michael and Catherine's wedding photos?
12   Who became Governor of California in October?
13   Which TV presenter was awarded the Faraday Prize for contributions to science?
14   What made taking your car into London that bit trickier in 2003?
15   Who was arrested on charges of child molestation on November 20th in Los Angeles, but subsequently cleared?

? **Tie-breaker**

Whose daughter is Rosanna Davison, Miss World, 2003, and what was the surprising venue for the contest that year?

The sixties

● ●

QUIZ 50
PART 1

1   In 1962, where did Russia attempt to send arms and establish a missile base? Who was the Soviet leader at this time?

2   England beat Germany in the World Cup in 1966; what was the score?

3   Who replaced Charles de Gaulle after his resignation as President of France in 1969?

4   John F. Kennedy, President of the United States: what did the F stand for?

5   Who was captured and shot in Bolivia in 1967?

6   In which year was Nelson Mandela sentenced to life imprisonment?

7   What is the name of the character played by Ursula Andress in the 1962 James Bond film *Dr No*?

8   Which vaccine was licensed for use in 1962?

9   In which year was colour introduced to the BBC and ITV in Britain: 1965, 1967 or 1969?

10 Who succeeded Harold Macmillan as prime minister in 1963?

11 What iconic symbol of the Cold War was initially constructed in 1961?

12 In which year did the famous Woodstock Music and Art Festival take place: 1967, 1968 or 1969?

13 Which country granted independence to the Congo in 1960?

14 Which actress starred in the film *Guess Who's Coming To Dinner* in 1967?

15 In which year was the book *Valley of the Dolls* published, and who was the author?

PART 2

1   In which year did Martin Luther King make his "I have a dream" speech: 1962, 1963 or 1967?
2   Who played Cathy and Reg in the British television play *Cathy Come Home*, first shown in 1966?
3   In which year did John Profumo admit that he had lied to the House of Commons and resign from office: 1963, 1964 or 1965?
4   In which year was Algeria granted independence by France?
5   In which year was the US animated television series *The Flintstones* first shown? What were the full names of its creators?
6   Which former SS Nazi administrator was hanged by Israel in 1962?
7   Whose version of the song 'Anyone who had a Heart' shot to No. 1 in 1964 and remains the biggest selling single by a female artist in the history of British pop music?
8   For which film did Elizabeth Taylor win the Academy Award for Best Actress in 1966?
9   Which children's television programme shown on ITV was first transmitted on July 30th, 1968?
10 What is the name of the inventor in *Chitty Chitty Bang Bang: The Magical Car*, and in which year was the book first published? Who was the author?
11 Name the two pilots who accompanied Commander Neil Armstrong on his 1969 mission to the Moon.
12 Who was appointed Poet Laureate in 1968?
13 What was the title of Maya Angelou's autobiography of the early years of her life, published in 1969?
14 In which year was Yasser Arafat elected chairman of the PLO: 1965, 1967 or 1969?
15 What was the title of the Beatles' second album, released in 1963?

? Tie-breaker
Which movie was the final film appearance for both Clark Gable and Marilyn Monroe, and in which year was it released?

Women's rights

● ●

QUIZ 51
PART 1

1   What limit was put on the women who were given the vote in Britain 1918?
2   Which amendment to the American constitution grants the right to vote regardless of sex?
3   Which country, in 1893, was the first to give women the vote in a national election?
4   Who became the husband of the progressive campaigner and CND founder, Dora Black?
5   Who founded the Women's Social and Political Union in 1903?
6   The first example of what medical facility was opened by Margaret Sanger in Brooklyn in 1916?
7   In which year did the Sex Discrimination Act come into force in the UK: 1947, 1963 or 1975?
8   Of which organization was Stella Rimington appointed the first female head in 1992?
9   Name the original 'rock chick' who died of a heroin overdose in 1970, at the age of just 27?
10 What distinction did the Australian feminist campaigner Edith Cowan achieve?
11 "The female of the species is more deadly than the male" - lines by which British author and poet?
12 Which Clapham-born activist pursued a career of fighting social causes in Victorian England, most notably the match-girls strike of 1888?
13 The National Women's Suffrage movement was founded in the US by Susan Anthony and Elizabeth Cady Stanton; was it founded in 1869, 1899 or 1919?
14 The Eurhythmics and Aretha Franklin collaborated on which woman-championing anthem in 1985?
15 What was Eve Ensler's controversial off-Broadway play of 1996, that has since become an oft-performed feminist favourite?

PART 2 – *Match the feminist work to its author.*

1   A Room of One's Own
2   The Female Eunuch
3   Fat is a Feminist Issue
4   I Know Why The Caged Bird Sings
5   Vindication of the Rights of Woman
6   The Color Purple
7   The Yellow Wallpaper
8   The Women's Room
9   Wide Sargasso Sea
10 The Second Sex
11 The Golden Notebook
12 The Feminine Mystique
13 Fear of Flying
14 Intercourse
15 The Beauty Myth

A   Alice Walker
B   Andrea Dworkin
C   Betty Friedan
D   Charlotte Perkins Gilman
E   Doris Lessing
F   Erica Jong
G   Germaine Greer
H   Jean Rhys
I   Marilyn French
J   Mary Wollstonecraft
K   Maya Angelou
L   Naomi Wolf
M   Simone de Beauvoir
N   Susie Orbach
P   Virginia Woolf

? Tie-breaker

Which important early feminist was the wife of philosopher William Godwin? Who was her famous daughter?

Name the year

● ●

QUIZ 52

PART 1 – *Give the dates for these events. Two points for spot-on, one point if within the figure in brackets either way.*

1   US Declaration of Independence (2)
2   Birth of William Shakespeare (6)
3   Magna Carta (5)
4   Death of Queen Victoria (1)
5   Execution of King Charles I (2)
6   Coronation of Queen Elizabeth II (1)
7   Mayflower lands in America (5)
8   *Wuthering Heights* published (10)
9   Battle of Waterloo (1)
10 French Revolution (1)
11 Spanish Armada (2)
12 Birth of Bill Clinton (3)
13 First FA Cup Final (2)
14 Norman Conquest (0)
15 First test match between England and Australia (5)

Did you know?

The Hundred Years' War was actually a series of conflicts between England and France between 1337 and 1453 (yes, we know, 116). The English longbows held the whip hand for the first phases of the war, but the inspiration of Joan of Arc and fighting on home soil meant that France was able to force England to cede most of its French territories by the end of the conflict.

PART 2 – *Name the year from the events given.*

1. Ronnie Scott's opens in London, Castro comes to power in Cuba, Peru's Alex Olmedo wins Wimbledon.
2. The Profumo affair, Kennedy assassinated, The Beatles have their first No1 hit.
3. *Today* newspaper launches, Prince Andrew becomes engaged to Sarah Ferguson, GLC is abolished.
4. Police forcibly eject peaceful protestors from the main camp at Greenham Common, South Africa cancel a cricket tour to England, Chelsea win the FA Cup after a replay against Leeds.
5. Maastricht Treaty on European Union signed, Nick Faldo wins his third and last Open Championship, Neil Kinnock resigns as Labour Party leader.
6. Lord Lucan is found guilty of murder in absentia, Martina Navratilova requests political asylum in the US, Dutch Elm Disease hits the UK.
7. John Hinckley attempts to assassinate President Reagan, IBM release their first personal computer, *Cats* premieres in the West End.
8. Algeria achieves independence, Elvis has four No1s totalling 15 weeks at the top of the charts, Graham Hill wins Formula One Championship for the first time.
9. Althea Gibson becomes first black player to win a Wimbledon singles title, *West Side Story* premieres on Broadway, *Sputnik 1* is launched.
10. Billie Jean King beats Bobby Riggs in The Battle of the Sexes, the Queen opens the Sydney Opera House, the US withdraws from Vietnam.

? *Tie-breaker*

Which English king was on the throne at the start of the Hundred Years' War in 1337? What was the name given to his son (who predeceased him)?

The Romans

● ●

QUIZ 53
PART 1

1 Who, according to legend, were the founders and first kings of Rome?
2 Which city was the centre of the eastern Roman Empire?
3 Who was the Queen of the Iceni who led a bloody rebellion against the Romans in the first century AD?
4 Who was the Carthaginian general who defeated the Romans at Cannae, but was eventually thwarted by Scipio at Zama?
5 What relation was Augustus Caesar (formerly Octavian) to Julius Caesar?
6 Who took Rome at the Battle of the Colline Gate and imposed a bloody dictatorship for two years from 82 to 80 BC?
7 Which land did the Romans call Hibernia?
8 What is the Cloaca Maxima?
9 Whose rape by the king's son precipitated the revolt that led to the establishment of the Roman Republic?
10 Who was the last of the seven Roman kings?
11 The Roman town of Aquae Sulis, known for its heated waters, lay on the same site as which modern English city?
12 Who is the Roman equivalent of the Greek god, Apollo?
13 What symbol did the Christians in Rome adopt when Marcus Aurelius resumed persecution of the faith?
14 Who made his horse, Incitatus, a member of the Senate?
15 What was begun in 122 AD in Britain?

Did you know?

The Roman Empire in the West fell in 476 when Rome itself finally fell to the Germanic tribes. The Eastern Empire, however, continued to flourish, centred on what is now the Turkish city of Istanbul. The Empire pushed into Eastern Europe, annexing Bulgar and Hungarian territory, and tried to push back eastwards, too. In 1204 the Crusaders conquered the city and established a 'Latin' empire, and 200 years later the city finally fell to the Ottoman Turks, never to return to Christian hands.

PART 2

1 Gallia, or Gaul, as the Romans knew it, encompassed roughly which modern European country?
2 Who was the Spanish-born Roman poet whose *Epigrams* provide an amusing account of Roman society and politics during the second half of the first century AD?
3 Who was the Egyptian queen loved first by Julius Caesar and later by Mark Antony?
4 Who led a massive slave rebellion against Rome in 73 to 71 BC?
5 Who wrote the witty and licentious series of tales translated as *The Metamorphoses*?
6 What is the modern city on the site of Roman Eboracum?
7 Who is the Roman god of War?
8 The Punic Wars were fought between Rome and which other city-state?
9 Who became Roman procurator of Judaea and Samaria in 26 AD?
10 Virgil's *Aeneid* follows his hero, Aeneas, after his flight from which epic military struggle?

? *Tie-breaker*

Who controlled most of Southern England from about 10 to 40 AD, and what name does Shakespeare give him?

World War II

●●●●●●●●●●●●●●●●●●●●●●●●●

QUIZ 54

PART 1

1   What name was given to the German army's method of lightning tactical strikes into new territory followed by consolidation and reinforcement?

2   In which part of France did the allies land in June 1944 in Operation Overlord?

3   Who designed the 'Bouncing Bomb', used with great success in the raids on the strategic dams of the Ruhr valley?

4   The German air force was the Luftwaffe; what was the name of their ground army?

5   What is the significance of December 7th, 1941, in the outcome of WWII?

6   Where did the Germans set up the defensive Winter Line?

7   What was the Barbarossa campaign?

8   What manufacture were the British fighter planes' machine guns in the Battle of Britain?

9   Who was the head of the Afrika Korps?

10 What was the name of the disastrous air offensive chronicled in the epic movie *A Bridge Too Far*?

11 What type of planes carried the bombs dropped on Hiroshima and Nagasaki?

12 By what name is the Ardennes Offensive, Von Runstedt's last-ditch counter-offensive in France in 1944, better known?

13 Who planted the briefcase of explosives in Hitler's war office on July 20th, 1944, in an attempt to assassinate the Führer?

14 Who were the ANZACs?

15 What was the Anschluss of 1938?

PART 2

1   What is significant about May 8th, 1945?

2   On which Japanese island did the Americans take control of vital Pacific airfields in March 1945, and raise a famously symbolic Stars and Stripes on the island's highest point?

3   Montgomery's Eighth Army was given which nickname during its African campaign?

4   What was the campaign name of the planned German invasion of Britain thwarted by the success of the RAF in the Battle of Britain?

5   Who was the Air Chief Marshal responsible for implementing the bombing raids on German industrial cities?

6   Who commanded the German Sixth Army at Stalingrad?

7   The captain of the besieged German battlecruiser, the *Graf Spee*, scuttled his boat while lying in which neutral port in 1939?

8   Which US general was given the nickname 'Old Blood and Guts'?

9   Who was in charge of German forces in Italy when the allies launched a double offensive in late 1943?

10   Which US general accepted the surrender of Japan in 1945?

11   Where did the Germans launch the first (almost) solely airborne infantry assault in May 1941?

12   Which French government minister was stranded in London when Paris fell, and became the leader of the Free French?

13   What was the M4 Sherman?

14   Which legendary German battleship went down off the coast of France in 1941, three days after sinking HMS *Hood*, the pride of the Royal Navy?

15   What name was given to the period after the German invasion of Poland, when the major powers of Europe were formally at war, but not actually doing much fighting?

? *Tie-breaker*

What were the three fighters most frequently flown in the air duels that constituted the Battle of Britain?

The seventies

● ●

QUIZ 55

PART 1

1　In which year was decimal coinage introduced in Britain: 1970, 1971 or 1972?

2　Which US president replaced Richard Nixon, who was forced to resign after the Watergate Scandal?

3　Who played Jack Carter in the 1971 British crime film *Get Carter*?

4　Who seized power in Uganda in 1971?

5　Which three actresses played the original Charlie's Angels?

6　Who wrote *Watership Down*, and in which year was it published?

7　The republic of Sri Lanka was formed in 1972. What was it known as before this?

8　Karol Wojtyla was elected to become what in 1978?

9　How many times did Ray Reardon win the snooker World Championship between 1970 and 1978: 4, 6 or 7 times?

10　Who is the only person to have filled all four of the Great Offices of State (Prime Minister, Chancellor of the Exchequer, Home Secretary and Foreign Secretary)?

11　Who reached number 10 in the UK charts in 1972 with 'Starman'? What was the title of the song on the B-side of this 7-inch single?

12　Which 1974 disaster movie teamed Paul Newman and Steve McQueen against a fire in a San Francisco skyscraper?

13　On which day in 1977 was the Queen's Silver Jubilee celebrated with streets and neighbourhoods holding organized parties for all their residents?

14　What was the name of the character played by John Travolta in the 1977 movie *Saturday Night Fever*?

15　Which noted non-violent anti-apartheid activist was killed in Pretoria, South Africa in 1977?

PART 2

1   Which country reverted to a monarchy in 1976 after its dictator General Franco died? What was the name of the new king, who still reigns today?

2   Who was prime minister when the three-day working week was declared in 1973?

3   Which 1975 film, directed by Milos Forman, was the first since 1934 to win all five major Academy Awards?

4   What was The Congo renamed in 1972?

5   Name the Pink Floyd album that appeared in 1975.

6   What were the names of the two unmanned scientific probes launched into space in 1977?

7   Which South African township came to the world's attention on June 16th, 1976, when mass protests erupted over the government's policy to enforce education in Afrikaans rather than English?

8   Name two of the three countries that joined the EEC in 1973.

9   Who played police constable George Dixon in the BBC television series *Dixon of Dock Green*? He always began each episode with a salute and a greeting: what was the greeting?

10 Which country hosted the summer Olympic Games in 1976?

11 Which English town was awarded city status by Queen Elizabeth II in 1977?

12 Which regime was overthrown in Cambodia in 1979? Who was the leader of this regime?

13 What was the name of Sid Vicious' (of the Sex Pistols) American girlfriend? In which city was he arrested for her murder?

14 Who is the author of *Roots: The Saga of an American Family*, published in 1976?

15 In which year did the Vietnam War end: 1973, 1975 or 1976?

? *Tie-breaker*
  In which year did Concorde begin its commercial flights: 1973, 1974 or 1976?

The 21st century - 2004

● ●

QUIZ 56
PART 1

1   Which special anniversary was commemorated on June 6th?
2   Where did the 2004 Summer Olympics take place?
3   Which village in Cornwall was hit by severe flooding in August?
4   In the US, which comedy series aired its final episode on May 6th, drawing an estimated 52 million viewers?
5   What was the name given to the epidemic that was spreading throughout southeast Asia?
6   Which former daytime television presenter represented the UK Independence Party in the 2004 election to the European Parliament?
7   Which ocean liner was christened by the Queen on January 8th?
8   Whose death did the Hutton Inquiry investigate?
9   Who won the Academy Award for Best Actor in a Leading Role for his portrayal of 'Jimmy' at the 76th Academy Awards ceremony in 2004?
10 Five British men were released from detention and landed back in the UK at RAF Brize Norton: from where were they released, and how many were immediately re-arrested for questioning?
11 What colour was the flour bomb that hit Tony Blair in the Chamber of the House of Commons during a session of Prime Minister's Questions? Which campaign group claimed responsibility?
12 To which country did the United States lift a ban on travel, ending travel restrictions to the nation that had lasted for 23 years?
13 Which country won the World Ice Hockey Championship in Prague?
14 Which religious film was released on Ash Wednesday?
15 How many Formula One World Championship titles did Michael Schumacher have under his belt after finishing second in the Belgian Grand Prix at Spa-Francorchamps: four, seven or eleven?

PART 2

1   What was reopened in September on the Isle of Man?
2   How many Academy Awards did *The Lord of the Rings: The Return of the King* receive at the 76th Academy Awards ceremony in 2004?
3   Who resigned as president of Haiti?
4   Which country banned smoking in all enclosed work places, including restaurants, pubs and bars, on March 29th?
5   Which controversial documentary film won the Palme d'Or at the Cannes Film Festival?
6   Following the Madrid bombings of March 11th, what did the new Spanish government announce four days later?
7   What was the nationality of the terrorists who took between 1000 and 1500 people hostage in a school in Beslan, Northern Ossetia?
8   What was the title of the album released by Green Day in September?
9   Queen Elizabeth II made a state visit to France to celebrate the 100th anniversary of the Entente Cordiale: what was the Entente Cordiale?
10 Which former president of the United States died on June 5th, aged 93?
11 Which Harry Potter film was released?
12 At which international airport did a section of the ceiling in a terminal collapse, claiming at least six lives?
13 Which world leader died in a Paris hospital on November 11th?
14 Which US baseball team won the World Series for the first time since 1918, breaking the 'Curse of the Bambino'?
15 Which legendary DJ died on October 26th, after 40 years of massive influence on popular music?

? *Tie-breaker*
Which television series began in 2004 and saw a chef troubleshooting failing restaurants?

Name the year

● ●

QUIZ 57
PART 1

1   In which year was *Gone With the Wind* released: 1910, 1922 or 1939?
2   In which year did Spike Milligan die: 2000, 2002 or 2004?
3   In what year did *Test Match Special* first broadcast ball-by-ball commentary: 1957, 1967 or 1977?
4   In which year did the artist Claude Monet die: 1846, 1889 or 1926?
5   In what year was the Penny Post introduced: 1818, 1840 or 1896?
6   What year did Marx and Engels publish The Communist Manifesto: 1848, 1888 or 1902?
7   In what year was the original Band Aid song the Christmas No1: 1980, 1984 or 1987?
8   In which year did the wearing of seat belts become compulsory: 1955, 1970 or 1983?
9   In which year was Napoleon's marriage to Josephine annulled: 1790, 1810 or 1822?
10 Greenpeace was established in 1933, 1960 or 1971?
11 In which year did the British Museum first open to the public: 1707, 1759 or 1808?
12 What year were driving tests made compulsory in the UK: 1935, 1951 or 1963?
13 In which year was Ruth Ellis the last woman hanged for murder in Britain: 1933, 1955 or 1970?
14 In which year did Edward III outmanoeuvre the French at the Battle of Crecy: 1219, 1346 or 1485?
15 In which year were Zip codes introduced in the US: 1899, 1946 or 1963?

History – Name the year

PART 2

1 In which year was James Cameron's film, *Titanic*, released: 1994, 1997 or 2001?

2 In which year was the first weather broadcast made by the BBC: 1923, 1933 or 1953?

3 In which year did scientists discover the link between the HIV virus and AIDS: 1984, 1990 or 1995?

4 When was the first match played at Lord's cricket ground: 1787, 1847 or 1877?

5 In what year were the railways privatized by the Labour government: 1926, 1935 or 1948?

6 In which year was Samuel Johnson's Dictionary published: 1699, 1755 or 1801?

7 In which year was Russia's first constitution formed: 1905, 1922 or 1929?

8 In which year was the British East India Company granted its charter: 1600, 1700 or 1800??

9 In which year was Princess Eugenie of York born:1985, 1990 or 1995?

10 In which year was Darwin's *Origin Of Species* published: 1859, 1884 or 1903?

11 In what year did Bowie release *Ziggy Stardust*: 1967, 1972 or 1977?

12 In which year was the first Wembley FA Cup Final: 1923, 1933 or 1953?

13 In which year did Brunel's suspension bridge at Clifton open: 1814, 1864 or 1898?

14 In which year did Niccolo Polo, father of Marco, visit Kubla Khan in what is now Beijing: 1266, 1344 or 1402?

15 In which year was the Commonwealth of Australia formed: 1888, 1901 or 1930?

? Tie-breaker

In what year did Edward VIII abdicate the throne: 1925, 1930 or 1936? Who was British PM at the time?

Myths and legends – The British Isles

●●●●●●●●●●●●●●●●●●●●●●●●●●

QUIZ 58
PART 1

1   Who rode naked through the streets of Coventry, having made a bargain with her husband that he would reduce taxes if she did so?
2   Who is the sworn love of Robin Hood?
3   From which village does Robin Hood come in most versions of the story?
4   The love of which woman lures the sons of Usna to their doom?
5   Who leaves the court of Hygelac, King of the Geats, to assist Hrothgar, King of the Danes, who has a problem with a local monster?
6   In the TV series of *Robin Hood*, with Michael Praed as Robin, which now-famous actor played Will Scarlet?
7   In Celtic lore, who is the Goddess of War and Death?
8   Who was the greatest of the Welsh bards?
9   Who was the Hound of Ulster?
10 Who was High King in Tara whilst the Hound was in his prowess?
11 His nemesis, Queen Maeve, was Queen of which Irish territory?
12 Who played Robin in *Robin Hood*, *Prince of Thieves*?
13 Who ventured to The Dark Tower to rescue his brothers and sisters from the Elf-King?
14 Who is the Sheriff of Nottingham's steward, who becomes a regular opponent of Robin Hood?
15 In Welsh mythology, who was the daughter of Llyr?

PART 2 – *Tales of the Once and Future King.*

1 Which castle housed the Round Table?
2 Which of the Knights of the Round Table had an encounter with a Green Knight?
3 Who was the father of King Arthur's bride, Guinevere?
4 Which masterpiece of Arthurian literature was published by William Caxton in 1485?
5 Who played King Arthur in the 2005 movie?
6 Uther Pendragon was Arthur's father; who was his mother?
7 Who was the forsaken wife of Lancelot?
8 Mordred was born after which lady tricked Arthur into lying with her?
9 And who played her in John Boorman's eighties film version of the tales, *Excalibur*?
10 In some versions of the stories, who is believed to have brought the Holy Grail to England?
11 Sir Bertilak is a key character in a story featuring Sir Gawain; by what name is he known in the story?
12 Who killed Gawain's brothers, Gareth and Gaheris?
13 According to legend, which King invited the Saxon armies into England?
14 What was the name of Arthur's foster-brother, true son of Sir Ector?
15 Which knight is with Arthur at the end and casts Excalibur into the Lake?

? **Tie-breaker**
Which two knights achieve the Holy Grail alongside Sir Galahad?

Ancient civilizations

● ●

QUIZ 59
PART 1

1 Which great civilization was brought down by the Spanish Conquistadores under Hernan Cortes?
2 What was the key city that gave its name to the age of Greek civilization between roughly 1600 and 100 BC?
3 *Gilgamesh* is the great epic poem of which ancient culture?
4 Was Plato a pupil of Socrates or vice versa?
5 Which Hebrew King conquered Jerusalem in 1005 BC?
6 Jerusalem fell again in 597 BC resulting in the exile of thousands of Jews to which territory?
7 In which modern country were the Olmec and Mayan the two earliest recorded civilizations?
8 Which country boasts an army of beautifully preserved terracotta warriors from about 250 BC?
9 What was Vatsayara's epic erotic work, completed in about 400 AD?
10 What form of communication was first used by the Egyptians as early as 3,000 BC?
11 Which politician, priest and designer of the Step Pyramid was made a god by the Egyptians some 2,000 years after his death?
12 Who was King of Macedonia between 336 and 323 BC?
13 What is the name of the Inca fortress lying above the Urumbamba River gorge?
14 In Homer's *Odyssey*, who recognizes Odysseus on his return to Ithaca?
15 Nineveh was the capital of which ancient Empire?

PART 2

1   True or false: Aristotle was once tutor to Alexander the Great.
2   Cyrus, Darius and Xerxes were rulers of which empire c. 500 years BC?
3   Which famous monument was built at Ephesus in Turkey in 550 BC?
4   Which peoples occupied the area of Canaan, including the city of Gaza around 1100 BC, and were often at war with the early Kingdom of Israel?
5   Which naval empire controlled large parts of the Mediterranean from North African and West Asian ports such as Tyre and Tripoli?
6   Who defeated the Spartans and their allies at Thermopylae in 480 BC?
7   Karnak, Giza and Memphis were important centres of which great ancient power?
8   Who was buried at Thebes in 1349 BC?
9   Atahualpa was the last Emperor of which long-standing South American civilization?
10   What destroyed Pompeii in 79 AD?
11   Who was the Carthaginian general who gave the Romans a hammering at Cannae, but was eventually defeated by Scipio at Zama?
12   Huitzilopochtli is the chief god of which people?
13   Who wrote the philosophical works, *Symposium* and *The Republic*?
14   The Minoan civilization was centred on which island, now part of Greece?
15   Where was the Pharos Lighthouse, one of the Seven Wonders of the World, completed in 275 BC?

? *Tie-breaker*

Who was the Babylonian leader who constructed the Hanging Gardens?

The eighties

• •

QUIZ 60
PART 1

1   Who became US president in 1981?
2   The Berlin Wall, dismantled in 1989, was how long: 16 km, 72 km or 155 km?
3   How many crew members died when the space shuttle *Challenger* exploded shortly after take-off, and in which year did this occur?
4   Who replaced Leonid Brezhnev as Soviet leader in 1982?
5   In which year did the American actor John Belushi die: 1980, 1982 or 1983?
6   What was the name of the hotel in Brighton in which the IRA detonated two bombs to coincide with the British Conservative Party Conference in 1984?
7   Who was the creator of the television soap opera *Brookside* and in which year did it make its debut?
8   What is the Russian word for the economic reforms introduced in 1987 by the Soviet leader Mikhail Gorbachev?
9   In which year did Iran and Iraq end their eight-year war?
10 Who won the men's and the women's Wimbledon championship in 1982?
11 On what date in 1985 was Live Aid held: July 6th, July 13th, July 17th?
12 Which 1988 Academy Award-winning film starred Tom Cruise as Charlie Babbitt and Dustin Hoffman as his brother Raymond?
13 What was the title of the book by Stephen Hawking published in 1988?
14 In which country was President Ceausescu executed in 1989?
15 What was the title of Duran Duran's third album, released in November 1983?

PART 2

1   What was the name of the ferry that capsized outside Zeebrugge in 1987?
2   In which year was Pope John Paul II wounded in an assassination attempt?
3   Who did Mikhail Gorbachev succeed as Soviet leader in 1985?
4   In which country did the Chernobyl disaster occur, and in which year?
5   Greenham Common peace camp was situated in which English county?
6   In which year did the Tiananmen Square protests take place: 1986, 1988 or 1989?
7   What was the title of the No 1 hit for Dexy's Midnight Runners in 1981?
8   Which film won Best Picture at the Academy Awards in 1985?
9   In which year was Benazir Bhutto elected prime minister, and of which country?
10 Which stage comedy by British playwright Willy Russell premiered in London in 1980?
11 Which country won the 1986 football World Cup, against whom, and in which country did this take place?
12 What was the name of the general who was defeated in the Panama general elections but ignored the result, causing the Americans to send in troops to remove him, and in which year did this take place?
13 Which Swedish prime minister was mysteriously assassinated in 1986?
14 What was the title of the book that disclosed secrets about the British secret service that caused a scandal upon its release in 1987 because the British government attempted to ban it? Who was its author?
15 Who was murdered in New York City on December 8th, 1980?

? *Tie-breaker*
  Who directed the 1980 musical film Fame?

The 21st century - 2005

●●●●●●●●●●●●●●●●●●●●●●●●●●●●

QUIZ 61
PART 1

1   What devastated much of the north-central Gulf Coast of the United States in August 2005?

2   Which Harry Potter book was published in 2005?

3   Which birthday did the Disneyland resort in California celebrate?

4   What overall majority did the Labour Party secure in the 2005 General Election?

5   George W. Bush was inaugurated in Washington, D.C. for his second term as president. True or false: he is the 41st president of the United States.

6   Which two titles did Camilla Parker Bowles assume after her marriage to Prince Charles?

7   Which well-known soap couple tied the knot the day before Camilla and Charles's marriage?

8   Which Member of Parliament appeared before a U.S. Senate committee to answer allegations of making money from the Iraqi Oil-for-Food Programme?

9   What is special about the Airbus A380, which made its first flight from Toulouse, France on April 27th?

10 Which country won the Eurovision Song Contest?

11 Adriana Iliescu was the oldest woman in the world to give birth: how old was she when she did so?

12 What did Sony officially unveil at E3 (the Electronic Entertainment Expo), the world's largest annual trade show for the computer and video games industry?

13 Which film was released, effectively completing the saga begun by George Lucas in 1977?

14 Who won the UEFA Champions League by defeating A.C. Milan in a penalty shootout in Istanbul, and what was the final score?

15 Which singer was acquitted of all charges in his child molestation trial?

PART 2

1   Which religious leader died on April 2nd? Who succeeded him?
2   As part of the Trafalgar 200 celebrations, Queen Elizabeth II conducted the International Fleet Review in the Solent: how many international warships did she review: 167, 177 or 187?
3   Live 8 took place in July to raise awareness of which campaign?
4   The International Olympic Committee awarded the 2012 Summer Olympics to London, which means London will become the first city to have hosted the Games three times. In which other years did it do so?
5   How many explosions rocked the transport network in London on July 7th?
6   On July 28th, what did the Provisional IRA issue a statement ordering?
7   In which venue did The Rolling Stones kick off their "A Bigger Bang" tour in August?
8   England won the Ashes for the first time since which year? Who captained the England team?
9   Which popular Irish comedian died on March 10th, aged 68?
10 What was added to the end of the year 2005?
11 What took place in Iraq on December 15th?
12 What did Jamie Oliver campaign to improve?
13 What was the title of Coldplay's concert tour that kicked off in June 2005? How many shows did they play in total: 96, 111 or 127?
14 What extension in London was completed, linking Canning Town to North Woolwich?
15 Who won the Academy Award for Best Actress in a Leading Role for her portrayal of "Maggie" at the 77th Academy Awards in 2005?

? *Tie-breaker*
Which soap celebrated its 20th anniversary on air with a special episode featuring video messages from a variety of departed characters?

Battles and generals

• •

QUIZ 62
PART 1

1 What is the highest British military honour for bravery?
2 What was the name given to Cromwell's cavalry division in the New Model Army?
3 The Battle of Lepanto saw the European alliance, the Holy League, defeat which opponent at sea?
4 Which is the only nation to have sailed up the Thames and sunk English ships since 1066?
5 Davy Crockett was killed in which famous battle?
6 Sir George White's successful defence of Ladysmith took place during which colonial conflict?
7 What was Sun Tzu's masterpiece of military strategy written in about 500 BC?
8 At which famous site, in 490 BC, did 10,000 Athenians defeat a Persian army five times that number?
9 What is the Russian equivalent of the SAS?
10 At which decisive battle did the Eighth Army finally drive the Germans out of Egypt?
11 Which British General became Governor of India, despite losing the US War of Independence?
12 Inchon was a successful US landing during which conflict?
13 At which port did Sir Francis Drake famously "singe the King of Spain's beard"?
14 Crecy, Poitiers and Agincourt were all examples of the formidable power of which English weapon?
15 Where did the British resistance take place in 1879, documented in the movie, *Zulu*?

Did you know?

The RAF has a training college, too, in Cranwell. The US trains its officers in Colorado Springs, and has a Naval Academy in Annapolis. The Army Academy has been situated in West Point, New York, overlooking the Hudson River, since its foundation in 1802.

History – Battles and generals

PART 2 – *Match the commander to the battle in which they fought.*

1 General Wolfe
2 Stonewall Jackson
3 Duke of Marlborough
4 Admiral Collingwood
5 Baden-Powell
6 General Sir Douglas Haig
7 Sir Thomas Fairfax
8 Robert Bruce
9 General Gordon
10 Marechal Ney

A Trafalgar
B Siege of Mafeking, Boer War
c Bannockburn
D Khartoum
E Battle of Naseby, English Civil War
F Siege of Quebec
G Waterloo
H Harpers Ferry, US Civil War
I Malplaquet, War of Spanish Succession
J Somme

? Tie-breaker
Where is the British Army Officer Training School? And its Royal Navy equivalent?

The nineties

● ●

QUIZ 63
PART 1

1   Which unpopular financial burden led to public demonstrations and hundreds of arrests in 1990?

2   Who did Manchester United beat in the Champions League Final to complete their historic treble?

3   Who was murdered in South London on April 22nd, 1993?

4   Who had to be rescued after five days in a capsized yacht during the 1997 Vendée Globe race?

5   What was the name of the operation launched by Western troops to liberate Kuwait?

6   Who became the first female US Secretary of State in 1997, the highest-ranking woman in US history?

7   In 1995 Eric Cantona was fined £20,000 and banned for nine months for kicking a fan at which ground?

8   Who announced the repeal of all apartheid laws in South Africa in 1991?

9   What made a rendezvous with the US space shuttle, *Discovery*, on 6th February 1995?

10 Two ten-year-old boys were convicted of the abduction and killing of which two-year-old in 1993?

11 Abdullah Ocalan was the leader of which group rebelling against the Turkish government in the 1990s?

12 Helen Clark became the first woman Prime Minister of which country in 1999?

13 Which state was readmitted to the United Nations General Assembly in 1994?

14 What connected Austria, Finland and Sweden on New Year's Day in 1995?

15 Which foreign dictator was placed under house arrest during his medical treatment in Britain in October 1998?

PART 2

1 Who won the Tour de France for the first time in 1999?
2 Which female serial killer confessed to six murders in 1991?
3 Which 1995 album went on to be the second best-selling album in chart history?
4 Who was the figure skater whose ex-husband organized an attack on her rival, Nancy Kerrigan?
5 Which year in the nineties was the Queen's 'Annus Horribilis', after various scandals and the Windsor Castle fire?
6 Who won a major football tournament in 1992, despite failing to qualify?
7 Who was murdered outside his home by Andrew Cunanan in 1997?
8 Who was given six years in prison for raping Desiree Washington in 1992?
9 In 1996 The Who played their first live gig for seven years at a Prince's Trust Concert in which location?
10 What new media format was launched commercially in September 1995?
11 Who made his first call for war on the US in August 1996?
12 Who replaced Bob Hawke as Australian Prime Minister in 1991?
13 Who was elected President of the Czech Republic in 1993?
14 In the 1997 General Election, who lost the safe Conservative seat of Harrogate to the Liberal Democrats after massive tactical voting?
15 Who was the Conservative Secretary of State for Defence who also lost his seat at that election?

? *Tie-breaker*

Police were caught on camera in LA in 1991 beating which suspect after a high-speed chase?

Myths and legends

● ●

QUIZ 64
PART 1

1   Odin is the principal god in which mythology?
2   And what name was given to his warrior handmaidens?
3   What was the gift of Prometheus to mankind, for which he was chained to a rock and tortured by the gods?
4   Which famous horror writer created the Cthulhu Mythos, an Edwardian world of occult activities and nightmare creatures?
5   Which Egyptian god wears the head of a jackal?
6   In Hindu mythology, which god is the Protector: Vishnu or Shiva?
7   What has a lion's body and an eagle's wings and head?
8   Where do fallen heroes end up in Norse mythology?
9   Mazda was a god of wisdom; does he feature in Hindu, Persian or Roman mythology?
10 In Greek mythology, which part of the Underworld is reserved for the really bad boys?
11 Who was thrown to the lions but saved by a lion that he had helped many years earlier?
12 Who is the Celtic sun-god?
13 What kind of creature was Fafnir, guardian of the treasure of the Nibelungs in German mythology?
14 The bunyip is the symbol of evil in which myths?
15 Who is the father of Lohengrin in German legend?

PART 2

1   The legends of which country tell the tale of Sigmund and his son, Sigurd?
2   A centaur has a man's torso and the hindquarters of which animal?
3   Clotho, Lachesis and Atropos are mythological creatures collectively known by what name?
4   In Norse mythology, what is the term for the "doom of the gods", a kind of Armageddon?
5   Which country's mythology is contained mainly within epic tales known as the *Edda*?
6   A silkie is part man and part which other creature?
7   What was the result when Pasiphae mated with a bull in Greek mythology?
8   In what form did Zeus seduce Leda?
9   Which white witch was the wife of Pwyll, Prince of Dyfed?
10 In Norse mythology, who is the mischief-maker who is constantly trying to undermine the gods?
11 Which Roman god has two faces, consistent with his role as the god of travel, open doors and new paths?
12 Who is the god of evil in Egyptian mythology?
13 What was Odysseus's homeland?
14 Zephyrus and Aeolus are gods governing what?
15 Who was the lover of the Irish bard (or knight, according to which version you use), Tristan?

? *Tie-breaker*

The expression "caught between Scylla and Charybdis" refers to an episode when the Argonauts rowed between these two deadly traps. What were Scylla and Charybdis?

Music
and
culture

Pop music - 6os

● ●

QUIZ 65

PART 1 – *Here are fifteen No1 singles from the early years of pop. Identify the artists who had the hit.*

1   'Cumberland Gap' (Feb '57)
2   'I Got You Babe' (Aug '65)
3   'Keep On Running' (Jan '66)
4   'I Heard It Through The Grapevine' (Mar '69)
5   'Do Wah Diddy Diddy' (Aug '64)
6   'It's Not Unusual' (Mar '65)
7   'Are You Lonesome Tonight?' (Feb '61)
8   'Needles and Pins' (Jan '64)
9   'You'll Never Walk Alone' (Oct '63)
10 'It's Only Make Believe' (Dec '58)
11 'Paint It Black' (May '66)
12 'Go Now!' (Jan '65)
13 'Silence Is Golden' (May '67)
14 'Summer Holiday' (Mar '63)
15 'Who's Sorry Now?' (May '58)

PART 2

1 Who presented the first ever *Top of the Pops* on New Year's Day, 1964?
2 True or False: Roy Orbison wore dark glasses because of an eye condition.
3 Which singer, better known as a comedian, had a No 1 hit with the weepy, 'Tears', in 1965?
4 And which other entertainer had the last No 1 of the decade in December, 1969? What was the song, still a favourite sing-a-long?
5 With which sixties band would you associate singer Allan Clarke?
6 Florence Ballard; Mary Wilson; who's missing from which band?
7 Which legendary rock 'n' roll star once employed Jimi Hendrix in his backing band?
8 What was the name of Elvis's manager from 1955?
9 What was The Who's 1969 album, a "Rock Opera" later turned into a bizarre movie by Ken Russell?
10 How old was Buddy Holly when he died in a plane crash in 1952: 22, 26 or 31?
11 What connects John Mayall's Bluesbreakers, Cream and Derek and the Dominoes?
12 What was the name of Elvis's backing band on many of his early hits?
13 Which of The Everly Brothers, The Righteous Brothers and The Isley Brothers contained no real brothers?
14 What was the one-off 1968 No 1 hit for The Crazy World of Arthur Brown, made famous by Brown's demented performance on *Top of the Pops*?
15 Which enduring star has earned himself the nickname, 'The Peter Pan of Pop'?

? **Tie-breaker**

Who was the UK's first Eurovision Song Contest winner in 1967, and with which song? Who came second the following year, and who was joint first in 1969 with 'Boom Bang-A-Bang'?

Food and drink

● ●

QUIZ 66
PART 1

1 From which country does sushi originate?
2 What is a bratwurst?
3 Chai is the Indian word for what?
4 Which is traditionally the hottest; rogan josh, korma, vindaloo, madras?
5 From what is caviar made?
6 What is bouillabaisse?
7 What is the old name for a Snickers bar?
8 What are marrons glacés?
9 Which celebrated London restaurant is owned and run by Ruth Rogers and Rose Gray?
10 What sauce accompanies the ham and eggs on a muffin in Eggs Benedict?
11 For what would a chef use a mandolin?
12 What is Italian cured pork belly?
13 What does en brochette mean?
14 Olives, anchovies and oil, blended into a paste and often used as an appetiser or accompaniment to bread: what is it?
15 The word 'Spam' is actually an abbreviation of what?

PART 2

1 Which aristocrat gave his name to a popular scented tea, often drunk without milk?

2 Sweden produced the Aktiebolaget Gasackumulator, but sensibly abbreviated the trade name to what?

3 Four rectangles of sponge, two pink, two yellow, in a block, wrapped in marzipan: what is it?

4 What is the Japanese marinade made from soy sauce, sake and mirin?

5 If an American offered you broiled food, how would it be cooked?

6 A sultana is a dried form of what?

7 The Greek dip, tzatziki, consists of cucumber mixed in what?

8 Which old-fashioned sweet and powerful Northern confectionery used to be taken by mountaineers in need of a fast energy hit?

9 What kind of fish is a kipper?

10 What term is used for a French cheese and ham toasted sandwich?

11 Gorgonzola and Roquefort are both blue cheeses sharing which other characteristic?

12 Which ingredient gives stroganoff its slightly grey tinge?

13 What is a flageolet?

14 Which country is the world's biggest coffee exporter?

15 American manufacturer Weber dominates the market in which catering accessory?

? *Tie-breaker*

What is the name of the legendary Californian restaurant in Yountville run by chef Thomas Keller? And what is Keller's equally well-regarded New York establishment?

Culture vulture

● ●

QUIZ 67
PART 1

1   Who painted the roof of the Sistine Chapel?
2   What is the name of the famous museum in St Petersburg?
3   Who wrote the opera, *Madame Butterfly*?
4   Who are the two warring families in Shakespeare's *Romeo and Juliet*?
5   What links St Paul's Cathedral to Greenwich Observatory and The Ashmolean Museum?
6   What was the relationship between Vanessa Bell and Virginia Woolf?
7   What is the more commonplace term for the branch of abstract expressionism called tachisme?
8   The Piazza San Marco, with its famous Basilica, is the dominant square in which European city?
9   With which instrument is the Spanish maestro, Andres Segovia, associated?
10 What were built to adorn Nebuchadnezzar's Palace south of Baghdad?
11 What was the literary magazine founded by Joseph Addison and Richard Steele in 1711?
12 A factory for manufacturing what was founded at Meissen in 1710?
13 Who was the French Renaissance humanist whose *Essais* (*Essays*) would become one of the most influential works of the period?
14 Which architect designed the Guggenheim Museum in New York?
15 What connects Rachel Whitread, Keith Tyson and Simon Starling?

PART 2

1 Which of Madrid's museums houses The Garden of Earthly Delights by Hieronymus Bosch?
2 Which famous theatre critic was the first person to use the f-word on live television in Britain?
3 In which country could you be given the Mosman Art Prize?
4 Sickert, Gore and Augustus John are all associated with which London-based group of artists?
5 Where was Monet's garden, where he painted the famous 'Waterlilies'?
6 What nationality was the painter Kandinsky?
7 Which novel by Gustave Flaubert was the subject of a famous obscenity trial on its release in 1856?
8 For what is artist Tom Keating best known?
9 With which musical instrument was the legendary Jacqueline Du Pré associated?
10 Who painted 'Symphonies in Grey' and Green and also White?
11 Which American essayist and philosopher wrote *Walden*, a celebration of simple living?
12 Which town, 50 miles from Paris, boasts Europe's finest Gothic Cathedral, with some of the most spectacular stained glass?
13 Which fine piece of John Rennie's London architecture now sits in Arizona?
14 Henry Moore and Barbara Hepworth were great friends who both operated in which artistic form?
15 Which artist and visionary was the founder of the Kelmscott Press in 1891?

? Tie-breaker

What are the four operas that make up Wagner's Der Ring Des Nibelungen (The Ring Cycle)?

The Beatles

● ●

QUIZ 68
PART 1

1   What was George Harrison's only solo No1?
2   What was the record label started by the band in 1968?
3   Who did Ringo replace as drummer in August 1962?
4   At whose trial did Paul McCartney have to explain the meaning of the song Helter Skelter?
5   And which was the first to top the US charts?
6   What role did Mark David Chapman play in the history of The Beatles?
7   'I Am The Walrus' featured on which 1967 EP release?
8   In which European city did The Beatles give a series of electrifying live performances in the months before they hit the big time?
9   Who managed The Beatles during their early successes, up until his death in 1967?
10 What was the Beatles' first movie, released in 1964 at the height of their popularity?
11 In 1966, The Beatles suffered serious harassment from government officials of which country after declining an invitation to a reception with the President's wife?
12 What connects 'Act Naturally', 'Yellow Submarine' and 'Don't Pass Me By'?
13 Which Beatles song is believed to be the most covered song of all time?
14 Which was the last year the Beatles played live: 1966, 1968, 1969 or 1970?
15 Which record producer is credited with being a vital ingredient in the band's success?

Did you know?

Whilst McCartney has remained a strong composer and solid live performer in his solo career, his biggest hits have all had a novelty element. His recent efforts have shown something of a return to the form that saw him have consecutive No1 hit albums in the early seventies with the fabulous *Band On The Run* and *Venus and Mars*, the follow-up.

PART 2

Name the Beatles album from the tracks given.

1   'Lovely Rita'/'Lucy In The Sky With Diamonds'/'A Day In The Life'
2   'A Taste of Honey'/'I Saw Her Standing There'/'Love Me Do'
3   'Across The Universe'/'For You Blue'/'Get Back'
4   'Tomorrow Never Knows'/'Yellow Submarine'/'Eleanor Rigby'
5   'Dizzy Miss Lizzy'/'You're Going To Lose That Girl'/'Ticket To Ride'
6   'Sexy Sadie'/'Glass Onion'/'Back In The USSR'
7   'Norwegian Wood (This Bird Has Flown)'/'Nowhere Man'/'Michelle'
8   'Hello Little Girl'/'Leave My Kitten Alone'/'Free As A Bird'
9   'She Came In Through The Bathroom Window'/'Come Together'/'Here Comes The Sun'
10 'Tell Me Why'/'Things We Said Today'/'Can't Buy Me Love'

? *Tie-breaker*

Name Paul McCartney's three No1 singles since the demise of The Beatles.

Food and drink

● ●

QUIZ 69
PART 1

1   What is the main ingredient of Spanish paella?
2   What shape is the pasta known as conchiglie?
3   What is the meringue dessert named after a ballet dancer?
4   What is the main ingredient of the Scottish soup, cullen skink?
5   And what is the main ingredient of the Russian soup, borscht?
6   John Dory, wahoo and hoki are edible types of what?
7   Mornay; sounds posh, actually simple; what is it?
8   Filippo Berro are best known in Britain for producing what culinary essential?
9   What is the name of the chilled tomato soup originally from Spain?
10 What naturally occurring agent assists in the setting of jam?
11 What kind of pastry is used to make profiteroles?
12 Dopiaza is a curry sauce centred on which main ingredient?
13 What name is given to a filo pastry parcel filled with nuts and soaked in honey?
14 Leftover potato fried up with onion and maybe other vegetables is known affectionately as what?
15 Frappé means what?

Music and culture - Food and drink

PART 2

1. In Indian cooking, chapattis, naan and roti are all types of what?
2. What is the traditional batter-based accompaniment to roast beef for Sunday lunch?
3. Which fictional hotel-owner declared his establishment unable to serve a Waldorf salad due to a lack of Waldorfs?
4. What is the Italian term for hors d'oeuvres, or starters?
5. What, essentially, is Chateaubriand?
6. Chow mein dishes in Chinese cuisine are served with what staple?
7. What name is given in schools for the traditional dessert of currant-filled sponge roll, usually served with custard?
8. Polenta is made with flour, water and what other ingredient?
9. Hummus is comprised of olive oil, chickpeas, garlic and which other principal ingredient?
10. Vegetables cut into fine strips are said to be served how?
11. What is a madeleine?
12. What are prunes?
13. A tin half-filled with water to allow slow cooking of, for example, a soufflé, is known as a what?
14. What is the name for small cubes of fried or toasted bread thrown on a salad or soup as a garnish?
15. Arran Pilot, Pink Fir Apple and Estima are all types of what?

? Tie-breaker

What was Shirley Conran's best selling book about keeping house?

Pop music - 70s

●●●●●●●●●●●●●●●●●●●●●●●●●●●

QUIZ 70
PART 1

1   In 1972, years after he was a rock 'n' roll pioneer, Chuck Berry had a No1 hit for the first time. Which novelty record brought him success?

2   Who embarked on a worldwide tour called the Rolling Thunder Review in 1975?

3   Who did Sid Vicious succeed as bass player in the Sex Pistols?

4   What, in 1975, was Queen's first UK Top 40 single?

5   Whose album, *Bridge Over Troubled Water*, was a No. 1 hit single (and album) on both sides of the Atlantic?

6   Which song, released in 1978, was John Peel's favourite, and was played at the legendary DJ's funeral?

7   'Tie A Yellow Ribbon Round The Old Oak Tree' was a massive hit for which pop combo?

8   David Gates was the lead singer in which soft-rock group?

9   Long blonde-haired singer Brian Connolly was the front man in which glam band?

10 What instrument did Ian Anderson, lead singer of Jethro Tull, play as he pranced around the stage in his tights?

11 'Stayin' Alive' and 'Night Fever', huge singles for the Bee Gees, were taken from the soundtrack to which box-office smash movie?

12 Shane Fenton enjoyed chart success under which alternative name?

13 In what cause did George Harrison think up the charity concert at Madison Square Garden on August 1st, 1971?

14 Which loved-up crooner was the songwriter and producer at the head of the Love Unlimited Orchestra?

15 *Songs In The Key of Life* was a classic release from which enduring soul singer and songwriter?

PART 2 - *Identify these classic seventies albums from the three tracks given.*

1   'Heaven Can Wait'/'All Revved Up With No Place To Go'/'Paradise By The Dashboard Light'
2   'Will Anything Happen?'/'Picture This'/'Sunday Girl'
3   'Cracked Actor'/'Time'/'The Jean Genie'
4   'Tiger'/'Money Money Money'/'Dancing Queen'
5   'Bring On The Night'/'Bed's Too Big Without You'/'Walking On The Moon'
6   'Dreams'/'You Make Loving Fun'/'Go Your Own Way'
7   'Sweet Painted Lady'/'Ballad of Danny Bailey'/'Candle In The Wind'
8   'Battle of Evermore'/'Black Dog'/'Stairway To Heaven'
9   'Needle and the Damage Done'/'Alabama'/'Heart of Gold'
10 'Sister Morphine'/'Wild Horses'/'Brown Sugar'

? *Tie-breaker*

Who had a No. 1 hit on both sides of the Atlantic with 'Three Times a Lady', and who was their lead singer on that track?

Did you know?

The Punk movement, which exploded in late 1976 and became headline news in '77, was brewing from the beginning of the decade. The Sex Pistols played their first live gigs in 1975, and "New Rose" by The Damned, claimed as the first punk single, was released on 22nd October, 1976. The Sex Pistols' *Anarchy in the UK* was released shortly after and the bandwagon was gathering momentum...

Culture vultures

● ●

QUIZ 71
PART 1 – *Match the painter to the work.*

1 Sandro Botticelli
2 Claude Monet
3 JMW Turner
4 Rembrandt van Rijn
5 Wassily Kandinsky
6 Pablo Picasso
7 David Hockney
8 Vincent Van Gogh
9 Canaletto
10 Pierre-Auguste Renoir

A 'Still Life: Vase With Twelve Sunflowers'
B 'A Bigger Splash'
C 'The Grand Canal and St Salute, Venice'
D 'Guernica'
E 'Water Lily Pond (Le Bassin Aux Nympheas)'
F 'Dance at La Moulin de la Galette'
G 'The Night Watch'
H 'The Blue Rider (Der Blaue Reiter)'
I 'The Birth of Venus'
J 'Rain, Steam and Speed'

Did you know?

Impressionism was never a specific school of art; it was more a loose bonding of a number of Paris-based artists in the nineteenth century. The term comes from the Monet painting, 'Impression, Sunrise', and Monet remains the artist who most encapsulates the idea of impressionism.

PART 2

1 Poet Seamus Heaney won the 1999 Whitbread Prize for his translation of which famous Anglo-Saxon work?

2 By what name is the architectural piece Bartholdi's 'Liberty Enlightening The World' better known?

3 What term is applied to the ceiling of a domed building, or an interior domed ceiling within a larger structure?

4 Which saintly figure composed some of the earliest choral music in record?

5 In which field did Ann Sofie Von Otter make her name?

6 What nationality was the famous engraver and watercolourist, Hokusai?

7 Which British architect, creator of the Pompidou Centre and the Millennium Dome, was charged with overseeing the design of Heathrow's Terminal 5?

8 Norwegian composer Edvard Grieg based his *Peer Gynt Suite* on a surreal play by which of his countrymen?

9 Whose bizarre plans for the Sagrada Familia in Barcelona remained incomplete on his death in 1926?

10 What is the common name given to Beethoven's Sixth Symphony?

11 Whose maid, Gabrielle, was the subject for many of his famous nude studies?

12 Which museum, built on the site of a defunct railway station, was opened in 1986 by President Mitterrand in Paris?

13 Tennyson's *Idylls of the King* are a narrative verse retelling of which classic tale?

14 What is the highest male singing voice?

15 Which female impressionist painter was the granddaughter of Fragonard and married Edouard Manet's brother, Eugene?

? Tie-breaker

Lyrical Ballads (1798) was an influential volume of poetry published jointly by which two luminaries of the time?

Clothes and fashion

● ●

QUIZ 72
PART 1

1. What kind of bag is named after a nineteenth century British Prime Minister?
2. Where would one wear espadrilles?
3. Which famous Chanel perfume was created by Ernest Beaux and launched in 1921?
4. What is a peruke?
5. Who was born Laura Mountney in Merthyr Tydfil in 1925?
6. Nick Kamen was seen in a famous advert, stripping down to which designer pants in a laundrette?
7. Which football club named their new stadium (first used in 1997) after their sponsor, a leading brand of sportswear manufacturer?
8. With what is Louis Vuitton associated?
9. What is the name of the frill often seen worn around the neck in Elizabethan portraits?
10. Which designer currently heads the Dior empire?
11. For what is Nicky Clarke best known?
12. What was Mary Quant's crucial stylistic contribution to women's attire in the 1960s?
13. And what was her equally racy variation on the theme in the early 1970s?
14. Which part of the body is left free in a properly-dressed toga?
15. Which famous designer of tennis clothing was asked to leave his job at Wimbledon after he designed a pair of "shocking" lace panties to be worn under a tennis skirt?

PART 2

1 Which supermodel was married to Richard Gere for four years in the early 1990s?
2 Whose 1947 'New Look' blew fashion thinking of the time wide open?
3 George Davis, former CEO of Next, lent his expertise and gave his name to the in-house clothing range of which retailer?
4 What name is given to a decorative silk shoulder sash for wearing a ceremonial sword?
5 Which fashion house does one associate with Formula 1?
6 Linda Evangelista, Christy Turlington and which other model often worked together and were known as 'The Trinity'?
7 What name is given to women's trousers that have the appearance of a skirt but have separate legs?
8 Which Croydon-born model pioneered the painfully thin 'waif look' in the 1990s?
9 Where would you normally wear a Homburg?
10 Provocative and After Five are scents promoted using which famous actress?
11 Who produces the perfumes Nu and Paris?
12 Who is credited with the design of the "little black dress"?
13 What was Sarah Jane Hutt the last Englishwoman to achieve, in 1983?
14 What name is given to a luxurious Tibetan cashmere shawl?
15 What would an American call a pair of tights?

? *Tie-breaker*
Where would you be likely to wear a peignoir, and of what material is it most likely to be made?

Rock legends

● ●

QUIZ 73
PART 1

1   Which singer/songwriter is known as The Boss?
2   Which artist used The Thin White Duke as one of his many alter-egos?
3   With which band was Peter Gabriel once lead singer?
4   Billy Corgan was the leading influence in which early nineties grunge band?
5   Annie Lennox had a No1 hit in the 80s as lead singer in which band?
6   Which US magazine, founded by Jann Wenner in 1967, is regarded by most as the doyen of rock publications?
7   What connects Neil Young, Leonard Cohen, Alanis Morissette and Joni Mitchell?
8   Who was the rock DJ, a great supporter of trad rock acts, who went by the nickname of 'Fluff'?
9   Roger McGuinn and Gene Clark are associated with which legendary sixties band?
10 Syd Barrett, who died in 2006, was the original singer in which avant-garde rock band?
11 Shaun Ryder was the lead singer in which anarchic Mancunian band at the end of the 1980s?
12 The enduring Chrissie Hynde has been at the forefront of which band for nearly thirty years?
13 During Live Aid, 1985, which established star flew from London to New York and played a set at both concerts?
14 Which famous and respected rock show on TV was hosted during its halcyon days by 'Whispering' Bob Harris?
15 Singer Don Van Vliet recorded and performed under what more familiar pseudonym?

Music and culture - *Rock legends*

PART 2 – *Name these classic bands from their line-ups.*

1   Kurt Cobain, Krist Novoselic, Dave Grohl
2   Axl Rose, Slash, Izzy Stradlin, Duff McKagan, Steve Adler
3   Ian Curtis, Peter Hook, Stephen Morris, Bernard Sumner
4   Robert Plant, John Bonham, Jimmy Page, John Paul Jones
5   Levi Stubbs, Duke Fakir, Obie Benson, Lawrence Payton
6   Gaz Coombes, Danny Goffey, Mick Quinn
7   Mackie Jayson, Brian Leiser, Huey Morgan
8   Tim Wheeler, Mark Hamilton, Rick McMurray, Charlotte Hatherley
9   Phil Lynott, Scott Gorham, Brian Robertson, Brain Downey
10 Hugh Cornwell, Jet Black, Dave Greenfield, Jean-Jacques Burnel
11 Andy Bell, Vince Clarke
12 Ian Brown, John Squire, Mani, Reni
13 Ritchie Blackmore, Tony Carey, Cozy Powell, Ronnie James Dio, Jimmy Bain
14 Geddy Lee, Alex Lifeson, Neil Peart
15 Dave Hill, Jim Lea, Noddy Holder, Don Powell

? *Tie-breaker*

After breaking up The Jam in 1982, which band did Paul Weller form, and who was the keyboard player who was the other main regular member?

Food and drink

● ●

QUIZ 74

PART 1 – *(Actually, just drink).*

1   What is the world's biggest selling single malt?
2   From what is calvados distilled?
3   Cloudy Bay Sauvignon Blanc is a celebrated wine of which country?
4   Jack Daniels is the most popular brand of what liquor in the UK?
5   Which cocktail is an odd mixture of champagne and Guinness (or any stout)?
6   Champagne and cassis (blackcurrant liqueur) comprise which aperitif?
7   "If you can't beat 'em, join 'em" was a successful advertising slogan for which brand of beer?
8   Australians couldn't give XXXX for anything other than what?
9   What French term is used for the main wine-waiter in a restaurant?
10 What is the traditional stirrup cup consumed before riding off on a hunt?
11 Cobra and Tiger are beers produced originally in which country?
12 Old Peculier is a brand of high-strength bitter from which brewery?
13 Strongbow is a best selling brand of which beverage?
14 What are the constituents of a dry Martini?
15 Which body takes upon itself control of the quality and integrity of beer making in the UK?

PART 2

1 Mateus Rosé is many a British youngster's introduction to wine drinking. Where is this popular quaffer produced?
2 Concha Y Toro is a massive wine-producing corporation in which country?
3 Trocken on a German wine would indicate what?
4 Tokaj is the blue-ribbon wine of which European country?
5 What grape is the main varietal in Chablis?
6 Brouilly, Morgon and Fleurie are all types of which style of wine, made principally from the Gamay grape?
7 If you were enjoying a glass of Gavi at source, which country would you be in?
8 What is the generic term for the sparkling wines native to Spain?
9 The Stellenbosch is a major wine-producing area of which country?
10 Which country produces Nyetimber sparkling wine?
11 Many dessert wines are made from botrytized grapes. Which means, basically, what?
12 A red Burgundy would be made principally from which grape varietal?
13 In the acclaimed 'wine movie' *Sideways*, to which grape varietal does Miles (Paul Giamatta) take exception?
14 St Emilion and Pomerol are both Appellations in which wine-growing region?
15 A French wine described as Syrah would be called what in Australia?

? Tie-breaker
Which two towns are the centres of the Champagne making area?

Pop idols

● ●

QUIZ 75
PART 1

1   Before his solo success, Robbie Williams had already had chart success as part of which act?

2   Until the Spice Girls and girl power, who were the UK's most successful girl-group?

3   Les McKeown was the singer in which teen heartthrob act from the seventies?

4   Who finished second behind Will Young in the first series of *Pop Idol*?

5   Heidi Range, after a brief spell in Atomic Kitten, became one of which successful girl group?

6   Who was the first of the original Spice Girls to leave the band?

7   Whose departure forced S Club 7 to change their name to simply S Club?

8   Who won the first BBC *Fame Academy* in 2002?

9   Brian McFadden left his wife Kerry and pursued a relationship with which Australian songstress?

10   'Don't Give Up On Us' (1976) was a No1 hit for TV heartthrob, David Soul. Which show made him famous?

11   Which show launched the careers of Liberty X and Girls Aloud?

12   Seventies pin-up David Cassidy was initially a member of which singing TV act?

13   'Rock On' (1973) was the breakthrough hit for which twinkly-eyed star?

14   Which Spice Girls single entered the US chart at No11, breaking the Beatles' long-standing record for the highest entry by a non-US act?

15   Whose 1999 album, *Millennium*, sold 1.13 million copies in its first week of release, setting a new US record?

Music and culture - Pop idols

PART 2

1   By what name are Liz McClarnon, Natasha Hamilton and Jenny Frost better known?
2   The Lynch sisters, Edele and Keavy, were an integral part of which Irish pop act?
3   With which band did the Appleton sisters, Nicole and Natalie, first achieve chart success?
4   After ending his relationship with the Spice Girls, what was Simon Fuller's next project in the manufactured pop act market?
5   Davy Jones was the singer in which artificial sixties pop act, the prototype for the modern pop groups?
6   *Introduction* was the Top 10 debut album from which singer-songwriter, a winner of a TV talent show?
7   Whose debut, *Sound of the Underground*, went to No2 in 2003?
8   And whose album, *Justified*, kept them off top spot?
9   Boyzone's 'No Matter What' was a song from which Andrew Lloyd-Webber musical?
10 What was Donny Osmond's singing sister called?
11 Tearaway Brian Harvey was singer in which successful boy-band?
12 Who is the mother of singer Peter Andre's son, Junior?
13 By what name are Elena Katina and Yulia Volkov better known?
14 Which talented youngster, now better known as an actress, had a No1 single, aged 16, with 'Because We Want To' in 1998?
15 'Changes' (2003) was No1 hit for which famous daughter?

? **Tie-breaker**
Which two names are missing?: Keith Duffy, Mikey Graham, Shane Lynch.

Pop music - 8os

● ●

QUIZ 76
PART 1

1   The classic Michael Jackson track 'Billie Jean' was taken from which huge-selling album?

2   What was the breakthrough single for Frankie Goes To Hollywood, its success almost guaranteed by the BBC's decision to ban it?

3   Who had a hit with 'Girls Just Wanna Have Fun', an archetypal beat-pop eighties song?

4   'When Doves Cry' was Prince's first US No1 single; which album, also a No. 1, was it taken from?

5   Which singer shot to short-lived stardom when she played at the Nelson Mandela concert in 1988, thrusting her eponymous debut album and single, *Fast Car*, to the upper reaches of the US and UK charts?

6   Which US all-girl group featured future solo artists Jane Wiedlin and Belinda Carlisle?

7   *Songs From The Big Chair* helped which act make it in the US as well as the UK?

8   Whose *Raising Hell* album was the first rap record to go platinum in the US?

9   Who were the UK's only Eurovision winners in the decade, with 'Making Your Mind Up' in 1981?

10 What took place on Saturday July 13th, 1985?

11 Chuck D and Flavor Flav were part of which Def Jam rap act that built up a huge following in the latter part of the decade?

12 What did Sony & Philips demonstrate for the first time at a joint press conference in April 1981?

13 Which Dire Straits album became the first to top 3 million sales just in the UK?

14 Which cover version provided Soft Cell with their only US hit and their biggest in the UK?

15 Who won Eurovision for Switzerland in 1988 with 'Ne Partez Pas Sans Moi'?

PART 2 - *Whose album? (They all reached No. 1).*
1   *Faith*
2   *Viva Hate*
3   *Welcome To The Pleasuredome*
4   *The Gift*
5   *Popped In Souled Out*
6   *Ghost In The Machine*
7   *Alf*
8   *Can't Slow Down*
9   *The Unforgettable Fire*
10 *Graceland*
11 *Dare*
12 *Hysteria*
13 *Seven and the Ragged Tiger*
14 *The Lexicon of Love*
15 *Misplaced Childhood*

? *Tie-breaker*

What was Madonna's first Top 10 single in the UK; and what was the title of her second album, which cemented her as an international superstar?

Song and dance

● ●

QUIZ 77
PART 1

1   According to the Noel Coward lyric, what are mad dogs and Englishmen alone in doing?

2   Who was the choreographer who produced the elaborate arrangements for many of the Warner and MGM show-stopping musicals of the thirties and forties?

3   Which leggy actress featured as Gene Kelly's dangerous love interest in a *Singin' in the Rain* dream sequence?

4   "Birds do it, bees do it, even educated fleas do it" - lines by which prolific US composer and lyricist?

5   The original ballroom programme on TV, *Come Dancing*, was created by the same man who conceived Miss World. Who was he?

6   In what 1957 film did Fred Astaire feature as Audrey Hepburn's dancing partner?

7   Who made his mark on Broadway in 1957 with the lyrics for Leonard Bernstein's *West Side Story*, and went on to compose his own musicals, including *Follies* and *A Little Night Music*?

8   Who starred in the 1980 film *Fame* and also sang the title track to 1983's *Flashdance*?

9   What does Jennifer Beals' wannabe ballet dancer do for a living in *Flashdance*?

10 In which stage and screen musical would you find a group of dancing Nazi storm troopers?

11 The Mazurka is a traditional dance of which country?

12 Which controversial musical was premiered on 28th March 1968, in New York's Biltmore Theatre?

13 What was the sexy dance troupe on the Kenny Everett show?

14 Which legendary choreographer directed *Cabaret* and was responsible for its dance numbers?

15 Fred Astaire is always associated with Ginger Rogers; which cousin-by-marriage of Ginger's danced with Fred in his first screen role?

Music and culture – Song and dance

PART 2 – *Match the song to the source material.*

1 'Bless Your Beautiful Hide'
2 'Brush Up Your Shakespeare'
3 'Secret Love'
4 'You'll Never Walk Alone'
5 'Ol' Man River'
6 'Tonight'
7 'Sit Down, You're Rocking the Boat'
8 'You Are My Lucky Star'
9 'Tomorrow'
10 'Blow, Gabriel, Blow'
11 'There's No Business Like Show Business'
12 'Thank Heaven For Little Girls'
13 'You're the One That I Want'
14 'Oh What A Beautiful Morning'
15 'Shall We Dance?'

A *Gigi*
B *Show Boat*
C *Guys and Dolls*
D *West Side Story*
E *Singin' in the Rain*
F *The King and I*
G *Annie*
H *Carousel*
I *Kiss Me Kate*
J *Calamity Jane*
K *Oklahoma!*
L *Anything Goes*
M *Seven Brides For Seven Brothers*
N *Grease*
P *Annie Get Your Gun*

? *Tie-breaker*
Whose singing voice replaced both Natalie Wood's in West Side Story, and Audrey Hepburn's in My Fair Lady?

Spot the lyric

● ●

QUIZ 78

PART 1 – *Identify the song from the lyrics – artist (original) and title, please.*

1   Stop making the eyes at me, I'll stop making the eyes at you./And what it is that surprises me is that I don't really want you to.

2   Life is a mystery, everyone must stand alone,/I hear you call my name, and it feels like home.

3   And I find it kind of funny,/I find it kind of sad,/The dreams in which I'm dying are the best I ever had.

4   Girls run around with no clothes on,/To borrow a pound for a condom./If it wasn't for chip fat they'd be frozen -/They're not very sensible.

5   Chain reaction running through my veins/Pumps the bass line up into my brain/Screws my mind until I lose control/And when the building rocks I know it's got my soul.

6   In one single moment your whole life can turn 'round,/I stand there for a minute starin' straight into the ground.

7   Last time that we had this conversation,/I decided we should be friends./Yeah, but now we're going around in circles,/Tell me, will this déjà vu never end?

8   You were working as a waitress in a cocktail bar,/When I met you./I picked you out, I shook you up and turned you around,/Turned you into someone new.

9   You own it, you better never let it go./You only get one shot, do not miss your chance to blow./This opportunity comes once in a lifetime.

10 I read the news today, oh boy,/10,000 holes in Blackburn, Lancashire.

PART 2

1   We don't need no education,/We don't need no thought control./No dark sarcasm in the classroom,/Teacher, leave them kids alone.

2   With the lights out, it's less dangerous/Here we are now – entertain us.

3   It's been seven hours and fifteen days,/Since you took your love away./I go out every night and sleep all day,/Since you took your love away.

4   I took her to a supermarket,/I don't know why, but I had to start it somewhere./So it started there.

5   Please allow me to introduce myself,/I'm a man of wealth and taste,/I've been around for a long, long year,/Stole many a man's soul and faith.

6   It's on Amerika's tortured brow/That Mickey Mouse has grown up a cow./Now the workers have struck for fame,/'Cause Lennon's on sale again.

7   And it's whispered that soon,/If we all call the tune,/That the piper will lead us to reason.

8   Welcome to a new kind of tension,/All across the alien nation,/Everything isn't meant to be okay.

9   She keeps her Moet and Chandon in a pretty cabinet./Let them eat cake, she says, just like Marie Antoinette.

10 Why is the bedroom so cold, turned away on your side? Is my timing that flawed, our respect run so dry?

? Tie-breaker
Today is gonna be the day/That they're gonna throw it back to you./By now, you should've somehow/Realised what you gotta do.

Culture vultures

●●●●●●●●●●●●●●●●●●●●●●●●●●●

QUIZ 79
PART 1

1 What term is used for making artistic images by attaching string, newspaper and such to a canvas or base?
2 Which French artist was known for painting only in blue?
3 Which London landmark was opened to the public in Bloomsbury, London, in 1759, six years after it was founded?
4 Picasso and Braque were the prime movers in which art movement?
5 Who produced the eighteenth-century moral/humorous series, *The Harlot's Progress* and *The Rake's Progress*?
6 What is the type of tower known as a campanile designed to hold?
7 Who is best known for the orchestral suite, *The Planets*?
8 Trafalgar Square, Regent's Park, Marble Arch and the rebuilt Brighton Pavilion are all the work of which architect?
9 Which poet won the Whitbread Prize in successive years in 1997 (*Tales From Ovid*) and 1998 (*The Birthday Letters*). (He died later in '98.)?
10 Which famous fourteenth-century palace of the Moorish dynasty lies at Granada in southern Spain?
11 Which early Gothic edifice, built to Maurice de Sully's twelfth-century design, dominates a section of Paris from its position on the Seine?
12 The Clore Gallery was a 1986 addition to which famous art gallery?
13 What did Jorn Utzon construct in Sydney between 1957 and 1973?
14 Which poet and artist has his illustrations to Dante's *Divine Comedy* on display at the Tate Gallery?
15 Domenico Scarlatti was known primarily as a composer for which instrument?

Music and culture – Culture vultures

PART 2
Match the composer to the opera
1 Ludwig van Beethoven
2 Gaetano Donizetti
3 Giacomo Puccini
4 Wolfgang Amadeus Mozart
5 Georges Bizet
6 Giaochino Rossini
7 Giuseppe Verdi
8 Benjamin Britten
9 Pyotr Tchaikovsky
10 Richard Strauss

A *La Traviata*
B *Fidelio*
C *Carmen*
D *The Magic Flute*
E *Eugene Onegin*
F *Lucia Di Lammermoor*
G *Billy Budd*
H *The Barber of Seville*
I *Der Rosenkavalier*
J *Madame Butterfly*

? Tie-breaker
Name the Three Tenors.

Did you know?

The Three Tenors have had many successful collaborations and concerts. They first got together on the eve of the 1990 World Cup Finals in Italy at the Baths of Caracalla in Rome, with renowned conductor Zubin Mehta leading the orchestra. Their rendering of 'Nessun Dorma', from Puccini's *Turandot*, was used as the theme for that tournament. They subsequently sang at the next three World Cup Finals, and sold millions of CDs. Opera purists have tended to mock their contribution to popularising the art form.

Food and drink - chefs

● ●

QUIZ 80
PART 1

1 Which TV chef led a high-profile campaign to improve the quality of school dinners in the UK?

2 Who was the face of Indian cookery on the BBC for most of the 70s and 80s?

3 Who is the feared and funny food critic for *The Sunday Times*?

4 Who was the pioneer TV chef who showed viewers how to achieve good home cooking while her husband Johnny hung around and got in the way?

5 Which flamboyant chef owns Mirabelle in Curzon Street, London?

6 Who hosts the long-running TV cookery game-show, *Ready Steady Cook*?

7 Who is chef/proprietor of the 3-Michelin-Star restaurant in Bray, Berkshire, The Fat Duck?

8 This village boasts another acclaimed 3-star restaurant, owned by Michel Roux; what is it?

9 Which prestigious London hotel houses Gordon Ramsay's No2 restaurant?

10 Hibiscus, Mr Underhill's and The Merchant House are all prestigious restaurants, and all based in which fortunate Midlands town?

11 What is Raymond Blanc's celebrated Oxfordshire country-house restaurant?

12 Fay Maschler is a famous food critic who has worked mainly for which newspaper?

13 Under what name does Nobuyuki Matsuhisa trade in his London restaurant?

14 Which "cheeky-chappie" chef, restaurateur and valiant champion of British cuisine was awarded an OBE in June 2006?

15 Who made his name at the Landmark Hotel before taking French Leave on TV and seeking sanctuary at the Carved Angel in Dartmouth?

PART 2 – *Match the cookery writer to the book.*
1   Nigel Slater
2   Gordon Ramsay
3   Rick Stein
4   James Martin (w/ Jean Cazelle)
5   Nigella Lawson
6   Darina Allen
7   Antonio Carluccio
8   Ruth Rogers and Rose Gray
9   Sophie Grigson
10 Jane Grigson
11 Simon Hopkinson
12 Tamsin Day-Lewis
13 Jamie Oliver
14 Elizabeth David
15 Hugh Fearnley-Whittingstall

A   *The River Cottage Cookbook*
B   *Food For Friends*
C   *Just Desserts*
D   *An Omelette and A Glass of Wine*
E   *Roast Chicken and Other Stories*
F   *Great British Dinners*
G   *A Year At Ballymaloe*
H   *The Art of The Tart*
I   *A Feast of Mushrooms*
J   *A Taste of the Sea*
K   *How To Eat*
L   *River Café Cookbook*
M   *Appetite*
N   *The Naked Chef*
P   *A Passion For Pasta*

? Tie-breaker
Who runs London's only restaurant to boast 3 Michelin Stars?

Pop music - 90s

●●●●●●●●●●●●●●●●●●●●●●●●●

QUIZ 81
PART 1

1   Beyoncé Knowles and her cousin, Kelly Rowland, were both in which late-90s r'n'b act?
2   Who embarked on a Blonde Ambition tour at the start of the decade?
3   True or False: The Spice Girls' debut single, 'Wannabe', made No1 in the UK and in the US.
4   Which country star appeared on the KLF's hit, 'Justified and Ancient'?
5   Which former member of NWA became the guiding force behind the emergence and success of Eminem?
6   Which teenage band had a No1 hit with 'Mmm-Bop'?
7   Rod Stewart, Sting and which other ageing rocker collaborated on the US No1 single, 'All For Love'?
8   Gwen Stefani started her career as lead singer in which band?
9   Who is the only other member of Take That to have a No1 hit, apart from Robbie Williams?
10 Which country artist's single, 'Ropin' The Wind', enjoyed eighteen weeks atop the US Billboard chart?
11 Who died, aged 45, on November 24th, 1991, ensuring his band achieved almost as much posthumous success as they did while he was alive?
12 Who had hits with covers of 'Killing Me Softly' and 'No Woman, No Cry'?
13 The Hindu Love Gods were a side project featuring Warren Zevon and members of which major band?
14 Dolores O'Riordan was lead singer with which successful Irish band?
15 'Baby One More Time' propelled which singer to instant stardom?

PART 2 - *Name the artist of the following hit albums.*
1   *I've Been Expecting You*
2   *Music For The Jilted Generation*
3   *Dookie*
4   *Funky Divas*
5   *Falling Into You*
6   *Mellon Collie and The Infinite Sadness*
7   *You've Come A Long Way, Baby*
8   *Nevermind*
9   *Vauxhall And I*
10 *The Bends*
11 *Boys For Pele*
12 *Ray of Light*
13 *Songs of Faith and Devotion*
14 *Jagged Little Pill*
15 *Dig Your Own Hole*

? *Tie-breaker*

Who caused controversy at the 1996 Brit Awards by interrupting Michael Jackson's performance with his own parody of the eighties icon?

Clothes and fashion

● ●

QUIZ 82
PART 1

1   With which retailer is the St Michael brand associated?
2   Which young actress has "La Bella Vita" tattooed just above her right buttock?
3   L'Air du Temps is a longstanding popular scent from which house?
4   A phillibeg is a type of what?
5   Who went from Chloe to Gucci in 2001?
6   Which British designer was associated first with the punk movement – she was heavily involved with Malcolm McLaren – and then known as a leading light in the extravagant dress of the New Romantics?
7   What type of wear is made by Loake and Grenson?
8   Czech model Eva Herzigova was best-known for endorsing which product in the 1990s?
9   Which shirt making company bought Calvin Klein in 2002?
10 The Rive Gauche chain was opened to sell the ready-to-wear range of which designer?
11 Which manufacturer of fashionable outdoor wear was founded in Basingstoke in 1865?
12 Who is famous for his polo label?
13 The race meeting at Ascot is known for its flamboyant displays of which fashion item?
14 In which Italian city was the Gucci house formed?
15 Which model was born Leslie Hornby in London in 1949?

PART 2

1 What is the one-piece top garment worn by many Indian women?
2 The Somerset town of Street boasts a well-established shopping village named after which local shoe manufacturer?
3 Where would you wear your very expensive Tag Heuer?
4 What is calico?
5 Italian house La Perla are best known for what?
6 Poison and Dolce Vita are both perfumes produced by which fashion house?
7 A décolleté garment is what exactly?
8 What Hindi-derived word describes a denim work garment consisting of trousers and a torso bib?
9 Why might you visit Toni & Guy?
10 Taffeta is a variety of which material?
11 What is a long round scarf made of feathers?
12 Which model appeared naked in a controversial Y2000 ad for Opium, an Yves Saint-Laurent perfume?
13 What is a wide-awake?
14 Which Knightsbridge store has become synonymous with haute couture?
15 What would a piece of René Lalique jewellery be made from?

? *Tie-breaker*

For what might you use Mehndi?

Song and dance

●●●●●●●●●●●●●●●●●●●●●●●●●●●

QUIZ 83
PART 1

1   Berlin's 'Take My Breath Away' was a hit after featuring in which 1980s action movie with Tom Cruise?

2   What was Joe Cocker and Jennifer Warnes' hit theme tune to *An Officer and A Gentleman* (1982)?

3   What musical sees a barn building competition become an excuse for some exuberant dancing?

4   Which Hollywood actor played Danny Zuko in the original 1973 London production of *Grease*?

5   A novel by Gaston Leroux provided the inspiration for which Andrew Lloyd Webber musical?

6   Which suspender-clad musical heroine vows, "When I go, I'm going like Elsie"?

7   In William Shakespeare's *Romeo and Juliet* (dir. Baz Luhrmann, 1996), a drugged-up Mercutio bursts into a rendition of which disco classic?

8   The 'Cell Block Tango' is a song and dance number in which musical of the stage and screen?

9   What song provides the soundtrack to Jennifer Grey and Patrick Swayze's triumphant last dance at the end of *Dirty Dancing*?

10 What would you be doing if you followed this lyrical advice: "It's just a jump to the left, And then a step to the right; With your hands on your hips, You bring your knees in tight"?

11 Groove Armada's 'I See You Baby' is used to choreograph a series of butt-shaking visuals in an advert for which make of car?

12 Who plays prison warden Mama Morten in the 2002 film version of *Chicago*?

13 Who tap-danced up the walls in his role as dancer George Cohan in *Yankee Doodle Dandy* (1942)?

14 Which dancer collaborated on the second part of *Song and Dance* by Andrew Lloyd Webber?

15 What was Baz Luhrmann's directorial debut, set around a dance contest in Australia?

Music and culture – Song and dance

PART 2 – *Strictly Come Dancing (unless otherwise specified, we only want the celebrity dancer's name).*

1   Who is the main compere of *Strictly Come Dancing*?
2   And who is his glamorous sidekick who conducts the back-stage interviews?
3   Which former contestant covered for her when she went on maternity leave in Series 2?
4   Who fronted the daily update programme for series 2?
5   Which professional has partnered Martin Offiah, Julian Clary and Colin Jackson?
6   And who is her professional partner, given to challenging the judges from time to time?
7   Which Series 3 contestant was relieved to be partnered by Ian Waite, as she stands at 5'10"?
8   Who won *Strictly Ice Dancing* in 2004 despite having half the preparation time of the other contestants?
9   Who presides over the amateur spin-off series *Strictly Dance Fever*?
10 Which three former *Eastenders* stars have come second, first and fifth in the three series?
11 Who is the only lady judge?
12 Who are the three Olympic athletes who have competed, all impressively?
13 Who had Brendan Cole pulling his hair out in series 3, but managed to survive until fourth out, despite being conspicuously the worst dancer?
14 Who won the 2005 Christmas Special, garnering a maximum 40 on the way?
15 Which former footballer and current pundit won a *Strictly African Dancing* contest in 2005 as part of the *Africa Lives* season?

? *Tie-breaker*

In the 2001 Broadway revival of The Producers, who starred as Max Bialystock and Leo Bloom, and later reprised their roles in the movie remake?

L'Amour

● ●

QUIZ 84
PART 1

1 Which song was The Beatles contribution to 'Our World' in 1967, the first live TV global link?
2 Who loves Angel, but returns to Alex because Angel cannot accept her past?
3 Who is the unrequited love of Cyrano de Bergerac?
4 Who loves Heathcliff but marries Edgar Linton?
5 Who is American actress Joanne Woodward's devoted husband?
6 Who fell in love on the set of *To Have and Have Not*?
7 John Rolfe, an English settler, married whom on April 5th, 1614, in Jamestown, Virginia?
8 Who was the chaste but loving correspondent of French abbess, Heloise?
9 "O my love's like a red, red rose/That's newly sprung in June." Famous words, but who wrote them?
10 Which Shakespeare character "never told her love, but let concealment like a worm I'th bud feed on her damask cheek."?
11 Which married couple duetted on the 1965 hit, 'I Got You Babe'?
12 After how many years of marriage do a couple celebrate their Pearl wedding anniversary?
13 To whom has Irish actress Sinead Cusack had a long marriage?
14 And who is happily married to Vanessa Redgrave's daughter, Natasha Richardson?
15 Which multi-lingual French singer, born in 1924, has sold over a hundred million records, mostly about l'amour?

Did you know?

Luhrman's exciting modern interpretation is one of a number of films made about Shakespeare's star-cross'd lovers. Perhaps the best straight version was the 1968 film by Franco Zefferelli bravely casting two unknown teenagers, Leonard Whiting and Olivia Hussey, in the leads. Before that, Arthur Laurents and Stephen Sondheim had plundered the plot line for their successful musical, *West Side Story*.

PART 2

1 What 1970 film features the line "Love means never having to say you're sorry"?

2 Which actress was "falling in love again" in the 1930 film *The Blue Angel*?

3 "Reader, I married him." Who were the bride and groom in this famous literary union?

4 What was the name of Kurt Cobain's rock star lover?

5 What was the name of Italian sonneteer Petrarch's love interest?

6 Which of Elizabeth Taylor's husbands did she marry twice?

7 What woman was the inspiration for the love songs 'Something' by George Harrison, and 'Wonderful Tonight' by Eric Clapton?

8 For what does the acronym S.W.A.L.K. stand?

9 Jane Austen's character Elizabeth Bennet famously fell for Mr Darcy, but who was her sister Jane's love interest?

10 What band declared in 1980 that 'Love Will Tear Us Apart'?

? Tie-breaker

Who played the star-cross'd lovers in Baz Lurhman's 1996 film William Shakespeare's Romeo and Juliet?

Culture vultures

● ●

QUIZ 85
PART 1

1   Gittern, dobro and balalaika are all types of what?
2   Which British nineteenth-century artistic movement wanted to move artistic and decorative pursuits away from the manufactured products introduced during the industrial revolution?
3   Which one-word term describes a painting or sculpture of the Virgin Mary cradling the dead Christ?
4   Which Amsterdam museum was first opened in The Hague in 1800, and houses some of the best works of Rembrandt, Vermeer and Hals?
5   Which modern composer wrote the well-received piece for strings and cello, 'The Protecting Veil', in 1987?
6   Which egg-shaped government building was completed by Norman Foster and team in 2003?
7   Rossetti, Holman Hunt and Millais were amongst the founders of which school of art?
8   Who wrote a 'Rhapsody In Blue', for piano, orchestra and jazz band?
9   Which French composer's most famous piece was his 1928 'Bolero'?
10 Which building, built by Walter Gropius at Dessau in the 1920's lends its name to a Germanic architectural movement?
11 Which majestic Joseph Paxton structure was erected in Sydenham in 1851, moved the following year and burned in 1936?
12 Apart from the original gallery and the new Tate Modern in London, where are the other two sites run by the Tate in Britain?
13 Which American artist died in 1986, aged ninety-nine; her most famous work was probably 'Red Poppy', subject of a US postage stamp?
14 Which influential Italian family posed as the Magi for Botticelli's 'Adoration of the Magi'?
15 What was built to George Bergstrom's design during WWII at Arlington, Virginia, near Washington DC?

PART 2 – *Match the work to the poet.*

1   *Whitsun Weddings*
2   *A Shropshire Lad*
3   *The Aeneid*
4   *Paradise Lost*
5   *The Hawk In The Rain*
6   'Anthem For Doomed Youth'
7   *The Rape of the Lock*
8   'In Memoriam'
9   'Ode On A Grecian Urn'
10 *Metamorphoses*
11 *Making Cocoa For Kingsley Amis*
12 'The Rime of the Ancient Mariner'
13 *Leaves of Grass*
14 'The Wasteland'
15 *Under Milkwood*

A   Ovid
B   Wilfred Owen
C   Philip Larkin
D   Walt Whitman
E   John Keats
F   Wendy Cope
G   John Milton
H   A.E. Housman
I   T.S. Eliot
J   Samuel Taylor Coleridge
K   Alexander Pope
L   Ted Hughes
M   Dylan Thomas
N   Alfred, Lord Tennyson
P   Virgil

? **Tie-breaker**
Who is the current Poet Laureate (as of August 2006), and whom did he succeed in 1998?

Pop music (21st century)

● ●

QUIZ 86

PART 1 – *Name the artist of these UK No. 1 singles.*

1   'Dry Your Eyes'
2   'When The Sun Goes Down'
3   'Just Like A Pill'
4   'You Said No'
5   'Freak Like Me'
6   'Dirty'
7   'Leave Right Now'
8   'Groovejet (If This Ain't Love)'
9   'Like Toy Soldiers'
10   'Somethin' Stupid'
11   'Maneater'
12   'Bring Me To Life'
13   'What Took You So Long'
14   'Five Colours In Her Hair'
15   'Stickwitu'

PART 2

1 Which liked and respected radio presenter's death saddened the music world in October 2004?

2 Which female singer had the No1 album of the year in 2001 and again in 2003?

3 *Hot Fuss* was the critically acclaimed debut from which US rock band?

4 Which sixteen-year-old released her debut album *The Soul Sessions*, in 2003?

5 What was the title of former guardsman James Blunt's massive debut album?

6 Chester Bennington is the pin-up vocalist with which nu-metal band?

7 Which solo female artist's 2002 debut sold 20 million copies and won her eight Grammies?

8 *Come With Us* was a UK No1 album in 2002 for which durable dance band?

9 In music terms, who is Curtis James Jackson III?

10 Who connects the Libertines with Babyshambles?

11 *By The Way* (2002) was a commercial breakthrough for which US rockers?

12 Who had immediate success with her debut album, *Call Off The Search*, in 2003?

13 Jake Shears and Ana Matronic share vocal duties in which rock-cum-cabaret act?

14 What was David Gray's 2002 follow-up to the massively successful *White Ladder* (1999)?

15 Which Invisible Band topped the album chart in 2001?

? *Tie-breaker*

In what year was Scottish singer K.T. Tunstall born?

On the radio

●●●●●●●●●●●●●●●●●●●●●●●●●●

QUIZ 87
PART 1

1   Who was Radio 1's first female presenter?
2   Who has become an institution presenting *I'm Sorry I Haven't A Clue* since what seems like the dawn of time but is actually 1972?
3   Which Rochdale-born presenter has been BBC Radio's champion of World Music, particularly African?
4   Fox FM is the local radio service for which city and county?
5   With which radio programme was the late Roy Plomley associated?
6   And who took over as regular presenter of this show after Michael Parkinson filled in for a short period?
7   Which educational institution first broadcast on BBC radio in 1971?
8   Which was the first commercial radio station to start broadcasting in England, in 1933?
9   Which nightly reading was launched on BBC radio in 1949?
10 What were transmitted by the BBC via Greenwich from 5th February 1924 to 5th February 1990?
11 In which year was *The Archers* first broadcast: 1951, 1961 or 1971?
12 What distinction did 'Flowers In The Rain' by The Move enjoy on September 30th, 1967?
13 What was the UK's first commercial radio station, which began broadcasting in the capital in 1973?
14 What was renamed as BBC Radio 4 in 1967?
15 Who has been presenting *Woman's Hour* since taking over from Sue McGregor in 1987?

Music and culture - On the radio

PART 2

1   What is the commercial rival to BBC Radio 3, launched in 1992?
2   Which rabbi became something of a cult figure with his observations in the *Thought For The Day* slot on Radio 4's *Today* programme?
3   All three members of TV's The Goodies had worked on which radio comedy, running from 1963 to 1974?
4   Which deep-voiced DJ hosted the *Friday Rock Show*, and used it to champion hard rock and heavy metal?
5   Which city is served by the commercial radio station, Radio Piccadilly?
6   Which of the following was NOT a radio show before being shown on TV: *The League of Gentlemen, Dead Ringers, Not The Nine O'clock News, Hancocks Half Hour*?
7   James Naughtie took over as a main presenter on *Today* on Radio 4 after the death of which well-loved regular in 1994?
8   Which presenter and writer hosts Radio 4's *Midweek* programme?
9   On what non-digital frequency is *Test Match Special* broadcast?
10 Who is the host of Radio 2's *Breakfast Show*, the country's most popular morning listening?
11 Who co-presented *The Evening Session* with Steve Lamacq for four years, and is also known for presenting TV coverage of Glastonbury alongside John Peel?
12 Which well-known comedy actress makes frequent appearances on *The Archers* as Debbie Aldridge?
13 Which long-running quiz show was first aired as a stand-alone programme on Radio 4 in 1967?
14 What is the light chat-cum-comedy show on Radio 4 hosted by Ned Sherrin?
15 Which Liverpudlian Radio 4 presenter is married to Adrian Chiles?

? **Tie-breaker**
    Which two female DJs hosted Radio 1's breakfast show between 1997 and 2004?

People and places

Who's who

● ●

QUIZ 88

PART 1 – *Here are ten well-known names. Can you match them to the real names of those individuals?*

1 John Peel
2 Jordan
3 Pink
4 Michael Caine
5 Judy Garland
6 Bono
7 Johnny Vegas
8 Enid Blyton
9 The Rock
10 Fat Boy Slim

A Paul Hewson
B Maurice Micklewhite
C Frances Ethel Gumm
D Mrs Daryl Walters
E Norman Cook
F Dwayne Johnson
G Michael Pennington
H Katie Price
I Alecia Moore
J John Ravenscroft

Did you know?

The Who played as The Detours and The High Numbers before settling on The Who. Favourites among the mods, their early hits were angry youth anthems, most notably 'My Generation' (1965). Forty years on, after twice retiring, and despite the death of two of the original members, they are still playing live gigs.

People and places – *Who's who*

PART 2

1 In which year was *Who's Who* first launched: 1779, 1849 or 1909?
2 Who starred in the famous film version of Edward Albee's play, *Who's Afraid of Virginia Woolf*?
3 What was Busted's third No. 1 single in February 2004?
4 Who had a Top 10 hit with 'Who Killed Bambi?' in 1979; was it Sid Vicious, Ten Pole Tudor or Jilted John?
5 The TV-soap nation was kept on tenterhooks for seven months in 1980 to find out what revelation?
6 Which film stars Bob Hoskins as a private eye (Eddie Valiant) alongside a seductive cartoon moll called Jessica?
7 Who Let The Dogs Out in 2000?
8 Which scriptwriter was largely responsible for the creation of Dr Who?
9 Who is Batman?
10 And who is his adversary, Oswald Cobblepot?

? Tie-breaker
Who were the four original members of The Who?

People and places

● ●

QUIZ 89
PART 1

1. Which comic creation of Belgian cartoonist, Hergé, first appeared in print in 1929?
2. Hattie Caraway was the first woman to appear where in 1932?
3. Who went missing during the Paris-Dakar rally in 1982?
4. Who formed, and became the first leader of the (Independent) Labour Party in 1893?
5. Who posted 95 theses attacking wrongs in the Roman Catholic system on a church door in Wittenberg in 1517?
6. Where is a famous annual Regatta, a sporting and social event, held every year on the Thames?
7. What were Catherine Hartley and Fiona Thornewill the first British women to achieve in 2000?
8. The Jameson Raid led to the resignation of which statesman as Premier of the Cape Colony?
9. Who, in 1610, was the first to observe, and name, Jupiter's four satellites?
10. Who was born in Tupelo, Mississippi, on 8th January 1935?
11. What was the incident that led to the resignation of Michael Heseltine from Margaret Thatcher's Cabinet in 1986?
12. What did the 1920 Treaty of Versailles bring into being?
13. Noel Gallagher of Oasis is frequently seen at the home matches of which football club?
14. Enver Hoxha declared which nation a Republic in 1946?
15. Who led the (then) fastest Antarctic expedition by a British team in 1981?

PART 2

1 Who was sent off as England exited the 2006 World Cup on penalties?
2 Which twentieth-century composer first used what is now called the dodecaphonic scale?
3 The Welland Ship Canal links which two masses of water in North America?
4 Who was the victim of assassin John Felton in 1628?
5 The Polish Corridor was established after World War I to provide Poland with access to the Baltic Sea via which city port?
6 Who was the author of the sporting classic, *The Compleat Angler*?
7 Pope Alexander VI was better known as the patriarch of which ambitious Italian family?
8 Sarah Churchill and Abigail Masham competed for the affections of which English monarch?
9 Which British statesman died aboard the HMS *Hampshire* in 1916?
10 What was Terence Rattigan's 1946 play based on a famous legal case, Archer v Shee?
11 The Swiss Guard are the personal guard of which figure of authority?
12 Which German Communist leader was executed in 1919, after an unsuccessful uprising?
13 Who led a British expedition to the South Pole in 1909?
14 In what field was Craig Claiborne a successful writer and critic in the US?
15 What was legalized by the US Supreme Court on 22nd January 1973?

? *Tie-breaker*

Against which sitting MP did BBC correspondent, Martin Bell, choose to stand on an anti-corruption platform at the 1997 election?

Wales

● ●

QUIZ 90
PART 1

1. On what date does St David's Day fall?
2. What is the highest peak in Wales?
3. Who is First Minister of the Welsh Assembly?
4. St David's and Milford Haven are coastal towns in which Welsh county?
5. The Llangollen Bridge straddles which river on northern Wales?
6. What narrow stretch of water separates Anglesey from the Welsh mainland?
7. What is the valley north of Cardiff that became a major mining centre in the nineteenth century?
8. What two colours sit behind the dragon on the Welsh flag?
9. In which position did the great JPR Williams make his name playing rugby for Wales?
10. What are the hills and beauty spots forming a National Park around and to the north of Merthyr Tydfil?
11. Who instigated a revolt against King Henry IV in 1400 and pronounced himself Prince of Wales?
12. Which goalkeeper is Wales' most-capped football international, with 93 caps?
13. What is the university town on the River Teifi at the very edge of Ceredigion county?
14. Which Welsh athlete won the Grand Boucle, the women's equivalent of the Tour de France, in 2006?
15. Which great Welsh footballer joined Juventus from Leeds United in 1957 for £65,000, a record fee at the time?

PART 2

1 Who are the only Welsh side competing in cricket's County Championship?
2 True or false: the Conservative Party lost every seat in Wales at the 1997 election.
3 What distinction did Jim Griffiths earn in 1964?
4 Which racecourse hosts the Welsh Grand National every year?
5 What is the annual August celebration of Welsh arts and culture, including the Gorsedd of Bards?
6 Where in Wales did Henry Tudor (who became Henry VII) land his troops in 1485?
7 Where were 144 people, mostly children, killed by a slag heap fall in 1966?
8 What is the Pistyll Rhaeadr, a notable sight in mid-Wales?
9 Who are the second largest party, and therefore the official opposition, in the Welsh Assembly?
10 Which river winds its way through the centre of Cardiff?
11 Who brought most of (modern) Wales, plus some border territories under his control and was acknowledged by the Saxon Kings of England in 1056?
12 Which former Union man was Rugby League player of the year in 1991 and 1993 and after his much-publicized code-switch to Widnes?
13 Who did Cardiff City beat in the 1927 FA Cup Final to become the only non-English side to win the trophy?
14 Who play at Stradey Park?
15 Peter Law won which Parliamentary constituency as an Independent after a row about candidacy?

? *Tie-breaker*

What is the Parliamentary seat for Anglesey called (the Welsh name is used), and which offspring of a former PM held it for the Liberal Party from 1929 to 1951?

The Emerald Isle

● ●

QUIZ 91
PART 1

1   What is celebrated on March 17th?
2   Who won Eurovision for Ireland with 'All Kinds of Everything'?
3   Who was elected First Minister of Northern Ireland in the first sitting of the new Assembly in 1998?
4   In what year did Dublin hold the title of European city of culture, 1991, 1994 or 2001?
5   The city of Dublin is on which river?
6   What is the highest peak in the Mountains of Mourne, making it the highest peak in Northern Ireland, and which peak in the Republic is higher?
7   A monument to which English hero was blown up in Dublin in 1966?
8   The Good Friday agreement, in which Ireland gave up its constitutional claim to Northern Ireland, was signed in which year?
9   Who was the manager of Northern Ireland when they beat Spain at the 1982 World Cup?
10 And who scored the only goal of the game?
11 In 1981, who was suspended from the House for calling Northern Ireland Secretary Humphrey Atkins a liar?
12 What became available for sale for the first time in the Republic in 1985?
13 *Mrs Warren's Profession*, *Arms and the Man* and *Pygmalion* are all works by which Nobel Prize-winning Irish playwright?
14 Colcannon is a traditional Irish side dish consisting primarily of what?
15 What city lies on the Shannon estuary?

Did you know?

No woman had held the most senior office in Ireland prior to 1990. Born Bourke and Leneghan, these two formidable women were both educated at Trinity College and both even held the same teaching post at the college. Maybe the current president will follow her predecessor into the role of UN Commissioner for Human Rights?

PART 2

1 According to the advert, it takes 119.6 seconds to do what?
2 What is Muckanaghederdauhaulia's claim to fame?
3 What sporting post did Lord Killanin hold between 1972 and 1980?
4 What name was given to Royal Irish Constabulary Reservists brought in by the British government in 1920?
5 Who won a seat in the House of Commons whilst in hunger strike in prison?
6 Which Irish activist entered the British Parliament in 1969 aged only 21?
7 Who landed in a German submarine at Banna Strand, Kerry, in 1916?
8 When is the Beltane festival, taken from the Irish-Gaelic name for the month in which it occurs?
9 Who retired from politics in 1973, aged ninety?
10 Roy Keane refused to play in the 2002 World Cup Finals after a row with which manager?
11 Leprechauns (or cluricaunes, as they are sometimes known) are said to perform what job for the fairies?
12 What was legalised in Ireland in 1997?
13 In what decade did the Potato Famine hit Ireland?
14 Which international cricket team was beaten by Ireland in a warm-up match in 1969?
15 Those who kiss the Blarney Stone are said to receive the 'gift of the gab'. Where is the stone located?

? *Tie-breaker*

Which two Mary's have been President of Ireland since 1990?

Births and deaths

● ●

QUIZ 92
PART 1

1 Which singer, who had great success with her debut album *No Angel*, has a birthday on Christmas Day?

2 True or false: Harry Potter and his creator, J. K. Rowling, share the same birthday.

3 How, and in what year, did American financier John Jacob Astor meet his end?

4 Which Irish novelist, whose first book was entitled *The Country Girls*, celebrates her birthday on December 15th?

5 Who was executed by Italian partisans as he attempted to flee Italy on April 28th 1945?

6 Which English former athlete, and the only man ever to win Olympic, World, Commonwealth and European 100 metres gold medals, celebrates his birthday on April 2nd?

7 In which city is Jim Morrison buried?

8 Which former prime minister of Britain died on January 24th 1965? Where is he buried?

9 How did Lady Jane Grey meet her end? How long had she been queen?

10 Which well-known physicist, author of *A Brief History of Time*, celebrates his birthday on January 8th?

11 Where was Freddie Mercury born?

12 Which former *Sex and the City* actress, renowned for her sense of fashion, has a birthday on March 25th?

13 In which city, and in which year, did Birmingham-born Tony Hancock take a drug overdose?

14 The vocalist and drummer Karen Carpenter died from a heart attack aged 32. What caused this?

15 Which Scottish biologist and pharmacologist, who played a major role in the development of penicillin, died on March 11th, 1955?

PART 2

1   Which English comedian and actor, who starred in four series of *Blackadder*, was born on January 6th, 1955?

2   Who had a successful career as a great cellist until the onset of multiple sclerosis, which eventually led to her tragically early death on October 19th, 1987?

3   Who was the lead singer of INXS who was found hanging in a Sydney hotel room in 1997?

4   Which actor was born on January 13th, 1977 and went on to play Legolas in *The Lord of the Rings* trilogy?

5   Whose final words are believed to be: "The executioner is, I believe, very expert; and my neck is very slender"?

6   Which *Shakespeare in Love* actress celebrates her birthday on September 28th?

7   In the Bible, when Cain kills Abel, he is asked by God as to his whereabouts. What reply does Cain give?

8   The German composer Johann Sebastian Bach suffered a stroke following what?

9   In which year was Queen Victoria born, and in which year did she begin her reign?

10 What happened to David Rizzio, Italian courtier to Mary Queen of Scots? Who instigated this?

11 Kate Hudson's mother's birthday is November 21st: who is she?

12 Where was Charles I executed?

13 Which poet wife committed suicide by gassing herself in 1963?

14 In the opera *Madame Butterfly*, how does Cio-Cio-San (Madame Butterfly) meet her end?

15 What were singer and actor Adam Faith's reputed last words?

? **Tie-breaker**
   "A single death is a tragedy, a million deaths is a statistic." Who is this quotation attributed to?

Quotes

●●●●●●●●●●●●●●●●●●●●●●●●●●●

QUIZ 93
PART 1

1   Who did Clement Freud describe as "Attila the Hen"?

2   "Edith Evans looks like something that would eat its young." An appraisal by which American wit?

3   "XX gives away all her old clothes to starving children. Well, who else are they going to fit?" Pauline Calf on which thin celeb?

4   "*Paradise Lost* is one of those books which the reader admires, lays down and forgets to take up again. Its perusal is a duty rather than a pleasure." Who is dismissing Milton's magnum opus?

5   "She's so hairy, when she lifted her arm I thought it was Tina Turner in her armpit." Joan Rivers on which singer?

6   "This man has child-bearing lips." Joan again; who this time?

7   "I'm not offended at all because I know I'm not a dumb blonde. I also know I'm not blonde." Who makes light of a bitchy remark?

8   "You have sent me a Flanders mare." Who, reportedly, on seeing his fourth wife?

9   "Being criticized by Geoffrey Howe is like being savaged by a dead sheep." Whose memorable appraisal of a political opponent?

10   "He can lie out of both sides of his mouth at the same time, and if he ever caught himself telling the truth, he'd lie just to keep his hand in." Harry Truman on which other US politician?

11   "Here lies a great and mighty king/Whose promise none relies on;/He never said a foolish thing/Nor ever did a wise one." Who composed this 'epitaph' for Charles II whilst the king was still very much alive?

12   "He was so mean it hurt him to go to the bathroom." Britt Ekland on which former boyfriend?

13   "He hasn't an enemy in the world, and none of his friends like him." Which other writer wrote this about George Bernard Shaw?

14   "He was not a serious politician. But his footwork should command respect. He is proof of the proposition that in each of us lurks one bad novel." Former MP, Julian Critchley, on which politician and novelist?

15   "My show is the stupidest show on TV. If you're watching it, get a life." Who said this in 1999?

People and places - *Quotes*

PART 2

1   "Reports of my death are greatly exaggerated." Who objected to a premature obituary?

2   "I married beneath me. All women do." Which twentieth century feminist and politician?

3   "Turn on, tune in, drop out." Whose advice about the wonders of LSD in the sixties?

4   "It is true that liberty is precious - so precious that it must be rationed." Whose political credo?

5   Who referred to the House of Lords as "Mr Balfour's Poodle"?

6   "In the future everyone will be famous for fifteen minutes." Who anticipated reality TV in the sixties?

7   "The wind of change is blowing through the continent." Who made this speech before the South African Parliament in 1960?

8   "A riddle wrapped in a mystery inside an enigma." What was Churchill describing?

9   "I know I have the body of a weak and feeble woman, but I have the heart and stomach of a king." Who is exhorting her troops?

10 "Nothing is certain but death and taxes." So said which US President?

11 "Ich bin ein Berliner." Who made this conciliatory, if inaccurate, post-war remark on a visit to Germany?

12 "The history of the world is but the biography of Great Men." Which biographer hyped his art thus?

13 "Men seldom make passes at ..." Complete this Dorothy Parker witticism.

14 "A Rose is a Rose is a Rose." Who managed to persuade people that this was a profound observation?

15 Who described England as "a nation of shopkeepers"?

? *Tie-breaker*

"You can fool all the people some of the time, and some of the people all of the time, but you cannot fool all the people all of the time." Which US President first used this phrase?

Around Britain

● ●

QUIZ 94
PART 1

1 Ambleside and Coniston Water are both to be found in which English beauty spot?
2 The town of Abergavenny lies at the southern end of which beautiful hilly region?
3 Which beauty spot in the south of England was designated an official National Park in March 2005?
4 In which county is The Eden Project located?
5 In which county is Knebworth House, home of the Lytton family and venue for many an outdoor rock concert or celebration?
6 In which beauty spot might you find the villages of Lower Slaughter, Great Rollright and Little Rissington?
7 Which ancient building is found on Holy Island off the coast of Northumbria?
8 What ancient monument is found two miles west of Amesbury in Wiltshire?
9 Which famous Welsh castle and garden lies just over the border from England to the south of Welshpool?
10 Whereabouts in London are the Royal Botanic Gardens situated?
11 Which old ancestral home of the Churchill family is found near Woodstock in Oxfordshire?
12 Which Royal residence in East Molesey in Surrey boasts a world-famous maze?
13 Which of the following castles is not in Scotland: Balmoral, Floors, Hever, Stirling?
14 Which county has the only stretch of coastline to be designated a National Park?
15 Castle Howard, Rievaulx Abbey and Fountains Abbey all lie within the boundaries of which English county?

PART 2

1   Who was the famous resident of Chartwell House for forty years during the twentieth century?
2   Tintagel Castle is linked with the deeds of which legendary figure?
3   Which Northamptonshire estate is the ancestral home of Princess Diana's family, the Spencers?
4   Which palatial Derbyshire residence is home to the influential Duchess of Devonshire, and was believed to have been the inspiration for Pemberley in Jane Austen's *Pride and Prejudice*?
5   True or false: the United Kingdom's smallest city is in Cornwall.
6   The village of Haworth in West Yorkshire is associated with which family?
7   Sissinghurst Castle has famous gardens designed and managed by which famous writer and gardener?
8   Anne Hathaway's Cottage near Stratford-upon-Avon is a beautifully preserved Cotswold cottage. Who was Anne Hathaway's husband?
9   Which Lancashire seaside town hosts annual illuminations in the autumn?
10 Which Cistercian abbey, made famous by Wordsworth's poetry and Turner's paintings, is situated on the River Wye north of Chepstow?
11 The Peak District lies primarily within which English county?
12 Which impressive feat of engineering is based in Llanberis in Wales?
13 Ulverston is home to a Museum devoted to which famous son of the small Lake District town?
14 Which castle to the north of Newcastle-upon-Tyne is known as the 'Windsor of the North'?
15 Which construction in the North West, built in 1894, is known to the locals as The Big Ditch?

? *Tie-breaker*

Which Midlands town boasts a beautifully preserved pump room and baths, opened in 1814 and lovingly restored and improved after flooding in 1998?

People and places

● ●

QUIZ 95
PART 1

1   Who gets locked in a boot with George Clooney in the 1998 thriller, *Out Of Sight*?
2   Who was the King of Jordan whose death in 1999 threatened the Middle East peace process?
3   The author, Isabel Allende, is the niece of the former President of which country, removed in a coup in 1973?
4   What was the last dynasty of the Russian Tsars?
5   Who was the legendary Manchester United manager who built up the club after the war and led them to victory in league, cup and Europe?
6   What was the occupation of Dr Bernard Spilsbury?
7   Which family ruled Florence through a powerful period of the city's history in the second half of the fifteenth century?
8   In 1944, Iceland gained independence from which country?
9   Which educational establishment was founded by King Henry VI in 1440?
10 Which theologian wrote *The Imitation of Christ*?
11 Who married Jacqueline Bouvier in 1953?
12 Who did John Major replace as Chancellor of the Exchequer in 1989?
13 What did Reverend Chad Varah set up at St Stephen Walbrook church in London in 1953?
14 Who led the team of weapons inspectors who failed to find much evidence of Weapons of Mass Destruction in Iraq after the US/British invasion?
15 In which country did a US force overthrow General Noriega in 1989?

Did you know?

It was the moving reports by the BBC's Michael Buerk that moved Geldof to act. An unlikely hero, the foul-mouthed Irishman showed huge stamina and commitment in getting his own way with anyone from politicians to aid-workers to sponsors to notoriously fickle musicians. Suggestions that he was trying to enhance his own career have been mocked by his continuing efforts to improve the lot of ordinary people in Africa.

PART 2

1   Who was the charismatic lead singer with eighties band, Culture Club?
2   How did Van Gogh lose his ear in 1888?
3   Which cinema legend died on Christmas Day, 1977?
4   Who was elected as the first President of the new Russian Federation in 1990?
5   *The Loom of Youth* is the only work of fiction by a writer with a much more famous and prolific brother. Who is he?
6   Elizabeth Gaskell's *Cranford* was based on which real Cheshire village?
7   In The Treaty of Guadeloupe Hidalgo in 1848, Mexico ceded which two territories (now states) to the US?
8   King Harold, defeated at the Battle of Hastings, was a member of which Saxon dynasty?
9   Which playboy footballer numbered Miss World Mary Stavin amongst his many girlfriends?
10   Which is the principal city and governing seat of Queensland in Australia?

? *Tie-breaker*

Where was the famine that prompted Bob Geldof to launch Band Aid and, later, Live Aid?

Who's who

● ●

QUIZ 96
PART 1

1 By which alternative first name is England cricketer Andrew Flintoff known?
2 Which comedian was known as the 'Cheeky Chappie'?
3 Which former World Footballer of the Year is often known simply as Zizou?
4 Who was the Lady With The Lamp?
5 What nickname did snooker player Ray Reardon's swept back hair and facial shape earn him?
6 Who did King Henry VIII describe as a 'Flanders Mare'?
7 In North American history, film and literature, who was Uncas?
8 Who was the original 'It Girl' from the golden age of silent cinema?
9 During the Wars of the Roses, what was the nickname of Richard Neville, The Earl of Warwick?
10 Which musician was known as 'Satchmo'?
11 What was the nickname of TV chef Graham Kerr?
12 Which great West Indian fast bowler was nicknamed 'Big Bird'?
13 Which seventies footballing hard man was known as 'Chopper'?
14 Who, in US western history, was Martha Jane Cannary?
15 Who did the press dub the Yorkshire Ripper?

Did you know?

Louis XIV ruled from 1643 to 1715, an extraordinary 72 years. The early years of his rule were presided over by the wily Cardinal Mazarin, after which Louis took personal control of state affairs. Many wars, religious arguments and treaties later, Louis died, leaving the throne to his great-grandson.

People and places – Who's who

PART 2 – *All these people are know by their initials. We just need their initials.*

1   Rowling. Children's writer.
2   Barrie. Author of Peter Pan.
3   Ewing. TV soap character.
4   Grace. English cricketer.
5   King. US blues singer.
6   Lovecraft. US horror author.
7   Williams. Welsh rugby player.
8   James. English writer of ghost stories.
9   James. English female crime novelist.
10 Byatt. English prize-winning novelist.
11 Yeats. Irish poet.
12 Griffith. American film director.
13 Fields. US comic and actor.
14 Gilbert. Victorian librettist.
15 Tunstall. Scottish songwriter and singer.

❓ Tie-breaker

Louis XIV was known by what flattering epithet during his long reign?

Tittle-tattle

•••••••••••••••••••••••

QUIZ 97
PART 1

1   How many husbands has Elizabeth Taylor had?
2   Who did Britney Spears and Christina Aguilera famously lock lips with at the 2003 MTV Video Music Awards?
3   Who was Tom Cruise married to before Nicole Kidman?
4   In the Australian soap opera *Neighbours*, which character's exit was written off-screen due to the sacking of the actor Shane Connor in 2004?
5   Which well-known actor is the father of Angelina Jolie?
6   Who was the first major American celebrity known to have died from an AIDS-related illness?
7   Which *Friends* actor is known to have struggled for years with prescription-drug and alcohol addiction?
8   Marilyn Monroe was linked with which two politician brothers?
9   Who is the father of former glamour model Jordan's first child, Harvey?
10   Why did Woody Allen and Mia Farrow separate in 1992 after a 12-year relationship?
11   *Rolling Stone* magazine called the lead singer of the now-defunct Hole, and widow of Kurt Cobain, 'the most controversial woman in the history of rock': who is she?
12   Which famous mafioso and boss did Frank Sinatra have a strong friendship with?
13   Who did former Westlife singer Brian McFadden form a relationship with after the break-up of his marriage to former Atomic Kitten singer Kerry Katona?
14   How many children does the singer Rod Stewart have?
15   Which stars of reality series *The Simple Life* had a huge falling out, but refused to divulge the reason why?

PART 2

1 Which comedian was actress Caroline Quentin formerly married to?
2 How many times has actress Patsy Kensit been married?
3 Whose daughter did Michael Jackson marry in 1994?
4 Who is Cherie Blair's well-known actor father?
5 What are the first names of actress Grace Kelly and Prince Rainier of Monaco's children?
6 Who was proven to be TV presenter Paula Yates's father after media allegations that it was not Jess Yates?
7 With whom did Elton John enter into a civil partnership in December 2005?
8 Who was caught in a compromising position with prostitute Divine Brown in a car on Sunset Boulevard, Hollywood in 1995?
9 How many times had Wallis Simpson been married before she married Edward VIII?
10 Who married the drummer of Mötley Crüe, Tommy Lee, in 1995, after knowing him for only 96 hours?
11 Which former rugby captain was Diana, Princess of Wales reputedly involved with?
12 Which Hollywood actress was arrested for shoplifting at Saks Fifth Avenue store in 2001?
13 Who, in April 2004, claimed to have had an affair with David Beckham whilst working as his personal assistant?
14 Which Girls Aloud singer was involved in an altercation with a nightclub toilet attendant in 2003, and subsequently charged with assault?
15 Which Hollywood actor was brought to trial in 1943 and accused of illegally having sex with a teenager on his yacht, but was later acquitted?

? Tie-breaker

What was Prince Harry's insensitive choice of costume when he attended a fancy-dress party in 2005?

People and places

● ●

QUIZ 98
PART 1

1   Which artist and general genius was born in Florence on 15th April, 1452?
2   What were discovered in the Wadi Qumran in 1947?
3   With what particular type of painting is the Elizabethan painter Sir Nicholas Hilliard associated?
4   On which ship did Cook undertake his exploration of the South Pacific?
5   Who did Hitler marry the day before they both committed suicide in 1945?
6   Prince Henry, 'The Navigator' was a Prince of which country?
7   Which poet created the unique metre known as Sprung Rhythm?
8   Which character from children's folklore was clad "from heel to head" in a coat "half of yellow and half of red"?
9   Who was tried and executed at Fotheringay Castle?
10 Who declared themselves independent of Pakistan in 1971?
11 Who was the Archbishop of Canterbury under King Charles I, executed in 1645 for High Treason?
12 The only Dutch Pope, Adrian VI, died in 1523. How many years would pass before another non-Italian would be elected: 110, 245 or 455?
13 Who was the original owner of Sulgrave Manor in Northamptonshire?
14 According to Jewish folklore, rather than the scriptures, who was Adam's first wife?
15 Who was sacked as a football pundit by ITV after making racist remarks about Marcel Desailly on air, albeit unwittingly?

PART 2 – *Who, in the 2005 general election, was elected to serve in the following constituencies?*

1   Blackburn
2   Kirkcaldy and Cowdenbeath
3   Henley
4   North Antrim
5   Richmond, Yorkshire
6   Bolsover
7   Winchester
8   Birmingham Ladywood
9   Belfast West
10 Vauxhall, London
11 Bethnal Green and Bow
12 Hull East
13 Hampstead and Highgate, London
14 Rushcliffe, Nottingham
15 Great Grimsby

? *Tie-breaker*
Which of the above MPs was returned with the biggest majority in the House?

Kings and Queens

● ●

QUIZ 99
PART 1

1   Who ascended to the throne on the abdication of Edward VIII?
2   What relation was George III to George II?
3   Which King died on 5th January, 1066?
4   True or false: King Edward VIII was crowned and abdicated in the same year.
5   Who were married in secret in 1533?
6   Who was the first reigning British monarch to visit Australia?
7   Which actress and showgirl was the mistress of King Edward VII?
8   In whose reign was Louis VIII of France offered the English throne in 1216 (he was never crowned)?
9   Harold Harefoot, King of England 1035–1040, was whose son?
10 Which English King was known as *Malleus Scotorum*, The Hammer of the Scots?
11 Who was the uncle of Richard II who acted as Regent throughout his minor years?
12 Who was the last of the Stuart monarchs?
13 Victoria, Alice, Helena, Louise and Beatrice. Whose daughters?
14 Who deposed Richard II in 1399?
15 Who was the elder daughter of the deposed King James II, and who was her husband?

> **Did you know?**
>
> Henry VIII's well-known proclivity for re-marrying left a very confused succession. His offspring all had different mothers and were of different faiths, so there was no unity between them, and plenty of unscrupulous lords waiting for an opportunity to exploit them. The fifteen years after his death were a particularly bloody period.

PART 2

1   Which two Kings ruled France from 1643 to 1774, a total of 131 years between them?

2   Who was crowned King of Italy in 1805?

3   The abdication of King Stanislav in 1795 saw the effective end of the independent monarchy in which country?

4   Who was the strong-willed Queen of the Netherlands who ruled for fifty years, including both World Wars, before abdicating in favour of her daughter?

5   Which immensely powerful 18th-century ruler was the only female head of the Hapsburg Empire?

6   Which dynasty of French Kings ruled from 1328 to 1589?

7   Who succeeded Duncan I as King of Scotland?

8   *Queen Cristina*, starring Great Garbo, was a 1933 biopic of a seventeenth-century queen of which country?

9   Who was crowned Holy Roman Emperor in 800 AD, by which time he controlled most of Western Europe?

10 In which country did Frederick I adopt the title of King in 1701 (it would remain a Kingdom until 1918)?

? Tie-breaker
Which three of Henry VIII's offspring ruled England?

Smith and Jones

● ●

QUIZ 100
PART 1

1 Which movie pits the heroes against an army of clones called Agent Smith?
2 Davy Jones was an actor and singer with which popular sixties act?
3 Who was the showjumper who was censured for giving a V-sign to the crowd in the seventies?
4 Who replaced Geraint Jones as England wicketkeeper after a run of 30 consecutive Tests for the Kent player?
5 What was the occupation of American folk hero Casey Jones?
6 Winston Smith is the main protagonist in which iconic twentieth-century novel?
7 Which Welsh athlete broke the marathon world record in 1984, and won the London marathon the following year?
8 What was The Smiths follow-up to their eponymous debut album called?
9 Which club did Alan Smith leave to join Manchester United in 2004?
10 Joey Jones won most of his caps for Wales whilst playing at left back for which football club?
11 What is London's principal meat market?
12 Eric Schmidt is Chairman and CEO of which US computer technology firm?
13 Why was the great All-Black flanker Michael Jones left out of their 1995 Rugby World Cup squad?
14 Who is the largest manufacturer of handguns in the US?
15 Who wrote the eighteenth-century novel, *The Life and History of Tom Jones, A Foundling*?

PART 2

1   Singing 'Walking In the Air' brought Aled Jones into the public eye as a youngster; to which Christmas favourite was it the theme?
2   In 1994, Alan Smith scored the winning goal for Arsenal in the Cup-Winners' Cup Final against which Italian side?
3   Which film marked the debut of former footballing hard man Vinnie Jones?
4   In which city is the main base of the Smithsonian Institution?
5   Robert Smith is the lead singer in which rock band?
6   Who was the voice of Darth Vader in the *Star Wars* movies?
7   Mel Smith and Griff Rhys-Jones (aka Alias Smith and Jones) were previously seen on TV in which satirical comedy series?
8   Dave Jones, once of Southampton until removed from his job after baseless and false accusations were made against him, is now manager of which other football club?
9   Who played the title role in the 1939 movie, *Mr Smith Goes To Washington*?
10 England fast bowler Simon Jones plays county cricket for which side?
11 By what name is singer Thomas Woodward, OBE, better known?
12 In which town does British retailer, WHSmith, have its headquarters?
13 Which 47-year-old began a relationship with 13-year-old Mandy Smith in 1983, marrying her six years later?
14 Which Smithfield born architect designed the Banqueting House at Whitehall in 1619?
15 Which movie won Tommy Lee Jones his only Academy Award, for Best Supporting Actor?

? *Tie-breaker*

Who played Mr and Mrs Smith in the 2005 movie of the same name?

Bonnie Scotland

● ●

QUIZ 101

PART 1

1   Who came first, Robert Bruce or William Wallace?
2   Which Scot captained the England cricket team in the 1970s?
3   Who are the only two Scottish golfers to have won The Open Championship since 1945?
4   Who wrote the six-part series of historical novels about fifteenth-century Scotland, *The Lymond Chronicles*?
5   Which two players jointly hold the goal-scoring record for the Scotland football team with 30 goals?
6   Which famous Scottish author lived at Abbotsford House?
7   Stronsay, Hoy and South Ronaldsay are all part of what?
8   Which Scottish artist's images of bar-rooms and motels became fashionable in the early twenty-first century?
9   What is the significance of Pan-Am Flight 103 in recent Scottish history?
10 How many seats did the Conservative Party win in Scotland in the 1997 election?
11 Which Scottish MP took over as leader of the Liberal Democrat party in 2006?
12 Who is the patron saint of Scotland?
13 Candlemas, Lammas and Martinmas are three of the Scottish quarter days; what is the other?
14 Which sport had a brief moment in the limelight when Scotland's women's team won an unexpected gold medal in the 2002 Winter Olympics?
15 From which mainland town would you sail to Stornoway in the Hebrides?

PART 2

1 Who was manager of the Aberdeen side that won the Scottish league in 1984 and 1985?
2 How many cities are there in Scotland?
3 Who were known as the Lisbon Lions?
4 Who was the last serving Prime Minister of the UK to be sitting in a Scottish constituency?
5 The Kirk is the informal name for what?
6 What took place on 23/24 June 1314?
7 What is Aberdeen Angus?
8 Who took over as manager of Rangers when Alex McLeish stood down at the end of the 2005–06 season?
9 Who led the Scottish Royalists, fighting on the side of King Charles I in the English Civil War?
10 Which 1707 act of parliament in both England and Scotland effectively created Great Britain?
11 Who was Mary MacGregor of Comar?
12 What did the Scotland act of 1998 reinstate?
13 The Firth of Tay links which two Scottish cities?
14 Who helped Charles Edward Stuart escape to Skye after the failure of the '45 rebellion?
15 *Elegies* was an award-winning 1985 poetry collection by which Scottish poet?

? Tie-breaker
In which year were the thrones of Scotland and England united under the Stuarts, and whose death precipitated this event?

Royals

●●●●●●●●●●●●●●●●●●●●●●●●●●●●●

QUIZ 102
PART 1

1   Of whom did Princess Diana say "Yes, I adored him. Yes, I was in love with him"?

2   Who in 1994 became the first senior member of the Royal family to convert to Roman Catholicism since the Act of Settlement was signed in 1701?

3   In which year did Elizabeth II inherit the throne?

4   Which university did Prince William attend?

5   Prince Harry caused controversy in January 2005 when he wore what sort of outfit to a fancy dress party?

6   Which photographer-cum-model was once romantically linked to Prince Andrew?

7   Ian Ball tried to kidnap which member of the Royal Family in 1970?

8   In 1987, a year after her death, jewellery owned by which former wife of a Royal was sold at auction for £31 million?

9   Which member of the Royal Family is often popularly referred to as Princess Pushy?

10 Princess Anne's daughter Zara Phillips has been romantically involved with which England rugby player?

11 What was retired at Portsmouth on December 11th, 1997?

12 Who is Princess Anne's second husband, whom she married in 1992?

13 Who was Lady Elizabeth Bowes-Lyon?

14 The Duchess of York has written a series of books for children. What is the name of her airborne title character?

15 Prince Philip was originally a subject of which European country?

Did you know?

The heir to the throne is Prince Charles; then his eldest son, William, and then Harry, William's brother. The Duke of York, Prince Andrew, is next, then his two daughters, followed by Edward and his daughter. Then comes Anne, her son, Peter and daughter, Zara. Then we're into Viscount Linley and the cousins.

PART 2

1   In what year was Prince Charles invested as Prince of Wales: 1963, 1969 or 1976?
2   And where did the investiture take place?
3   In November 2003 a baby was born to the Count and Countess of Wessex. What did they name her?
4   After Prince Harry, who is next in line to the British throne?
5   Who designed the wedding dress worn by Lady Diana Spencer at her wedding to Prince Charles in 1980?
6   What is the Queen's official residence in Scotland?
7   In 1917 King George V changed the royal family name to Windsor. What was it before and why was it changed?
8   What was the name of the gardener with whom Princess Margaret had an eight-year affair in the 1970s?
9   Where did the wedding of Prince Charles and Lady Diana take place in 1981?
10 Whose centenary was celebrated on August 4th, 2000?

? *Tie-breaker*

Who did Prince Edward marry and what title did she adopt?

United States

●●●●●●●●●●●●●●●●●●●●●●●●●●●●

QUIZ 103
PART 1
1   Which is the Golden State?
2   Which state's voting was the subject of much dispute at the end of the 2000 Presidential election?
3   Which US state has the largest surface area?
4   Hawaii is a collection of islands; on which of the islands is the capital, Honolulu, situated?
5   The Grand Canyon lies in which US state?
6   What is the largest city on the Pacific Northwest seaboard, in the state of Washington?
7   Which US state means "flat water" in the native language?
8   Where is Kent State University, where the National Guard shot dead four students during a peaceful demonstration in 1970?
9   The Golden Gate Bridge is a feature of which US city?
10 What is known as The Windy City?
11 Which state in the union is the least populated: New Mexico, Rhode Island, Alaska or Wyoming?
12 Which state is the Lone Star state?
13 Which state borders on four Great Lakes (all except Lake Ontario)?
14 What artificial border signifies the break between the Northern and Southern states of the US?
15 Which is the only US state with a population greater than New York State?

Did you know?

The United States began when Delaware became the first state to be admitted to the new constitutional order in 1787, followed by Pennsylvania and New Jersey. The others have been added gradually over the years, the last two, Alaska and Hawaii, in 1959

PART 2 – *Match the state to the capital city.*

1   Arizona
2   Florida
3   Nebraska
4   Utah
5   New Mexico
6   Illinois
7   Tennessee
8   Wisconsin
9   Massachusetts
10 Rhode Island

A   Boston
B   Springfield
C   Tallahassee
D   Madison
E   Santa Fe
F   Nashville
G   Phoenix
H   Lincoln
I   Providence
J   Salt Lake City

? **Tie-breaker**
Which six states comprise the region of New England?

Vive la France!

●●●●●●●●●●●●●●●●●●●●●●●●●●●●●

QUIZ 104
PART 1
1 What is France's national anthem?
2 What do the French call the English Channel?
3 In which year was the Eiffel Tower completed: 1808, 1889 or 1922?
4 What is the name given to a gendarme's traditional headgear?
5 Charlotte Corday assassinated which French revolutionary in 1793?
6 L'Hotel des Invalides contains which famous tomb?
7 In French literature, who is Harpagon?
8 The first French king called Charles was called Charles The Bald; what nickname was applied to the second?
9 In which department would you find the cave paintings of Lascaux?
10 Which French statesman was known as L'Eminence Rouge?
11 The king's son and heir was known by what title during the Middle Ages?
12 The oriflamme was last carried at the Battle of Agincourt in 1415, a resounding defeat for the French. What was it?
13 What was the name given to the French civil wars between 1648 and 1653?
14 Who is often known in France as La Pucelle?
15 Which Englishwoman is the bestselling writer of all time in France?

PART 2

1   In 2006, according to official statistics, the population of France was just over 35, 65 or 95 million people?
2   Which major French city lies on the channel of the River Loire on the Atlantic coast?
3   In 1995, Jacques Chirac took over from whom as President of France?
4   With which sport is the great Jean-Claude Killy associated?
5   What was used in the French penal system for the last time in 1977?
6   Which philosopher and writer declined the Nobel Prize for Literature in 1964?
7   Which brothers showed the first motion picture to a paying audience in 1895 at the Grand Café in Paris?
8   Which Frenchman became a national hero when he won the 1983 French Open Tennis, the first home winner since 1946?
9   Which city is famous for perfume?
10 Which great Royal Renaissance chateau lies on the River Seine to the south east of Paris?
11 Who has won the most Rugby Union caps for France (111)?
12 The fabled Three Rivers of France are the Dordogne, the Tarn and which other?
13 Henri IV (Henri of Navarre) was the first king in which major French dynasty?
14 The modern departments of Landes, on the Atlantic coast, and Gers, make up which famous former region of peasant France?
15 On the French flag, the tricoleur, which colour is on the left?

? *Tie-breaker*
What year did the French Revolution begin?

London town

●●●●●●●●●●●●●●●●●●●●●●●●●●●

QUIZ 105
PART 1

1   What is used to mark the residence or workplace of a famous person in London?
2   Which area in the West End houses many of London's finest nightspots and restaurants, as well as most of its seedier nightlife?
3   Which underground line is denoted in brown on the map of the tube?
4   Which London park lies to the south of The Mall and the north of Birdcage Walk?
5   What was Monica Ali's bestselling debut novel, from 2004, about life in multi-cultural London?
6   Liverpool Street, Marylebone, King's Cross: what is missing?
7   Which *Eastenders* stars switched on the Oxford Street Christmas lights in 1986?
8   Which is next in this sequence of road bridges: Westminster Bridge, Lambeth Bridge, Vauxhall Bridge ... ?
9   What is The Old Lady of Threadneedle Street?
10 Under which bridge was Italian banker Roberto Calvi found hanging, the victim of a suspected, but unsolved, crime?
11 With which other London team did Wimbledon share a ground before decamping to Milton Keynes?
12 The Almeida Theatre is situated in which area of London?
13 St Bartholomew's and Guy's are what kind of educational establishment?
14 Which annual event takes place between Putney and Mortlake?
15 Which great London sporting venue is to be found on St John's Wood Road?

PART 2

1   Which famous diarist chronicled both the Great Fire and The Plague in the reign of King Charles II?
2   To what was the name of Gillespie Road tube station changed in 1932 to reflect its proximity to a stadium?
3   Which theatre, perhaps best known for ballet, was the first to open north of the Thames in 1963?
4   Which King started the construction of The Tower of London?
5   Which British composer's 2nd Symphony was named his 'London Symphony'?
6   Who wrote the novel, *London Fields*, published in 1989?
7   Which famous Hampstead pub was a favourite retreat of the Romantic poets Shelley, Keats and Byron?
8   What is the name of the Egyptian obelisk that stands on the Embankment?
9   Which underground line was the first to open, in 1863?
10 Who lived at 221b, Baker Street?
11 What is the famous toy shop located on Regent Street?
12 In which area of London do Del and Rodney live in *Only Fools and Horses*?
13 Which musical features the famous London song, 'The Lambeth Walk'?
14 Of the football league teams within the M25, who has the most westerly ground?
15 Portobello Road is home to a market specializing in what?

? *Tie-breaker*

In which year was the first London Marathon run, and who were the first sponsors?

People and places

● ●

QUIZ 106
PART 1

1   Which soap actress gave an honest account of her struggle against cocaine addiction in her 2006 bestselling autobiography, *The Other Side of Nowhere*?
2   In what kind of arena do indoor cycling races take place?
3   By what other name was St Petersburg known in the twentieth century?
4   What nationality was the writer and thinker, Erasmus?
5   Which war does Laurie Lee play a part in according to his autobiography, *As I Walked Out One Midsummer Morning*?
6   The 1668 anti-French Triple Alliance was agreed between Holland, England and which other nation?
7   In British politics, what did the Limehouse Declaration create in 1981?
8   Which Australian city is built around Port Jackson?
9   In 1969, where did The Beatles make their last public performance?
10 What was unveiled in Trafalgar Square on 31st January 1867?
11 Who did Hitler make Foreign Minister in 1938?
12 Who was kidnapped by the Symbionese Liberation Army in 1974?
13 Who were granted land rights by the Treaty of Waitangi in 1840?
14 Which European country only gave women the vote as recently as 1971?
15 Which US Republican Senator initiated the anti-Communist witch-hunts in the 1950s?

PART 2

1   Who stunned the pop world with her debut single 'Wuthering Heights', which remains her only No1 single?
2   Who was made Israel's first woman PM in 1969?
3   What links Tolstoy and Prokofiev?
4   1600 Pennsylvania Avenue is the address of which famous building?
5   What were the SALT talks during the Cold War?
6   T. S. Eliot's *Murder In The Cathedral* is a play about the murder of which historical figure?
7   Which Italian city, capital of Piedmont, lies on the River Po?
8   Which country did Ian Smith declare a Republic in 1970?
9   Who is the only Scot to have won the US Masters golf tournament?
10 Where were 300 unarmed protestors shot and killed by South African police in 1976?
11 Which event saw John Mitchell, HR Haldeman and John Erlichman sent to prison in 1975?
12 Egypt was united with which other country to (temporarily) form the United Arab Republic in 1958?
13 True or false: in 1834 The Tolpuddle Martyrs were executed for forming what was effectively the first trade union.
14 Who was the commentator who uttered the immortal lines "They think it's all over ... it is now!" during the 1966 World Cup Final?
15 Imre Nagy was executed in 1958 for his part in the revolt of which country against Soviet rule?

? Tie-breaker
Who was elected as the first woman speaker in the House of Commons in 1992?

The Emerald Isle

● ●

QUIZ 107
PART 1

1   Where in Ireland will you find Phoenix Park?
2   Can you name the second most successful Irish pop/rock act after U2?
3   Who founded the Fianna Fail party in 1926?
4   How many players are there in a hurling team?
5   The N7 trunk road will take you from Dublin to which western town?
6   What was the old seat of the High Kings of Ireland?
7   Who finished runner-up in the 1999 Formula One Driver's Championship?
8   Who remains the youngest player to play in the World Cup Finals?
9   True or false: there is no Roman Catholic cathedral in Dublin.
10 Which Irish PM added his signature to that of Margaret Thatcher on the 1985 Anglo-Irish Agreement?
11 What name is given to the collection of basalt columns on the north coast of County Antrim?
12 Who was the charismatic frontman with the Irish rock band, Thin Lizzy?
13 What is the longest river in Ireland, running mainly North to South?
14 True or false: the town of Wexford does not lie in Wexford county.
15 Which small group of islands lie offshore of Galway Bay?

People and places – *The Emerald Isle*

PART 2

1 Which famous college actually constitutes the University of Dublin?
2 Who captained Northern Ireland in the 1958 World Cup and Spurs to the double in 1961?
3 Which county lies on Ireland's East coast, immediately south of Dublin?
4 Which Irishman was awarded a KBE by the British government in 1986 for his charitable work?
5 Connacht, Ulster, Meath, Munster; what is missing?
6 Christy Ring, Nicky Rackard and Brendam Cummins are well-known exponents of what?
7 By what name is famous Irishman David Howell Evans better known?
8 Who is the only rider from the British Isles to win the Tour de France?
9 Which writer's life is remembered every year in Dublin on 16th June with the Bloomsday celebrations?
10 The Twelve Bens are a group of hills located in which beauty-spot in western Galway?
11 Which Irish golfer has made an excellent media career as a commentator and writer and golfing wit in the US?
12 Monsignor James Horan campaigned for the opening of which cog in Ireland's transport infrastructure in County Mayo?
13 Cormac's Chapel is part of which collection of important historic buildings in County Tipperary?
14 Which thirty-something songwriter belatedly hit the big-time with his 2002 album, *O*?
15 Who was the strong-willed nineteenth-century politician who organized and unified the Irish Home Rule MPs in the House of Commons?

? Tie-breaker

When was the last time Ireland won the rugby 5/6 Nations Championship: 1967, 1985 or 1996?

Who's who

●●●●●●●●●●●●●●●●●●●●●●●●●●●●

QUIZ 108

PART 1 – *Identify the surname shared by the following pairs.*

1   George's right-hand girl and Andrew's right-hand man
2   Great Olympian and thespian dynasty
3   Scottish speed merchant and *Next Generation* skipper
4   Model triple athlete and Match of the Day pundit
5   Jelly-baby Who and Bucks Fizz babe
6   *Dynasty* Dame and Celtic Warrior
7   Low-carb guru and Mr Guitar
8   Deadpan comedian/actor and Kink
9   World Cup Winner and Ali G
10 English footballing brace and Minder's boss
11 Actress-cum-MP and controversial black Senator
12 The third man of golf and a Hole lot of trouble
13 Springbok batsman and ageing Rolling rocker
14 Formula One entrepreneur and basketball legend
15 Red Shoes and Golden Boots

Did you know?

Marilyn Monroe the legend has always been a bigger star than Monroe the actress. Her film output was patchy, although it includes a handful of gems (*Seven-Year Itch, Some Like It Hot, The Misfits*). Her private life was sensational: three high-profile marriages, being the first woman to appear on the centrefold of Playboy and a suspicious and tragic death guaranteed her immortality.

PART 2 – *Match the imaginary to the real.*

1   Mrs Daryl Walters
2   Tracy Marrow
3   Hector Hugh Munro
4   Norma Egstrom
5   Harry O'Dowd
6   Niomi McLean-Daley
7   Phyllis Primrose-Pechey
8   Joel Chandler Harris
9   Archibald Leach
10 Daniel Carroll

A   Peggy Lee
B   Boy George
c   Fanny Craddock
D   Danny La Rue
E   Enid Blyton
F   Cary Grant
G   Uncle Remus
H   Saki
I   Ice T
J   Ms Dynamite

? *Tie-breaker*

What was Marilyn Monroe's name when she was born, and to what was the surname changed when she was baptized?

Births and deaths

● ●

QUIZ 109

PART 1 – *Name the oldest and youngest person in each group.*

1 Tiger Woods, Johnny Depp, Mike Tyson, Gwen Stefani
2 Brad Pitt, Nicolas Cage, Steffi Graf, Kurt Cobain
3 Britney Spears, Kelly Clarkson, Scarlett Johansson, Justine Henin-Hardenne
4 Prince Andrew, Michael Jackson, John Travolta, Peter Jackson
5 Michael Jordan, Keanu Reeves, Naomi Campbell, Helena Bonham-Carter
6 Bono, Prince, John McEnroe, Pat Cash
7 Princess Anne, Tony Blair, Stephen King, Joanna Lumley
8 Orlando Bloom, Reese Witherspoon, Michael Owen, Serena Williams
9 Muhammad Ali, Michael Palin, Jeffrey Archer, Tony Jacklin
10 Billy Connolly, Barry Manilow, John Major, Pele

Did you know?

Bruce Lee died of a cerebral oedema, possibly caused by an allergy to a prescription drug unwittingly administered to him. He was only thirty-two, and was just starting to get the recognition in the US, where he was born, that he already enjoyed in Hong Kong. His son, Brandon, was equally ill-fated, shooting himself accidentally, aged 28, while on the set of the movie, *The Crow*.

People and places – Births and deaths

PART 2 – *Identify the year from the births and deaths. Two points for spot-on, one point for a year either way.*

1 Joining Us: Donny Osmond & Billy Bragg. Leaving Us: Humphrey Bogart & Oliver Hardy

2 Joining Us: Kirsten Dunst & Prince William. Leaving Us: Ingrid Bergman & Grace Kelly

3 Joining Us: Ben Ainslie & Ronan Keating. Leaving Us: Maria Callas & Bing Crosby

4 Joining Us: Ellen MacArthur & Colin Farrell. Leaving Us: Agatha Christie & Howard Hughes

5 Joining Us: Mary Quant & Judi Dench. Leaving Us: Bonnie and Clyde & James Dillinger

6 Joining Us: Samantha Fox & Mike Tyson. Leaving Us: Lenny Bruce & Walt Disney

7 Joining Us: Ewan McGregor & Dido. Leaving Us: Ogden Nash & Jim Morrison

8 Joining Us: Wayne Rooney & Keira Knightley. Leaving Us: Philip Larkin & Marc Chagall

9 Joining Us: Whitney Houston & Lena Zavaroni. Leaving Us: Sylvia Plath & Patsy Cline

10 Joining Us: Paula Radcliffe & Monica Lewinski. Leaving Us: Bruce Lee & JRR Tolkien

? Tie-breaker

In which year did Stanley Kubrick die in the same month Brooklyn Beckham was born?

People and places

● ●

QUIZ 110
PART 1

1   What was the name given to Henry Kissinger's softly-softly approach to Cold War tensions?
2   The sandstone rock in Australia's Northern Territories known as Uluru was formerly known as what?
3   Who is the only Croatian to have won the men's singles at Wimbledon?
4   What had two heads in Austria and one in Germany?
5   What was formally ceded to Britain (it remains under British sovereignty) by the Treaty of Utrecht in 1714?
6   Who was elected leader of the Social and Liberal Democrat Party in 1988?
7   Which reformer was excommunicated by Pope Leo X in 1521?
8   The final entry in whose diary was written on the 31st may, 1669?
9   In 2001, where did the heir to the throne kill the king and most of his family before finally killing himself?
10 In which county is Chequers, the Prime Minister's country residence?
11 The fifteenth-century Paston Letters are a fascinating study of domestic life in which English county?
12 Gozo is a secondary island and part of which predominant island state?
13 The Battle of Sedgemoor saw the end of the Duke of Monmouth's rebellion against the crown in 1685. What else is significant about the battle?
14 Which former White House aide was involved in the Iran–Contra affair but somehow got away with a suspended prison sentence?
15 What was the famous Parisian prison stormed by mobs in 1789, a key moment in the Revolution?

Did you know?

The Games has proved a reasonably successful combination of celeb TV and sports show. Various C-listers compete against each other in various disciplines, and at the end of the series a gold medal winner is announced for the men and women. The third series' winner, Kirsty Gallagher, took over as female presenter for Series 4.

PART 2

1 Where does the Northern Ireland Assembly convene when it is in session?
2 Who challenged John Major's leadership of the Conservative Party in 1995, but was defeated in the ballot?
3 Where did Israeli commandos rescue 100 passengers from a hijacked aircraft in 1976?
4 Which actress is married to the retired footballer Lee Chapman?
5 What office did Lanfranc hold under William The Conqueror from 1070?
6 Ridley and which other Protestant cleric were burnt in Oxford during the reign of Queen Mary I?
7 Who was President of the Weimar Republic between 1925 and 1934?
8 Who was the ship's captain involved in The Mutiny On The Bounty?
9 What did Pope Gregory XIII persuade the Roman Catholic countries of Europe to adopt in 1582?
10 Who was the model and society girl at the heart of the scandal involving cabinet Minister John Profumo?

? Tie-breaker

Who were the two presenters for the first Series of The Games, Channel 4's reality athletics show, launched in 2003?

Around Britain

● ●

QUIZ 111
PART 1

1 What is the county town of Suffolk?
2 Which river runs through the heart of Nottingham?
3 In which city is Scone Palace, site of the crowning of the old Scottish kings?
4 Clifford's Tower is all that remains of which city's castle?
5 Which town, birthplace of Charles Dickens, houses a museum in his honour?
6 With whom is the Liverpool tourist attraction, The Cavern Club, associated?
7 Which city's main non-Roman Catholic church is St Giles' Cathedral?
8 Which city boasts a fabulous School of Art designed by Charles Rennie Mackintosh?
9 To what is the newly built BALTIC centre on the banks of the Tyne in Gateshead devoted?
10 Which two cities lie within the boundaries of the county of Devon?
11 Which English town is often referred to, especially in literary works, as Old Sarum?
12 Which town to the north of London was a major Roman centre called Verulamium?
13 From which English city would you take a ferry to the Isle of Wight?
14 Which holiday resort town is at the heart of the Devon coastal area known as 'The English Riviera'?
15 Which decommissioned pleasure-boat now sits in Leith docks in Edinburgh?

Did you know?

Warwick Castle, the splendidly intact fortified mediaeval castle, and Alton Towers, the pleasure park, are both owned by the Tussaud's Group, who own and run the famous waxworks museum in London.

PART 2
Name the town or city in which each of these attractions is located
1   The Royal Pavilion
2   The National Football Museum
3   The Ashmolean Museum
4   The Jorvik Viking Centre
5   Sally Lunn's House & Museum
6   Fitzwilliam Museum
7   The Cider Museum
8   Albert Dock
9   The Deep
10 Cadbury World
11 Roman Bath and Pump Rooms
12 Ironbridge Gorge Museum
13 Warwick Castle
14 National Museum of Photography, Film & Television
15 Palace of Holyroodhouse

? **Tie-breaker**
Most of the area around Middlesbrough, now referred to as Teesside, was once part of which county?

Celebrity couples

● ●

QUIZ 112
PART 1

1   Who is actress Billie Piper's former husband, with whom she maintains a cordial friendship?
2   Who is the celebrity girlfriend of rugby player Gavin Henson?
3   Mike Todd, Arthur Miller, Eddie Fisher, Richard Burton. Who is the odd one out?
4   Which British soap actress's cocaine addiction was splashed across the tabloids by her ex-husband and mother-in-law?
5   Who has been married to Michael Jackson (20 months) and Nicolas Cage (3 months)?
6   Who was Madonna's first husband?
7   Which rugby star was romantically linked with Diana, Princes of Wales?
8   Whose marriage to R. Kelly was annulled when a court revealed she was only 15 at the time, and had lied about her age?
9   With whom did Kenneth Branagh have a much publicized relationship after his split from Emma Thompson?
10 Who served divorce papers on Mia Farrow while she was on the set of *Rosemary's Baby*?
11 Eric Clapton's former wife, Patti, was previously married to which other rock star?
12 Who did Tom Cruise divorce in August 2001?
13 And who gave birth to a daughter by Cruise in 2006?
14 Who has enjoyed a long marriage to actress Phoebe Cates, despite a 16-year gap in age?
15 Which Irish actress has been married to Jeremy Irons for nearly thirty years?

PART 2 – *Match the hubby and spouse (current or ex).*

1   David Beckham
2   Keith Chegwin
3   David Arquette
4   John Cleese
5   Elvis Presley
6   Mike Tyson
7   Liam Gallagher
8   Nikki Sixx
9   Humphrey Bogart
10 Lenny Henry
11 Vincente Minnelli
12 Brad Pitt
13 Jamie Redknapp
14 Lee Majors
15 Jude Law

A   Louise Nurding
B   Judy Garland
C   Dawn French
D   Jennifer Aniston
E   Victoria Adams
F   Farrah Fawcett
G   Sadie Frost
H   Priscilla Beaulieu
I   Patsy Kensit
J   Lauren Bacall
K   Connie Booth
L   Robin Givens
M   Courteney Cox
N   Donna D'Errico
P   Maggie Philbin

? *Tie-breaker*

What was Zsa Zsa Gabor's legendary reply when asked by an interviewer how many husbands she had had?

Tittle-tattle

● ●

QUIZ 113
PART 1

1 Which celebrity couple were photographed sitting on golden thrones at their wedding in 1999?

2 Which Hollywood actor made offensive anti-Semitic remarks when arrested for drunken driving in 2006?

3 Who admitted to adultery in a television interview with Jonathan Dimbleby in 1995?

4 Who was arrested for performing a lewd act (alone) in a public restroom in a Beverly Hills park in 1998?

5 In June 2005, why was Russell Crowe arrested and charged with second-degree assault by New York police?

6 Two years after her sister's coronation, Princess Margaret became embroiled in a public scandal over her wish to marry whom?

7 Who – Ant or Dec – married long-term girlfriend, make-up artist Lisa Armstrong, in July 2006?

8 Which royal prince's name was linked with Koo Stark?

9 Who is actor John Travolta married to?

10 Whose hair caught on fire whilst filming a Pepsi commercial in 1993?

11 Which Hollywood actor, renowned for having starred as Charlie Chaplin in *Chaplin*, has been sent to jail on several occasions for drug offences?

12 Who left his wife Della for TV presenter Anthea Turner, and married her in 2000?

13 Which actress daughter of Henry was known as Hanoi Jane because of her anti-Vietnam war activities in the 1970s?

14 Who was ribbed mercilessly by the two regular panellists, Paul Merton and Ian Hislop, on *Have I Got News For You* about the scandalous revelations by the tabloids about his private life?

15 What nickname was given to the group of artists that included Dean Martin, Frank Sinatra and Peter Lawford?

PART 2 – *Match the celebrities, wife to husband.*

1   Esther Rantzen
2   Pamela Stephenson
3   Sheila Hancock
4   Melanie Griffith
5   Vanessa Paradis
6   Hattie Jacques
7   Goldie Hawn
8   Keeley Hawes
9   Jane Asher
10 Zoë Ball
11 Cher
12 Sarah Michelle Gellar
13 Jennifer Saunders
14 Katie Price
15 Marilyn Monroe

A   Antonio Banderas
B   Gerald Scarfe
c   Norman Cook
D   John Le Mesurier
E   Sonny Bono
F   Adrian Edmondson
G   Peter Andre
H   Freddie Prinze, Jr.
I   Arthur Miller
J   Matthew McFadyen
K   Kurt Russell
L   Desmond Wilcox
M   Johnny Depp
N   John Thaw
O   Billy Connolly

❓ *Tie-breaker*

Who is the father of Jordan's son, Harvey, and by which previous boyfriend had she become pregnant but chosen termination?

Who's who

● ●

QUIZ 114
PART 1

1   Who is Hollywood actress Kate Hudson's famous mum?
2   Young British actress Rachael Stirling (*Tipping The Velvet*) is the daughter of which acting Dame?
3   Who was Carrie Fisher's mum, who didn't come out well in Carrie's book?
4   Who is Judy Garland's daughter?
5   Who is Warren Beatty's actress sister?
6   How did Sofia Coppola get a major part in *Godfather III*?
7   Who are Martin Sheen's two well-known actor sons?
8   Which former footballer of the year had a brother called Bradley and cousins called Paul and Martin?
9   Which young player in the England ODI squad (Aug 06) had a test-playing father?
10 Who was Olivia De Havilland's sister?
11 Which TV presenter has a former Ryder Cup captain as her father?
12 Who is the actress daughter of Janet Leigh (of *Psycho* fame)?
13 Which successful designer is the daughter of one of The Beatles?
14 Who is boxer Nigel Benn's footballing cousin?
15 Which young test cricketer is a cousin of boxer, Amir Khan?

PART 2 – *Match the character to their nickname.*

1　Edith Piaf
2　Frank Sinatra
3　Joan Bakewell
4　Joan of Arc
5　Johnny Cash
6　Lesley Hornby
7　Margaret Thatcher
8　OJ Simpson
9　Richard Cromwell
10　Michael Holding
11　Harbajan Singh
12　William Perry
13　Ron Harris
14　Joe Louis
15　Nigel Benn

A　Thinking Man's Crumpet
B　Chopper
C　Juice
D　Little Sparrow
E　The Brown Bomber
F　Whispering Death
G　The Fridge
H　Maid of Orleans
I　The Dark Destroyer
J　Ol' Blue Eyes
K　The Turbanator
L　Attila the Hen
M　Tumbledown Dick
N　Twiggy
P　Man in Black

? *Tie-breaker*

Which two post-war England cricket captains have had sons who have also played test cricket for England?

People and places

● ●

QUIZ 115
PART 1

1   Tom Jones and Prince were born on the same day (June 7th). How many years separate them: 10, 18 or 26?
2   How has the uprising against excessive foreign influence in China in 1900 become known?
3   What was the great church built by Ivan The Terrible on Red Square?
4   President Sukarno was the first President of which country when it was made a Republic in 1945?
5   With the creation of what do we associate the name of Thomas Chippendale?
6   Sugar Loaf Mountain looms over the harbour of which South American city?
7   Which Spanish city boasts the Moorish palace known as the Alhambra?
8   Who was the author of the pillar of cynicism, *The Devil's Dictionary?*
9   Sir Robert Mark and Sir David McNee were consecutive holders of which civil post?
10   Which island did Columbus discover on his journey to reach the Americas in 1492?
11   Who hosted, and won, the first Rugby Union World Cup in 1987?
12   Where did an unknown number of British subjects die in an airless cell in 1756?
13   What was Nan Winton the first woman to do on TV in 1960?
14   When the Korean War began in 1950, who invaded whom?
15   Who was sworn in as the first woman President of Argentina in 1974?

PART 2

1   The British PM Henry Temple was better known by which title?
2   What title did Benjamin Disraeli hold?
3   Who was the last single British Prime Minister?
4   Which PM once fought a duel with Lord Castlereagh?
5   What is Margaret Thatcher's middle name?
6   Which Liverpool constituency did Harold Wilson hold from 1950 to 1983?
7   True or false: no Cambridge graduates have been PM since the war.
8   Which Labour PM was married to Gladys Mary Baldwin?
9   Which former PM is buried in Bladon in Oxfordshire?
10 Who was the Liberal PM from 1908 to 1916?
11 William Grenville's short-lived government achieved which major piece of legislation in March 1807?
12 Who was shot by John Bellingham in the lobby of the House of Commons?
13 Which PM of less than one year's standing was born in Canada?
14 Which PM married a niece of Churchill's?
15 Who is Tony Blair's father-in-law?

? Tie-breaker
In what way did Hungarian Prime Minister Ferenc Gyurcsany commit a political faux pas in 2006?

Flags and symbols

● ●

QUIZ 116
PART 1

1 The 'golden arches' is another name for which food-related corporate symbol?
2 Which British political party has a red rose as its symbol?
3 In typography, what is the name given to a device not part of the standard character set, and used decoratively or as a pictogram?
4 Which English football team's crest is a cockerel sitting atop a football?
5 What is the equilateral cross with bent arms sacred to Hinduism that has taken on a more sinister meaning in the twentieth century?
6 Who governs heraldry in England and Wales?
7 On a standard clothing label, what does a crossed-out black triangle represent?
8 And how about a crossed-out hollow square with a hollow circle inside?
9 The International Red Cross is represented by a red cross on a white background. How is its Islamic counterpart represented?
10 Which charitable organization is represented by the outline of a candle wrapped in barbed wire?
11 What does a pair of crossed swords symbolize on a map?
12 The World Wide Fund for Nature has what animal as part of its logo?
13 What fashion house's symbol is a pair of interlocked letter 'C's?
14 Which sign of the zodiac is symbolized by the Ram?
15 What NCO rank does a single-bar chevron on the sleeve represent in the British military?

Did you know?

Heraldry is a unique terminology that appears complex. In fact, the basics are quiet easy to learn as there are only a few colours and shapes, but the complexity arises with the inclusion of personalized crests and charges (animals or objects from the "real world"). Different countries have different rules and terms for the same thing, to add to the confusion. Conclusion: avoid!

PART 2 - *Which country's flags are being described?*

1　Horizontal stripes - from top to bottom, red/white/red.
2　Red circle on white background.
3　Vertical stripes - from left to right, green/white/orange.
4　Vertical stripes - from left to right, green/white/red.
5　Horizontally divided into white top, red bottom.
6　White background with red maple leaf; vertical red stripes on left- and right-hand edges.
7　Blue cross (with vertical line to left of centre) on white background.
8　Yellow cross (with vertical line to left of centre) on blue background.
9　Nine horizontal stripes of alternating blue and white; a white cross on a blue background in top left-hand corner.
10　Yellow star in the centre of a red background.

? **Tie-breaker**
In heraldry, what would a field, or, with bars, sable, mean?

Bonnie Scotland

● ●

QUIZ 117

PART 1

1 What is the name of the river that flows into the heart of Glasgow?
2 Who was the MP for North Lanarkshire (later Monklands East) from 1970 until his death in 1994?
3 Which Scottish footballing legend once taunted his English opponents by sitting on the ball during an international?
4 Which famous Scot is known affectionately as 'The Big Yin'?
5 How many years separated the opening of the Forth Bridge, for rail traffic, and the Forth Road Bridge: 43, 60 or 74?
6 Is the population of Scotland just over 3 million people, just over 5 million or just over 7 million?
7 What is the Saltire?
8 How old was Robbie Burns when he died in 1796: 37, 47 or 57?
9 What is Scotland's highest peak, also the highest in Great Britain?
10 Where do Scotland play their home rugby union matches?
11 Which grim event in Scottish history took place on 13th March 1996?
12 Which Scot is the youngest ever winner of the World Snooker Championship?
13 Whose death in 2000 necessitated an election for a new leader of the Scottish Executive?
14 Apart from the Royal Bank of Scotland and The Bank of Scotland, what is the third major Scottish bank?
15 Who bought the remote Fair Isle in 1954?

People and places – *Bonnie Scotland*

PART 2

1 Which Scottish town in the Cairngorms is the premier British skiing centre?
2 As of July 2006, which Scot is the UK's No1 tennis player?
3 Which of Shakespeare's plays is often referred to in theatrical circles simply as "The Scottish Play"?
4 Which economist and philosopher published his *Wealth of Nations* in 1776?
5 Who became the UK Parliament's youngest MP when he won Ross, Cromarty and Skye for the SDP in 1983?
6 Which is the most remote of the habitable Scottish islands, lying some 100 miles off the coast?
7 Who was the manager of the Scottish football team during their disastrous 1978 World Cup campaign, where they entered as one of the favourites and were eliminated in the group stage?
8 Mel Gibson's *Braveheart* was a fanciful and romantic account of the life of which Scottish warrior?
9 Which city is the centre of the North Sea oil industry?
10 What is Mons Meg, one of the sights of Edinburgh Castle?
11 Where is the Scottish Grand National run?
12 St Andrews golf course is found on the coastline of which Scottish county?
13 Who wrote a series of novels incognito, which became known as The Waverley Novels, as *Waverley* was the first in the sequence?
14 In which town are the Highland Games centered around every year?
15 Which pair of brothers made their Rugby Union debuts for Scotland against France in January 1986?

? *Tie-breaker*

Who won 100 metres gold at the Moscow Olympics in 1980, and why is the achievement sometimes belittled?

People and places

• •

QUIZ 118
PART 1

1   Which right-wing Italian Prime Minister was narrowly defeated in the 2006 election?
2   Which law, of enormous benefit to writers and their dependants, was passed through Parliament in 1709?
3   To which island was Napoleon exiled after his defeat and abdication in 1814?
4   What was the given name of the Haitian politician known as Papa Doc?
5   WPC Yvonne Fletcher was killed at which London location in 1984?
6   A ride for help by which US patriot was the subject of a narrative poem by Henry Longfellow?
7   What was the name of Zimbabwe's capital before it became Harare?
8   What weapon did the Germans use for the first time at Ypres in 1915?
9   In 1964 Tanganyika and Zanzibar combined to form which new country?
10 In 1980 Princess Beatrix became Queen of which country after the abdication of her 71-year-old mother (who lived until 2004!)?
11 What is the name of the strait separating Turkish Asia from mainland Europe? And which poet and adventurer swam it in 1810?
12 The Battle of Lewes in 1264 was fought between Henry III's troops and those of which rebellious nobleman?
13 Who became the first Western rock star to play in the old Soviet Union in 1979?
14 Who won a libel case against the *Daily Mirror* in 1959 after they alleged he was homosexual?
15 What happened when Sarah Ann Henley threw herself off Clifton Suspension Bridge in 1885?

Did you know?

The legend has it that Genevieve's steadfastness and prayers saved her city from Attila the Hun's armies. Later, when Childreric also besieged the city, she managed to smuggle eleven boatloads of grain through enemy lines to feed the starving people. An institute for teaching and nursing exists in her name, as well as an abbey.

PART 2

1   Who was Josef Dzhugashvili?
2   Who is Baron Greenwich?
3   Which favourite of Queen Elizabeth I was married to Amy Robsart?
4   Who is the mother of Rod Stewart's children, Liam and Renee?
5   By what name are Currer, Ellis and Acton Bell better known?
6   Both John Milton and Andrew Marvell worked as a secretary for which high-ranking English politician?
7   Who was the first Prime Minister of India?
8   Which famous jazz musician had the Christian names Edward Kennedy?
9   Who gave up the title of Viscount Stansgate to pursue a career in the House of Commons?
10 Who deposed King Idris of Libya in 1969?

? **Tie-breaker**
Saint Genevieve is the patron saint of which major European city?

Births and deaths

● ●

QUIZ 119
PART 1

1 Which famous daughter of Judy Garland celebrates her birthday on March 12th?
2 Where is Queen Elizabeth I buried?
3 Which James Bond actor was born March 21st, 1946?
4 "Reports of my death have been greatly exaggerated." Whom is this quotation attributed to?
5 Who shot Billy the Kid?
6 In which river did English novelist Virginia Woolf drown herself?
7 Who founded the electronics and computer company Amstrad and celebrates his birthday on March 24th?
8 What was the name of the children's nanny, probably murdered by Lord Lucan in 1974 (convicted in absentia June 19th, 1975)?
9 Where was English writer Rudyard Kipling born?
10 The artist Vincent Van Gogh and lead singer of Nirvana, Kurt Cobain, died in the same manner. How?
11 Who is the eldest grandson and first grandchild of Queen Elizabeth II and the Duke of Edinburgh, born on November 15th, 1977?
12 Whose final words were "The rest is silence"?
13 Which Formula One racing driver, brother of Michael, celebrates his birthday on June 30th?
14 Which member of the Monty Python team was born in Weston-Super-Mare, Somerset in 1939?
15 In the opera *Carmen*, how does Carmen meet her end?

People and places – *Births and deaths*

PART 2

1. Which star of *Trainspotting* and *Moulin Rouge* celebrates his birthday on March 31st?
2. Who was the American inventor of the Kodak camera who shot himself in 1932?
3. Where were pop group the Bee Gees born?
4. Which English Poet Laureate died in Rydal Mount in 1850?
5. In which English county was the artist John Constable born?
6. Who was the author of *Pygmalion*, born in 1856?
7. Which former tennis player, whose after-tennis life has been plagued by scandal, was born on November 22nd, 1967?
8. The Italian composer Giacomo Puccini died of throat cancer in which year?
9. Where was the artist Pablo Picasso born?
10. Which pint-sized Aussie pop star was born on 28 May 1968?
11. Who was born Anna Mae Bullock and celebrates her birthday on November 26th?
12. Which television presenter, famous for her fast and accurate mathematical calculations, celebrates her birthday on Christmas Eve?
13. Where in Pakistan was former cricketer turned politician Imran Khan born?
14. Whose final words were "I die a Queen, but I would rather die the wife of Culpepper."
15. In which German city was Karl Marx born?

? *Tie-breaker*

Which well-known singer was born in Stoke-on-Trent on February 13th, 1974?

Around Britain

● ●

QUIZ 120
PART 1

1 Which motorway would you take to get from London to Swindon?
2 A famous old steam railway route linked Carlisle to which other northern town?
3 Southend and Sheerness overlook which stretch of water?
4 The Great Ouse and the River Nene both empty into which east coast inlet?
5 The M40 cuts through which range of hills once it gets beyond the M25?
6 Which motorway links Glasgow and Edinburgh?
7 The M62 crosses the Pennines, linking which two major cities?
8 Take the A47 from Leicester to Norwich. What is the biggest town you pass en route?
9 True or false: The English–Scottish border follows the path of Hadrian's Wall.
10 What carries you northwards through the Thames if you are travelling on the M25 to the east of London?
11 Cardiff and Weston-Super-Mare face each other across which expanse of water?
12 Rochester, Chatham and Gillingham all lie at the outlet of which river?
13 The Menai Bridge links mainland Britain to which other land mass?
14 The M54 to Telford veers off westwards from which other motorway?
15 Which group of islands lie to the southwest of Land's End?

Did you know?

The distance from London to Glasgow is actually less than half the length of mainland Britain. The cities are 397 miles apart, whereas the journey from Land's End on the south-west tip of Cornwall to John O'Groats at the northern end of mainland Scotland is 868 miles.

PART 2

1   Which are furthest north, the Orkneys or the Shetland Islands?
2   Which city has the third largest population in England, after London and Birmingham?
3   Which lies furthest east, Nottingham, Lincoln, Rotherham or Stoke-on-Trent?
4   Which lies furthest south, Winchester, Dover, Bath or Canterbury?
5   Which lies furthest east, Brighton, Eastbourne, Cambridge or Ipswich?
6   Which lies furthest south, Leeds, Liverpool, Blackpool or Hull?
7   Which lies furthest north, Cambridge, Oxford, Ipswich or Cheltenham?
8   Which lies furthest west, Newcastle, York, Aberdeen or Leeds?
9   Which of the four main Channel Islands is the largest in area, Alderney, Guernsey, Jersey or Sark?
10 Which lies furthest east, Glasgow, Bristol, Carlisle or Cardiff?

? Tie-breaker
Name the five other counties bordering Hampshire.

People and places (US presidents)

● ●

QUIZ 121
PART 1

1   Which famous presidential speech ended in a description of democracy as "a government of the people, by the people and for the people"?
2   Which president made the Gettysburg Address?
3   Who was Nixon's running-mate and vice-president?
4   Three presidents have been awarded the Nobel Peace prize. Name one.
5   Which US president signed the Civil Rights Act, outlawing racial discrimination, in 1964?
6   Which two former presidents died on 4th July, Independence Day, in 1827, exactly fifty years after the Declaration?
7   What distinction did James Buchanan hold when he was elected president?
8   What is the minimum age for a president?
9   Who was the first Roman Catholic president?
10 What is the official title of the wife of the president of the US?
11 Who, in 1972, was the first US president to visit China?
12 What was nickname of Andrew Jackson, the seventh president?
13 Who was the oldest president to take office?
14 Which future president was part of the committee that drafted the Declaration of Independence?
15 What does 'W' in George W. Bush stand for?

PART 2 – *Match the man to his dates.*

1 Abraham Lincoln
2 Calvin Coolidge
3 Richard Nixon
4 Dwight D Eisenhower
5 Franklin D Roosevelt
6 George Washington
7 Thomas Jefferson
8 John Quincy Adams
9 Lyndon B Johnson
10 Theodore Roosevelt
11 Ronald Reagan
12 Harry S Truman
13 Gerald Ford
14 Thomas Woodrow Wilson
15 Ulysses S Grant

A 1953–1961
B 1974–1977
C 1923–1929
D 1901–1909
E 1869–1877
F 1861–1865
G 1825–1829
H 1801–1809
I 1789–1797
J 1933–1945
K 1963–1969
L 1913–1921
M 1945–1953
N 1981–1989
P 1969–1974

? ***Tie-breaker***
In what month do the Presidential Elections take place, and how often?

The Big Apple

● ●

QUIZ 122

PART 1

1 What colour are the iconic New York cabs?
2 Which is the only New York City borough on the US mainland?
3 Who was Mayor of New York at the time of the September 11th attacks in 2001?
4 What apocalyptic 2004 film sees New York hit by a freak tidal wave and then submerged under masses of ice and snow?
5 Which music club, central to 1960s avant-garde and punk rock, is found at 315, Bowery?
6 Which New York landmark was a gift from the French in the 1880s, to celebrate a century of independence?
7 New York provides the setting for which 1949 song and dance spectacle starring Gene Kelly and Frank Sinatra?
8 What film follows the progress of students at the fictional New York High School of Performing Arts?
9 In what song would you find 'the boys of the NYPD choir still singing 'Galway Bay'?
10 What was the name of Andy Warhol's original New York studio?
11 In what film does George Peppard (as Paul Varjak) say "And I always heard people in New York never get to know their neighbours"?
12 Katz's Deli on the Lower East Side of Manhattan was made famous by a notoriously 'fake' scene in which movie?
13 Name the two Major League baseball teams from New York City.
14 Central Park lies within which New York City borough?
15 What is at the confluence of 42nd Street and Broadway?

People and places – *The Big Apple*

PART 2

1   What is the name of the financial quarter of New York?
2   What is the peninsula at the southern tip of Brooklyn?
3   Which stunning Art Deco corporate skyscraper, built between 1928 and 1930, was William van Alen's contribution to the New York skyline?
4   What was the venue for Velvet Underground's last gigs with Lou Reed in 1970, which produced a memorable live album?
5   What is the name of the tower the New Yorkers defiantly intend to build on the site of the World Trade Center?
6   New York was taken by the British in 1664; from whom did they take the colony?
7   Who made *Escape From New York*, an exciting adventure film that presents New York as a no-go area used as a hands-off prison for extreme criminals?
8   Excluding its television mast, how tall is the Empire State Building: 381m, 365m, or 348m?
9   What does the Statue of Liberty hold in her right hand?
10   What was Tom Wolfe's 1987 novel, an outstanding appraisal of the moral torpor afflicting New York City in the eighties?

? Tie-breaker

Which two venues in Queens have hosted the US Tennis Open since the professional era began in 1968?

Did you know?

New Yorkers love their sport. Even soccer, not a notable American game, had its moments in New York. When the North American Soccer League opened in the 70s wealthy backers paid a fortune to bring in the best foreign stars (sound familiar?). In those halcyon days Beckenbauer, Neeskens and even Pele turned out for the New York Cosmos. It never caught on.

People and places

• •

QUIZ 123

PART 1

1   Which great English fast bowler, later a not-so-great commentator, died in 2006?
2   In a statement often attributed to feminist writer Gloria Steinem, a woman needs a man like what?
3   Who was the longest-serving Prime Minister in Britain in the twentieth century?
4   True or false: Author John Buchan was once Governor-General of Canada?
5   Who was the mover behind the Popish Plot of 1678?
6   The Midlands seat of Warwick and Leamington was held for many years by which Conservative Prime Minister?
7   Who became President of Russia in 2000?
8   On which country did Britain and France declare war in 1854?
9   Who was arrested in his Belgrade home after an armed siege in 2001?
10 Which country is linked to Switzerland by the Simplon rail tunnel under the Alps?
11 Which Pakistani PM was executed by the military junta that deposed him in 1979?
12 Which country passed the controversial Land Acquisition Act in 2000?
13 Which Arab state gained independence from the UK on 19th June 1961?
14 Which British trading organization was often known as "John Company"?
15 Who once described himself to the General Dental Council as a practitioner of 'dentopedalogy, the science of opening your mouth and putting your foot in it'?

PART 2

1 Which New Zealander was the first man to put his foot on the summit of Mount Everest?

2 Tenochtitlan, the Aztec capital, lies beneath which teeming modern city?

3 Which flowers sprang from the blood spilled from Adonis when the bull gored him?

4 The Roman roads Ermine Street and the Fosse Way meet at which city?

5 In 1997, who became the youngest Conservative leader for over 200 years?

6 Winston Churchill, John Simon and which other politician were in the Cabinet during both World Wars?

7 Who was the Norwegian explorer who beat Scott to the South Pole?

8 Which other organization sued the World Wrestling Federation and contested its right to market itself using its initials?

9 Which astronomer was often consulted by Catherine De Medici?

10 Of which institution did painter Joshua Reynolds become the first President in 1768?

11 Which was the fiftieth, and last, territory to join the United States, in 1959?

12 Which sporting arena was built for the British Empire Exhibition in 1924 and 1925?

13 In which modern country is Mount Ararat, the supposed resting place of Noah's Ark?

14 Which of the following does not have a border with Austria: Hungary, Slovenia, Poland, Italy?

15 Who achieved credibility as an actress/singer as Roxie Hart in *Chicago* and cemented it with a long run performing Lloyd Webber's *Tell Me On A Sunday*?

? Tie-breaker

Who was the famous diplomat who started off working for Louis XVI, survived the revolution and Napoleon, and engineered the Bourbon restoration?

London town

● ●

QUIZ 124
PART 1

1   What is the most expensive property on a monopoly board?
2   In the rhyme, what question is asked by the Bells of Old Bailey?
3   On which street can you find Harrods' store?
4   Who became Mayor of London in 1397?
5   Which temporary exhibition in the 1970s attracted a record number of visitors to the British Museum?
6   A train to Devon would be taken from which London station?
7   To which London address would you go if you needed verification of your birth?
8   The Serpentine winds its way around which London park?
9   Which king oversaw the building of the original Westminster Abbey?
10 Who painted 'Sun Breaking Through The Fog, Houses of Parliament' in 1904?
11 Which London University college has a formidable reputation for teaching sciences?
12 By what name is the skyscraper at 1, Canada Square, better known?
13 What other London tourist attraction sits next to Madame Tussaud's on Marylebone Road?
14 What is London's, and indeed the UK's, major fish market?
15 Chancery Lane and Gray's Inn are London places associated with which profession?

PART 2

1 Who wrote and had a hit with the folk song, 'Streets of London'?
2 Which underground station lies between Bond Street and Westminster on the Jubilee Line?
3 Which independent theatre lies just off the High Street in Islington?
4 Oxford Circus is the intersection of Oxford Street and which other street?
5 Where did a nightingale sing?
6 What is the collective name for the four main legal societies in London?
7 Which other station lies on the Euston Road between Euston and King's Cross?
8 The M11 connects London with which other city?
9 *London Calling* was a critically acclaimed 1979 album by which rock band?
10 Cross London Bridge from the city, and in which borough would you find yourself?
11 A stroll from Westminster Bridge to Blackfriars would take you along which promenade?
12 Which twentieth-century composer wrote *A London Symphony*?
13 In which part of London did the Jack the Ripper murders take place?
14 What is the Archbishop of Canterbury's London residence?
15 Which of these London clubs has never won the FA Cup: Charlton Athletic, Chelsea, Fulham, West Ham United?

? Tie-breaker

In the last few years London has consistently had six of the Top Ten tourist attractions in the UK. Name these six.

Science and nature

The natural world

●●●●●●●●●●●●●●●●●●●●●●●●●●●●

QUIZ 125
PART 1

1 Broccoli, sprouts and cauliflower are all members of which family of plants?
2 What is Ragged Robin?
3 A quail is a small form of which other game bird?
4 What is a cross between a male horse and a donkey called?
5 By what other common name is the belladonna lily known?
6 To what family does the bandicoot belong?
7 Roderick Rat, Hammy the Hamster and GP the guinea pig all featured in which children's TV show?
8 What causes nettles to sting?
9 Which naturalist's work with gorillas was filmed in the biopic, *Gorillas In The Mist*, starring Sigourney Weaver?
10 What is the science of dividing creatures into similar groups?
11 What kind of creature lives in a holt?
12 Amber is made from the resin of which tree?
13 True or false: apart from human beings, the only other creatures known to suffer from sunburn are pigs.
14 What kind of creature is a flying fox?
15 Which is bigger, a weasel or a stoat?

Did you know?

Over half the world's birds belong to the order, *Passeriformes*, the perching birds. They number over 5,000 species and include most garden birds and songbirds. They have separate toes, for clinging, so are rarely found in watery habitats. The largest *Passeriformes* are ravens; most are medium-sized or smaller birds.

PART 2 – *How good is your Latin? Match these common names to their Latin equivalent.*

1 Foxglove
2 Weeping willow
3 Raven
4 Goldfish
5 Grapefruit
6 Pot marigold
7 Sperm whale
8 Whooper swan
9 Housefly
10 Wolf

A Cygnus cygnus
B Canis lupus
C Calendula officinalis
D Musca domestica
E Physeter macrocephalus
F Digitalis purpurea
G Carassius auratus auratus
H Corvus corax
I Salix sepulcralis
J Citrus x paradise

? ## Tie-breaker
Which wandering sea bird boasts the largest wingspan of any bird?

Blinded by science

● ●

QUIZ 126
PART 1

1   What is signified by the letter K in The Periodic Table?
2   In which year did CDs become commercially available; 1976, 1982 or 1986?
3   What is the chemical annotation for carbon dioxide?
4   What is the name of the process whereby a solid transmutes into a gas without becoming liquid on the way?
5   Who discovered dynamite by effectively 'wrapping' unstable nitroglycerine in finely ground rock?
6   What are the chemical elements that compose natural salt, and what is its symbol?
7   By what name are helium, argon, radon, krypton, xenon and neon called?
8   Only compounds that contain which element can be described as organic?
9   Who isolated potassium and sodium from molten potash and soda?
10 What is the term for chains of repeated groups of atoms, e.g. DNA, proteins?
11 Apart from the dominant oxygen and hydrogen, which other two elements are found in the hydrosphere?
12 What is the equivalent of Chemistry at Harry Potter's school, and who teaches it?
13 What did Scottish scientist Charles Macintosh invent?
14 What was the name of the computer that beat World Chess Champion Gary Kasparov in 1997?
15 Who invented the mercury thermometer?

Did you know?

Once No8 is reached on this scale, the wind is at gale force, and No12 indicates a hurricane or typhoon. Both hurricane and typhoon are terms for what is properly termed a tropical cyclone, an area of low pressure heated suddenly by rising warm air and causing freak results.

PART 2

1   Which gaseous compound causes the smell of rotten eggs?
2   From what is aluminium extracted?
3   What was the ground-breaking 'thought experiment' proposed by an Austrian scientist in 1935?
4   What element bears the letters Hg in The Periodic Table?
5   What is the opposite of fluidity in a liquid?
6   Messier numbers are allocated to what?
7   Movement produces which type of energy?
8   What are produced in the endocrine glands?
9   Is acidity indicated by a pH higher or lower than water?
10 True or false: an isobar connects two points of equal temperature on a weather map.

? Tie-breaker

What would be used to measure wind speed? And what scale is used to grade wind?

The natural world

●●●●●●●●●●●●●●●●●●●●●●●●●●●●

QUIZ 127
PART 1

1   What is the world's tallest bird?
2   A hoglet is the young of which common garden mammal?
3   True or false: A typical earthworm has a total of ten hearts.
4   What name is given to an animal that chews its cud?
5   If a bird is a palmiped, what does that signify?
6   Philomel is a poetic name, with its origins in Greek mythology, for which bird?
7   Which former comedian went on to become presenter of BBC's *Spring Watch* programme, and a major authority on British birds?
8   Blue gum and ironbark are species of which genus of Australian tree?
9   What is a sidewinder?
10 A capybara is the world's largest example of which genus of mammal?
11 What is the common name of *Atropa belladonna*, a poisonous plant with purple flowers and cherry-like fruit?
12 On which group of islands did Charles Darwin study finches to better help him understand the process of natural selection?
13 John Audubon is famous for painting what?
14 How does a grasshopper make its familiar humming noise?
15 How many humps would you find on a Bactrian, or Asian, camel?

Did you know?

Potatoes probably originated in South America in the Andes. They were introduced into Europe by the Spanish conquistadors in the early 16th century, and into Britain by the pirate-adventurers, Raleigh and Drake, in the latter part of that century. The tuber has remained a staple part of our diet ever since, and a major economy crop, especially in Ireland, where potato blight has caused many a famine over the years.

PART 2 – *Which is the odd one out, and why?*
1 radish, chervil, coriander, rosemary
2 chamois, impala, dingo, springbok
3 topaz, talc, feldspar, carbon
4 chough, shrike, lynx, teal
5 alpaca, John Dory, snapper, sturgeon
6 gopher, lemur, macaque, bush baby
7 chestnut, willow, elm, pine
8 shiitake, fool's cap, porcini, chanterelle
9 onion, chive, turnip, garlic
10 gannet, stork, flamingo, heron

? *Tie-breaker*

Which of these is not a variety of potato: Maris Piper, Rosie's Larder, Golden Wonder, Pink Fir Apple

In the garden

●●●●●●●●●●●●●●●●●●●●●●●●●●●●

QUIZ 128
PART 1

1 Azaleas are a type of what?
2 What is the art of growing plants exclusively in pots?
3 What name is given to the art of cropping hedges or bushes into artistic shapes?
4 What is gardening without soil?
5 In which year was *Gardener's World* first broadcast: 1959, 1965 or 1968?
6 What was the actual first name of the landscape designer known as Capability Brown?
7 *How Does Your Garden Grow?* was the precursor to which famous radio show?
8 What was held for the first time in 1913 in the grounds of the Royal Hospital?
9 Bushy stunt virus and spotted wilt virus both tend to affect which edible plant type?
10 If a flower is campanulate, what is the main characteristic of its flowers?
11 What name is given to a shaded walk with pillars and cross-beams for trailing vines?
12 What is also called moonwort and satinpod?
13 With which garden is the famous gardener and writer Vita Sackville-West associated?
14 Why wouldn't you want convolvulus on your borders?
15 In what kind of soil would an ericaceous plant survive best?

Did you know?

This lady was one of the first true gardeners; more of an arranger of plants than a schematic designer. Her approach was more that of a painter, using garden and plants rather than canvas and brushes.

PART 2

1   What name is given to a small parcel of land rented out at low rates for those with limited wealth to grow crops and vegetables?

2   *Walden* is which writer's story of a year living amongst plants and trees in quiet solitude?

3   Edwin Beard Budding, a Gloucestershire engineer, is credited with the first design of what inestimable garden aid?

4   With what specific style of gardening would you associate Bob Flowerdew?

5   Who wrote the seventeenth century poem, 'The Garden'?

6   Which *Gardener's World* presenter had the longest run on the programme?

7   Which Cotswold garden was created by Major Lawrence Johnston in the 1920s and acquired by the National Trust in 1947?

8   Which popular gardening programme featured Alan Titchmarsh, Tommy Walsh and Charlie Dimmock renovating other people's gardens?

9   Which great garden designer became head gardener at Chatsworth in 1826?

10 Who was the gardener on *Blue Peter* from 1974 until 1987, a year before his death?

? *Tie-breaker*

Who was the Surrey-born gardener and writer who worked alongside Edwin Lutyens on many of his architectural projects?

Do the maths

● ●

QUIZ 129
PART 1

1   A number which can only be divided by one and itself.
2   Who wrote *Principia Mathematica*, published in 1687?
3   What branch of mathematics includes sines, tangents and cosecants?
4   In a right-angled triangle, the square of the hypotenuse is equal to the sum of the squares of the other two sides. What is this?
5   The fraction 9/40 is represented alternatively by what percentage: 17.5, 18, 22.5 or 27.5?
6   What is the Latin for pebble?
7   What is the 3-D version of a triangle?
8   Fermat's Theorem concerns which mathematical construct?
9   6 and 28 are the first two in which sequence of numbers?
10 What is the average of the following numbers: 6, 8, 14, 17, 21, 30?
11 What is the mean of the following numbers: 6, 8, 14, 17, 21, 30?
12 What is binary 1000 in decimal numbers?
13 What is a triangle with two of its three sides equal?
14 What name is given to a parallelogram with four equal sides but no right angles?
15 What letter generally signifies the horizontal axis on a graph?

Did you know?

Until the use of the electronic calculator was allowed in school exams, immensely complicated books of tables were used to calculate complex equations. The tables were devised as an aid by the Muslims, and the first person to produce them in a coherent form in the West was Henry Briggs, in 1617.

PART 2

1 4 x 18
2 3 x 22 + 6
3 83 + 45 + 119
4 83 + 55 – 109
5 Double 46 – 23 + 4
6 Half of 112 – 3 + 18 x 3
7 One third of 42 doubled and deducted from 99
8 126 ÷ 3, x 4, – 20
9 45 ÷ 9, x 3, – 2 doubled
10 Square root of 81, – 4, x 10, + 31. What is the square root?

? *Tie-breaker*

What is the next in this sequence of Fibonacci numbers: 3, 7, 10, 17, 27, 44, 71 … ?

The human body

● ●

QUIZ 130
PART 1

1   What is the total number of bones in the human body: 154, 206 or 237?
2   What is the name of the largest artery in the human body?
3   True or false: Crohn's disease is a chronic inflammatory disease of the lungs.
4   What is myopia?
5   Which part of the body is the axilla?
6   What is the name of the bone extending from the shoulder to the elbow?
7   What acid is found in the stomach?
8   What is the name of the muscle that covers the shoulder joint?
9   What is the name of the virus that causes glandular fever?
10 Which muscle is unattached at both ends?
11 What is rubella otherwise known as?
12 Name the three different forms of adult teeth.
13 What is the name of the skin disease characterized by loss of pigmentation?
14 What does 'vascular' relate to?
15 Name the two female sex hormones.

PART 2

1 Which is the largest organ within the human body?
2 What are the names of the upper and lower jaw bones?
3 True or false: more muscles are used when frowning than when laughing.
4 How many nerve cells does the brain contain: 10,000 million, 100,000 million or 300,000 million?
5 On which part of the body is the hallux found?
6 What are the names of the two most common forms of hernia?
7 What is stomatology the study of?
8 What is the hardest substance in the human body?
9 What is the name of the muscle that makes up a large proportion of the shape and appearance of the buttocks?
10 MRI scans are used to demonstrate pathological or physiological alterations of living tissues: what do the letters MRI stand for?
11 In the eye, what is the centre of the iris called?
12 What is an epistaxis?
13 What is the word used to describe abnormally low blood pressure?
14 What is the type of plastic surgery that is used to improve the function or appearance of a person's nose?
15 What is the name of the inner and longer of the two bones of the forearm?

? **Tie-breaker**
What is the common name for a singultus?

Space – The final frontier

●●●●●●●●●●●●●●●●●●●●●●●●●●

QUIZ 131
PART 1

1   Which spacecraft enabled the first moon landing?
2   Who became the oldest man in space when he went up in 1998, aged seventy-seven?
3   Which constellation depicts the twins?
4   In which year did the first Chinese pilot go into space: 1979, 1994 or 2003?
5   Who, in 1961 was the first US astronaut to fly in space, aboard *Freedom 7*?
6   What is the sole constituent of the atmosphere of Mars?
7   What lies above the Troposphere and below the Ionosphere?
8   What is the brightest star in our celestial sphere?
9   Christa McAuliffe was amongst those killed aboard which ill-fated mission?
10 Ganymede, Callisto and Pasiphae are all satellites of which planet?
11 The Asteroid Belt lies between which two planets?
12 What post was first held by John Flamsteed (appointed 1675), and then by Edmund Halley from 1720 to 1742?
13 What is Hale-Bopp, first sighted in 1995?
14 What was placed in the earth's orbit by Discovery in 1990?
15 What name is given to a dust or gas cloud in space, visible through a telescope?

Did you know?

When the moon is closest to the earth in its orbit, its position is known as the perigee; when at its furthest, the apogee. These unusual words have no other application, and have found no place in general language. (Unlike, for example, nadir and zenith, with are both words relating to positioning of celestial bodies.)

PART 2

1   Which of the nine planets in our solar system is furthest from the Sun?
2   What name is given to the study of the universe?
3   What was the new type of space station launched by the Soviets in 1986?
4   Lovell, Swigert and Haise were the astronauts aboard which famous mission?
5   Who was the pilot of *Vostok 1*, launched on April 12th, 1961?
6   Which non-European state is deemed a "co-operating state" with the European Space Agency?
7   Where are the headquarters of the European Space Agency?
8   From where was the first US space launch (*Explorer 1*, 1958) made?
9   What is the significance of 186,000 miles per second?
10 The constellation of Sagittarius is representative of what figure?

? *Tie-breaker*

What is the basic unit of measurement for vast distances in space (1 being equivalent to 3.26 light years)?

The natural world

●●●●●●●●●●●●●●●●●●●●●●●●●

QUIZ 132

PART 1 – *Can you give the collective nouns for these animals? We've even given you the answer; you just need to sort them out.*

1 Bees
2 Deer
3 Whales
4 Monkeys
5 Lions
6 Wolves
7 Puppies
8 Fish
9 Race horses
10 Oxen

A shoal
B pack
C swarm (or grist)
D yoke
E pride
F litter
G string
H herd
I school
J troop

Did you know?

Ducks have three different collective nouns. In the water, they are a Paddling, on the ground a Badelynge, and in flight a Flush, a Pump or a Team.

PART 2 – *That was too easy. These are a bit harder. But we've been kind and given you the answers again. All you have to do is mix and match.*

1   Polecats
2   Boars
3   Goldfish
4   Lapwings
5   Ravens
6   Starlings
7   Clams
8   Budgerigars
9   Tigers
10 Peacocks

A   muster
B   unkindness
C   sounder
D   bed
E   troubling
F   ambush
G   chatter
H   chine
I   deceit
J   murmuration

? *Tie-breaker*
Which birds would make a terrible nuisance of themselves if a 'descent' of them lived close by your house?

Blinded by science

● ●

QUIZ 133
PART 1

1 Meteorology is the study of what?
2 What percentage of the earth's atmosphere consists of nitrogen: 35%, 66% or 78% approx?
3 What word did James Joyce's *Ulysses* contribute to particle physics?
4 What name is given to frozen carbon dioxide, commonly used in stage shows?
5 True or false: sound waves will not travel through a vacuum.
6 Who first devised the periodic table?
7 What is the chemical symbol for tungsten?
8 What is the SI unit of energy?
9 How many pairs of equal sides must a parallelogram contain?
10 Name the odd one out: krypton, xenon, hydrogen, helium.
11 What name is given to the gas-filled space above the liquid in a sealed container?
12 Who was the first woman to win a Nobel Prize for scientific achievement?
13 What name is given to the interference caused to wave patterns by an object or gap?
14 In which household substances would you find alkyl benzene sulphonate?
15 What is 50% of the diameter of a circle?

Did you know?

The study of fossils is known as palaeontology. Whilst fossils have always existed, it is only since Darwin's *Origin of Species* that these mineral remains have been put into context and helped mankind date the various periods in the development of the earth and its inhabitants.

PART 2

1   Which element has the symbol Cu?
2   True or false: a concave lens has the effect of making things look smaller.
3   Which great scientist, born 1791, spent some of his formative years as an assistant to Sir Humphry Davy, before going on to become a brilliant innovator in the electrical field?
4   Who was born in Ulm in 1879? (OK, a lot of people; we're after the famous scientist!)
5   True or false: helium is lighter than hydrogen
6   A pyromaniac has a dangerous obsession with what?
7   What constitutes about 70% of manufactured glass?
8   A pascal is a measure of what?
9   When is REM (rapid eye movement) likely to occur?
10 Which vitamin assists in blood clotting?

? *Tie-breaker*
What is the name given to fossilized dinosaur dung?

Cats and dogs

● ●

QUIZ 134
PART 1

1　Which sitcom featured a pet capuchin monkey called Marcel?
2　Which TV programme featured dogs called Shep and Petra?
3　In the works by Hergé, what breed is Tin Tin's dog Snowy?
4　Bast is the feline-headed god of which ancient civilization?
5　Who is the cat in the famous series of cartoons by Bill Watterson?
6　Which eighteenth-century literary figure is said to have praised his cat, Hodge, as "a very fine cat indeed"?
7　Pal was the first dog to portray which famous collie on screen?
8　Who was 'The Mystery Cat'. in TS Eliot's *Old Possum's Book of Practical Cats*?
9　Who was the author of the classic children's novel, *101 Dalmatians*?
10　A cat called Jonesy appears in which series of sci-fi movies?
11　What does the black cat statue on Highgate Hill in London celebrate?
12　How did it become easier to have a pet dog in 1988?
13　Whose behavioural observations of pets were recorded in *Catwatching* and *Dogwatching*?
14　What breed of dog is Scooby-Doo?
15　Who has feline friends called Arlene and Nermal?

Did you know?

Alice's Adventures In Wonderland was born out of a story told by the Reverend Charles Dogson (Lewis Carroll) on a river trip. One of the girls on the trip, Alice Liddell, asked for a written version of the tale. Two years later the manuscript of Alice's adventures underground was complete and published as Alice's Adventures In Wonderland with illustrations by John Tenniel.

PART 2

1   The Siamese cat from Sheila Burnford's *The Incredible Journey*.
2   The HMV dog sitting on the gramophone player
3   The dog in *The Magic Roundabout*
4   The Clinton family cat
5   Paris Hilton's dog
6   The Darling family dog in *Peter Pan*
7   John Lennon's cat
8   Hermione Grainger's cat
9   Bill Sikes' dog in *Oliver Twist*
10 The Hound of Hell

A   Crookshanks
B   Elvis
C   Nana
D   Nipper
E   Cerberus
F   Bullseye
G   Dougal
H   Tao
I   Tinkerbell
J   Socks

? Tie-breaker

Name the two cats in Alice's Adventures In Wonderland.

The natural world

QUIZ 135
PART 1

1. Denmark is situated between the North Sea and which other?
2. Which Alaskan mountain is the highest point in the USA?
3. What links the Mediterranean Sea to the Atlantic Ocean?
4. Lake Geneva straddles which two countries?
5. The Cook Strait divides the north and south land-masses of which country?
6. Which English river feeds the Manchester Ship Canal?
7. The coastal resorts of Croatia are on which sea?
8. What is the name scientists give to the single continent that comprised the earth's entire landmass about 240 million years ago?
9. The Pennines forms a natural border between which two rival counties of England?
10. Which island nation lies off the southeast tip of India?
11. The majority of the Gobi Desert lies within the boundaries of which country?
12. Green beryl is the proper name for which valuable gem mineral?
13. Which enormous mass of water lies at the north end of Tanzania between Kenya and Uganda?
14. Which occupies the bigger area, the Gulf of Mexico or the Mediterranean Sea?
15. Mont Blanc is the highest peak in which mountain range?

Did you know?

On Wednesday, July 19th, 2006, the hottest temperature ever recorded in the UK was measured at the Royal Horticultural Society garden at Wisley in Surrey. During a summer heatwave, the thermometer hit 36.5° C.

PART 2 – *Identify which of these places extends furthest north (not counting colonized islands).*

1   Spain, Portugal, Italy
2   United Kingdom, Poland, Ukraine
3   Zimbabwe, Angola, Botswana
4   Sudan, Saudi Arabia, Thailand
5   Afghanistan, Japan, Turkey
6   Crete, Sardinia, Corsica
7   Iraq, Iran, Israel
8   Burma, Nepal, India
9   China, North Korea, Mongolia
10 Norway, Sweden, Iceland
11 Sydney, Perth, Brisbane
12 Miami, New Orleans, Los Angeles
13 Amsterdam, London, Kiev
14 Rome, Venice, Florence
15 Washington, San Francisco, Chicago

? *Tie-breaker*

Which country boasts the world's hottest recorded temperature?

The natural world

●●●●●●●●●●●●●●●●●●●●●●●●●●●●

QUIZ 136
PART 1

1 By what name is a formicary more commonly known?
2 Culpeper's is a business name associated with what?
3 If the female part of a plant is the pistil, what is the name of the male counterpart?
4 Who is the patron saint of animals?
5 Which familiar bird has the odd Latin name, *Troglodytes troglodytes*?
6 Which creature is named for its habit of living in a cast-off shell of a mollusc?
7 The locust belongs to which family of insects?
8 What is the name given to the creeping mint plant often used as a restorative tea?
9 What type of bird is a widgeon?
10 What is a lamprey?
11 True or false: only female ducks quack.
12 Which character in *Friends* owned a monkey called Marcel?
13 Spraint are the droppings of which mammal?
14 If you spotted a wobbegong on a visit to Australia, what would you have seen?
15 What oil is made from the seed of the flax plant?

PART 2 – *What is the familiar name given to the young of the following animals?*

1 Deer
2 Eel
3 Pigeon
4 Hare
5 Lion
6 Pig
7 Sheep
8 Cat
9 Elephant
10 Duck
11 Fish
12 Frog
13 Grouse
14 Zebra
15 Kangaroo

? Tie-breaker

To what classification of animals do squid and octopi belong?

Computers

● ●

QUIZ 137
PART 1

1   Which Windows release happened on October 25th, 2001?
2   What is Microsoft's competitor to the Sony Playstation?
3   What did Steve Jobs and Wozniak form in 1976?
4   Which manufacturer produces a range of portable PCs called Latitude?
5   Shawn Fanning created which file-sharing service, which had major repercussions on the music industry?
6   A byte contains how many bits?
7   What is Adobe's graphics package designed to compete with QuarkXPress?
8   What is the bespoke music jukebox and download software package for an Apple computer (now also widely used on PCs)?
9   Which Seattle-based e-tailer, the market leader in selling media products online, launched in 1995, made its first net profit in 2003?
10 What was the early computer language developed by IBM in the 1940s for engineering application?
11 Which part of the Microsoft Office package is the specialist database?
12 Which company, formed by Larry Page and Sergei Brin, was incorporated on 7th September 1998?
13 Which is the odd one out: Mac OSX, Linux, COBOL, MS Windows NT?
14 WiFi has begun to replace which wired option in many networks?
15 Which e-tailer made the fortunes of Martha Lane-Fox and Brent Hoberman?

Science and nature – Computers

PART 2 – *Explain these computer/Internet terms.*

1 ISP
2 GIF
3 ISP
4 URL
5 DIVX
6 AOL
7 ISDN
8 bps
9 LAN
10 CD-RW
11 WAP
12 SMS
13 HP
14 TCP
15 SQL

? *Tie-breaker*
Which kind of computer connection uses a trident symbol as its icon? What is the full name for this type of connection?

The natural world

● ●

QUIZ 138
PART 1

1 What is the largest British carnivore?
2 In which year was the Royal Horticultural Society founded: 1750, 1804 or 1874?
3 Where the cell walls of plants are made up of cellulose, what constitutes the cell walls of fungi?
4 Salamanders are often thought of as lizards, but are in fact from which other family of amphibians?
5 What is widely believed to be the fastest flying insect?
6 By what common name is the flower impatiens often known?
7 Which TV programme featured a monkey called Judy and a lion called Clarence?
8 Mouldiwarp, crode and modywart are all old country names for which creature?
9 What plant, often used in flower arrangements, is also known as baby's breath?
10 Armadillos are native only to which part of the world?
11 "One for sorrow/Two for joy;" so runs the first two lines of the folklore rhyme about magpies. But what does three signify?
12 The avocet is the symbol of which ornithological organization?
13 What is the common name of the small arctic whale with a long spiral tusk, *Monodon monoceros*?
14 A documentary about which animal was voted the public's favourite natural history programme?
15 The windhawk is another name for which bird of prey?

PART 2

1   The Apennine Mountains form the backbone to which European country?
2   Which of the world's oceans covers the largest area?
3   Snaefell Pike is the highest point on which island?
4   What is a sirocco, other than a Volkswagen car: is it a river in Peru, an Asian rodent or a dry African wind?
5   The Isle of Sheppey lies off the coast of which English county?
6   Which Scottish river flows eastward through the Grampian hills and empties into the North Sea near Aberdeen?
7   What is the historically significant mountain pass between Afghanistan and Pakistan?
8   Which is the largest of the Great Lakes across North America (the name is a giveaway)?
9   The Arabian Sea lies to the west of India; what stretch of water lies to the east?
10   Which dormant volcano is Africa's highest peak?
11   Which one of these is not one of the Mediterranean Balearic islands: Ibiza, Majorca, Lanzarote, Minorca?
12   What is the desert covering about 100,000 square miles in southwest Africa?
13   Which is the world's deepest sea, going down to around 30,000 feet?
14   Which is the bigger land mass, Iceland or Ireland?
15   Cape Horn, the southernmost tip of South America, lies on the coast of which country?

? Tie-breaker
Where might you find the Gutenberg discontinuity?

Blinded by science

● ●

QUIZ 139

PART 1

1. Which metallic element, atomic number 50, has the symbol Sn?
2. In which year did Louis Braille finish his system of reading using dots in relief for blind people: 1834, 1888 or 1925??
3. What do we call a three-dimensional picture created by lasers?
4. Which German scientist invented the mercury thermometer in 1714?
5. Where are Hell, Ptolemaeus, Birmingham and Archimedes?
6. What contribution to cinema did Herbert Kalmus invent in 1922?
7. What is measured in hertz?
8. "A body will remain stationary or travelling at a constant velocity unless it is acted upon by an external force." Which law?
9. Who produced the first wireless telegraph in 1895?
10. Acid will turn a litmus paper what colour?
11. What was invented by Hans Lippershey, a Dutch optician, in 1608?
12. Who devised the spinning mule (1779), one of the machines that revolutionized the fabric-making industry?
13. What anaesthetic was dentist Horace Wells the first to use in the US in 1844?
14. Which ingredient makes saliva a natural anti-bacterial?
15. Who discovered the process of vulcanizing rubber, which would eventually lead to the use of tyres?

Did you know?

The nineteenth century was a period of rapid change and extraordinary innovation. Just as the microchip changed lives dramatically towards the end of the twentieth century, so the synthesising of natural resources into energy for propulsion, light, heat and manufactured goods changed the face of the Western world back then. Computers have moved us on apace, but without the nineteenth-century inventors, there would be no computers.

PART 2

1 Which scientific accolade was created by an endowment from a man who died in 1896?
2 What is measured in ohms?
3 Who published *Experiments and Observations In Electricity* in 1752 in the United States?
4 How many elements make up the Lanthanides group: 6, 10 or 14?
5 How many imperial gallons of oil in a barrel?
6 What piece of apparatus is used to measure the resistance of a conductor?
7 "Heat will always flow from a hotter object to a colder one and not the other way round." Which law?
8 What is calcium oxide commonly called?
9 What can you do if you have scotopic vision?
10 What was the Blucher, built by Robert Stephenson in 1814?

? Tie-breaker

In 1892, which invention of James Dewar guaranteed happier picnics for evermore?

Cats and dogs

● ●

QUIZ 140
PART 1

1   What is the name of Harry's owl in the Harry Potter stories?
2   And which character in the books can shapeshift into the form of a tabby cat?
3   Whose famous film dog is called Toto?
4   Which film features a dog called Harvey owned by a boy called Elliot?
5   What did the three little kittens lose in the nursery rhyme?
6   What breed of dog is Lady in *Lady and the Tramp*?
7   Which dog became a legend for its loyalty to Edinburgh policeman John Gray?
8   Who provides the voice for Puss-in-Boots in *Shrek 2*?
9   Buck is the main character in which classic animal drama by Jack London?
10 What is the name of the god when in cat-form in Garth Nix's *Sabriel* trilogy of fantasy books for older children?
11 What is name of the cat in Disney's *Pinocchio*?
12 Who voiced the heroic beagle Lou in *Cats and Dogs*?
13 Who is the naughty scruffy dog in Lynley Dodd's stories for children?
14 Which famous literary figure owned a cat called Hodge and would feed it oysters?
15 Which cat has sidekicks called Choo Choo, Benny The Ball and Fancy Fancy?

PART 2

1   What is the name of Dr Who's robotic dog companion?
2   Which cartoon dog had a muskrat (Muskie) and a gopher (Vince) for his companions?
3   What is the name of the Himalayan cat in *Meet The Parents*?
4   What is the name of Ursula Moray Williams' Witch's Cat?
5   Which character in books and films for children has a pet monkey called Chee-Chee?
6   What is the name of the hound in Disney's *The Fox and The Hound*?
7   What was the name of the cat who lived at 10 Downing Street when John Major was in residence?
8   What was the name of the *Blue Peter* tortoise?
9   Who owns a cartoon dog called Dogmatix?
10 Which household product has traditionally used a scampering Labrador puppy in its advertising?
11 Which Bond villain was often filmed stroking a white Persian cat?
12 Which character was the object of numerous double-entendres about her cat, Tiddles, in the sitcom *Are You Being Served*?
13 Which comic character had a scruffy mutt called Gnasher?
14 What is the name of the bulldog who occasionally beats Tom up in *Tom and Jerry*?
15 What was the name of General Melchett's pigeon, shot and eaten by Blackadder, for which he was court-martialled and sentenced to death?

? Tie-breaker
In the children's TV show, what colour are Roobarb and Custard respectively?

The natural world

● ●

QUIZ 141
PART 1

1 Which Scottish Loch is the largest lake on mainland Britain?
2 Centred in a famous National Park in California, what is the highest waterfall in the US?
3 Which islands lie in the Indian Ocean to the east of the coast of Kenya and Tanzania?
4 It is well known that Everest is the world's highest mountain, but which is the second?
5 The Aegean Sea is a part of the Mediterranean Sea between Greece and which other country?
6 The Cape of Good Hope lies at the southern tip of which continent?
7 The Great Barrier Reef lies off the coast of which country?
8 What sort of wind registers 8 on the Beaufort scale?
9 The Coast of Labrador lies on the Atlantic coast of which country?
10 Which river starts in Lake Tear of Clouds and spills into the New York Bay?
11 Sumatra, Borneo and Timor are all island components of which country?
12 The Bering Straits separate which two continents?
13 What is the world's largest island?
14 Which sea represents the lowest point below sea level in Europe?
15 Which is the longest river in France, emptying into the Bay of Biscay on the Atlantic coast?

PART 2 – *Name the male and female of the given animal.*
1   Goat
2   Polar bear
3   Ass
4   Deer
5   Duck
6   Swan
7   Sheep
8   Kangaroo
9   Horse
10 Fox
11 Wolf
12 Chicken
13 Hawk
14 Badger
15 Turkey

? *Tie-breaker*
The UK shipping area formerly known as Finisterre was changed to what in 2002?

Medicine

● ●

QUIZ 142
PART 1

1   What term is a given to a fully qualified, but still junior, hospital doctor?
2   An obstetrician is concerned particularly with which branch of medicine?
3   Which famous surgeon performed the world's first heart transplant in 1967?
4   What unfortunate and embarrassing complaint is officially known as nocturnal enuresis?
5   By what name is rubella also known?
6   If you are afflicted by an epistaxis, what have you got?
7   BCG is an inoculation against what?
8   The herb hypericum is credited with great healing qualities. What is its common name?
9   What is an STD?
10 What is sometimes referred to as Grand Mal?
11 What relatively common affliction is known formally as a hemicrania?
12 Allergic rhinitis is better known as what?
13 An ENT department in a hospital looks after what?
14 In 1978, Louise Brown was the first person to be born by what method?
15 What type of bandage would a surgeon apply to a bleeding artery?

PART 2

1 A surgeon puts you back together, but who puts you out while they do it?
2 At what point does protocol dictate that a Doctor revert to Mr or Mrs as an honorific?
3 An oncologist is a specialist in which field?
4 Where in the body is the calcaneus bone?
5 Psoriasis is an affliction of what?
6 What is hypertension more commonly called?
7 If you have myopia and a strabismus, what's your problem?
8 A podiatrist is a specialist in which area of the anatomy?
9 An inoculation against varicella could prevent what, in layman's terms?
10 Exposure to which creatures increases the risk of Lyme disease?
11 What is the oath taken by all medical practitioners?
12 Moorfields Hospital specializes in the treatment of what?
13 What is the ancient Chinese medicine that uses needles to stimulate pressure points, or meridians?
14 By what initials is the hospital 'superbug', which preys on the infirm, known?
15 Whilst leucocytes (white blood cells) are vital antibodies, an excess of them often signifies which often-fatal disease?

? *Tie-breaker*

George Jorgensen was the first person to undergo which life-changing operation in 1952?

The natural world

● ●

QUIZ 143
PART 1

1   What is the world's largest desert, more than three times the size of any other?
2   What is the American word for corn?
3   Which bird has the keenest sense of smell, largely using that sense to find food?
4   What type of crossbreed dog did medieval poachers develop, because they were barred, as commoners, from owning hunting hounds?
5   In 1935, Charles Richter developed a scale for measuring what?
6   A lepidopterist takes an interest in which creatures?
7   The monkey-puzzle tree was originally native to which South American country?
8   The importing from North America of which woodland creature led to the rapid decline of the red squirrel in Britain?
9   The Jean Bernard in France is the world's deepest what?
10 Which bird, native to the Andes, is the world's largest bird of prey?
11 Watercress, commonly used in salads, is related to which family of flowers?
12 How many separate islands make up the US state of Hawaii: 8, 14 or 18?
13 The Moh scale measures the hardness of which elements?
14 In which century were rabbits introduced to Britain: the 2nd century BC, the 9th century or the 12th century?
15 Ornithophobia is fear of what?

Did you know?

Polecat is a misnomer for these creatures, which are in fact members of the weasel family (subgenus: *Putorius*). The European polecat is a flesh-eating mammal (the ranker the flesh the better for these yucky fellas), and this family includes the domestic ferret, widely used in poaching and rabbiting.

PART 2 – *We give you ten plants and ten alternative names. We want you to match them up.*

1   antirrhinum
2   sweet briar
3   carnation
4   iris
5   wild hyacinth
6   larkspur
7   rowan
8   laburnum
9   aquilegia
10 cuckoo pint

A   fleur-de-lis
B   lords and ladies
C   delphinium
D   eglantine
E   columbine
F   mountain ash
G   snapdragon
H   bluebell
I   golden chain
J   gillyflower

? *Tie-breaker*

Why is the goose barnacle thus named?

Sports
and
pastimes

Sporting chance

● ●

QUIZ 144
PART 1

1 In squash, each game is played until one player scores how many points?
2 Where is the famous American Football stadium called the Rose Bowl?
3 Who was the first American cyclist to win the Tour de France?
4 On which racecourse is the St Leger annually run in September?
5 Which sporting event took place for the first time in Chamonix in France in 1924?
6 Who beat Muhammad Ali in 1978 to assume his World Heavyweight title?
7 Which rider won a rare hat-trick of Badminton, Burghley and Lexington in 2003?
8 Goldie versus Isis would be a race between whom?
9 Who became World Heavyweight Champion by beating Ken Norton after Muhammad Ali retired in 1979?
10 The New England Patriots compete in which American sport?
11 Which side were beaten 111–13 by England in a group match at the 2003 Rugby Union World Cup?
12 Goose Tatum, Meadowlark Lemon and Curly Neal are all star attractions in which sporting outfit?
13 Who became Britain's first-ever gold medal winner at the World Championships when she won the 200 metres backstroke in 2003?
14 Shotokan and Goju-ryu are different styles of which sport?
15 Who won three consecutive Rugby Union Premiership titles in England from 2003–05, despite never finishing top of the league?

PART 2 – *All these competitors have been world champions. Match them to their sport.*

1   Marvin Hagle
2   Nicole Cooke
3   Alison Fisher
4   Charlie Magri
5   Stephanie Cook
6   Chris Boardman
7   Jansher Khan
8   Alex Marshall (Scotland)
9   Andy Fordham
10 Kate Howey

A   Modern pentathlon
B   Men's 4000 metres individual pursuit (cycling)
C   Judo
D   Snooker
E   Bowls
F   BDO Darts Championship
G   Boxing (middleweight)
H   Boxing (flyweight)
I   World Road Race Championship (cycling)
J   Squash

? Tie-breaker

Which Englishman was President of FIFA from 1961–74? And who succeeded him?

Did you know?

The Englishman above was a low-key figurehead who adopted a hands-off diplomatic role to the job. His successor, although allegedly guilty of innumerable misdemeanours, did a lot to promote football in the non-European continents. The current incumbent, Sepp Blatter, is certainly no diplomat, giving opinions, often erroneous and ill-considered, about subjects far beyond his demesne.

Olympic Games

● ●

QUIZ 145
PART 1

1   Which seventeen-year-old won three gold medals at the Sydney Olympics and two more in Athens four years later?
2   Which cocky star won successive decathlon gold medals in the 80s?
3   Which country was Nadia Comaneci, the first gymnast to score a perfect 10 in Olympic gymnastics, representing?
4   Which US city hosted the 1996 Games?
5   Where will the 2008 Games be held?
6   Which US athlete won the discus gold medal at four successive Olympics between 1956 and 1968?
7   True or false: Britain won both men's and women's long jump gold at the 1964 Tokyo Games.
8   How does the Olympic motto, Citius Altius Fortius, translate?
9   Who speared her way to javelin gold in 1984?
10 Who is the only man in Olympic history to win a treble of 5,000 metres, 10,000 metres and marathon?
11 Who won the women's modern pentathlon for Britain at Sydney in 2000?
12 Who won light heavyweight gold in the 1960 Olympic boxing?
13 In which sport did Rodney Pattisson win consecutive golds in 1968 and 1972?
14 Which Northern Ireland athlete won the women's pentathlon gold in Munich in 1972 and became an instant national hero?
15 Leslie Law was awarded gold in the 2004 three-day-event after which German rider was found to have infringed the rules?

PART 2 – *All these individuals won gold medals at the Games; all we need is the sport in which they were competing. If athletics, give the discipline; if swimming, give the stroke. Some individuals may have been part of a team.*

1   Chris Hoy, Athens, 2004
2   Captain Mark Phillips, Munich, 1972
3   Chris Finnegan, Mexico City, 1968
4   Darren Campbell, Athens, 2004
5   Kitty Godfree, Antwerp, 1920
6   Sean Kerly, Seoul, 1988
7   Audley Harrison, Sydney, 2000
8   Jason Queally, Sydney, 2000
9   Martin Cooper, LA, 1984 and Seoul, 1988
10 David Wilkie, Montreal, 1976
11 Lord David Burghley, Amsterdam, 1928
12 Sarah Webb, Athens, 2004
13 Chris Boardman, Barcelona, 1992
14 Tim Foster, Sydney, 2000
15 Dick McTaggart, Melbourne, 1956

? **Tie-breaker**
Which Australian legend led out the country's Olympic team at the 2000 Olympics in Sydney, and which event did she subsequently claim the gold medal?

Sporting A-Z

● ●

QUIZ 146
PART 1

A   The voice of cricket
B   Pride actually came after this fell (from use)
C   Italy's World Cup captain and star
D   Only winner of Champion Hurdle ('84) and Gold Cup ('86)
E   Eleven times champion Jockey
F   Rotterdam's finest
G   Olympian Essex girl, OBE
H   Prince of British boxing
I   Captain of Pakistan
J   Welsh hurdler and ballroom dancer
K   Home of Gloucester RFC
L   Brits on rugby tour
M   Record cap-winner for Germany
N   The Golden Bear
O   So good at Bolton they named him twice
P   1980's Brazilian Formula One World Champion
Q   Won Britain's first gold in Sydney, 2000
R   England's Captain Courageous
S   Doncaster, Chelsea and Scotland's rapid striker
T   Martial art that went Olympic from 2000
U   Rory or Tony
V   Went for a paddle and blew the Open
W   2006 Ryder Cup skipper
Y   Denizens of Bootham Crescent
Z   Elegant Pakistan and Gloucestershire batsman

? Tie-breaker

Name Wisden's five cricketers of the twentieth century, chosen in 2000.

Did you know?

First published in 1864, Wisden *Cricketer's Almanac* is known as the Bible of Cricket. Wisden selects its five Cricketers of the Year each year and it is considered one of the game's highest accolades. Until recently the criteria were mainly based on the previous English summer, but the list now reflects the year's cricket worldwide more accurately.

Sporting chance

● ●

QUIZ 147
PART 1

1   Who accompanied Steve Redgrave in the last three of his five Olympic gold medal winning rows, and went on to win a fourth gold himself in Athens in 2004?
2   Supermodel Jodie Kidd has represented England at which sport?
3   What name is given, in rowing and other sports, to a heat of 'lucky losers' giving them a second chance to qualify for the nest stage of the competition?
4   In what year was the Boat Race run for the first time: 1798, 1877 or 1919?
5   What was Susan Brown's sporting 'first' in 1981?
6   Which high-profile sportsman refused to be drafted into the US army in 1967?
7   What took place for the first time in Louisville, Kentucky, in 1875?
8   Who skippered an all-woman crew in *Maiden* in the 1990 Whitbread round-the-world yacht race?
9   True or false: Enrique Iglesias was once on the books of Real Madrid as a goalkeeper.
10 What caused the cancellation of the Cheltenham festival in March, 2001?
11 Which athlete holds the British record for women at 100, 200 and 400 metres?
12 Who is England's most-capped Rugby Union international, with 114?
13 The main showcourt at the US tennis Open at Flushing Meadow is named after which great US player?
14 Who was the great Australian fly-half who amassed 911 points in 72 tests in the 80s and 90s?
15 Who took over sponsorship of the Rugby Union Premiership for the 2005-06 season?

PART 2

1   49er, Finn, Tempest and Laser are all classes of what?
2   Who, in 1998, became the first British team to win Rugby Union's Heineken Cup when they beat holders, Brive, in the final?
3   What is the name of Pittsburgh's American Football team?
4   Jane-Owe Waldner of Sweden enjoyed a long career at the top level of which sport?
5   In football, before squad numbers came in, what number would a right-winger traditionally wear?
6   Which indoor ball game originated in Harrow School in the middle of the nineteenth century?
7   Where is golf's US Masters held every year?
8   What was significant about Jack Johnson's victory in the 1908 World Heavyweight bout against Tommy Burns?
9   The All England Club at Wimbledon is a home to lawn tennis and which other sport?
10 Who added the World Equestrian title to her European title in August 2006, and what is the name of the horse she rode on both occasions?

? *Tie-breaker*
Name the three Welsh winners of the World Snooker Championship.

Football - the greats

● ●

QUIZ 148
PART 1

1   Who is Edson Arantes do Nascimento?
2   Which star of Portugal and La Liga made his debut for Sporting Lisbon aged 16?
3   Who did Alex Ferguson bring to Old Trafford from Brondby for £500,000?
4   Who was the Brazilian winger known as "Little Bird"?
5   Which great Mexican forward was one of the pioneers of gymnastic goal celebrations during his time with Real Madrid?
6   Which Italian forward was European and World Footballer of the Year in 1993?
7   Which Romanian playmaker was termed "The Maradona of the Carpathians"?
8   Which Argentinian led the Fiorentina attack for much of the nineties?
9   With which club has the durable Paolo Maldini played his entire career?
10 Who was the legendary black-shirted Russian goalkeeper of the fifties and sixties?
11 Which goalkeeper captained Italy in the 1982 World Cup Final?
12 Which brothers retired from international football after a 3-2 defeat by Brazil at the 1998 World Cup?
13 Which great all-round player became the first overseas coach to win a domestic trophy in England?
14 Who inspired Napoli to its first Serie A title in 1986-87?
15 Which imperious German defender was known as "Der Kaiser"?

PART 2 - *Match the player to the country for whom he played his international matches.*

1 Liam Brady
2 Nandor Hidegkuti
3 Jozef Masopust
4 Zbigniew Boniek
5 Juan Schiaffino
6 Jean Tigana
7 Hans Krankl
8 John Charles
9 Ruud Krol
10 Morten Olsen
11 George Weah
12 Franco Baresi
13 Hristo Stoichkov
14 Berti Vogts
15 Roger Milla

A *Uruguay*
B *Wales*
C *Hungary*
D *Czechoslovakia*
E *Cameroon*
F *Italy*
G *Republic of Ireland*
H *Bulgaria*
I *Poland*
J *Liberia*
K *Holland*
L *France*
M *Austria*
N *Denmark*
O *(West) Germany*

? **Tie-breaker**
Who was the captain of the great Brazilian side of 1970? And by what score did they beat Italy in the final?

Transportation

●●●●●●●●●●●●●●●●●●●●●●●●●●●●●

QUIZ 149
PART 1

1 QANTAS is the biggest airline of which country?
2 Which stretch of water in the Lake District was used by Malcolm and Donald Campbell for their water speed record attempts?
3 Where did a Boeing 737 crash in 1989, killing 46 people?
4 Which playboy millionaire set a transcontinental air-speed record in 1937 in a private monoplane?
5 What landed at Bahrain and Rio de Janeiro on 21st January, 1976?
6 In which year was Brunel's steamship, *The Great Eastern*, launched: 1838, 1858 or 1878?
7 What airline was founded in Russia in 1923?
8 What did the USAF's *Lucky Lady* become the first aeroplane to do in 1949?
9 Who, in 1930, flew to Australia in a Gypsy Moth called *Jason*?
10 What did the Montgolfier Brothers demonstrate on 4th June, 1783?
11 Who was the first person to cross the Channel in an aeroplane?
12 Where did two trains collide in West London on October 5th, 1999, killing 31 people?
13 Who is the articulate and aggressive CEO of Irish budget airline Ryanair?
14 The first section of motorway built in England was constructed as a by-pass to which Lancashire town?
15 To which destination was the Piccadilly Line extended in December, 1977?

Did you know?

The Trans-Manchurian is a branch of the famous Trans-Siberian link. A third link, the Trans-Mongolian, offers another option. The Trans-Siberian itself clocks in at 9,288 km, taking about seven days and crossing eight time zones.

PART 2

1   Which airline operates out of Dubai?
2   A ferry sailing from Portsmouth would land in which French port?
3   Whose name has come to mean a lounge car on a British train or a sleeping car on a US train?
4   Whose daughter, Gina, broke the women's water-speed record in 1990?
5   What is the name of the scenic luxury train route from Pretoria to Cape Town?
6   According to the Senate investigation, how many people went down with the *Titanic*: 779, 1523 or 1894?
7   Which other ship, a sister to *Titanic*, sank in 1916 when it hit a mine, although with significantly less loss of life?
8   Which company completed the 'Big Four' of the railway networks alongside LMS, Southern and LNER prior to nationalisation in 1948?
9   Which airline has been running the longest without a break?
10 Which city is served by Prestwick Airport?

? Tie-breaker
Which two Russian cities are linked by the Trans-Manchurian railway?

History of the Ashes

● ●

QUIZ 150

1 Who led England in the notorious Bodyline series in 1932–33 in Australia?

2 Who scored a triple hundred when England logged the Ashes record score of 903–7?

3 Who, in 1999, became the first bowler for 100 years to take a hat-trick in an Ashes test?

4 Who, in 1972, took sixteen wickets in the match for Australia at Lord's, but would play only six tests for his country?

5 Which early fast bowler, nicknamed The Demon, took 14 wickets in a test in 1882?

6 Who captained England when they won back the Ashes after twelve years in 1970–71 in Australia?

7 And who was his main strike bowler in that series?

8 Fast bowlers hunt in pairs: who was Dennis Lillee's partner?

9 Who scored a brilliant double hundred at Trent Bridge in 1938, an innings Don Bradman rated as the best he saw?

10 Which batsman hit a 75 ball hundred on a tricky pitch to win a famous Oval test in 1902?

11 Who was the last player to score a double hundred in an Ashes test for England?

12 Steve Waugh scored ten hundreds against England; how many did Don Bradman score: 12, 15 or 19?

13 Who scored centuries in three consecutive tests for England on the 1986–87 tour to Australia?

14 Who is the only player to have taken ten wickets in an innings in an Ashes test?

15 How many of his 29 tests as Captain against England did Allan Border win: 13, 16 or 20?

PART 2 - *Summer 2005.*

1   Who was the only test debutant on either side in the first test?
2   Who was the man of the match in that first test at Lord's?
3   Who came into the Australian side to replace the injured Glenn McGrath for the second test?
4   Who was the not-out Australian batsman at the end of the thrilling match?
5   How was the last batsman dismissed?
6   Who scored the first hundred of the series in the first innings of the third match at Edgbaston?
7   And who saved the Aussies with a fighting hundred in the fourth innings?
8   Who took six wickets in the Australian first innings to give notice of his ability to reverse-swing the ball?
9   Who scored his maiden hundred against Australia in the first innings of the fourth test?
10   Who was dropped from the Australian team, and replaced by the tyro, Shaun Tait?
11   Who was the substitute fielder who ran out Ricky Ponting, initiating an uncharacteristic gripe from the normally chivalrous Aussie captain?
12   Who became the only batsman to score two hundreds in the series with 129 at The Oval?
13   Who scored a vital half-century to keep Kevin Pietersen company as he kept the Aussies at bay on the last day?
14   Who took most wickets in the series for England?
15   Who was the only Australian batsman to average over 40 in the series?

? *Tie-breaker*
How many did wickets did Shane Warne take in the series?

Football League

● ●

QUIZ 151
PART 1

1   Who sponsored the Football League Championship in 2006–07?
2   Who play at the Priestfield Stadium?
3   Who returned to the League in 2006 after a previous incarnation went into liquidation in 1962?
4   Which league side play at Layer Road?
5   In 2005, who became the first former winners of the European Cup to slip into the third tier of the league?
6   Who won the league in 1960 but haven't played in the top flight since 1976?
7   Who are Stoke City's local rivals?
8   Who are the most recent top division winners not to be playing that division in 2006–07?
9   Peter Taylor left which Northern club to become manager of Crystal Palace in 2006?
10 Who has spent the last decade ground-sharing with two local Rugby clubs?
11 Which manager took Barnet FC into the league but left after disagreements with the club's owner, Stan Flashman?
12 Whose ground saw Premiership football in 2002–03 and 2003–04, but not involving their own team?
13 Whose relegation to the Conference in 2005–06 meant league football would not be played at the Abbey Stadium?
14 Who play by the seaside at Bloomfield Road?
15 Which former player took over as manager of Ipswich Town following the departure of Joe Royle in 2006?

Sports and pastimes – Football League

PART 2 – *Identify the football league teams from their nicknames (none played in the Premiership in 2006–07).*

1 Seagulls
2 Stags
3 Tangerines
4 Mariners
5 Black Cats
6 The Bees
7 Cobblers
8 Latics
9 Tractor Boys
10 The Rams
11 Terriers
12 Bluebirds
13 Hatters
14 Canaries
15 Shakers

? Tie-breaker

Which three league clubs share the nickname, The Robins, and which of the three has the bird on the club badge?

321

A good walk spoiled

● ●

QUIZ 152
PART 1

1   Which left-handed golfer won the US Masters in 2004 and 2006?
2   Which prewar golfer is the only Englishman to have won seven Majors?
3   And which more modern player is the only one to have won six?
4   Who was captain of the successful European team at the 2004 Ryder Cup?
5   Where does the annual World Matchplay Tournament take place?
6   What was the venue for the ill-tempered Ryder Cup contest known as The War On The Shore?
7   Which Zimbabwean golfer won the USPGA (twice) the PGA Order of Merit (twice) and the Open Championship in the 1990s?
8   Which Swedish player, dominant in the women's game, caused controversy by taking up an invitation to play in a men's US tour competition?
9   Who is the only British player to have won back-to-back US Masters titles?
10 Who, in 1970, became the first British golfer to win the US Open for fifty years?
11 How many non-US players have won the Masters: 9, 12 or 19?
12 Who was the last English golfer to win the European Order of Merit?
13 Who was the first winner of the US Women's Open in 1987?
14 Where was the venue for the first Ryder Cup to be held outside the US or Britain?
15 Which Irishman holed the putt that sealed the 2002 Ryder Cup victory for Europe?

PART 2

1   Which Mexican-born American won both the US Open and the Open Championship in 2006?
2   The Masters tournament was conceived by which great American golfer?
3   Who won the World Matchplay Championship three years running in the 1990s and again this century, thereby becoming the first six-time winner?
4   Who was the last left-hander to win the Open Championship?
5   When Tiger Woods won his twelfth major, the 2006 USPGA, whose record of eleven majors did he pass to put him second behind Jack Nicklaus?
6   Which US rookie defied the odds to win the 2003 Open Championship, but has never threatened in a Major since?
7   Which course, in 2006, hosted the Open Championship for the first time since 1967?
8   Nick Faldo won two of his three Open Championships at which course?
9   Whose winning putt sparked off the controversial US celebrations at Brookline in the 1999 Ryder Cup?
10 Who is the only Canadian to have won a major championship?
11 Who won the PGA Order of Merit in 2003 and 2004?
12 True or false: Jean Van De Velde is the only French golfer to have played in the Ryder Cup.
13 Which Australian won the Open Championship for three consecutive years in the 1950s?
14 Who was Europe's Ryder Cup captain when they wrested the trophy from the US in 1985, after 28 years?
15 The abiding memory of that contest is of which European golfer standing, arms out wide, after holing the winning putt?

? *Tie-breaker*
Which three South African golfers have won the US Open since the war?

Horses

● ●

QUIZ 153
PART 1

1   For what is Cowdray Park in Sussex famous?
2   A Chincoteague, a Shetland or a Dartmoor are all types of what?
3   What head-control for a horse comes in a standing or running form and is banned in dressage competition?
4   What falls between a trot and a full gallop?
5   What name is given to the training exercise where a horse will circle the trainer, occasionally prompted by a 10m long line?
6   What colour is a piebald horse?
7   What is the name given to the scabby eruptions that sometimes occur behind a horse's knee?
8   What name is given to amateur racing over fences for hunting horses?
9   What is the name for the seatless leather leg protectors worn as an extra layer over riding trousers?
10 Where does the famous horse race, Il Palio, take place around the main square?
11 Which sporting event is held annually on the estate of the Duke of Beaufort in Gloucestershire?
12 Which twentieth-century allegorical novel features farm-horses called Boxer, Molly and Clover?
13 A horse with a golden coat and pale mane and tail is generally termed what?
14 What is the surname of the sisters Josephine, Diana and Christine, authors of well over a hundred horse and pony books for children between them?
15 Which late sixties band wrote a famous song about a Chestnut Mare?

Sports and pastimes - Horses

PART 2 - *Match the horse's name to the description.*

1 Don Quixote's horse.
2 Frank Hopkin's mustang, as seen in the movie with Viggo Mortensen.
3 Alexander The Great's mount.
4 The misnamed old nag in *Steptoe and Son*.
5 Dick Turpin's horse.
6 The mount of Tonto, Roy Rogers' sidekick.
7 The cabbie's horse in C.S.Lewis's *The Magician's Nephew*.
8 Napoleon's horse, named after one of his victories.
9 Eight-legged horse in Norse mythology.
10 The horse ridden by Death inTerry Pratchett's *Discworld* novels.

A Scout
B Bucephalus
c Binky
D Rosinante
E Marengo
F Black Bess
G Hidalgo
H Sleipnir
I Hercules
J Strawberry, then Fledge

❓ Tie-breaker

Who were the stablemates of Black Beauty at Birtwick Park?

Sporting chance

● ●

QUIZ 154

PART 1

1   Who turned the Five Nations into a six?
2   Which Spanish rider won the Tour de France five consecutive times in the 1990s?
3   With which sport would you associate Kareem Abdul-Jabbar?
4   In which athletics discipline is Roman Sebrle (pronounced Sheb-ro-lay) the current world record holder?
5   Gillian Sheen in 1956 remains Britain's only gold medallist in which sport: fencing, archery or judo?
6   What number would a scrum-half wear in rugby union?
7   Who remains the only Australian to have won the Formula One World Championship?
8   Which small but big-hearted grey won the nation's hearts with his performances at the Cheltenham Gold Cup, including a memorable win in 1989?
9   Rugby Union's Calcutta Cup is played annually between England and which other side?
10   Which two international cricket teams compete for the Wisden Trophy?
11   Who defeated Mike Tyson on June 8th, 2002?
12   Droopy's Scholes won a rare Grand National and Derby double in which sport in 2004?
13   What colour is the innermost ring on an archery target or butt?
14   Karen Briggs, Sharon Rendle and Nicola Fairbrother have all been World Champions at which sport?
15   Who led South Africa to their victory in the 1995 Rugby Union World Cup?

Sports and pastimes - *Sporting chance*

PART 2 - *Match the team to the sport in which they compete.*

1   Adelaide Crows
2   LA Lakers
3   Tampa Bay Rowdies
4   Queensland Reds
5   Poole Pirates
6   Sheffield Eagles
7   Toronto Maple Leafs
8   Baltimore Orioles
9   Scottish Saltires
10 San Francisco 49ers

A   American Football
B   Baseball
C   Cricket
D   Ice Hockey
E   Aussie Rules Football
F   Speedway
G   Rugby Union
H   Rugby League
I   Basketball
J   Association Football

? *Tie-breaker*

What were the names of the two boats Dennis Conner skippered to success in the America's Cup in the 1980s?

Did you know?

Dennis Conner won the Cup three times in the decade, twice representing Australia, and once New Zealand, even though he himself is an American. Conner was a genuine yachtsman, not a millionaire having a bit of fun; he had won a medal in the Olympics before setting his stall out to win the America's Cup.

The World Cup

● ●

QUIZ 155
PART 1

1   Geoff Hurst scored a hat-trick in the 1966 Final. Who scored England's other goal in that game?
2   Who was the last England manager to fail to get the team to the Finals?
3   Who scored a hat-trick as Italy beat Brazil in a 3-2 thriller in 1982?
4   Who started off the 2002 Finals with a bang by beating holders, France, 1-0 in the opening game?
5   Who provided the shock of the 1994 tournament by eliminating holders Germany?
6   Who is the only Englishman to have top-scored in a World Cup Finals tournament?
7   Who scored a magical solo goal as Scotland beat Holland 3-2 in a thriller in 1978?
8   Who were the first team to lose the final on penalties?
9   True or false: Wales has never qualified for the World Cup Finals.
10 Who scored the winner as West Germany came from 2-0 down to beat England 3-2 in the 1970 Finals?
11 Who was in goal for England when Maradona cheated and scored his "Hand-of-God" goal?
12 Who knocked Portugal, Spain and Italy out of the 2002 Finals?
13 In 1978, with Argentina needing a heavy win to go through, who succumbed 6-0 in pathetic fashion?
14 Who are the only team to have had two men sent off in a World Cup final?
15 Who opened England's 1982 Finals campaign with a goal in the first minute of a 3-1 group win over France?

PART 2

1   In which city did the first Final take place?
2   Who presented the trophy to 1934 winners, Italy?
3   Who scored a hat-trick as Brazil routed France 5-2 in the semi-finals in 1958?
4   Which two sides fought out the Battle of Santiago, a disgraceful apology for a football match in 1962?
5   Who remains the top scorer in a single Finals tournament, with 13 in 1958?
6   Which Polish striker was top scorer in 1974?
7   Which was the highest-scoring Final?
8   Which English referee awarded a penalty in the first minute of the 1974 Final?
9   And in the same game, whose man-marking of Johann Cruyff was a crucial factor in West Germany's victory?
10 True or false: The Charlton brothers, Bobby and Jack, became, in 1966, the first brothers to play in a World Cup Final?
11 Which country finished third on their first and only appearance in the Finals in 2002?
12 Who is the only outfield player to have played in four Finals tournaments?
13 Which Englishman took the Republic of Ireland to successive Finals in 1990 and 1994?
14 Who put England into the last eight with a goal deep into extra time to clinch a 1-0 win over Belgium in 1990?
15 Who achieved personal redemption by scoring a penalty as England beat Argentina 1-0 in 2002?

? *Tie-breaker*
Who was sent off after Slaven Bilic conned the referee in a 1998 semi-final, thus missing the Final, and who replaced him?

Sporting chance

● ●

QUIZ 156
PART 1

1   Who was the last British male to contest a Grand Slam Final (the 2006 US Open, not completed)?

2   Who did Virginia Wade beat in her women's singles final victory at Wimbledon in 1977?

3   True or false: *Question of Sport* presenter Sue Barker once won a Grand Slam tennis title.

4   Whose long-standing record did Martina Navratilova beat when she won her ninth women's singles title at Wimbledon?

5   Who was the last player to complete a career Grand Slam (all four Grand Slam tournaments)?

6   And which title has evaded both Pete Sampras and (so far, as of 2006) Roger Federer?

7   Gustavo Kuerten won successive French Open Championships in 2000 and 2001. Which country does he represent?

8   How old was tennis player Maureen 'Mo' Connolly when she first won the US Open in 1951?

9   Which woman tennis player beat the sexist Bobby Riggs in a much-publicized match in 1973?

10 Who beat her compatriot, Kim Clijsters, in three Grand Slam finals in 2003 and 2004?

11 Which 30-year-old was a teary winner of the 1998 ladies' singles at Wimbledon, after losing the 1993 and 1997 finals after winning the first set?

12 In 1997, who became the first Frenchman to contest a Wimbledon men's singles final for 51 years?

13 In 1988, who ended Martina Navratilova's run of six consecutive women's singles titles at Wimbledon?

14 What do multiple Grand Slam winners Jim Courier, Guillermo Vilas, Mats Wilander and Ivan Lendl have in common?

15 In 1991 and 1992 who won 6 of the 8 Grand Slam ladies' singles titles, but never won Wimbledon, losing the '92 Final to Steffi Graf?

Sports and pastimes – Sporting chance

PART 2

1. Who was the coach of England's successful side in the 2003 Rugby Union World Cup?
2. With which sport would you associate Walter Payton, Vince Lombardi and Elroy Hirsch?
3. Who was the rival of Zola Budd whom the South African-born runner accidentally tripped in the 1984 Olympics 3,000 metres final?
4. Which politician captained the British team to their 1971 Admiral's Cup victory?
5. What major change overtook Rugby Union in 1995?
6. Which stimulant saw an athlete banned for the first time for drug use at the 1968 Olympic Games?
7. Who, in 1992, became the first non-US team to win the World Series baseball competition?
8. What nickname was given to the fight between Muhammad Ali and George Foreman in Kinshasa, Zaire, in 1974?
9. Who won the 2002 yacht race, the Route du Rhum, in *Kingfisher*?
10. In baseball, who is the all-time home run leader?
11. What are found at Belle Vue, Mildenhall, Hall Green and Crayford?
12. Which US jockey resurrected his career by coming to Europe in 1979 after a bad patch in the States?
13. Which German rider was second to Lance Armstrong on three of his winning Tours de France?
14. Who won the Men's Hockey gold medal for the second consecutive Olympic Games in Athens in 2004?
15. Which horse won the Gold Cup in three consecutive years from 2002, but sadly died in 2005?

? Tie-breaker

Who were the two players, known as The Woodies, who dominated men's doubles tennis in the 1990s, especially at Wimbledon?

Games and pastimes

● ●

QUIZ 157
PART 1

1   Which English writer wrote the rules for many card games, most notably whist?
2   Who was World Chess Champion from 1866 to 1894?
3   In the US it is tic-tac-toe; what is it in Britain?
4   Which Englishman challenged for the World Chess Championship in 1993, but lost to Gary Kasparov at the final hurdle?
5   What colour is the Academic in Cluedo?
6   What was Eric Bristow's nickname when he was a consistent challenger for the World Darts title?
7   Which 1981 design has earned Chris Haney and Scott Abbott a vast amount of money?
8   How many successful pots will a snooker player make to achieve a maximum break of 147?
9   How many points does a cannon score in a game of billiards?
10 Which is the strongest suit in bridge?
11 How many tiles are there in a Mah Jong set: 24, 96 or 144?
12 In which card game can a player score "one for his nob" simply by turning over a jack?
13 Which game was once known as Taw, a word that is still used as a term within the game?
14 In three card brag, a prial is another term for what?
15 How many counters are on the board at the start of a game of backgammon?

PART 2

1   What is the Japanese logic puzzle that caught the global imagination
    in 2005?
2   In piquet, a carte blanche earns ten points at the start of the game. How?
3   Judit Polgar is the most accomplished female chess player in history.
    Which country does she represent?
4   Omar Sharif was a formidable exponent of which classic indoor pursuit?
5   Which young Dutch player won the 2006 World Darts Championship,
    beating the holder, his countryman Raymond Van Barneveld, in the final?
6   Who was the first US chess champion?
7   And who was his long-time Soviet rival?
8   Which other Russian master and long-time champion did Gary Kasparov
    beat to become World Chess Champion in 1985?
9   Which game, released in the fifties, involves manoeuvring pieces
    representing armies to facilitate world domination?
10 How many cards are dealt to each player in gin rummy?
11 What game are the children playing in C. S. Lewis' book when Lucy
    discovers Narnia?
12 Which popular card game of the eighteenth century was played with a
    deck of 40, with the 8s, 9s and 10s removed?
13 What name is given to a crossword with less straightforward clues?
14 David Sklansky is a player, author and authority on which increasingly
    popular card game?
15 In what game might you play a Squop, a Scrunge, or even a Boondock?

? **Tie-breaker**

*How many points is the word 'scrabble' worth in Scrabble (by adding 'crabble'
to an already existing S), with one of the Bs on a double-letter score, and the E
on a double-word score?*

The Olympic Games

●●●●●●●●●●●●●●●●●●●●●●●●

QUIZ 158
PART 1

1   In which year did Steve Redgrave win the first of his five gold medals?
2   Which Swiss tennis player has won an Olympic gold medal?
3   In what way were medals in some disciplines slightly devalued in Moscow in 1980 and Los Angeles four years later?
4   Who went from Laser in 2000 to Finn in 2004, and still won gold for Britain?
5   Which city will host the 2010 Winter Olympics?
6   Which other rowing team won their event in Sydney in 2000, in addition to Steve Redgrave's boat?
7   Which Olympic sport comes in freestyle and Greco-roman?
8   Which Canadian won super-heavyweight gold in 1988?
9   Who partnered Nathan Robertson to a silver medal in the badminton in Athens in 2004?
10 Who was the British women's team's only gold medal winner in Sydney in 2000?
11 Who set a long jump world record at the 1968 Olympics that stood for another 23 years?
12 Which US athlete won an amazing nine gold medals between 1984 and 1996, including four consecutive long jump titles?
13 Where did the first postwar games take place, in 1948?
14 Who rode the great Laurieston to equestrian gold in both the individual and team 3-Day Event in 1972?
15 Who beat perennial favourites Canada to win the 1936 Olympic ice hockey tournament?

PART 2

1 Who won the 100 metres in Seoul in 1988 but was later disqualified for cheating?
2 Who cleaned up the golds in the table-tennis in 1996 and 2000?
3 Which martial art was introduced as a formal Olympic sport in 2000 in Sydney?
4 Which two Kathys won bronze medals at 400 metres in 1984 and 2000?
5 Who carried the British flag at the Athens Olympics, her fourth, having won judo medals in 1992 and 2000?
6 Which British skier won an Olympic bronze medal in 2002, only to be disqualified for inadvertently taking a proscribed cold remedy?
7 Which sisters won the ladies' doubles title at the Sydney games in 2000? And which of them won the singles?
8 At which Games were eleven Israeli athletes murdered by the Black September group?
9 Who pioneered the modern method of going backwards over the high jump bar?
10 Who won gold for Britain in the 400 metres hurdles in Mexico City in 1968?
11 And which all-time great US athlete won the same event in 1976 and 1980?
12 Who became the first African country to win a football gold medal in 1996?
13 Which Austrian skier won the blue-ribbon event, the downhill, in Innsbruck in 1976?
14 Who got the silver medal in the 400 metres in Atlanta in 1996 (the gold might as well have been given to Michael Johnson before the race)?
15 In Athens in 2004, Chile's Nicolas Massu won two gold medals in which sport?

? *Tie-breaker*
Which two skaters won individual figure skating gold for Britain in 1976 and 1980?

Cricket

● ●

QUIZ 159

PART 1

1 What was the venue for Don Bradman's final test match in 1948?
2 Who was the first Australian bowler to take 300 test wickets?
3 Who was the first Indian player to play 100 tests?
4 Which two Sri Lankan batsmen broke the record for the highest partnership in test cricket in 2006, scoring 624 against South Africa?
5 In which year did the first ODI take place between England and Australia: 1963, 1971 or 1975?
6 Who, in 1987, became the first batsman to pass 10,000 test runs?
7 Which of these Australian captains ended their test career with the highest batting average: Steve Waugh, Allan Border, Greg Chappell?
8 Who captained Australia to their first World Cup title?
9 In the final of that tournament, which England batsman got himself out trying a reverse sweep when on course to win the match with ease?
10 Which other West Indies legend played for Somerset at the same time as Viv Richards?
11 Who play at Fenner's?
12 What was the venue for Brian Lara's record-breaking 400 against England in 2004?
13 Who is India's leading test wicket-taker?
14 Who became England's youngest test player in 1949, and played his last test an extraordinary 27 years later?
15 Which brothers are the two leading run-scorers in tests for Zimbabwe?

PART 2

1   Who was the umpire at the centre of the ball-tampering storm in the Final test between England and Pakistan in 2006?

2   Who was the great Australian all-rounder of the 1950s who batted in the high middle order and opened the bowling with Ray Lindwall?

3   Who were the opposition for Bangladesh's first test in 2000?

4   Who were the two West Indies spinners of the 1950s immortalized in the lines of a song as "those two little pals of mine"?

5   True or false: David Gower never scored a hundred against South Africa.

6   Who is the former Australian test captain who retired as a commentator on British TV at the end of the 2005 season?

7   England's star of the 2006 summer, Monty Panesar, plays for which county side?

8   Which quick bowler, with a short but furious test career was known as The Typhoon?

9   By what name was Pakistani batsman Mohammed Yousuf known before converting to Islam?

10 Where is the famous test ground called Eden Gardens?

11 Makhaya Ntini replaced which fearsome fast bowler as Shaun Pollock's opening partner?

12 Who was the Pakistani umpire with whom Mike Gatting had a notorious slanging match on the 1987-88 tour?

13 West Indies won the first two cricket World Cups; who prevented a hat-trick?

14 Which overseas player scored a triple hundred for Somerset during the 2005 county season?

15 Who hit his highest test score of 194 against Bangladesh at the start of the 2005 season?

? *Tie-breaker*

In the 1999 World Cup, Australia beat South Africa in a memorable semi-final where the scores finished level. Whose prodigious hitting took SA to within a whisper of the Final? And who, in a previous match between the sides, put down Steve Waugh, and probably cost his side the chance to put the Aussies out at an early stage?

Fast cars

• •

QUIZ 160
PART 1

1   Which manufacturer's cars were used by Crockett in *Miami Vice*?

2   Which car, made by an old Italian company (owned by Volkswagen) hit the market at over $1million in December 2005, and clocked 0–60 in 2.5 seconds?

3   In 1896 the speed limit for motor cars was increased from 4mph to what speed?

4   Knight Rider drove a customized version of which road car?

5   The popular American roadsters known as Dodges are made by which motor company?

6   Voted sports car of the seventies, which Ferrari won the first Cannonball Run in 1970?

7   Who produced the V12 powered Miura, the fastest production car around in the 1960s?

8   Which legendary designers came up with the Testarossa for Ferrari?

9   What is the name of the Plymouth Fury with a killing rage in Stephen King's novel?

10 Which great rally driver died of a brain tumour in 2005, four years to the day after he became World Champion?

11 What car is Max driving in *Mad Max II*?

12 Who released the T70 racing car in 1965?

13 In *Die Another Day* the Bond movies reverted to which classic car-makers after a flirtation with BMW?

14 Which company produced the S7 in 2001, after honing their skills by fine-tuning Mustangs for Ford?

15 What was the name of the Dukes of Hazzard's Dodge Charger?

PART 2

1 Which city has historically been the centre of America's automotive industry?
2 How did motor racing driver Graham Hill die?
3 The first of what took place in Le Mans in 1906?
4 What came between the Elite and the Elise?
5 Who is the only man to have won the World Championship as a Formula One driver and as a motorcyclist?
6 Where is the annual TT racing festival held?
7 True or false: Jacques Villeneuve was the last F1 driver to win the Indy 500.
8 Where is the Daytona 24-hour race held?
9 Where is the racing circuit known as Albert Park?
10 In 2005 who won his seventh Le Mans 24-Hour race to beat Jacky Ickx's long-standing record?

? *Tie-breaker*

Who was the fastest amateur celebrity in Top Gear's Star In A Reasonably-Priced Car, prior to the 2006 series when a new car was introduced?

Did you know?

The car used for series eight was a Suzuki Liana. The fastest time was recorded by the show's resident driver, The Stig (Mark2), with Nigel Mansell not far behind. Racing driver Damon Hill was only fractionally faster than the top amateur. Two celebs, Terry Wogan and the late Richard Whiteley, were slower than the show's featured blind driver, Billy Baxter, a Bosnian war veteran.

The Premiership

● ●

QUIZ 161
PART 1

1 Who are the only side to have gone through a Premiership season unbeaten?
2 Which Sheffield United striker scored the Premier League's first goal in 1992?
3 Who managed Newcastle to second place in the Premiership in 1996 and 1997?
4 Which three promoted sides from 2000–01 became the first to all avoid relegation the following year? (They were all still there in 2006–07.)
5 Who were the first winners of the newly-created Premiership?
6 Who were promoted to the Premiership for the first time in 1998 after winning a play-off final against Sunderland on penalties after the game finished 4–4?
7 Who, in 2001, was the only Manager of the Year not to have won the Premiership title?
8 Who came on as a substitute for Wigan in May 2006, and was sent off before he touched the ball for pulling down Freddie Ljungberg?
9 What was the SAS forward line that led Blackburn to the title in 1995?
10 How many sides have played every season in the Premiership since its inception?
11 Who scored a hat-trick in 4.5 minutes against Arsenal in 1994?
12 Who bucked a trend in 2004–05 by becoming the first team in Premiership history to be bottom of the table at Christmas but avoid relegation?
13 Who are the only side to concede 100 goals in a Premiership season (1993–94, 22 teams)?
14 Which side played their first season in the premiership in 2006–07?
15 Chelsea hold the record for fewest goals conceded in a Premiership season, in 2004–5. Was it 11, 15 or 21?

PART 2 – *All these players signed for a Premiership club in the summer of 2006. Match them to the selling club.*

1 Dimitar Berbatov (Tottenham Hotspur)
2 Emile Heskey (Wigan Athletic)
3 David James (Portsmouth)
4 Jimmy Floyd Hasselbaink (Charlton Athletic)
5 Benni McCarthy (Blackburn Rovers)
6 Tomas Rosicky (Arsenal)
7 Dirk Kuyt (Liverpool)
8 Andrei Shevchenko (Chelsea)
9 Danny Shittu (Watford)
10 Michael Carrick (Manchester United)
11 Damien Duff (Newcastle United)
12 Jimmy Bullard (Fulham)
13 Andrew Johnson (Everton)
14 Nicolas Anelka (Bolton Wanderers)
15 Julio Arca (Middlesbrough)

A *Sunderland*
B *Fenerbahce*
C *Feyenoord*
D *Queens Park Rangers*
E *Birmingham City*
F *Tottenham Hotspur*
G *Manchester City*
H *Bayer Leverkusen*
I *Porto*
J *Middlesborough*
K *Crystal Palace*
L *Borussia Dortmund*
M *Chelsea*
N *Wigan Athletic*
O *AC Milan*

? **Tie-breaker**
In 1992, on the opening day of the first Premiership season, how many overseas players took the field at the start of various games: 11, 23 or 30?

Quotes - sporting remarks

● ●

QUIZ 162

PART 1 (unless otherwise specified, just tell us who said it).

1   "Anyone who sees me go anywhere near a boat again, ever, you've got my permission to shoot me."

2   "Son, when you participate in sporting events, it's not whether you win or lose, it's how drunk you get." Wise words from which TV character?

3   "No gentleman ever takes exercise."

4   "Isn't that nice, the wife of the Cambridge president is kissing the cox of the Oxford crew."

5   "I don't want to sound paranoid, but that electronic line judge knows who I am."

6   "I want to keep fighting because it is the only thing that keeps me out of hamburger joints. If I don't fight, I'll eat this planet."

7   "People want to try to find a new Pele. They couldn't do that. You don't find another Beethoven, you have only one Michelangelo. In music you have only one Frank Sinatra and in football you have only one Pele."

8   "I'm not the next Anna Kournikova. I want to win matches."

9   "The decathlon is nine Mickey Mouse events and the 1500 metres."

10   "The lead car is absolutely unique – apart from the car behind, which is identical."

11   "The human equivalent of beige." Which British star is comedienne Linda Smith describing?

12   "I don't like this new law because your first instinct when you see a man on the ground is to go down on him."

13   "There's a touch of Julie Andrews syndrome. Her deal with nicey-nicey Cadbury's sums it up: fit but square." Who is *The Guardian* describing?

14   "When XXXXXX plays well, he wins. When he plays badly, he finishes second. When he plays terribly, he finishes third." Which golfing legend is Johnny Miller describing?

15   "He is so dedicated to the perfection of his own batting technique that he is sometimes oblivious to the feelings and aspirations of his team-mates." Of whom is this a description?

PART 2

1   "Some people think football is a matter of life and death. I don't like that attitude. I can assure them it is much more serious than that." Who uttered this now-famous quote?

2 "I'm going to sue Alan Hansen as he used to make me head all the balls. If I get Alzheimer's in ten years, I'm going to take civil action against him." Who?

3 "You've won the World Cup once, now go out and win it again." Who, and precisely when?

4 "He wears a No. 10 jersey. I thought it was his position but it turns out to be his IQ." George Best's appraisal of which later player?

5 "For those of you watching in black and white, Spurs are in the yellow strip." An early blooper in the career of which long-standing commentator?

6 "I wouldn't say I was the best manager in the business, but I was in the top one." Whose modest self-appraisal?

7 "Jesus was a normal, run-of-the-mill sort of guy who had a genuine gift, just as XXXXXX has." Who is Glenn Hoddle comparing with his Saviour?

8 "Football's football. If that weren't the case it wouldn't be the game it is." An eloquent summary from which pundit and interviewer?

9 "He's the worst finisher since Devon Loch. When he's in a clear shooting position he's under orders to do just one thing ... pass." Ron Atkinson on which of his former charges?

10 "I'd rather buy a Bob the Builder CD for my two-year-old son." What doesn't appear to be on Jason McAteer's shopping list?

11 "Our performance today would not have been the best looking bird but at least we got her in the taxi. She weren't the best looking lady we ended up taking home but she was pleasant and very nice, so thanks very much and let's have a coffee." Which quirky manager of recent vintage?

12 "In some ways, cramp is worse than having a broken leg." Which master of the gaffe struggles with his medical knowledge?

13 "He's not a tackler. I've told him don't bother tackling because you can't tackle. I'm fed up saying that to him. When he does go into tackles he doesn't know how to do it and ends up getting a booking." Who is Alex Ferguson describing?

14 "As we went out on the pitch he handed me a piece of paper. It was the evening menu for the Liverpool Royal Infirmary." Jimmy Greaves remembers which legendary hard man?

15 "That'll be the Samaritans. They usually call me this time of day." Whose witticism after a mobile phone goes off at a post-match press conference?

? *Tie-breaker*

"They'll be dancing in the streets of Raith tonight." What is the flaw in David Coleman's commentary?

Sporting chance

● ●

QUIZ 163
PART 1

1   The Canadian Grand Prix circuit is named after which Canadian driver, a victim of one of the sport's many fatal crashes?
2   Guiseppe Farina of Italy won the first Formula One World Championship in which make of Italian car?
3   Which Finnish driver won four consecutive World Rally Championships from 1996 to 1999 in his Mitsubishi?
4   Which circuit saw Brazilian legend Ayrton Senna lose his life?
5   Which Argentinian driver won four Formula One World Championships in the fifties?
6   Which British motorcyclist was World Superbike Champion four times in the 1990s?
7   What car did Michael Schumacher drive in his first World Championship winning year?
8   Jenson Button earned his first Grand Prix win in Hungary in August 2006. How many races did it take him to win: 46, 80 or 113?
9   Which other circuit used to host the British Grand Prix on alternate years to Silverstone?
10 In which discipline is Tony Rickardsson of Sweden a four-time World Champion?
11 What is Lella Lombardi the only woman to have achieved?
12 Which British motorcycling legend died of cancer in 2003; ironic given the horrific crashes he survived as a rider, notably in 1982 when he smashed both his legs?
13 And which Australian Honda rider won five titles from 1994 to 1998?
14 And who matched him by making it five in a row in 2005?
15 Who is the only French driver to have won the Formula One World Championship?

PART 2

1   Who scored the winning drop goal in the 2003 Rugby Union World Cup Final?
2   In Rugby League, for what is the Harry Sunderland Trophy given?
3   True or false: Enrique Iglesias was once on the books of Real Madrid as a goalkeeper.
4   For which small country was Marc Girardelli a rare World Champion (in skiing)?
5   Who became Three-Day-Event World Champion in August 2006 at Aachen in Germany?
6   In which sport did Katherine Grainger and Cath Bishop win a silver medal at the 2004 Athens Olympics?
7   Who has captained the All Blacks at Rugby Union a record 51 times?
8   Which horse won the Champion Hurdle in 1998, 1999 and 2000?
9   Sammy Sosa is a legend in which American sport?
10 Who has been Champion Jockey in National Hunt racing every year since 1996 (as of Aug '06)?

? *Tie-breaker*
Nigel Benn, Chris Eubank and Michael Watson all fought at the same time at which weight?

Horse racing

● ●

QUIZ 164
PART 1

1   Which chase, a major event in the sporting calendar, takes place at Aintree every year?
2   Who was Champion Jockey on the flat in 2004 after a gap of nine years?
3   What is France's premier flat race?
4   And what is the annual series of races that represent the pinnacle of the US season?
5   Which ill-fated horse won the 1981 Derby by a record ten lengths?
6   Who finally won the Derby at his 28th attempt in 1953, aged 49?
7   What is the name of Sheikh Mohammed's Dubai-based horse-racing stables?
8   What is the other major race that takes place in the same week as the Cheltenham Gold Cup?
9   Purple, gold braid, scarlet sleeves, black velvet cap, gold fringe. Whose colours?
10 Where is the Tote Ebor handicap run?
11 Who rode Oath, Kris Kin and North Light to Derby success in recent years?
12 Why did the 1993 Grand National end in farce?
13 What is the venue for the Irish Grand National?
14 How many separate bets are involved in a Yankee?
15 What was first used at the art of the Chesterfield Stakes at Newmarket in 1965?

PART 2 – *Match the horse and the triumphs.*

1   Hedgehunter
2   Lammtarra
3   Oh So Sharp
4   Rooster Booster
5   Garrison Savannah
6   Nijinsky
7   See You Then
8   High Rise
9   Mister Mulligan
10 Troy
11 Alleged
12 Kicking King
13 Arkle
14 Aldaniti
15 Desert Orchid

A   Grand National 1981 (Bob Champion)
B   Derby 1968 (Lester Piggott)
C   Arc de Triomphe 1977, '78 (Lester Piggott)
D   Gold Cup 1964, '65, '66 (Pat Taaffe)
E   Grand National 2005 (Ruby Walsh)
F   2,000 Guineas, Derby and St Leger 1970 (Lester Piggott)
G   Gold Cup 1989 (Simon Sherwood)
H   Champion Hurdle 2003 (Richard Johnson)
I   Gold Cup 2005 (Barry Geraghty)
J   1,000 Guineas and Oaks 1985 (Steve Cauthen)
K   Derby 1979 (Willie Carson)
L   Gold Cup 1991 (Mark Pitman)
M   Champion Hurdle 1985, '86, '87 (Steve Smith-Eccles)
N   Derby and Arc de Triomphe 1995 (Walter Swinburn/Frankie Dettori)
P   Gold Cup 1997 (Tony McCoy)

? **Tie-breaker**
Which two of the five classics in the flat season are for fillies only?

Football - European Cups

● ●

QUIZ 165

PART 1 – *The European Cup and Champions League*

1 Which side won the first five European Cups?

2 And which Portuguese side broke their grip in 1961?

3 Which side, Champions of England in 1955, were denied a place in the European Cup by the absurd prejudice and shortsightedness of their own FA?

4 Who was the manager of Porto when they won the trophy in 2004?

5 Who scored both goals as Ajax won the second of their hat-trick of trophies in 1972?

6 Who reached the final for the first time in 2000, and again in 2001, but lost both?

7 And which two English sides did they beat in the quarter-final and semi-final in 2001?

8 Who, in 1993, became the first (and still the only) French team to lift the trophy?

9 Who scored the decisive goal as Chelsea beat Arsenal in the quarter-final in 2003–04?

10 When Real Madrid beat Eintracht Frankfurt 7–3 in a breathtaking final, which two players scored all Real's goals?

11 Where will (or did!) the 2007 final take place?

12 Which young substitute scored the only goal in the 1995 final as Ajax beat AC Milan?

13 Who was the last English player to score in a Champions League final?

14 Who scored twice as Man United became the first English side to lift the trophy in 1968, beating Benfica 4–1?

15 Apart from four-time winners Bayern Munich, which other two German sides have won the trophy?

PART 2 – *(some answers refer to less prestigious competitions).*

1 In 1963, who became the first English side to win a European trophy?
2 Which Italian side won the last Cup Winner's Cup Final at Villa Park in 1999?
3 And who scored the winner for Chelsea as they beat Stuttgart 1–0 in the 1998 final?
4 Who are the only Turkish side to have won a European trophy, beating Arsenal on penalties in the 2000 UEFA Cup final?
5 Who won the UEFA Cup in 2005, thereby becoming the first Russian side to win a European trophy?
6 Who scored twice for Celtic as they lost the 2003 UEFA Cup Final 3–2 to Porto?
7 Who are the only other Scottish side to have played in a UEFA Cup final? (They lost in 1987.)
8 Whose only European trophy was the 1981 UEFA Cup?
9 What was the name of the UEFA Cup until 1971?
10 The first winners of the tournament after that name change were Spurs in 1972. Which other English side did they beat in the final?
11 Who was manager of Aberdeen when they won the 1983 Cup Winner's Cup final against Real Madrid?
12 Who came back from an aggregate 3–0 deficit against Steaua Bucuresti in a thrilling UEFA Cup semi final in 2006?
13 Which Ukrainian side, playing under the Soviet banner, gave one of the great European performances when they dismantled Atletico Madrid in the 1986 Cup Winner's Cup final?
14 Which British side lost the Cup Winner's Cup final of 1961 and 1967, but eventually won the trophy in 1972, their last European final?
15 Four sides have won all three major European trophies. Which of this list is the odd one out: Ajax, Barcelona, Bayern Munich, Juventus, Liverpool.

? ***Tie-breaker***

Which three English sides ensured the European Cup stayed in the country from 1977 to 1982?

Olympic Games

● ●

QUIZ 166
PART 1

1   Who was Britain's Golden Girl at Athens in 2004, winning both the 800 metres and 1,500 metres?
2   Which black American athlete pooped Hitler's Aryan party by winning four gold medals at the 1936 Berlin Games?
3   Who won all seven swimming events he entered in 1972?
4   Which nation has won two of the three Women's Football competitions held at the Games since 1996?
5   How many Olympic medals did Colin Jackson win?
6   Janica Kostelic has won four gold medals for Croatia in which sport?
7   Which Finnish athlete won both the 5,000 metres and the 10,000 metres at successive Games in 1972 and 1976?
8   Which increasingly popular winter sport was introduced as an official Olympic event in 1998?
9   The Biathlon at the Winter Olympics consists of skiing and which other discipline?
10 Who hosted the 1976 Olympics and became the only host nation not to win a gold medal?
11 Which is the only Norwegian venue to have hosted a Winter Olympics?
12 Peter Snell won the 800 metres and 1,500 metres in Tokyo in 1964. Which country did he represent?
13 Who was the Olympic boxing light-heavyweight gold medallist in 1960?
14 Eddie 'The Eagle' Edwards entertained the crowds with his ineptitude in which event?
15 Katarina Witt won successive golds at figure skating in 1984 and 1988 representing which country?

PART 2 – *Match the winner to their event.*

1   Ard Schenk (Hol)
2   Ulrike Meyfarth (Ger)
3   Duncan Goodhew (GB)
4   Jan Zelezny (Cze)
5   Alberto Tomba (Ita)
6   Michael Phelps (US)
7   Olga Korbut (USSR)
8   Bradley Wiggins (GB)
9   Pietro Mennea (Ita)
10 Kip Keino (Ken)
11 Alberto Juantorena (Cub)
12 Victor Saneyev (USSR)
13 Anatoly Bondarchuk (USSR)
14 Abebe Bikila (Eth)
15 Mark Todd (NZ)

A   Slalom skiing
B   Gymnastics
C   Hammer
D   400 metres and 800 metres
E   High jump
F   Javelin
G   Equestrian sports
H   200 metres
I   100 metres and 200 metres butterfly
J   Marathon
K   100 metres breaststroke
L   Cycling
M   Speed skating
N   Triple jump
P   3,000 metres steeplechase

? *Tie-breaker*
Name the five disciplines that make up the modern pentathlon.

Cricket

● ●

QUIZ 167
PART 1

1   Who replaced the injured Michael Vaughan against India in March 2006 and scored a hundred on his debut?
2   Who is the highest run-scorer in tests for South Africa?
3   Which West Indian batsman has two of the three highest test scores in history to his name?
4   Who hit a double hundred in 153 balls for New Zealand against England in Christchurch in 2000–01?
5   What was the former name (prior to 1999) of the Pura Cup, the first-class domestic competition in Australia?
6   Which phenomenal all-rounder took 235 wickets for the West Indies, and also scored 8,000 runs at an average over 57?
7   Which fidgeting England batsman was known as 'Rags'?
8   Who made 107 consecutive test appearances for Australia between 1993 and 2002?
9   Which current player has taken most wickets for England of all those still playing (as of September '06)?
10 Which Australian media baron blew apart cricket with a commercial 'circus' in the 1970s?
11 Who reached the test double of 1,000 runs and 100 wickets in the fastest time, 21 matches?
12 And who is the only Zimbabwean player to have reached this landmark?
13 And who is the only current New Zealand player to have reached it (as of September '06)?
14 Which Englishman was the first to pass 300 test wickets?
15 Which England wicketkeeper has completed the most test dismissals (as of September '06)?

PART 2 – *Give the counties with which these stars are associated.*

1   Gordon Greenidge (WI)
2   Clive Rice (SA)
3   Ken McEwan (SA)
4   Bishen Bedi (Ind)
5   Richard Hadlee (NZ)
6   Asif Iqbal (Pak)
7   Mike Procter (SA)
8   Wayne Daniel (WI)
9   Waqar Younis (Pak)
10 Farokh Engineer (Ind)
11 Murray Goodwin (Zim)
12 Alvin Kallicharran (WI)
13 Glenn Turner (NZ)
14 Barry Richards (SA)
15 Paddy Clift (Zim)

? *Tie-breaker*

Who has taken most test wickets for Pakistan, and who was his opening partner in many of the matches?

Mixed
bag

QUIZ 168
DIRTY DOZEN - PLAYING BY NUMBERS
A different challenge – each question has multiple answers – only the correct number of answers may be given, e.g. for no. 6, each players first six answers will be taken and any extra ones will be ignored.

1   In The Matrix, who does Morpheus believe to be "The One"?

2   Who were the TV chefs who called themselves Two Fat Ladies?

3   Who were King Lear's three daughters?

4   Name the four capital cities lying on the Danube.

5   Name the five New York boroughs.

6   Name the six "major" novels of Jane Austen?

7   What are the Seven Deadly Sins?

8   Name the G8 countries.

9   Name the nine countries that border Germany.

10   Who were the Top 10 Great Britons in the Millennium poll
     conducted by the BBC?

11   Which eleven states formed the Confederate rebels in the
     American Civil War? (Seven initially and four later.)

12   Which twelve creatures represent the Chinese years?

Did you know?

In the Great Britons poll, Michael Crawford, who had been
interviewed on Parkinson that week, finished in 17th place. No disrespect
to Mr Crawford, a talented performer, but if the poll were run now he
would struggle to make the top 200.

QUIZ 169
DIRTY DOZEN - SPORTING CHANCE

1   Who is the only man to have successfully defended an Olympic 100m title?

2   Who are the two German men who have won the Wimbledon singles title?

3   Who was the great trio known as The Three Ws of West Indian cricket?

4   Name the five Premiership clubs for which French striker Nicolas Anelka has played.

5   Name the five players with the most caps for Scotland (as of Sept. 2006)

6   Name the six England batsmen with over 2,500 runs and an average over 50.

7   Name the seven all-time top scorers in the Premiership (as of
    Sept. 2006)

8   Name the eight UK winners of the Formula One World
    Championship.

9   Name the last nine players to have debuted for England at cricket
    while playing for Lancahsire.

10 Name the ten events that make up a Decathlon.

11 Name the England team that started against Argentina in the epic 1998 World Cup match.

12 Name the European 2006 Ryder Cup team.

Did you know?

The substitutes used by England in that momentous game were Paul Merson, Gareth Southgate and David Batty. Despite the eventual defeat on penalties, it was one of England's best World Cup performances, notwithstanding Glen Hoddle spoling things afterwards by trying to lay the blame for defeat at the feet of one man.

QUIZ 170
DIRTY DOZEN - THAT'S ENTERTAINMENT

1   Who was The One And Only in 1991?

2   What three films have earned Tom Cruise Best a Best Actor
     nomination at the Academy Awards?

3   Which three films make up Kevin Costner's 'Baseball Trilogy' even
     though they are unconnected?

4   **Name the six mainstream films directed entirely by Quentin Tarantino.**

5   **Name the five winners of *I'm A Celebrity, Get Me Out Of Here*.**

6   **Name the six protagonists in Friends.**

7   Name the seven books in the Narnia series by CS Lewis.

8   Name the seven actors who have won two Best Actor Academy Awards, and the only actress to have won four.

9   Name Abba's nine No1 singles.

10 **Name the ten basic dances in Strictly Come Dancing.**

11 **Name the eleven studio albums recorded and released by David Bowie in the 1970s (1970-79).**

12 **What were the top 12 titles in the BBC's survey The Big Read, a search for the nation's most popular novel?**

Did you know?

A similar pool was carried out by Waterstone's a few years earlier, for the best book of the twentieth century. The same winner came out, and three others in the top 12 were the same. The winner even came top in a German poll conducted at the same time as The Big Read.

Mixed bag

●●●●●●●●●●●●●●●●●●●●●●●●

QUIZ 171
PART 1

1 How old was the Queen on her birthday in April 2006?
2 Which Emmerdale actress is married to footballer Harry Kewell?
3 What does Oxfam actually stand for?
4 What is the name of the Israeli Parliament?
5 By what name is St Stephen's Day more commonly known in modern times?
6 What was founded by Octavia Hill in 1895, and is now an integral part of our cultural heritage?
7 Grand Lodges and Grand Orients are European branches of which order?
8 Where is La Fenice Opera House?
9 In which US state was the Ku Klux Klan formed in 1865?
10 Who is the First Minister of the Treasury?
11 Which U2 song finally knocked Bryan Adams' 'Everything I Do, I Do It For You' off No1 after its mammoth 16-week stay?
12 What was the name of the Abba Hits album that shot the group back to No1 during the mid-nineties Abba revival?
13 Who took over from Jack Straw as Foreign Secretary?
14 Which politician's daughter was the surprise winner of the 2005 series of *I'm A Celebrity Get Me Out Of Here*?
15 Who made a last-gasp move from Arsenal to Chelsea before the August 31st transfer deadline in 2006?

PART 2

1 Which country provided most of the locations for the epic film version of *The Lord of the Rings*?

2 Who was trade union leader who became the first President of Poland after the collapse of the Soviet regime?

3 Who took over the Swingometer for the BBC's General Election coverage after the death of Robert Mackenzie?

4 True or false: Winston Churchill was an Old Etonian.

5 What was the emblem of the Confederate States which was dropped because it was too easily confused with the Yankees' Stars and Stripes?

6 Which election victory was the first to be correctly predicted by a Gallup poll?

7 Which town near the Welsh border is famous for its second-hand bookshops and holds an annual literary festival?

8 How many times did Tim Henman lose in the semi-finals at Wimbledon?

9 How many members are there in the US Senate?

10 Which European city is served by Schiphol airport?

11 What are Ashford Carbonell, Nempnett Thrubwell and Nether Wallop?

12 Which rock star once went by the alter-ego 'The Thin White Duke'?

13 Which country fought a battle for independence from France, led by the FLN under Ahmed Ben Bella?

14 The Camorra of Naples is a branch of which organization?

15 True or false: Steve McManaman scored for Liverpool in a Champions League Final.

❓ *Tie-breaker*

What is missing from the Cluedo board: hall, kitchen, lounge, conservatory, billiard room, study, library, dining room?

A-Z

● ●

QUIZ 172
PART 1

A   Spiders
B   Capital city of Romania
C   Barry McGuigan
D   French painter of the early twentieth century
E   International language, devised in 1887
F   British painter, grandson of psychoanalyst Sigmund
G   Reproductive cell
H   Hardwood tree of the walnut family
I   Light entertainment performed in the interval of a larger drama
J   English author, best known for *Three Men In A Boat*
K   Pakistani city and seaport
L   Nickname of blues singer Huddie Ledbetter
M   A whirlpool in Scandinavia
N   Canadian province, literally New Scotland
O   Leader of Uganda deposed by Idi Amin
P   English batsman, born in South Africa, member of current test team
Q   Irish footballer, now owner of Sunderland
R   West Indian fast bowler of the 1970s
S   Goodbye in Japanese
T   Popular TV drama about female POWs in Japan in WWII
U   English left-arm spin bowler of the 60s and 70s
V   Instrument of the harpsichord family
W   English evangelist, founder of the Methodist church
Y   US university in New Haven, Connecticut
Z   Anti-Roman Jewish sect

? Tie-breaker
Who wrote (or painted, more accurately), The Ultimate Alphabet, a popular book of pictorial puzzles?

Did you know?

The Ultimate Alphabet was a series of clever paintings; each painting depicted a variety of subjects representing a particular letter of the alphabet. The answers were deliberately not printed until a later edition of the book.

Mixed bag

● ●

QUIZ 173
PART 1

1 In which movie is the lead character served by a valet called Riff-Raff and a maid called Magenta?
2 What is the sign of the zodiac for April 21 to May 20?
3 Which club rugby union side are known as 'The Saints'?
4 Which job did 34-year-old Rebekah Wade land in 2002?
5 What name has been given to 30th January, 1972 in Ireland's troubled history?
6 Which African country was formerly known as French Sudan?
7 Which former partisan leader became head of state in Yugoslavia after WWII?
8 Bertie Bassett was a character made up of what type of confectionery?
9 Who were admitted to football's 1992 European Championship finals only after Yugoslavia were ejected on political grounds, and went on to win the competition?
10 Which revolutionary leader and his red-shirts were at the heart of the struggle to unify Italy?
11 In 1980 the SAS stormed and occupied which country's London embassy?
12 Which French painter is associated with a fruitful ten-year stay in Tahiti?
13 Which former state of the Soviet Union has its capital in Tbilisi?
14 Tallahassee is the administrative centre of which US state?
15 What do William Shakespeare, Michael Faraday and Edward Elgar have in common?

PART 2 – *Match these pop stars to the movies in which they appeared.*

1 Iggy Pop
2 Ice Cube
3 Damon Albarn
4 David Bowie
5 Mick Jagger
6 Kylie
7 Madonna
8 Snoop Doggy Dogg
9 Roger Daltrey
10 Bob Dylan
11 Cher
12 Ice-T
13 Whitney Houston
14 David Essex
15 Roland Gift

A *Merry Christmas, Mr Lawrence*
B *That'll Be The Day*
C *New Jack City*
D *The Delinquents*
E *Three Kings*
F *Scandal*
G *Desperately Seeking Susan*
H *Face*
I *Silkwood*
J *Cry-Baby*
K *Starsky and Hutch*
L *Performance*
M *Lisztomania*
N *The Bodyguard*
P *Pat Garrett and Billy The Kid*

? **Tie-breaker**

Which one from the list in part 2 has won an Oscar for their acting? And for which movie?

Red

●●●●●●●●●●●●●●●●●●●●●●●●●●●

QUIZ 174

PART 1

1   In nature, what is a Red Admiral?
2   Which classic movie features a character called Scarlett O'Hara?
3   Where did The Red Army undertake The Long March in 1934?
4   In 1968, who had a novelty Christmas No1 with 'Lily The Pink'?
5   In which state of the US is the city of Baton Rouge?
6   Which fictional character rescued condemned French aristocrats during the Revolutionary terror?
7   Which Italian politician was murdered by The Red Brigade in 1978?
8   What is the red line on a London Underground map?
9   What do you get when red and blue are mixed?
10 In the Six Nations Rugby Union tournament, which team plays in red?
11 What is usually caused by the Streptococcus pyrogenes group of bacteria, symptoms being a rash and a fever?
12 On which annual London march would the supporters wear a pink triangle?
13 Which part of France produces the great red wines known as Clarets?
14 Who sang about '99 Red Balloons'?
15 Flea and Anthony Kiedis are members of which rock band?

PART 2

1   What colour was Prince's beret?
2   With which football club did England international Trevor Cherry win a league championship winner's medal?
3   What is known as Red Crescent in many Muslim countries?
4   Who is the lead singer with Simply Red?
5   What was Stephen Crane's classic account of the US Civil War?
6   Whose only UK No1 hit was a cover version of Neil Diamond's 'Red Red Wine'?
7   What is "shepherds' warning"?
8   Lee Harvey Oswald shot John F. Kennedy, but who shot Oswald?
9   Who appeared alongside Bill Murray in *Lost In Translation*?
10 Apart from Lancashire, which other first-class cricket county XI use the red rose as their emblem?
11 What was Pink's first UK No1 in June, 2001?
12 Which heroic tales feature a character called Will Scarlet?
13 Which racing team in Formula One are associated with bright red cars (albeit adorned in recent years with various sponsors' logos)?
14 What is the heraldic term for red, or scarlet?
15 Who played Sapphire in the TV series *Sapphire and Steel*?

? Tie-breaker

Apart from Red Rum, which other 'Red' horse has won the Grand National in recent years?

Acronyms

● ●

QUIZ 175
PART 1
1   What does DVD stand for?
2   What four-letter acronym is generally used for the US space exploration operation?
3   What are the SAS?
4   Which government department goes by the acronym MAFF?
5   DAB radios are increasingly common; what is DAB?
6   What would you be doing if we went abroad for a spot of TEFL?
7   What does BSc after someone's name indicate?
8   What is PEP?
9   Often referred to as Wrens, what is the WRNS?
10 What is the four-letter acronym for the Government intelligence and communications office in Cheltenham?
11 If Britain joined the EMS what would they be party to?
12 Which UK stores group are often referred to as JLP?
13 A degree from UCLA means you studied where?
14 What occupation would someone with FRCVS after their name probably be in?
15 A member of the NUJ would be what?

PART 2

1   Which corporation is known as 'Auntie' or 'The Beeb'?
2   UNICEF is a United Nations charity looking after what?
3   A member of the NFU would probably do what for a living?
4   An HGV licence allows the holder to do what?
5   What does an ISP provide?
6   An American lawyer of the rank of DA holds what office (in full)?
7   Who were you voting for if you ticked SDP in the 1983 general election?
8   Who would belong to the LSO?
9   What sort of affliction is an RSI?
10 If you were banged up for GBH what was the full name of your crime?
11 Which Latin abbreviation is often used instead of the words 'for example'?
12 Which party, generally known by a three-letter acronym, provided the rebellious opposition to the racist apartheid regime in South Africa prior to its breakdown?
13 In the retail world, what is POS?
14 What is SSP?
15 What is the brief of the government department generally known as the DTI?

? *Tie-breaker*
What are you if you are awarded an MBE?

Crime and punishment

● ●

QUIZ 176
PART 1

1 By what name are Myra Hindley and Ian Brady better known?
2 The murderers of which 13-year-old were freed in 1997, eighteen years after their conviction?
3 Who was arrested on January 5th, 1981 on suspicion of murdering thirteen women?
4 The murder of a pensioner, 81-year-old Mrs Grundy, and the suspicions of her daughter, Angela, led to the arrest and conviction of which serial killer?
5 Who poisoned his second wife, Cora Turner, to be with Ethel Le Neve, his secretary?
6 What was the extraordinary gesture made by George Ryan, Governor of Illinois, two days before leaving office in 2003?
7 Which Cambridgeshire village was the location for Ian Huntley's murder of two young girls?
8 Who murdered Sharon Tate, actress wife of film director, Roman Polanski?
9 Where did murderer John Christie live?
10 By what name was the killer David Berkowitz known when police were on his trail?
11 Who was the first person to be executed in the US after the death penalty was reinstated in 1976?
12 What were the names of the Kray twins?
13 And whose South London gang fought a long turf war against the Krays?
14 Who was found hanged in a Birmingham cell whilst awaiting trial on New Year's Day, 1995?
15 Who admitted to acts of necrophilia and cannibalism as well as 15 murders in 1992?

Mixed bag - Crime and punishment

PART 2

1 Which fictional prison was the setting for the TV sitcom, *Porridge*?
2 The total sentences handed out to the Great Train Robbery gang was how many years: 201, 307 or 512?
3 Which asylum for the criminally insane opened in Berkshire in 1863?
4 Which city houses a jail called Strangeways?
5 Whose conviction for murder was overturned in 1998, 45 years after he was hanged for the crime?
6 Who was given a four-year sentence for perjury (he would serve two) on July 19th, 2001?
7 True or false: Whilst a sixth former at school, Stephen Fry was sent to prison for credit card fraud.
8 How did the life sentence for Colin Pitchfork in 1988 make crime history?
9 Which footballer spent 44 days in Barlinnie Prison in Glasgow in 1995 for an on-pitch assault?
10 The Maze prison in Northern Ireland was formerly known by what name?

? Tie-breaker

What was the fate of the famous grave-robbers, Burke and Hare?

Did you know?

Burke and Hare's killing spree lasted eleven months; the recipient of their grisly endeavours was an Edinburgh surgeon, Dr Robert Knox, who used the corpses for dissecting demonstrations. Hare's wife Margaret and Burke's lover, Helen MacAulay, were also in on the scheme. Unbelievably, Knox was never prosecuted for his compliance in the murders.

Money, money, money

● ●

QUIZ 177
PART 1

1   What name was given to 19th October, 1987, by the business community?
2   Who founded Microsoft and became one of the world's wealthiest men?
3   UK supermarket chain Asda are owned by which US giant?
4   What is the US equivalent of the *Financial Times*?
5   What type of bank account is the US equivalent of a current account?
6   What is the name of the German Central Bank?
7   Jessops made their name retailing what?
8   What was the principal currency of Italy prior to the introduction of the common currency, the Euro?
9   What are Scott Adams faux-business-advice newspaper cartoons, now a major publishing syndicate in their own right?
10 True or false: McDonalds own one third of sandwich chain Prêt A Manger?
11 What does HMV stand for?
12 Which newspaper was founded in 1821 in Manchester?
13 What was the value of a guinea?
14 Stelios Hadji-Ioannou was the founder of which successful travel-related company?
15 Supertax, best known these days from Monopoly, was introduced by which Chancellor in 1909?

Did you know?

The Tokyo Stock Exchange began trading in 1878, when capitalist sympathizers were beginning to have a greater influence in the Japanese economy and government. The exchanges of various cities were merged during WWII to form one central exchange in Tokyo, and the postwar rise of the Japanese stock was meteoric; by 1990 they were the dominant global exchange. The 1990s saw a major crash, but the Nikkei still stands as the third index after New York and London.

PART 2

1   What was first introduced into the British economy at a rate of 10% in 1799, to fund the Napoleonic War effort?
2   Which merchant bank was brought to its knees by 'rogue trader' Nick Leeson in 1995?
3   What, in full, is the CBI?
4   Travellers' cheques were introduced by the American Express company in which year: 1891, 1921 or 1951?
5   Where is the US bullion reserve held?
6   The collapse of which US company in 2001 led to an investigation and a number of sweeping changes to the way businesses are monitored and audited?
7   What was the name given to the vast loans given by the US to help European allies during and after the Second World War?
8   What happened on 29th October, 1929?
9   What year did the Australian dollar become the currency of that country: 1946, 1956 or 1966?
10 By what name was HSBC bank formerly known?

? *Tie-breaker*

What are the names given to, respectively, the Tokyo and Hong Kong stock indexes?

Mixed bag

● ●

QUIZ 178

PART 1

1 Who will be King if Prince Charles predeceases Elizabeth II?
2 What is the line between Pennsylvania and Maryland, which constitutes a theoretical border to the southern states of the US?
3 Which legendary country singer died, aged 30, in a plane crash in 1963?
4 The 38th parallel separates the two halves of which divided country?
5 Pentland and Leith are parts of which Scottish city?
6 Which Prime Minister was murdered by her bodyguards in 1984?
7 Who was the Chancellor of England executed by Henry VIII for refusing to back the King's break from the religious authority of Rome?
8 Where is Britain's National Railway Museum?
9 Which of Jesus' speeches features the Lord's Prayer?
10 Who won a *Celebrity Stars In Their Eyes* with an absurd impression of Rolf Harris?
11 Where would you be holidaying if you flew into Arrecife airport?
12 Who is Nicolas Cage's film director uncle?
13 What sport would you be watching if you saw the Miami Heat play the Utah Jazz?
14 What is the favourite food of Paddington Bear?
15 Who won an Oscar in 1972 for his part as Popeye Doyle in *The French Connection*?

PART 2

1 On what date does All Fool's Day fall?
2 How many pairs of chromosomes are there in the body: 6, 23 or 180?
3 Which famous publication came about after the King held a meeting at Hampton Court in 1604?
4 What are ten cables in length?
5 What is the Wiltshire residence of the Marquess of Bath, now used as a visitor attraction and safari park?
6 Which TV presenter was a Labour MP from 1974 to 1986, and later an MEP for the UK Independence Party?
7 What was the party this individual formed after leaving the Independence Party?
8 Which famous English painter painted a number of scenes around Dedham Vale in rural Suffolk?
9 What is the capital city of Sri Lanka?
10 Whose life is commemorated with a moveable holiday in the US on the third Monday of January?
11 Who is the country's most senior legal figure?
12 Which fashion item, considered appealing by the majority of men, was first marketed in the US in 1940?
13 Who lost her heart to a Starship Trooper in 1978?
14 Which coin ceased to be legal tender in the UK in 1961?
15 Which British sailor was the first to complete a solo non-stop journey around the earth in 1969?

? *Tie-breaker*
Which confectionery was marketed with the slogan "Made to make your mouth water," and by what name is it now known?

Mixed bag

● ●

QUIZ 179
PART 1

1 Who succeeded Leslie Crowther as the host of *Stars In Their Eyes*?
2 What colour were Coldplay in 2001?
3 Who is the Naked Chef?
4 Which city in Florida is home to Disneyworld?
5 Who wrote the series of portraits in music, *Enigma Variations*?
6 Which disgraced peer was sentenced to four years for perjury in 2001?
7 Stamford Raffles founded what in 1819?
8 Who became Ireland's first Prime Minister in 1921?
9 Who was the leader of the Shi'ite administration in Iran after the overthrow of the Shah in 1979?
10 In which year was Margaret Thatcher first elected Prime Minister?
11 John Steed and Emma Peel were better known as what?
12 Which year saw the start of the Interregnum in English history?
13 By what colloquial name is the Japanese ritual seppuku better known?
14 Which is the longest river flowing entirely in Europe, and into which sea does it empty?
15 Who was the blonde in Abba?

PART 2

1 Which charismatic football manager was known as Ol' Big Head?
2 In 1969, which cricketer was the first black person to be awarded a peerage by the British?
3 In 1856 the island of Van Diemen's Land was renamed as what?
4 What would you expect to buy from a milliner?
5 Where were sixty-six people killed at a football match in January, 1971?
6 Who was the main anchor of Channel 4 News when the channel launched in 1982?
7 Which famous London landmark has a Clock Tower and a Victoria Tower?
8 By what name are the stewardships of Stoke, Burnham and Desborough better known?
9 Which English tenor's voice prompted Britten to create the role of Peter Grimes especially for him?
10 UK elections normally take place on which day of the week?
11 Who was the inventor of the whirlpool bath?
12 Who is "bonny and blithe and good and gay"?
13 What was the pioneering science programme first shown on the BBC in 1965?
14 The book and film *Cry Freedom* concerned the anti-apartheid activities of which white South African journalist?
15 What is the name of Cherie Blair's father?

? *Tie-breaker*
Who led the Referendum Party in the 1997 election, and against which sitting Tory, the MP for Putney, did he choose to stand in person?

A-Z

● ●

QUIZ 180
PART 1

A South Africa's national liberation movement
B Landlocked country to the north of South Africa and west of Zimbabwe
C One-piece dress worn by the Ancient Greeks
D Russian Imperial Parliament, now the Russian lower house
E Greek god of love and passion, has a statue in Piccadilly circus
F British novelist, creator of Horatio Hornblower
G The diet that ranks carbohydrates according to their effect on blood glucose levels
H William Joyce, wartime traitor
I Assisted reproduction in which fertilization is accomplished outside the body
J Marches in protest at unemployment in the NE in 1936
K Japan's greatest film director
L Italian film actress
M Israeli Secret Service
N Swimming
O US artist, particularly noted for painting flowers
P Cheese with a distinctive orange rind
Q Bird, native to Central America
R Alternative therapy centred around the feet
S Yugoslav-born tennis player
T Transport and General Workers Union
U Poetic drama by Dylan Thomas
V Sedative drug, proprietary name for diazepam
W Alternative (US) name for a nightjar
Y Young Women's Christian Association
Z US rock musician, died in 2005

? ## Tie-breaker
In which century did the modern Latin alphabet come into being?

Did you know?

> The letters of the alphabet each represent a phoneme or sound in speech. However, not all words follow the phonetics of the individual letters. Argument continually rages about whether phonetic or pronunciation spelling is a good thing to help children learn more difficult words – psychology or si-COL-oh-gee?

Big business

● ●

QUIZ 181
PART 1

1 Which entrepreneur is the founder and CEO of the Virgin group of companies?
2 Which entrepreneur made his reputation as the owner of the Amstrad Computing Company?
3 In 1985, Rupert Murdoch bought half of which major US filmmaking company?
4 Who started a huge global corporation with a local five-and-dime store?
5 Which newspaper published the first colour supplement in 1962?
6 What form of advertising was banned in all forms in 2003?
7 Where did Deborah Meaden replace Rachel Elnaugh?
8 Who fronted the BBC series *Troubleshooter*, advising ailing business on ways to improve their performance?
9 Which UK landmark was bought by millionaire Peter de Savary in 1987?
10 Boots The Chemists were started and are still based in which city in England?
11 Where is the Lutine Bell found?
12 Who introduced Premium Bonds?
13 Who conceived and hosted the US TV show, *The Apprentice*?
14 What is the ERM?
15 Stuart Rose was appointed to revive the fortunes of which high street chain in 2004?

Did you know?

The London Stock Exchange was formed in 1801. It recently moved its centre of operations to more discreet premises on Paternoster Square; the old trading floor had been rendered largely redundant by technology. The motto of the LSE is *dictum meum pactum* - my word is my bond.

Mixed bag - Big business

PART 2 - Link the guru to the biography or work.

1 Mark McCormack
2 J.K. Galbraith
3 Donald Trump
4 Jim Collins
5 Tom Peters
6 Stephen R Covey
7 Robert Kiyosaki
8 Kenneth Blanchard
9 Charles Handy
10 John Maynard Keynes

A *Rich Dad, Poor Dad*
B *In Search of Excellence*
C *The Seven Habits of Highly Effective People*
D *The One Minute Manager*
E *Good To Great*
F *The Affluent Society*
G *What They Don't Teach You At Harvard Business School*
H *General Theory of Employment, Interest and Money*
I *The Art the Deal, The Art of Survival & The Art of The Comeback*
J *The Age of Unreason*

? Tie-breaker

Which organization launched a takeover bid for the London Stock Exchange after their bid of $2.4 billion in March 2006 was summarily rejected?

Mixed bag

● ●

QUIZ 182
PART 1

1 Who seized power in Uganda in 1971?
2 Which WWII warship is on display on the Thames, having been decommissioned in 1971?
3 Harold II lost the Battle of Hastings largely because he had marched straight from a resounding victory at which site in the north of England?
4 The merchant adventurer Marco Polo was operating out of which European city?
5 Who made the first revolver in 1835?
6 For what is the Napa Valley in California best known?
7 What did the US buy from Russia for $7.2million in 1867?
8 Which Labour MP faked his own death and fled to Australia in the 1970s?
9 What is the ladies' equivalent of the Ryder Cup?
10 From which city did Muhammad lead his people to Medina in the great flight known as the Hegira?
11 In which mountain range does Yosemite National Park sit?
12 In which century was calculus introduced into mathematical study?
13 Who wrote the dramatic choral work *Carmina Burana*?
14 Who was found hanging in a Stuttgart cell on May 9th, 1976?
15 What is the name of the Hogsmeade sweet shop?

Did you know?

Established in 1890, the Yosemite National Park covers approx 761,000 acres. It features the 13,000-foot peak, Mount Lyell and Yosemite Falls, the highest waterfall in the US. The word Yosemite means grizzly bear and the park is named after the river that runs through its heart. The photographer Ansel Adams took a series of famous black-and-white shots of the park; prints of these images were a 'must-have' accessory in the 1980s.

PART 2 – *Spot the odd one out.*

1   Mount Etna, Mount Baker, Kilimanjaro and Popcatapetl.
2   Michael Bentine, Peter Sellers, Ronnie Corbett and Spike Milligan.
3   Goneril, Portia, Regan, Cordelia.
4   *Northern Lights, The Glass In The Smoke, The Subtle Knife, The Amber Spyglass.*
5   Latvia, Lithuania, Moldova, Estonia.
6   Charlie Higson, Paul Whitehouse, Ricky Gervais, Mark Williams.
7   James Callaghan, Neil Kinnock, Michael Foot, John Smith.
8   Aramis, Porthos, Stelios, Athos.
9   Pestilence, Famine, Death, Misery.
10   Paul Weller, Rick Buckler, Joe Strummer, Bruce Foxton.

? *Tie-breaker*

If you went to see The Bulls play the Warriors in Bradford, what sport would be you be watching, and which town would the away team be representing?

Mixed bag

● ●

QUIZ 183
PART 1

1   Which revolutionary was captured and killed by Bolivian soldiers in 1967?
2   Which French feminist and philosopher was the author of *The Second Sex*?
3   What was founded in 1865 as the New Christian Mission by William Booth?
4   Which student revue was the stepping stone for a generation of comedians, including most of the Monty Python team?
5   Which Tchaikovsky piece was written to celebrate the defeat of Napoleon's armies?
6   Which island was originally named Van Diemen's Land?
7   Mikhail Baryshnikov defected to the US whilst on tour with which famous Russian ballet company in the 1970's?
8   What is the highest peak in the Alps?
9   Who relinquished the title of Viscount Stansgate in order to continue as an MP?
10 Which pair of brothers formed the Methodist Society in 1738?
11 By what name is the Communists' 5,000-mile retreat from Jiang-shi province in 1934–35 now known?
12 By what name are the Falkland Islands known in Argentina?
13 What is the regional name for the sun-drenched, tourist-filled southern Portuguese coast?
14 Who is Vera Brittain's politician daughter?
15 What colour of habit is associated with Cistercian monks?

Did you know?

Born in Lucca in 1858 into a musical family, Giacomo Puccini is arguably the most popular composer of operas. He created only twelve works, but all are performed with regularity, especially in the US. His breakthrough work was *Manon Lescaut* in 1893. Puccini died after surgery for throat cancer in 1924.

PART 2

1   A ruby anniversary denotes how many years of marriage?
2   What is produced by the islets of Langerhans in the pancreas?
3   The *Mabinogion* contains much of the mythology of which country?
4   In which county is the village of Borstal, site of the first juvenile detention centre?
5   What would Juan Herrera be called if he were English?
6   Whose Emperors were protected by the Praetorian Guard?
7   Which poem by John Keats is set de facto on the 20th January?
8   What is the capital city of Iran?
9   Which nation celebrates a famous anniversary on 26th January?
10 The site of many US space launches, Cape Canaveral, lies in which state?
11 Who was cleared of killing her two baby sons in a landmark case in 2003?
12 What do Americans celebrate on the first Monday of September with a public holiday?
13 Which Jewish festival takes place in the month of Nisan (Mar–Apr)?
14 What did Lisburn, Newport, Newry, Preston and Stirling have in common in 2002?
15 What ran aground off Brittany in 1978, spilling about 200,000 tons of oil?

? **Tie-breaker**
Which Puccini opera premiered at La Scala on 18th February, 1904? And in which city is this famous Opera House?

Mixed bag

● ●

QUIZ 184
PART 1

1   What is the legal age for drinking in the United States?
2   What was the location for a 1977 meeting of Commonwealth authorities to agree to ban links with the apartheid regime in South Africa?
3   Which are the highest ranking angels?
4   Where will you find the Sea of Tranquillity?
5   Into what fearsome creature could Aaron's rod turn?
6   "Honi soit qui mal y pense," is the motto of which famous order?
7   What is the largest internal organ in the human body?
8   The liquor kirsch is a distillation made from what?
9   Which college, a part of London University, was founded by Sidney James Webb, Baron Passmore?
10 Whose debut novel was *Desperate Remedies*?
11 The two West Country chalk white horses are found at Westbury and which other location?
12 What was the diet created by Audrey Eaton in the 1980s?
13 True or false: the FBI has responsibility for overseeing US agents in foreign territories.
14 Which Irish organization translates into English as "ourselves alone"?
15 What is the significance of July 1st in North America?

PART 2

1   What is the common name of the creeping mint, *Mentha pulegium*, used in medicinal teas?
2   How long was the Anglo-Chinese lease agreement on Hong Kong, which ran out in 1997: 50, 99 or 200 years?
3   What fizzy drink was patented by Dr John Pemberton in the US in 1886?
4   Where do Washington, Lincoln, Jefferson and Roosevelt rest in harmony?
5   The Colorado beetle is a notorious destroyer of which food crop?
6   Where did Cuban rebels, backed by the US, land in 1961, causing one of the most serious flashpoints in the Cold War?
7   Who played Queen Elizabeth I in the second series of *Blackadder*?
8   Who was convicted and executed for carrying out the bombing in Oklahoma City in 1995?
9   Pocahontas was the daughter of the chief of which tribe of American Indians?
10 What comes after Maundy Thursday?
11 Who was the principal architect behind the Houses of Parliament?
12 What was the name given to the great Turkish Empire in the Middle Ages, established in the late thirteenth century?
13 Gerry Adams is the leader of which party in Westminster?
14 By what name are devotees of the Church of Jesus Christ of Latter-day Saints more commonly known?
15 Which tanker ran aground in Alaska, spilling 120 million gallons of crude oil?

? *Tie-breaker*
Of which mountain were Chris Bonington and Ian Clough the first to scale the north face in 1962?

Capital punishment

●●●●●●●●●●●●●●●●●●●●●●●●●●●

QUIZ 185
PART 1 – *Match the capital to the country.*
1   Nairobi
2   Brussels
3   Oslo
4   Havana
5   Bucharest
6   Islamabad
7   Tripoli
8   Ankara
9   Berne
10 Ottawa
11 Tbilisi
12 Santiago
13 Nassau
14 Helsinki
15 Ouagadougou

A   Bahamas
B   Switzerland
C   Burkina Faso
D   Canada
E   Norway
F   Cuba
G   Finland
H   Georgia
I   Libya
J   Kenya
K   Chile
L   Pakistan
M   Romania
N   Belgium
P   Turkey

Mixed bag – Capital punishment

PART 2 – *Match the city to the famous landmark.*

1 New York
2 Cape Town
3 Berlin
4 Warsaw
5 Budapest
6 Madrid
7 Singapore
8 Florence
9 Moscow
10 Rome
11 Munich
12 San Francisco
13 Istanbul
14 Paris
15 Edinburgh

A Table Mountain
B Uffizi Gallery
C Raffles Hotel
D Galata Tower
E Brandenburg Gate
F Filmore Street
G Arthur's Seat
H Buen Retiro Park
I Central Park
J Gellert Baths
K St Peter's Basilica
L Montmartre
M Jablonowski Palace
N St Basil's Cathedral
O Frauenkirche

❓ Tie-breaker

What is the capital of Australia and in which state does it lie?

Faiths

● ●

QUIZ 186

PART 1

1 The priests of which religion are known as Brahmans?
2 Which Swiss city was the centre of sixteenth-century Calvinism?
3 The *Adi Granth* is the holy book of which faith?
4 Who founded the Church of Scientology, beloved of so many Hollywood stars?
5 The *Tipitaka* are scriptures central to which faith?
6 Followers of which religion are required to pray five times per day?
7 Kislev, Iyyar and Tammuz are what?
8 *The Watchtower* is the journal of which religious organization?
9 In 1649 Alexander Ross produced the first English translation of what?
10 What is the Jewish word for 'proper', as applied to food and many other substances?
11 Parsees are followers of which faith?
12 What is the 1st November in the Christian calendar?
13 The term Haji means a Muslim man has undertaken which pilgrimage?
14 What is the name of the original Buddha?
15 Who was the leader of the Lollards in the late fourteenth century?

PART 2

1   *The Tablet* is a journal reflecting the beliefs of which faith?
2   What is the Islamic word for the Testimony of Faith, one of the Five Pillars of Islam?
3   "The cause of suffering is craving" is one of which faith's Four Noble Truths?
4   Which holy book consists of 114 chapters and 6,236 verses?
5   What is a yarmulka?
6   What role does Jesus play in Islam?
7   What does 16th July, 622 signify in the Christian calendar?
8   The Golden Temple at Amritsar is holy to which religion?
9   Who was chosen to rule the Muslims after the death of Muhammad?
10 What is the word for the final peace in Buddhism?
11 What name is given to the Sunday prior to Easter Sunday?
12 What relationship is Fatima to Muhammad?
13 Which peaceful doctrine was founded by Mahavira in the sixth century: Sufism, Jainism or Sikhism?
14 Which river possesses purifying qualities in the Hindu faith?
15 By what name is the New Christian Mission, founded by William Booth in 1865, now known?

? **Tie-breaker**

What date is Epiphany, and what is its alternative name?

A–Z

● ●

QUIZ 187

PART 1

A Digging mammal with an armoured carapace
B Mountainous kingdom wedged between India and Tibet
C Author *Heart of Darkness* and *Lord Jim*
D Young protégé of the Three Musketeers
E Hard outer surface of an insect
F Star of controversial seventies TV drama, *A Bouquet of Barbed Wire*
G Where the Toon army stand at St James's Park
H Native American immortalized by Longfellow
I Prosecution of a public official by the State
J Vocal Rolling Stone
K Austrian Art Nouveau artist, perhaps best known for 'The Kiss'
L Ocean liner sunk by a U-boat in 1915
M Only city and capital of Monaco
N Actor and author of best selling autobiography, *The Moon's A Balloon*
O Mediterranean culinary herb
P *Punica granatum*, a shrub with edible fruit
Q Society of Friends
R Superman, seventies version
S Na_2CO_3
T Literary and legendary Queen of The Fairies
U Largest loyalist party in Northern Ireland
V Induction of male sterility
W Gaspar, Melchior, Balthasar
Y Zany comedy series with Rik Mayall, Adrian Edmondson and Nigel Planer
Z Star of the Brazilian side at the 1982 World Cup

? *Tie-breaker*
Which Nationwide Conference side (2006–07) also have a ground called St James's Park? And what is their nickname?

Did you know?

> Brazil in 1982 was regarded by many as the best international side never to have won the World Cup (perhaps the Dutch side of the 1970s might dispute that). The sublime midfield included Socrates, Falcao and Cerezo as well as our mystery 'Z'. They fell in an epic match with Italy, a Paolo Rossi hat-trick exposing the flaws in the Brazilian defence.

Mixed bag

● ●

QUIZ 188
PART 1

1   Which city hosts the annual Fringe Festival in August, probably Britain's premier arts festival?
2   Which England winger became the first European Footballer of The Year in 1956?
3   What is the type of crisp silk often used in formal dresses?
4   Who is the only British golfer to have won the British Open 1996–2006?
5   What colours is a piebald horse?
6   Where did Captain Arthur Phillip land with his 750 convicts in 1788?
7   Who, in August 2006, became the first player, other than World No2 Rafael Nadal, to beat World No1, Roger Federer?
8   The Babington Plot was a plan to assassinate which English monarch?
9   In which British city could you visit the Belgrade Theatre?
10 By what name is the yellow helianthus better known?
11 Who scored the England goal not scored by Geoff Hurst in the 1966 World Cup Final?
12 What were the Costa Ricans the first to export to Europe?
13 What connects these Caribbean islands in these years: Dominican Republic (1965), Grenada (1983) and Haiti (1994)?
14 Who published *The Wealth of Nations* in 1776, an early treatise on economic affairs?
15 Frederick Forsyth's *Day of the Jackal* is a fictionalized account of an assassination attempt on which European statesman?

Did you know?

"I love thee to the depth and breadth and height/My soul can reach, when feeling out of sight," the poet carries on. It is the 43rd sonnet out of 44 in this popular Victorian collection.

PART 2 – *Identify the counties in which these towns are located.*

1   Basingstoke
2   Stoke-on-Trent
3   Boston
4   Blackburn
5   Milton Keynes
6   Hastings
7   Devizes
8   Harrogate
9   St. Austell
10 Kendal
11 Colchester
12 Swansea
13 Royal Leamington Spa
14 Mansfield
15 Gateshead

? *Tie-breaker*

"How do I love thee? Let me count the ways." Name the poet who penned this line in Sonnets from the Portuguese.

Mixed bag

● ●

QUIZ 189
PART 1

1 Who wrestled the monster Grendel to death in Anglo-Saxon lore?
2 How old was Adrian Mole in Sue Townsend's original 'Secret Diary'?
3 Whose debut album, *The Raw and The Cooked*, caused a stir in the eighties?
4 Who was the husband of Helen of Troy and the brother of Agamemnon?
5 Where did the Campbells perform a notorious massacre of the Macdonalds?
6 Who made his first solo flight across the Atlantic in 1927?
7 Which two politicians led the coalition government during the First World War?
8 Which national treasure won three Grand Nationals in the 70s?
9 Which historic theatre on the South Bank of the Thames in London re-opened in 1997?
10 *The Right Stuff*, starring Sam Shepard, was the story of which legendary US test pilot?
11 Who were the inventors and pioneers of balloon flight?
12 Who was the leader of the fascists in the Spanish Civil War?
13 What is Professor Dumbledore's first name in the Harry Potter books?
14 Who co-wrote the Communist Manifesto with Karl Marx?
15 Who was appointed captain of the England football team in succession to David Beckham in August 2006?

PART 2

1 Which Bedfordshire Wild Animal Park first opened its doors to the public in 1931?

2 Nintendo's first foray into the toys and games market was the manufacture of which product from the nineteenth century?

3 Which country's political set-up includes the Likud party?

4 What is now celebrated on the third Sunday of June each year?

5 What is the location of the European Court of Justice?

6 In 1976, who went on strike for the first time for 46 years?

7 Where did the first discotheque, the Whiskey-A-Go-Go, open in 1963?

8 Which orchestra performed for the first time in Manchester's Free Trade Hall in 1858?

9 Which US city holds an annual Mardi Gras carnival on Shrove Tuesday in February?

10 Where did the first Public School for Girls open in 1854?

11 Which London children's hospital admitted its first patient in 1852?

12 Which country has Damascus as its capital city?

13 How many of Bobby Moore's 108 games for England were as captain: 45, 75 or 90?

14 Which unlikely association memorably heckled PM Tony Blair during a speech on June 8th, 2000?

15 What came out of the Whitechapel Bell Foundry in 1858?

? Tie-breaker

Gordon Brown seems to have been Chancellor of the Exchequer forever; who actually preceded him?

Celebration time

• •

QUIZ 190
PART 1

1   On what day of the year would children in the US go Trick or Treating?
2   Which country's New Year celebrations are traditionally ended with a parade or display of paper lanterns, often in the shape of fabulous creatures?
3   In which year did the Woodstock Festival take place?
4   What is the Hindu Autumn festival, held in the month of Kartikka in honour of Lakshmi (it also signifies the Hindu New Year)?
5   What is the name of the Jewish New Year Festival, which falls in Tishri (Sep/Oct)?
6   Which public festival in Munich has become largely an excuse to drink lots of beer?
7   What is the cause of the US public holiday on the second Monday of October?
8   Whose birthday, on the 2nd October, is a cause for celebration in India?
9   What moveable feast is usually held in the US on the last Thursday in November?
10 What was Gabriel Axel's wonderful 1987 Academy Award-winning (Best Foreign Film) Danish film culminating in a lavish party?
11 What was the name of the bowl of spiced wine passed around and drunk in celebration at Christmas and New Year in Anglo-Saxon England?
12 What is the name of the Jewish 8-day Feast of Lights, usually falling in the early part of December on the Western calendar?
13 What does Jools Holland call his annual New Year's Eve music show?
14 What term do the Americans use for a stag night?
15 Eid ul-Fitr is a happy time for Muslims, celebrating the end of what?

Mixed bag - Celebration time

PART 2

1 The Christmas holidays officially end with which January 6th Feast Day?
2 At a wedding, whose job is it to toast the bridesmaids?
3 Who released a single, 'Celebration', from an album called *Celebrate* in 1980?
4 'Cumpleanos Feliz' is a Spanish song generally sung to celebrate what?
5 What Jewish celebration represents the coming of age of a girl or boy?
6 What type of celebration originated in Berlin in 1989?
7 Which Jewish feast celebrates the Exodus, the freeing of the ancient Israelites from slavery?
8 Ruby or Jade is the birthstone for which month?
9 The Carnevale in Venice is famous for the wearing of what elaborate accessory?
10 Where is the largest annual public St Patrick's Day Parade and Party held?

? Tie-breaker

● Who had a UK No1 hit in 1981 with 'It's My Party'?

Did you know?

The song was a cover of a 1963 Lesley Gore number, which reached No1 in the US. Brian Ferry also covered it on his 1973 album, *These Foolish Things*. The song is a teen tragedy – the singer is complaining because Johnny has ditched her and given his ring to Judy. A vengeful sequel, 'Judy's Turn To Cry' was perhaps a step too far!

Mixed bag

● ●

QUIZ 191

PART 1

1 Ten cohorts, each approximately six hundred men, make up what Roman military unit?

2 Which Olympic gold medal winner caused a furore by posing naked for Playboy magazine in 1988, especially since she was from a Communist-run country?

3 What was Peter O'Donnell's long-running cartoon (1963–2001) in the Evening Standard?

4 Which blood vessels conduct blood away from the heart, and what is the largest of them?

5 Who was the flying ace hero of Capt WE John's adventure stories?

6 In the Chinese calendar, what animal is associated with 2007?

7 What did King George buy for £21,000 in 1762?

8 David was Solomon's father; who was his mother?

9 Who told the Arabian Nights tales to the Sultan, thus saving her life and changing his ways?

10 Which Irish dramatist was arrested and imprisoned for IRA activities?

11 By whom is Minnehaha loved?

12 Which creatures are referred to scientifically as chiroptera?

13 Who, in 2005, put some cash into Potteries football club, Port Vale?

14 Who is Margaret Drabble's equally well-known author sister?

15 Who painted a famous 'Blue Boy'?

PART 2

1 Who painted the famous 'Adoration of the Magi', hanging in the Uffizi Gallery?
2 Which town lies at the mouth of the River Wear?
3 What is name for the condition whereby people seek admission to hospital with bogus conditions?
4 Which right-wing Peer was killed by an IRA bomb whilst aboard his boat in 1979?
5 Who was accused of handing over secret documents concerning the sinking of the *Belgrano* during the Falklands War to left-wing MP, Tam Dalyell?
6 In what year was the State of Israel proclaimed: 1922, 1948 or 1969?
7 Who predicted that everyone would be "famous for fifteen minutes"?
8 Who managed Huddersfield Town to three successive league titles in the 1920s?
9 Who is the current Secretary of the United Nations (Aug '06)?
10 What is the large North American arctic deer, unusual for the fact that both the male and female have antlers?
11 Which late South African cricket captain was convicted of match-fixing in the late nineties?
12 What was the newspaper launched by Eddie Shah in 1986?
13 Which order of priests was founded by Ignatius Loyola in 1534?
14 Which territorial wars were ended by the 1902 Peace of Vereeniging?
15 By what name is writer Charles Dodgson better known?

? *Tie-breaker*

Who set James Thomson's 'Rule Britannia' to music?

All my colours

● ●

QUIZ 192
PART 1

1. Who said it loud, 'cause he was black and he was proud?
2. What is broken orange pekoe?
3. With which tinned foodstuff is the Jolly Green Giant especially associated?
4. Before they came to power, what was the name given to the paramilitary wing of Hitler's Nazi party?
5. The Crown Prince of which country holds the title Prince of Orange?
6. What was the title of Coldplay's breakthrough single?
7. Which children's book features an appalling child called Violet Beauregarde?
8. Which Canadian singer-songwriter released an album called *Blue* in 1971?
9. Who was the servant and confidant of Queen Victoria, played by Billy Connolly in a 1997 film?
10. Which University award sporting Purples, as distinct from the Blue given by Oxford and Cambridge?
11. In which bestselling video game does the character Cyan Garamonde appear?
12. Under what name do musicians Emily Saliers and Amy Ray record?
13. What helpful publication for businesses was rolled out on a national basis in 1973?
14. Billie Joe Armstrong is the lead singer in which contemporary band?
15. Who wrote the popular song, 'Blue Moon'?

Did you know?

The first Old English sheepdog used in the sponsorship was Shepton Dash. After the popularity was established, and Shepton Dash was at retirement age, a breed champion was sought to replace him. The result was Fernville Lord Digby, who would be chauffeur-driven to his assignments to ensure he was looking his best. He had three stunt doubles for all that demeaning physical work, and he made a fortune for Cynthia Harrison, his owner.

PART 2

1   Who played Inspector Jacques Clouseau in *The Pink Panther* movies?
2   Which goalkeeper moved from Norwich to West Ham in the summer of 2006?
3   Ian Gillan and David Coverdale both sang with which seventies hard-rock band?
4   Which country has an Orange Free State?
5   Where do performers hang out while they are waiting to go on stage?
6   Which Spanish city is famous for its orange groves and trees?
7   Who made the film, *The Purple Rose of Cairo*?
8   What colours do Aston Villa play in?
9   Who is Alicia Moore?
10   What word, meaning dust in Urdu, describes the deliberately anonymous colour of army camouflage gear?

? *Tie-breaker*
Which paint company uses an Old English sheepdog as its mascot?

Mixed bag

●●●●●●●●●●●●●●●●●●●●●●●●●●

QUIZ 193
PART 1

1 When does the Spring Bank Holiday occur?
2 The show *Crazy People*, broadcast on the BBC in 1951, would soon become which legendary comedy programme?
3 In which artistic field did Ansel Adams operate?
4 What was found in a Dutch lorry stopped in Dover on 18th June 2000?
5 What name is given to a sorcerer's companion, often taking an animal form, and who will sometimes assist him in his magic?
6 Which actor appeared in the most *Carry On* films?
7 Who was in charge of the crew and the rigging on board ship?
8 What would a cooper make?
9 What name is given to the peaceful overthrow of the Communist regime in Czechoslovakia?
10 What, in 1860, began distributing mail through a series of way-stations in the US?
11 Which astronomy programme was first broadcast on TV in 1957?
12 In what year did the BBC televize the FA Cup Final for the first time: 1938, 1948 or 1958?
13 What was broadcast live on current affairs radio for the first time on June 9th, 1975?
14 Which major English reference work was published over a period of 44 years between 1884 and 1928?
15 Which European country is ruled by a Chamber called the Vouli Ton Ellinon?

PART 2

1   What would an American court issue to enforce someone's appearance?
2   What is the longest river in France, and where does it discharge?
3   In which city was the first Macdonald's opened in 1954?
4   Who was the leader of the Communist Party in Romania who was executed after that country gained its independence from the Soviet Union?
5   Whose Winter Olympic exploits made them jointly Sports Personality of the Year in 1984?
6   What did Oscar Wilde describe as "The unspeakable in pursuit of the uneatable"?
7   Who won the first World Cup in 1930, and in which city was the final played?
8   What are yarg, gouda and taleggio?
9   Which country gained independence from Pakistan in 1971?
10 Which Archbishop of Canterbury drew up the Book of Common Prayer?
11 What is a dog called Pickles reported to have found in 1966?
12 Which theatre is home to English National Opera?
13 Which African country provided a sensational start to the 2002 World Cup by beating holders France in the opening game?
14 Which strait links the Black Sea and the Sea of Marmara in Turkey?
15 Which Welsh writer and thinker wrote *A History of Western Philosophy*?

❓ *Tie-breaker*

Where did Alfred Nobel first demonstrate dynamite in 1867: was it in a Surrey Quarry, a Danish lake or an extinct volcano in Northern Italy?

Mixed bag

● ●

QUIZ 194

PART 1

1 Thomas Arne's opera, *Alfred*, brought which jingoistic tune to the British nation?
2 Which cerebral affliction can often lead to premature senility?
3 What is peculiar about Lake Eyre in Australia?
4 Who was executed by Queen Mary I whilst still a teenager after her uncle tried to put her on the throne?
5 Which Indonesian tourist centre was rocked by a terrorist attack in 2002?
6 Which cartoon graced the pages of the *Daily Express* from 1920 to 1948?
7 What kind of animal was Mick The Miller?
8 In which year was Nelson Mandela freed from Robben Island prison?
9 Who gave birth to baby Leo on 20th May 2000?
10 Which island was partitioned after a Turkish invasion in 1974?
11 In what year was the Great Fire of London: 1566, 1666 or 1726?
12 On which river is the Grand Canyon?
13 What is NaCl commonly known as?
14 If you had a trachoma, which part of your body would be afflicted?
15 What is the currency of South Africa?

PART 2 – *Match the husband and wife.*

1   Gwen Stefani
2   Judy Finnegan
3   Britney Spears
4   Madonna
5   Kelly Preston
6   Mimi Rogers (1)
7   Lulu
8   Emma Thompson
9   Ingrid Bergman (2)
10 Kim Basinger
11 Jennifer Saunders
12 Pamela Stephenson (2)
13 Sylvia Plath
14 Lady Antonia Fraser (2)
15 Ffion Jenkins

A   William Hague
B   Alec Baldwin (2)
C   Billy Connolly (2)
D   Roberto Rossellini (2)
E   Harold Pinter
F   Ted Hughes
G   Kevin Federline (2)
H   Maurice Gibb
I   Richard Madeley
J   Gavin Rossdale
K   Sean Penn (1)
L   John Travolta
M   Tom Cruise
N   Greg Wise (2)
P   Ade Edmonson

? **Tie-breaker**
Name Frank Sinatra's four wives.

Mixed bag

● ●

QUIZ 195

PART 1

1 Whose assassination in 1981 was a blow to the peace process in the Middle East?
2 By what nickname is the sect, The Unification Church, often known?
3 Which British athlete ran the world's first four-minute mile?
4 Who had a hit with a cheesy lounge cover version of Oasis' 'Wonderwall'?
5 Which dissident writer, perhaps the best known of the anti-Soviet authors, wrote *One Day In The Life Of Ivan Denisovich*?
6 Sirimavo Bandaranaike became the world's first woman Prime Minister when she was elected to preside over which nation's affairs in 1960?
7 Which TV character was wont to call his wife a "silly old moo"?
8 What was the name of the cross-channel ferry that sank near Zeebrugge in 1987?
9 What is the name of the great Milanese Opera House?
10 Which comedian swam the English Channel for Sport Relief in 2006?
11 Who devised the theory of Natural Selection in his work *Origin of Species*?
12 Which Treaty ratified the formation of the EEC in 1957?
13 Which opponents of the Russian government are based around the southern city of Grozny?
14 With whose musical works are Richard D'Oyly Carte and the Savoy Theatre indelibly linked?
15 In 1985, what did the unfortunate Kevin Moran achieve whilst playing for Manchester United?

PART 2

1 'Every Part of Me's Bleeding' and 'The Hut' are works by which controversial modern artist?

2 Which scientific breakthrough by Crick and Watson was also a major contributor to crime-fighting and justice?

3 Nicholas Breakspear is the only British person to achieve what?

4 Which jewellery stores package all their merchandise in distinctive blue boxes?

5 Braeburn, Emmett's Peachy, Jonagold, Laxton's Superb. Which is the odd one out?

6 Who was shot from behind by Bob Ford in 1882?

7 *Nashville Skyline* was an influential album by which major artist?

8 The Trans-Siberian railway runs between which two Russian cities?

9 What comes between a Magnum and a Rehoboam?

10 Which pact between barons and the King of England was signed at Runnymede in 1215?

11 Whose power to prevent the presentation of a play was withdrawn in 1968?

12 What was Helen Sharman's distinction in 1991?

13 What was the former name of the Vietnamese capital of Ho Chi Minh City?

14 A philibeg is a variety of which traditional dress?

15 Which legally elected Chilean President was murdered during a right-wing coup sanctioned and backed by the United States?

? *Tie-breaker*

In Terry Deary's popular series of amusing books for children, Horrible Histories, how are the Greeks and the Vikings described in the respective titles?

Black and white

● ●

QUIZ 196

PART 1 – *Black*

1 Harry Potter's guardian
2 Parliamentary official
3 Henry Rollins' hard-core punk band
4 Palestinian paramilitaries responsible for the Munich Olympics massacre
5 2006 Brian De Palma film based on James Ellroy novel
6 Toxic spider with a reputation for husband-munching
7 Royal Irish Constabulary Reserve Force
8 New Zealand cricket team
9 American comedy actor
10 Hip-hoppers who like to Pump It
11 A kind of sunflower
12 Kahlua and vodka
13 Susan Hill's classic ghost story
14 Account of the Battle of Mogadishu
15 All Saints' final No1

Mixed bag – Black and white

PART 2 – *White*
1   Jack and Meg
2   Snooker's Whirlwind
3   Impressive Swiss Alp
4   Australian who played cricket for England
5   Chef-proprietor of Le Manoir Aux Quatre Saisons
6   Ron Shelton's 1992 basketball comedy
7   Jack London novel
8   Soul singer and love machine
9   Maurice Micklewhite
10 Disney's first feature
11 E. B. White's classic
12 Government policy report
13 French captain at Euro 2000
14 Billy Idol's showstopper
15 D.H. Lawrence's first published novel

? *Tie-breaker*

Which European Cup-winning Italian side play in black and white stripes?
From which English side did they get the idea for the strip?

A-Z

• •

QUIZ 197
PART 1

A   Napoleonic victory over Austrian and Russian armies in December 1805
B   French poet, author of *Les Fleurs du Mal* in 1857
C   Roughly 590 to 505 million years ago
D   He built the first motorcycle and patented the internal-combustion engine
E   The origin and history of words
F   Expressionist art using vivid coloration
G   It is used to measure radiation
H   Official records of Parliament
I   Austrian city, capital of the Tyrol region
J   Became PM of France in 1997
K   Gold territory in Canada that saw a mass rush in 1896
L   Region of north-east France, historically linked to Alsace
M   Mother of Lourdes and Rocco
N   Inventor of condensed milk
O   Messianic football manager and former NI international
P   They ruled England from 1154 to 1485
Q   Norwegian leader during Nazi occupation, shot as a traitor at the end of the war
R   25th US President, died in 1919
S   African country, capital Dakar
T   Child star of many Hollywood movies, born in 1928
U   Former Soviet state to the south of the Aral Sea
V   They sacked Rome in 455 but were later destroyed by Belisarius of Byzantium
W   Scene of a massacre of Sioux Indians by US troops in 1890
Y   Serbia, Bosnia, Montenegro, Slovenia, Croatia as was
Z   Italian theatre, opera and film director, best known here for his 1968 movie of *Romeo and Juliet*?

❓ *Tie-breaker*

What name is given to the alphabet used in many Slavic countries, including Russia?

Did you know?

Many of the main European languages supplement their alphabet by using diacritics (marks) to indicate emphasis or pronunciation on certain letters. The French mark soft c's and indicate how to inflect e's; the Germans use umlauts to accentuate certain vowel sounds. English is unusual in having no diacritics in standard use.

Christmas quiz

● ●

QUIZ 198
PART 1

1 Which annual Christmas event was first broadcast on TV in 1957?
2 Which chapel hosts the Festival of Nine Lessons and Carols on Christmas Eve?
3 What was Christmas Island's unwelcome "first" in 1957?
4 How many ghosts appear to Scrooge in Charles Dickens' novel *A Christmas Carol*?
5 In what classic Christmas song do "treetops glisten, and children listen to hear sleigh bells in the snow"?
6 What song was a UK Christmas number one for both Harry Belafonte (1957) and Boney M (1978)?
7 St. Nicholas is patron saint of which country?
8 In Cuba in 1970 Christmas Day lost its status as an official national holiday. In what year was it reinstated?
9 Father Christmas is known by various names – Santa Claus in the US, Pere Noël in France, La Befana in Italy. What do Germans call him?
10 Each Christmas-time a spruce tree graces Trafalgar Square in London. It is a gift to Britain from which country?

Mixed bag – Christmas quiz

PART 2 – *Who has these Christmas No. 1s?*

1   'Just Walkin' in the Rain' (1956)
2   'It's Only Make Believe' (1958)
3   'Return to Sender' (1962)
4   'Green Green Grass of Home' (1966)
5   'Lily the Pink' (1968)
6   'Two Little Boys' (1969)
7   'Long-haired Lover From Liverpool' (1972)
8   'Lonely This Christmas' (1974)
9   'There's No One Quite Like Grandma' (1980)
10 'Save Your Love' (1982)
11 'Mistletoe and Wine' (1988)
12 'Earth Song' (1995)
13 'Can We Fix It' (2000)
14 'Somethin' Stupid' (2001)
15 'Mad World' (2004)

? *Tie-breaker*

In which film did Bing Crosby first sing the perennial favourite, 'White Christmas'? Who wrote it?

Mixed bag

• •

QUIZ 199
PART 1

1 Which Derby winner was kidnapped and never found?
2 Which other country singer is the sister of Crystal Gayle?
3 Which famous manuscript was printed in Mainz in 1455?
4 Nelson caused a scandal by keeping which aristocrat as a permanent lover and mistress?
5 Who presented *Gladiators* alongside ex-professional footballer, John Fashanu?
6 What was first worn by a Mr Lorillard at the Tuxedo Park Country Club, NY in 1886?
7 What lies between the head and the abdomen on an insect's body?
8 Bridgetown is the capital city of which Caribbean island?
9 Who succeeded Bamber Gascoigne as the host of *University Challenge*?
10 Gary Oldman and Ethan Hawke have both been married to which Hollywood star?
11 A journey from John Wayne airport to Schipol airport would take you between which two cities?
12 The Pyrenees form a border between France and which country?
13 Alcmene was Herakles' mother; who was the father?
14 In which country did Simon De Montfort carry out a brutal crusade against the Cathars?
15 What is the Russian word for restructuring?

Did you know?

Membership of the EU currently stands at 25. Britain was in the second wave in 1973, which took the number to nine. Few west European nations remain outside the group: Norway and Switzerland, two countries legendary for neutrality, and Iceland, geographically remote and independent. Many newly independent East European states are likely to be candidates for membership in the next decade.

Mixed bag – Mixed bag

PART 2 – *Pick the odd one out.*

1. *The Hobbit; The Belgariad; The Silmarillion; The Two Towers*
2. Khalid Boulahrouz; Damien Duff; Eidur Gudjohnsen; William Gallas;
3. Lincoln; McKinley; Hoover; Kennedy
4. Faris Alam; Pete Burns; Jodie Marsh; Michael Barrymore
5. David Owen; David Steel; Shirley Williams; Roy Jenkins
6. Trygve Lie; Kurt Waldheim; Desmond Tutu; Boutros Boutros-Ghali
7. FORTRAN, COBOL, C++, GOCAL
8. Doon Mackichan; Lisa Tarbuck; Sally Phillips; Fiona Allen
9. Sally Gunnell; Colin Jackson; Linford Christie; Kelly Holmes
10. Frank Lampard; Owen Hargreaves; Jamie Carragher; Steven Gerrard

? Tie-breaker

Which two countries are due to be admitted to the European Union in 2007?

Mixed bag

●●●●●●●●●●●●●●●●●●●●●●●●●

QUIZ 200
PART 1

1 'Genie In A Bottle' was a first US And UK No1 for which pop artist?
2 By what name is the fictional character Bruce Wayne generally known?
3 Who was the last Australian woman to win Wimbledon?
4 Before becoming a C-list celebrity, what was the occupation of Paul Burrell?
5 Who accompanied Bill Brewer, Jan Stewer, Peter Gurney, Peter Davy, Daniel Whiddon and Harry Hawk to Widecombe Fair, according to the song?
6 The first commercial railway in Britain linked Stockton with which other North Eastern town?
7 Which player has made the most appearances in the Premier League, as of September 1, 2006?
8 By what name is Lac Leman known in Britain?
9 What is Marcus Bentley's role in *Big Brother*?
10 Romania, Ukraine and Georgia all have a coast on which inland sea?
11 Which city lies at the very north of Australia, on the coast of the Timor Sea?
12 Which city has the Pirelli skyscraper on its skyline?
13 Which high-profile Premiership manager was accused of taking bungs in a BBC Panorama programme broadcast in September 2006?
14 Which chocolate bar was the "sponsor" for the 2006 series of *Celebrity Love Island*?
15 Whose widow was called Hatshepsut?

PART 2

1   What is the chemical annotation for carbon dioxide?
2   Jemmy Pitcher, Lucy Lockit and Polly Peachum appear in which opera?
3   The Menai Bridge connects what to the Mainland?
4   What links the Atlantic Ocean to the Mediterranean Sea?
5   Who was the last British tennis player to win a Wimbledon singles title?
6   Which terrorist group was widely held to be responsible for the destruction of the Twin Towers on September 11th, 2001?
7   Whose discovery that microbes are the cause of infections led to huge advances in medical practice?
8   In what might you find lollo rosso, curly endive and red chard?
9   What is the traditional monetary unit of Portugal?
10 Who was the son of Uther Pendragon and Igrayne?
11 What was the name given to the scandal that led to President Nixon's resignation in 1974?
12 What is the constituency of the Conservative party leader, David Cameron?
13 Which instrument of terror was established by the church in 1478?
14 Who briefly lit up *Brookside* as the heartbreaker Beth Jordache?
15 Which Champion jockey was suspended in 2006 after allegations of race-fixing?

? Tie-breaker
Which three former Soviet states now border with Poland?

A-Z

●●●●●●●●●●●●●●●●●●●●●●●●●

QUIZ 201

PART 1

A   Capital city of Paraguay
B   First man to run a mile in under four minutes
C   The prostitute to whom Jeffrey Archer was alleged to have paid money
D   Residence of the chief magistrate and effective ruler in the Middle Ages of Venice
E   Basque separatist movement
F   Italian film director
G   Chinese tree with beneficial seeds, also called maidenhair
H   US escapologist
I   International Monetary Fund
J   Roman poet, best known for *Satires*
K   Russian seat of government
L   German-born American singer
M   Costal region of Central America (mainly Nicaragua) on the Caribbean
N   Capital city of Cyprus
O   A creature that can digest any form of food
P   Actress, married to Laurence Olivier
Q   Spanish football coach, deputy to Alex Ferguson at Manchester United
R   US jazz saxophonist
S   Capital city of Korean Republic
T   Light batter used in Japanese cuisine
U   Capital of Mongolia
V   Heavy metal guitarist
W   Pope John Paul II
Y   Japanese criminal organization
Z   US heavy rock band, known for long beards

Mixed bag - A-Z

? Tie-breaker
What number is denoted by the Roman numerals MCCXLIV?

Did you know?

> The Roman system of allocating a letter to indicate a numeric quantity was copied from the Greeks. It is a simple and logical system once the rules are learned. Thousands are indicated by placing a line above a smaller quantity, so V with a line above it would be 5,000, not five.

Mixed bag

● ●

QUIZ 202
PART 1

1 Who became chairman of the Palestine Liberation Organization in 1969?
2 Where do the Eurotunnel trains stop between Waterloo and France?
3 What is the blemish known formally as a comedo?
4 Which leader of the Peasant's Revolt of 1381 was stabbed to death by the Mayor of London?
5 The port of Tripoli is now the capital of which modern country?
6 In culinary terms, what is a stuffed sheep's stomach?
7 What is the chain of furnishing stores founded by Terence Conran?
8 Who became the UK's first £1 million footballer when he moved from Birmingham City to Nottingham Forest?
9 What was the name of the part of Czechoslovakia annexed by Hitler in 1938?
10 In 1956 the Soviets brutally oppressed an uprising in which Iron Curtain state?
11 Who sailed round the world single-handed in *Gypsy Moth IV*?
12 Who dreamed of a ladder reaching from the earth to the heavens?
13 Who introduced the Centigrade thermometer in 1742?
14 What was the character, Geraldine, in *The Good Life*?
15 Which city was pipped by London for the 2012 Olympic Games?

Did you know?

West Wing star, Martin Sheen, has been arrested numerous times for making political protests. The Democrats have often asked him to stand for office, but his stock response is that they are confusing celebrity for credibility.

PART 2

1 Which former FA Cup winner was a co-host on *Gladiators*?
2 Who kept score in *Shooting Stars* and who played the character?
3 Who connects *Cold Feet* with *The Fast Show*?
4 Who were Terry Collier and Bob Ferris?
5 Whose biography was entitled *In The Best Possible Taste*?
6 *Hetty Wainthropp Investigates* produced an easy and fun role for which redoubtable actress?
7 Who joined Sooty on his show in 1957, two years after it started?
8 Who plays department head, Harry Pearce, in *Spooks*?
9 Lindsay Duncan, a genuinely great actress, first appeared on TV as Scrubba in which double-entendre laden sitcom?
10 Which Lancastrian comedienne provided topical songs for consumer programme *This Life*, prior to becoming a megastar?

? Tie-breaker

What are the names of President Bartlet's wife and three daughters in The West Wing?

Mixed bag

● ●

QUIZ 203
PART 1

1   What is the name of the major Australian airline?
2   What relation was the recently deceased Queen Mother to Edward VIII, the King who abdicated?
3   Silicon Valley, a centre for new technology industries in the US, is in which state?
4   Which brothers conceived of and compiled the first *Guinness Book of Records*?
5   What were first featured in daily papers in 1970, and have remained a staple of the tabloids ever since?
6   Where was Jeanne d'Arc (Joan of Arc) burned at the stake in 1431?
7   In what way did the British electorate increase in 1928?
8   Why is the silverfish misnamed?
9   In which hills does the River Liffey rise before pouring into the sea at Dublin?
10 How was Bulgarian defector, Georgi Markov, poisoned in 1978?
11 Saddam Hussein's invasion of which country in 1990 provoked the first Gulf War?
12 Who was executed at Fotheringay Castle in 1587?
13 What runs from Paris to Istanbul via Munich and Sofia?
14 Who wrote the lyrics to Andrew Lloyd-Webber's early musicals?
15 What lamps, used by miners, are named after their inventor, Sir Humphry?

PART 2

1 Which British engineer researched and tested the first jet engine in 1937, only to have the idea rejected as unworkable by his employers?

2 What name was given to Indian locals recruited to the British army in the Empire days?

3 Who became the first woman president of Ireland in 1990?

4 Mad Hatter, Dormouse, Cheshire Cat, March Hare; which is the odd one out?

5 Who replaced David Blunkett as Home Secretary?

6 Which modern city was once known as Byzantium?

7 Who was the envoy of the Archbishop of Canterbury taken hostage in Lebanon in 1987 whilst suing for the release of other hostages?

8 Where is cult rock star, Jim Morrison, buried?

9 Which Russian nuclear reactor exploded in the worst non-military nuclear disaster recorded to date?

10 Which playwright, a contemporary of Shakespeare's, was killed in a tavern brawl?

11 Which seabird is believed to bring bad luck to any sailor who kills one?

12 Who wrote the blackly humorous poems about children, *Cautionary Tales*?

13 The famous surfing paradise, Bondi Beach, lies on the coast of which city?

14 Which city lies at the foot of Table Mountain?

15 *Mother Courage* and *The Caucasian Chalk Circle* are expressionist works by which major twentieth-century dramatist?

? *Tie-breaker*

What name was given to the chaotic months at the end of 1978, beginning of 1979, when strikes and unrest led to the downfall of the Labour government?

Mixed bag

●●●●●●●●●●●●●●●●●●●●●●●●

QUIZ 204
PART 1

1   An affair with Antonia De Sancha ended the political career of which former Tory minister?

2   An affair with Sara Keays ended the political career of which former Tory minister?

3   Which (now Sunday) newspaper was first published in 1843: *The Observer*, *The Sunday Sport* or *The News of the World*?

4   Which legendary entertainment club opened in Paris in 1889?

5   Why would an archer need a fletcher?

6   Which cartoonist created the off-beam and insightful cartoons, *The Far Side*?

7   Which great sociological record was undertaken in 1085–86 in England?

8   Which party won its first council seat in 1993?

9   Which island in Europe gained independence from Britain in 1964, after being annexed in 1800?

10 Where would you most likely find a proscenium arch?

11 Under what name did Agatha Christie write a number of romantic novels?

12 Which genuine saint's death was tragically overshadowed by the hyperbole surrounding the passing of Princess Diana four days previously in 1997?

13 What is the name of the barber in Rossini's opera, *The Barber of Seville*?

14 Germany's activities in central Europe obscured the invasion of which country by the Soviet Union in 1939?

15 Which Caribbean island was invaded by US troops in 1983?

PART 2

1 Which heroine of the Crimean War is regarded as the founder of modern nursing?
2 Which PM was married to Clementine Ogilvy Hozier?
3 Which tennis player retired in 2006, and was the only current player to have won all four Grand Slam titles during his career?
4 One of the Five Pillars of Islamic faith is fasting during the daylight hours of which month?
5 President Nasser of Egypt's nationalization of which local resource prompted a confrontation with Britain and France?
6 What does a thermostat control?
7 Of which party was Oswald Moseley a member prior to forming the British Union of Fascists?
8 Which German expression is often used instead of look-a-like?
9 Where is Ulan Bator?
10 How much, in decimal coinage, is a guinea?
11 Roy Liechtenstein was a major player in which modern art movement?
12 Where was the seat of the French collaboration government in World War II?
13 Who converted the Saxon King Aethelbert of Kent to Christianity in 597 AD?
14 Whose wife is turned into a pillar of salt after she turns to watch the destruction of Sodom?
15 In 1685, an illegitimate son, the Duke of Monmouth, rebelled against which king, his father?

? *Tie-breaker*
In which month does Remembrance Sunday fall?

A-Z

• •

QUIZ 205
PART 1

A	Home of the gods in Norse mythology
B	A bird
C	Welsh name for Cardiff
D	Plan for reparations from Germany after First World War
E	Philosophy dealing with the nature of being
F	One of the two official languages of Belgium
G	Florentine early-Renaissance painter
H	US librettist, often worked with Richard Rodgers
I	A group of Native American Indian tribes (NOT a single tribe)
J	Political group controlled by Robespierre after the French Revolution
K	Dr 'Bones' McCoy in *Star Trek*
L	Swedish winger, had spells at Arsenal and Everton
M	Medieval siege engine similar to a catapult
N	Largest lake in British Isles, in Northern Ireland
O	British top class golfer of the 60s and 70s, now a commentator
P	Essentially, the process of swallowing
Q	US politician with a reputation for stupid remarks
R	A gladiator fighting with a net and trident
S	Genus of bacteria
T	Militant Sri Lankan rebels
U	Proper name for the womb
V	Very High Frequency
W	First woman candidate for US Presidency
Y	Capital city of Cameroon
Z	Much-capped Spanish goalkeeper

? *Tie-breaker*

Phyllis Pearsall compiled the first London A-Z in which decade: the 1890s, the 1930s or the 1950s?

Did you know?

Pearsall was the founder of the Geographer's A-Z company. Frustrated when she got lost in London using an out-of-date map, she compiled her own from a London garret, and delivered the first 250 copies in a wheelbarrow! The term 'A-Z' has become the generic term for a London Street Atlas, despite the presence on the market of a number of others.

End games

● ●

QUIZ 206
PART 1

1   Which book in the Bible deals with the prophecies of the end of the world?
2   The end of a railway line or bus route is generally called what?
3   Who wrote the *End of the Affair* (1951), a book about infidelity and obsession in postwar London?
4   What do football commentators generally use to describe the end of a match?
5   How old was Mozart when he died: 29, 35 or 42?
6   Which novel did Charles Dickens leave unfinished at his death?
7   What single word has come to stand for an apocalyptic, biblical end of days?
8   What is sometimes added to a novel or story to round up certain loose ends or provide a coda to the story?
9   Which young star of *My Own Private Idaho* and *Stand By Me* died of a drug overdose in 1993 aged only 23?
10 Who played the last match of a twenty-year career in an emotional Flushing Meadow show court at the 2006 US Open?
11 Who wrote about *The Restaurant At The End Of the Universe*?
12 Who was substituted by manager, Graham Taylor, in his last match for England at Euro '92?
13 Which Irish playwright wrote the 1950s play, *Endgame*, in French?
14 How old was the poet Keats when he died: 25, 30 or 35?
15 Who played The Omega Man, who believed he was the last healthy man on earth, in the film of that name?

Mixed bag – End games

PART 2 – *Match the last lines to the literary works.*

1   I lingered around them under that benign sky; watched the moths
    fluttering among the heath and the harebells, listening to the soft wind
    breathing through the grass, and wondered how anyone could ever
    imagine unquiet slumbers for the sleepers in that quiet earth.

2   It is a far, far better thing that I do, than I have ever done; it is a far, far
    better rest that I go to, than I have ever known.

3   Who can tell?

4   After all, tomorrow is another day.

5   Nately's whore was hiding just outside the door. The knife came down,
    missing him by inches, and he took off.

6   Very few castaways can claim to have survived so long at sea as Mr Patel,
    and none in the company of an adult Bengal tiger.

7   She died last month at the age of Eighty Two.

8   What immortal hand or eye/Dare frame thy fearful symmetry?

9   Now at last they were beginning Chapter One of the Great Story which no
    one on earth has read: which goes on forever: in which every chapter is
    better than the one before.

10 Beauty is truth, truth beauty, - that is all/Ye know on earth, and all ye need
    to know.'

A   C.S. Lewis, *The Last Battle*
B   Margaret Mitchell, *Gone With The Wind*
C   Emily Brontë, *Wuthering Heights*
D   Isaac Asimov, *I Robot*
E   John Keats, 'Ode on a Grecian Urn'
F   Joseph Heller, *Catch 22*
G   Charles Dickens, *A Tale of Two Cities*
H   Wilkie Collins, *The Moonstone*
I   William Blake, 'The Tyger'
J   Yann Martel, *Life of Pi*

? Tie-breaker
What does Rick say to Louis in the last line of Casablanca?

End games

● ●

QUIZ 207
PART 1

1 Who died when soul singer Gloria Jones lost control of her Mini on September 16th, 1977?
2 Which rock star was found hanging in a Sydney hotel room in November 1997?
3 Which of the following World War I poets survived the conflict: Wilfred Owen, Rupert Brooke, Seigfried Sassoon?
4 Suffragette Emily Davison's death was an act of both suicide and protest. How did she die?
5 Where did Thomas à Becket meet his death at the hands of four knights in 1170?
6 Which England cricketer died in 2002 when he crashed his Porsche in Australia?
7 Who shot John Lennon outside his apartment building in 1980?
8 Where, in 1984, did an IRA bomb nearly succeed in an attempt on PM Margaret Thatcher's life? (She survived but five died.)
9 Where was French revolutionary Jean Paul Marat when Charlotte Corday stabbed him to death in 1793?
10 After numerous failed attempts, how did poet Sylvia Plath finally succeed in killing herself in 1963?
11 Whose 1994 suicide note featured the line 'better to burn out than to fade away', a lyric from Neil Young's song My My Hey Hey?
12 Which pop star died from a heart attack linked to anorexia nervosa in 1983?
13 Sheriff Pat Garrett shot and killed which outlaw in 1881?
14 Name the former Rolling Stone found dead in his swimming pool in 1969.
15 Which Cameroon international collapsed during a game against Colombia in 2003 and died shortly afterwards?

Mixed bag – End games

PART 2 – *Match the dying words (sometimes apocryphal) to their speaker.*

1   *Holding his beard aside from the block*: This hath not offended the king.
2   They couldn't hit an elephant at this distance.
3   Let not poor Nelly starve.
4   Goodnight my darlings, I'll see you tomorrow.
5   Why not, why not, why not. Yeah.
6   I am just going outside and may be some time.
7   How's the Empire?
8   On, my country! How I Leave my country!
9   All my possessions for a moment of time.
10 I shall hear in heaven.
11 Patriotism is not enough. I must have no hatred or bitterness towards anyone.
12 *On being asked to renounce the devil on his deathbed:* This is no time for making new enemies.
13 Either this wallpaper goes or I do.
14 Independence forever.
15 The executioner is, I believe, very expert; and my neck is very slender.

A   Anne Boleyn
B   Captain Lawrence Oates
C   US President John Adams
D   Charles II
E   Edith Cavell
F   Elizabeth I
G   George V
H   John Sedgwick, US General
I   Ludwig van Beethoven
J   Oscar Wilde
K   Thomas More
L   Timothy Leary
M   Noël Coward
N   Voltaire
P   William Pitt

? Tie-breaker

Which three rock 'n' rollers were killed in a plane crash in 1959, known as 'the day the music died'?

Answers

Books and literature

QUIZ 1
PART 1

1 George Eliot **2** Thomas Hardy **3** Victor Hugo **4** Edith Wharton **5** Joseph Conrad **6** Emily Brontë **7** Anthony Trollope **8** Leo Tolstoy **9** Bram Stoker **10** Laurence Sterne **11** James Joyce **12** D.H. Lawrence **13** Emile Zola **14** Henry James **15** F. Scott Fitzgerald

PART 2

1 Anthony Trollope **2** *Wuthering Heights* by Emily Brontë **3** Dostoevsky's Brothers Karamazov **4** Fanny Price **5** Don Quixote **6** Arthur C Clarke **7** Mr Rochester in Jane Eyre **8** *Fanny Hill* **9** *Shangri-La* **10** *Alexandre Dumas* **11** *Diary Of A Nobody* **12** Daphne Du Maurier **13** *Hedgehogs* **14** *Tom Sawyer* **15** *Giant Despair* ***Tie-breaker*** Count Fosco, Anne Catherick

QUIZ 2
PART 1

1 Etymology **2** In court; a beak is a magistrate **3** James Pitman **4** Spoonerism **5** Painkiller **6** Axiomatic **7** The clergy **8** Euphony **9** Harmony **10** Weight **11** Sherry **12** Ni **13** Plutocracy **14** Suburbs **15** 22

PART 2

1 B **2** C **3** C **4** A **5** B **6** B **7** C **8** B **9** C **10** A ***Tie-breaker*** Playing a song on the piano

QUIZ 3
PART 1

1 Films **2** *Roots* **3** Joyce Grenfell **4** Catherine Cookson **5** Samuel Johnson **6** Jack Kerouac **7** *Zen and The Art of Motorcycle Maintenance* **8** Dave Pelzer **9** Nick Hornby **10** Pamela Stephenson **11** *Wisden Cricket Annual* **12** Germaine Greer **13** Maya Angelou **14** James Herriot **15** Mars and Venus

PART 2

1 E **2** H **3** I **4** F **5** G **6** C **7** J **8** B **9** A **10** D ***Tie-breaker*** Agriculture and animal husbandry

Answers - Books and literature

QUIZ 4

PART 1

1 Jealousy **2** Ariel **3** Regan **4** Coriolanus **5** Richard III **6** Falstaff **7** Thomas Mowbray, Duke of Norfolk **8** Adonis **9** 154 **10** *Titus Andronicus* **11** Kill Claudio **12** Agincourt **13** Puck **14** Malvolio **15** *Two Gentlemen of Verona*

PART 2

1 Horatio **2** Syracuse and Ephesus **3** *Twelfth Night* **4** *Mark Antony* **5** John of Gaunt **6** *Winter's Tale* **7** Birnam Wood **8** *Taming of the Shrew* **9** Mariana of the Moated Grange **10** *Rosencrantz und Guildenstern Are Dead* **11** Gloucester **12** *As You Like It* **13** Tybalt **14** Cloten **15** *Love's Labours Lost* **Tie-breaker** Nick, a weaver, Pyramus

QUIZ 5

PART 1

1 Jelly **2** Knowledge **3** Discography **4** Mrs Malaprop **5** Earthquakes **6** Red tape **7** Cold Turkey **8** Dog Days **9** Carpentry **10** Aboard ship **11** Verbatim **12** Under the skin **13** German **14** Plebiscite **15** Gamma

PART 2

1 busy **2** free to talk **3** excellent **4** mate **5** great minds think alike **6** got to go **7** stay in touch **8** thank you **9** be back soon **10** have a nice day **11** later **12** please call me **13** any **14** bye for now **15** forward **Tie-breaker** Pandemic

QUIZ 6

PART 1

1 Louisa May Alcott's Little Women **2** Oxford **3** Anthony Horowitz **4** *Watership Down* **5** *Georgia Nicolson* **6** *Illustration* **7** *Raymond Briggs* **8** *Bucket* **9** *A dragon egg* **10** *Mr Tickle* **11** *Nautilus* **12** *Hans Christian Andersen* **13** *Jacqueline Wilson* **14** 1877 **15** *Farthing Wood*

PART 2

1 The Edge Chronicles **2** *The Very Hungry Caterpillar* **3** *A genie* **4** *A wolf* **5** *Mrs Tiggywinkle* **6** *Holly Short* **7** *Quentin Blake* **8** *Poacher* **9** *Lemony Snicket* **10** *Otter* **11** *Rosemary Sutcliff* **12** *Treasure Island* **13** *The Jolly Roger* **14** *Enid Blyton* **15** *Horrid Henry* **Tie-breaker** Peter, Susan, Edmund and Lucy Pevensie

QUIZ 7
PART 1
1 Rosamunde Pilcher **2** John Grisham **3** John Galsworthy **4** Maeve Binchy **5** Richard and Judy **6** John Fowles **7** The Earl of Asherton **8** Shogun **9** Alex Garland **10** *The Liar* **11** *Tipping The Velvet* **12** Michael Dobbs **13** Ben Elton **14** H.G.Wells **15** Umberto Eco
PART 2
1 N **2** K **3** F **4** G **5** C **6** P **7** M **8** E **9** D **10** H **11** A **12** I **13** B **14** L **15** J
Tie-breaker Robert Harris

QUIZ 8
PART 1
1 A prompt **2** Off-Broadway **3** Drama colleges **4** Peter Nichols **5** Alan Bennett **6** Agatha Christie **7** Oscar Wilde's *The Importance of Being Earnest* **8** Euripides **9** Brian Friel **10** Sean O'Casey **11** Aeschylus **12** Royal Shakespeare Theatre **13** John Arden **14** Richard Burbage **15** The Globe
PART 2
1 J **2** E **3** H **4** I **5** B **6** F **7** M **8** N **9** C **10** L **11** O **12** A **13** K **14** G **15** D
Tie-breaker *The Comedy of Errors, The Servant of Two Masters*

QUIZ 9
PART 1
1 *Da Vinci Code* by Dan Brown **2** Jane **3** Minette Walters **4** Edinburgh **5** Temperance Brennan **6** Bulldog Drummond **7** The Earl of Asherton **8** He is in a wheelchair **9** Raymond Chandler, Philip Marlowe **10** P.D. James **11** Robert Crais **12** Venice **13** Peter Ackroyd **14** John Buchan **15** Professor Moriarty
PART 2
1 F **2** I **3** B **4** C **5** A **6** G **7** J **8** E **9** D **10** H ***Tie-breaker*** Shrewsbury, Derek Jacobi

QUIZ 10
PART 1
1 Muggles **2** Squib **3** A phoenix **4** Voldemort **5** Cedric Diggory **6** James and Lily **7** Gilderoy Lockhart **8** R.A.B. **9** Slytherin **10** Nymphadora **11** Ginevra **12** Potions **13** Bellatrix Lestrange **14** Julie Walters **15** Peeves
PART 2
1 Diagon Alley **2** Argus Filch **3** Snape **4** Buckbeak **5** Lavender Brown **6** Cornelius Fudge **7** St Mungo's **8** Centaurs **9** Mad-Eye Moody **10** Parvati Patil **11** Madame Rosmerta **12** Fleur Delacour **13** Katie Bell **14** Zoe Wanamaker **15** Trevor ***Tie-breaker*** Prof (Filius) Flitwick, Charms

Answers - *Books and literature*

QUIZ 11

PART 1

1 Ishmael; Isaac **2** 40 days **3** Bethsaida, a village on the northern shore of the Sea of Galilee **4** The Apocrypha **5** Mark (Bible scholars believe Mark was written around 70 AD); Matthew and Luke **6** 600 years old **7** Zebedee **8** Reuben, Simeon, Levi, Judah, Dan, Naphtali, Gad, Asher, Issachar, Zebulun, Joseph and Benjamin; Dinah **9** Samuel **10** Golgotha **11** 27 **12** A priest and a Levite **13** His followers lowered him over the city wall in a basket **14** Eutychus. Paul kept talking on and on until midnight. Poor Eutychus was overcome by sleep, fell out of the window and was taken for dead. But Paul put his arms around Eutychus and declared him alive and well **15** Mount Sinai; two stone tablets

PART 2

1 Two cities destroyed by God for their sins **2** The Pentateuch **3** King David and Bathsheba **4** First Thessalonians (the letters of Paul predate all four of the Gospels. It is believed Paul wrote First Thessalonians around 50 AD, 20 years after Jesus was crucified and 20 years before the first of the Gospels, Mark, was written) **5** 39 and 46, respectively **6** 33 years **7** Latin **8** Thomas (hence the expression "doubting Thomas") **9** That in 40 days Nineveh would be destroyed **10** ... my cup runneth over." **11** Purim (Purim is a light-hearted festival celebrated in early spring, on the 14th day of Adar in the Jewish calendar) **12** 1384 (John Wycliffe first translated the entire Bible from Latin into English, completing the task the year he died, 1384) **13** Over 2000 **14** The Gutenberg Bible; 1455 **15** 1611 *Tie-breaker* Enos

QUIZ 12

PART 1

1 Harold Pinter **2** Science Fiction and Fantasy **3** Coleridge **4** *Oscar and Lucinda* **5** A children's book (for Under 11's) **6** They are husband and wife **7** John Updike **8** Best crime novel **9** *Vernon God Little* by DBC Pierre **10** Toni Morrison **11** Arundhati Roy **12** Roddy Doyle **13** Sport **14** Female novelists **15** 1969

PART 2

1 G **2** H **3** J **4** E **5** B **6** C **7** D **8** I **9** A **10** F *Tie-breaker* William Trevor, Ireland

QUIZ 13

PART 1

1 Mary Shelley's *Frankenstein* **2** *Return of the Native* **3** *Bleak House* **4** One written in the form of a sequence of letters **5** Steinbeck's *The Grapes of Wrath* **6** Herman Hesse **7** *Gulliver's Travels* by Jonathan Swift **8** T.S. Eliot **9** *Heart of Darkness* **10** Honoré De Balzac **11** *Moby Dick* by Herman Melville **12** Pasternak's *Doctor Zhivago* **13** Verdi's *La Traviata* **14** *Lady Chatterley's Lover* **15** *Robinson Crusoe*

PART 2

1 J **2** A **3** M **4** I **5** B **6** C **7** P **8** G **9** N **10** E **11** L **12** F **13** D **14** K **15** H *Tie-breaker* Horace Walpole

QUIZ 14

PART 1

1 anxiety/worry **2** love letter **3** right word/appropriate word **4** in good faith/genuine **5** off the peg/ready to wear **6** social climber **7** Holy War **8** seasickness **9** caught in the act **10** home help/nanny **11** best work (of an artist or writer) **12** the list of characters in a play **13** commoners **14** injured **15** seize the day/seize the moment

PART 2

1 Litter **2** Interest **3** Stamp **4** Cabinet **5** Hooker **6** Pitch **7** Snow **8** Express **9** Current **10** Needle **11** Slug **12** Skate **13** Squash **14** Application **15** Reserve

Tie-breaker Overall

QUIZ 15

PART 1

1 *Great Expectations* **2** *Nicholas Nickleby* **3** *Martin Chuzzlewit* **4** *Hard Times* **5** *Pickwick Papers* **6** *Dombey and Son* **7** *Bleak House* **8** *Oliver Twist* **9** *Our Mutual Friend* **10** *David Copperfield*

PART 2

1 *Pickwick Papers* **2** Portsmouth **3** Catherine **4** *Oliver Twist (Oliver!)* **5** Shipping **6** Keeley Hawes **7** *The Old Curiosity Shop* **8** David Lean **9** Dorrit **10** French Revolution **11** Dotheboys Hall **12** *Mystery of Edwin Drood* **13** Andrew Davies **14** Gillian Anderson **15** Diana Rigg ***Tie-breaker*** Dora (Spenlow) and Agnes (Wickfield)

QUIZ 16

PART 1

1 Scarborough **2** William Congreve's *The Way of the World* **3** T.S. Eliot **4** Peter Ustinov **5** Chekhov's *Three Sisters* **6** More, it is the cry for an encore **7** Cottesloe **8** JM Synge's *Playboy of the Western World* **9** Noel Coward **10** Aphra Behn **11** Papering the house **12** *Rosencrantz and Guildenstern Are Dead* **13** John Osborne's *Look Back In Anger* **14** Abbey **15** John Webster

PART 2

1 *Dr Faustus* (Marlowe) **2** *Pygmalion* (Shaw) **3** *The Ideal Husband* (Wilde) **4** *The Country Wife* (Wycherley) **5** *She Stoops To Conquer* (Goldsmith) **6** *The Birthday Party* (Pinter) **7** *Glengarry Glen Ross* (Mamet) **8** *The Cherry Orchard* (Chekhov) **9** *The Merchant of Venice* (Shakespeare) **10** *The Caucasian Chalk Circle* (Brecht) ***Tie-breaker*** Stanislavsky

QUIZ 17

PART 1

1 Tom Clancy **2** *The Time-Traveller's Wife* **3** 80 **4** Charles Frazier **5** Catherine Cookson **6** Frederick Forsyth **7** *Angels and Demons* **8** James Patterson **9** Robert Ludlum **10** Jean M Auel **11** Don De Lillo **12** Jilly Cooper **13** Philippa Gregory **14** Jackie Collins **15** *Bravo Two Zero*

PART 2

1 I **2** M **3** N **4** J **5** H **6** E **7** B **8** L **9** P **10** F **11** A **12** D **13** K **14** G **15** C

Tie-breaker *The Sport of Queens*

QUIZ 18

PART 1

1 Gentleman-thief **2** Charlie and Lola **3** *Alice Through The Looking-Glass* **4** Eeyore **5** Milly-Molly-Mandy **6** He is the vampire hero in a best-selling series of children's books **7** Captain Underpants **8** Thomas The Tank Engine **9** *Just William (Brown)* **10** *The Gruffalo* (created by Julia Donaldson) **11** Dr Ernest Drake **12** An elephant **13** *Goosebumps* **14** A small rabbit **15** Shirley Hughes

PART 2

1 K **2** G **3** E **4** A **5** I **6** C **7** M **8** N **9** F **10** J **11** D **12** P **13** H **14** L **15** B

Tie-breaker Julian, Dick, Anne, George (Georgina) and Timmy, the dog

QUIZ 19

PART 1

1 Theoden **2** Strider **3** Denethor **4** Tom Bombadil **5** Bill **6** Merry **7** Shelob **8** Deagol, strangled by Smeagol **9** Melkor **10** The Eagles **11** Palantir **12** Mithrandir **13** Gloin **14** Anduin **15** Glorfindel

PART 2

1 Treebeard **2** Lembas **3** A Balrog **4** Mirkwood **5** Barleyman Butterbur **6** Shadowfax **7** Illustration **8** Weathertop **9** The Grey Havens **10** Christopher **11** Mithril mail **12** Sharkey **13** Lord of the Nazgul or Ringwraiths **14** Ithilien **15** Barad-Dur **Tie-breaker** Arwen, Elrond

Cinema and television

QUIZ 20
PART 1
1 Liza Minnelli **2** Cannes **3** *The Aristocats* **4** *Top Gun* **5** Cate Blanchett **6** *E.T.* **7** Thomas Keneally **8** Isaac Asimov **9** An imaginary giant rabbit **10** Paul Newman and Robert Redford **11** *Citizen Kane* **12** Marilyn Monroe **13** Eddie Murphy **14** *Dr Strangelove* **15** *Romeo and Juliet*
PART 2
1 *Alfie* **2** A VW Beetle **3** Johnny Weissmuller **4** Scar **5** He isn't really there **6** *The Seven Samurai* **7** Thomas More **8** Ealing Studios **9** Michael Nyman **10** Julie Walters **11** *Crocodile Dundee* **12** They both spend most of the film dressed as women **13** Steven Soderbergh **14** Virginia Woolf **15** Truman Capote ***Tie-breaker*** T-Birds and Pink Ladies

QUIZ 21
PART 1
1 Status Quo **2** Anita Dobson **3** Christopher **4** The General Store **5** El Dorado **6** Prince Michael of Moldavia **7** Roger Tonge **8** False. The first programme was *This Is Five* **9** 1989 **10** The Duchess **11** Frank was married twice, first to Chrissy, then to Lyn **12** Drums **13** Her husband, Richard Hillman **14** Emma Jackson **15** Barnes
PART 2
1 M **2** O **3** J **4** I **5** A **6** K **7** C **8** H **9** L **10** F **11** E **12** D **13** N **14** G **15** B
Tie-breaker Wendy Crozier

QUIZ 22
PART 1
1 *Last of the Summer Wine* **2** Huxtable **3** Rembrandts, 'I'll Be There For You' **4** Wilfrid Brambell and Harry H. Corbett **5** New York City **6** Warren Mitchell **7** Manuel **8** *The Liver Birds* **9** Godber **10** Mrs Miggins **11** His stapler **12** Baseball pitcher (for the Boston Red Sox) **13** John Sullivan **14** "Go on, go on" **15** Richard
PART 2
1 Grace Brothers **2** Dwayne Dibley **3** Samantha in *Bewitched* **4** Emma Chambers **5** Roz Doyle **6** Dentist **7** Jim Hacker **8** Gordon Kaye **9** A goat **10** *The Brittas Empire* **11** From the hat he always wears **12** Vicar **13** Barbara Eden **14** *To The Manor Born* **15** *Two Pints of Lager and a Packet of Crisps* ***Tie-breaker*** Jane Turner and Gina Riley

QUIZ 23

PART 1

1 John McClane **2** Bruce Lee **3** David Carradine **4** John Malkovich **5** Jackie Chan and Owen Wilson **6** Alan Rickman **7** *The Long Kiss Goodnight* **8** *The Warriors* **9** John Travolta and Nicolas Cage **10** Sean Connery **11** Helm's Deep **12** Drew Barrymore, Cameron Diaz and Lucy Liu **13** (John) Rambo **14** Clive Owen and Keira Knightley **15** Patrick Stewart

PART 2

1 L **2** E **3** G **4** N **5** I **6** C **7** H **8** M **9** F **10** K **11** A **12** B **13** J **14** D **15** P

Tie-breaker Henry Fonda, Burt Lancaster, Kevin Costner, Kurt Russell

QUIZ 24

PART 1

1 *The Man With The Golden Gun* **2** *Diamonds Are Forever* **3** *Live and Let Die* **4** *Tomorrow Never Dies* **5** *For Your Eyes Only* **6** *On Her Majesty's Secret Service* **7** *You Only Live Twice* **8** *Licence To Kill* **9** *Goldfinger* **10** *From Russia With Love* **11** *Goldeneye* **12** *Never Say Never Again* **13** *Die Another Day* **14** *The World Is Not Enough* **15** *The Spy Who Loved Me*

PART 2

1 F **2** J **3** C **4** H **5** I **6** D **7** A **8** G **9** B **10** E ***Tie-breaker*** Walther PPK

QUIZ 25

PART 1

1 *Cheers* **2** *Six Feet Under* **3** Sydney Bristow **4** David Lynch **5** James Garner **6** *Starsky and Hutch* **7** *ER* **8** *Will and Grace* **9** John Goodman **10** Elle MacPherson **11** George Costanza **12** *Arrested Development* **13** Johnny Carson **14** Eva Longoria **15** Cliff Huxtable

PART 2

1 L **2** K **3** D **4** P **5** H **6** N **7** I **8** E **9** J **10** B **11** C **12** M **13** G **14** A **15** F

Tie-breaker 50.15 million

QUIZ 26

PART 1

1 A werewolf **2** *Ultraviolet* **3** Anita Blake **4** Edgar Allan Poe **5** Kitsune **6** 27 **7** Vampires and werewolves **8** Anne Rice **9** Banshees **10** Tower of London, where both were executed

PART 2

1 Gary Oldman **2** Christopher Lee **3** Quentin Tarantino **4** 1922 **5** Lon Chaney **6** Freddy **7** Bela Lugosi **8** James Whale **9** George Romero **10** Boris Karloff **11** Wes Craven **12** *Carrie* **13** *The Ring* **14** *Saw* **15** *The Texas Chainsaw Massacre*

Tie-breaker *The Flying Dutchman*

QUIZ 27

PART 1

1 1985 **2** Michael Rose **3** Well 'Ard **4** Patsy Palmer **5** Her "sister", Kat, and her "uncle" Harry **6** Chloe **7** Grant Mitchell **8** Alan was black and Jim was a racist **9** E20 **10** Jill Halfpenny **11** Nephew; Ted Hills is Kathy's brother **12** David and Lorraine **13** Phil Daniels **14** Doctor **15** Barry Evans and Natalie Price, Ian Beale and Melanie Healy

PART 2

1 E **2** P **3** H **4** L **5** D **6** M **7** J **8** C **9** N **10** A **11** G **12** F **13** K **14** B **15** I

Tie-breaker Ash, Adi, Ronny, Kareena; Tariq

QUIZ 28

PART 1

1 Motion Picture Academy Awards **2** *From Here To Eternity* **3** *Hamlet* **4** Andrews was overlooked for the part of Eliza Doolittle, despite being a success on the London stage in the role. The part went to the more Hollywood-friendly Audrey Hepburn **5** John Wayne in *True Grit* **6** *Crash/Brokeback Mountain* **7** Katharine Hepburn **8** Barbra Streisand **9** Gary Cooper **10** Jack Nicholson and Helen Hunt **11** Bruce Springsteen **12** Loretta Lynn **13** *'Moon River'* **14** *L.A. Confidential* **15** *Chicago* in 2003

PART 2

1 C **2** E **3** G **4** F **5** B **6** H **7** I **8** J **9** A **10** D *Tie-breaker* Hilary Swank; *Boys Don't Cry* (2000) and *Million Dollar Baby* (2005)

QUIZ 29

PART 1

1 Vulcan **2** Antony Stewart Head **3** *Hitchhiker's Guide To The Galaxy* **4** Avon **5** A hologram **6** Joss Whedon **7** *Firefly* **8** Kendra **9** *Voyager* **10** Superman **11** Whoopi Goldberg **12** *Stargate SG-1* **13** An angel in human form **14** *A For Andromeda* **15** *The Muppets*

PART 2

1 Patrick Stewart **2** Gene Roddenberry **3** Jemima Rooper **4** Edward James Olmos **5** *Farscape* **6** A Klingon **7** Borg **8** Kochanski **9** Wilkins **10** The three witches in Charmed **11** Drusilla **12** Odo **13** Oz **14** *V* **15** Servalan *Tie-breaker* Cordelia Chase, Wesley Wyndham-Price

QUIZ 30

PART 1

1 *Rocky Horror Picture Show* **2** Mary Poppins **3** Quentin Tarantino **4** *Seven Brides For Seven Brothers* **5** *The Italian Job* **6** *Casablanca* **7** *Gone With The Wind* **8** *The Blues Brothers* **9** *Airplane!* **10** Roger Moore **11** Anthony Perkins in *Psycho* **12** Gary Cooper **13** Anjelica Huston as *Morticia Addams* **14** Alfred Hitchcock **15** The Oscar ceremony

PART 2

1 *Russell Crowe* **2** *Chariots of Fire* **3** *Monty Python and the Holy Grail* **4** Ben Kingsley as Gandhi **5** *Moulin Rouge* **6** Marilyn Monroe in *The Seven Year Itch* **7** Elizabeth Taylor **8** *When Harry Met Sally* **9** Mozart (Tom Hulce) in *Amadeus* **10** Jamie Lee Curtis (Wanda) berates Otto (Kevin Kline) in *A Fish Called Wanda* **11** Groucho Marx **12** Marlon Brando as Don Corleone in *The Godfather* **13** *Wall Street* (Michael Douglas as Gordon Gecko) **14** Michelle Pfeiffer as Catwoman in *Batman Returns* **15** *Catch-22* **Tie-breaker** "I know."

QUIZ 31

PART 1

1 William Hartnell **2** The Master **3** Sonic screwdriver **4** Skaro **5** Sophia Myles **6** Bonnie Langford **7** Brigadier Lethbridge-Stewart **8** The Time Lords **9** Jo Grant **10** Russell T Davies **11** Pauline Collins **12** Captain Jack **13** Torchwood **14** Hats **15** Terry Nation

PART 2

1 Christopher Eccleston **2** Peter Cushing **3** They played different regenerations of the Doctor's Time Lord companion, Romana **4** Jackie Tyler (Camille Coduri) **5** Pure mathematics **6** Tom Baker **7** Peri **8** Bad Wolf **9** Peter Purves went from being a companion to a *Blue Peter* presenter **10** Peter Kay **11** Peter Davison **12** Paul McGann **13** Cardiff **14** Jagrafess **15** 1963 **Tie-breaker** Sarah Jane Smith, K9

QUIZ 32

PART 1

1 Jim Bowen **2** Michael Parkinson **3** Charlie Fairhead **4** Alan Dale **5** Evelyn Waugh **6** Tyne Daly **7** Big Ted, Humpty, Jemima, Little Ted and Hamble **8** Rachel **9** *Tenko* **10** Mary Alice Young **11** True: she joined the cast in 1984 **12** *Peak Practice* **13** Jane Seymour **14** Chris Evans **15** *'Unchained Melody'*

PART 2

1 Nigel Planer, Rik Mayall and Adrian Edmondson, respectively **2** Rebel **3** Hear'say **4** The Springfield Nuclear Plant **5** Kenny Everett **6** The Six Million Dollar Man **7** Judith Keppel **8** Gareth Blackstock **9** *Poldark* **10** *ER* **11** *Songs of Praise* **12** HMP Larkhall **13** No. 42 **14** Worzel Gummidge **15** *Changing Rooms* **Tie-breaker** Walter 'Wolfie' Smith (in *Citizen Smith*), Robert Lindsay

QUIZ 33

PART 1

1 *The Untouchables* **2** *Get Shorty* **3** *Gangs of New York* **4** *The Big Sleep* **5** *The Grifters*
6 *Double Indemnity* **7** *The French Connection* **8** *Chinatown* **9** *Blood Simple* **10** *Angels With
Dirty Faces* **11** *The Maltese Falcon* **12** *Mean Streets* **13** *Bonnie and Clyde* **14** *Road To
Perdition* **15** *Scarface*

PART 2

1 Frances McDormand **2** Michelle Pfeiffer **3** Elliott Gould **4** Kathleen Turner and William Hurt
5 George Clooney, Frank Sinatra **6** Helen Mirren **7** *The French Connection* **8** Madonna
9 Angelina Jolie **10** Edward G Robinson **11** Pam Grier **12** Al Pacino **13** Guy Ritchie
14 Jessica Rabbit **15** Linda Fiorentino ***Tie-breaker*** Ellen Barkin; New Orleans, where the
film is set

QUIZ 34

PART 1

1 Oliver Postgate **2** Purple **3** A cabbage **4** Jacqueline Wilson **5** Scruffty **6** *Blue Peter*
7 *Today Is Saturday, Watch And Smile* **8** Mrs (Bridget) McClusky **9** A pineapple under the sea
10 *Dawson's Creek* **11** *The Demon Headmaster* **12** Morph **13** Lord Belborough **14** *Biker
Mice From Mars* **15** Down a psychedelic helter-skelter

PART 2

1 Jimmy Saville **2** Postman Pat **3** Helga **4** Rugrats **5** Cut-throat Jake **6** Prince Charles
7 The Angels **8** "By the power of Greyskull" **9** *Banana Splits* **10** *Fireman Sam*
11 *Dr Teeth and the Electric Mayhem* **12** The three Goodies provide the voices **13** *Magpie*
14 An old, saggy cloth cat, baggy, and a bit loose at the seams **15** *Press Gang* ***Tie-breaker***
Leonardo, Raphael, Donatello and Michelangelo

QUIZ 35

PART 1

1 Second World War **2** *Hill Street Blues* **3** Jane Tennison **4** Lynda La Plante **5** Forensics/
pathology **6** Ken Stott **7** Inspector Lynley **8** Spender **9** Ken Stott **10** David Jason
11 Jeremy Brett **12** Gordon Jackson **13** Claire Goose **14** Ken Stott **15** Rowan Atkinson

PART 2

1 F **2** A **3** M **4** N **5** J **6** B **7** H **8** G **9** P **10** L **11** E **12** D **13** I **14** K **15** C
Tie-breaker Matthew McFadyen and Keeley Hawes. They fell in love, got married and had
children.

QUIZ 36
PART 1
1 *Annie Hall* **2** A leopard **3** Richard Curtis **4** *The Pink Panther* **5** Kenneth Williams and Sid James **6** Spencer Tracy **7** Buster Keaton **8** It's Cary Grant's real name **9** *Heathers* **10** Jerry Lewis, Eddie Murphy **11** *The Graduate* **12** Eric Idle and Robbie Coltrane **13** True. She appeared in the first movie. **14** Groucho Marx **15** *National Lampoon*
PART 2
1 I **2** H **3** J **4** G **5** M **6** L **7** B **8** C **9** E **10** N **11** F **12** A **13** P **14** K **15** D
Tie-breaker Adam Sandler, Drew Barrymore

QUIZ 37
PART 1
1 Mr Burns **2** Jacqueline Bouvier **3** Dan Castellaneta **4** Van Houten **5** Tracey Ullman **6** Willie **7** *Treehouse of Horror* **8** The Be-Sharps **9** Kelsey Grammer **10** The Waltons **11** He ate it **12** Buddhism **13** The family dog **14** Troy McClure **15** Duff
PART 2
1 Waylon J Smithers **2** Judge **3** 'Simpsons Roasting On An Open Fire' **4** Ricky Gervais **5** Prinicipal Skinner (Harry Shearer) **6** Mayor Quimby **7** "Fat Tony" D'Amico **8** *Itchy and Scratchy* **9** An elephant **10** Anything for left-handed people **11** Manjula **12** Julius Hibbert **13** Jessica **14** Edna Krabappel **15** Winona Ryder ***Tie-breaker*** Herschel, rabbi

QUIZ 38
PART 1
1 "You're fired!" **2** Roger Cook **3** Jade Goody **4** Keith Harris and Orville **5** *The Games* **6** *Celebrity Love Island* **7** Dermot O'Leary **8** Jordan (Katie Price) and Peter Andre **9** *The Osbournes* **10** *Castaway 2000* **11** Jack Dee **12** *Survivor* **13** Tourette syndrome **14** Anne Diamond **15** *Changing Rooms*
PART 2
1 J **2** F **3** H **4** E **5** G **6** I **7** B **8** A **9** D **10** C ***Tie-breaker*** *The Simple Life*

QUIZ 39
PART 1
1 John Le Mesurier **2** Royston Vasey **3** Mystery Machine **4** Lucy Davis **5** Terry Wogan **6** Egg **7** Vinegar Tits **8** 'The Chicken Song' **9** Paul Gross **10** *The Goodies* **11** Bill Bixby; Lou Ferrigno **12** Buffy Anne Summers **13** Sheena Easton **14** Ludwig was a mechanical violin-playing egg **15** Anthony Stewart Head

PART 2
1 David Jason and Terry Scott **2** 23rd **3** Lionel Stander; Freeway **4** Richard Baker **5** Laura Palmer **6** C. J. Parker **7** "Herbidacious" **8** False: *Countdown* was the first programme aired and made its debut on November 2nd, 1982 **9** *The Wombles* **10** Joanna Lumley and David McCallum **11** Antony **12** Lassiter's **13** Dr Jennifer Melfi **14** (August 14th) 2000 **15** Jack Bauer
Tie-breaker Roj; Gareth Thomas

QUIZ 40
PART 1
1 Millennium Falcon **2** Chewbacca, a Wookie **3** Tatooine **4** Keira Knightley **5** Hoth **6** Bail Organa **7** Endor **8** Red Five **9** John Williams **10** Gungan **11** *Star Wars Episode IV: A New Hope* **12** Admiral Ackbar **13** Darth Sidious **14** Bib Fortuna **15** General Grievous

PART 2
1 P **2** H **3** I **4** E **5** F **6** A **7** M **8** J **9** D **10** L **11** N **12** G **13** K **14** C **15** B
Tie-breaker Qui-Gon Jinn, Liam Neeson

QUIZ 41
PART 1
1 Frankie Howerd **2** Alec Guinness **3** Japan **4** *The Wicker Man* **5** Jane Fonda **6** Richard E Grant **7** Ed Wood **8** Quentin Tarantino **9** Donald Sutherland, Alan Alda **10** Keyser Soze **11** *Cry-Baby* **12** Roger Corman **13** Jimmy Cliff **14** Mike Leigh **15** It was in Latin

PART 2
1 A borstal **2** *The Texas Chain Saw Massacre* **3** Peter Greenaway **4** John Walters **5** *Nine Songs* **6** Brad Pitt **7** Austin Powers **8** Stanley Kubrick **9** *Crash* **10** Vincent Price **11** Brigitte Bardot **12** *Easy Rider* **13** *Dark Star* **14** Kurt Russell **15** Kevin Bacon
Tie-breaker Venice; Julie Christie and Donald Sutherland

QUIZ 42

PART 1

1 The war **2** Angela Rippon **3** Angie Watts (by her husband, Den, in Eastenders) **4** Russell Harty **5** Beth Jordache and Margaret Clemence **6** Martin Bashir **7** *Nationwide* **8** Sue Ellen's sister, Kristin Shepard **9** *Blackadder Goes Forth* **10** Nelson Mandela **11** *Pride and Prejudice* **12** *Hancock's Half Hour* ('The Blood Donor' episode) **13** Diana, Princess of Wales **14** Trigger **15** Michael Howard

PART 2

1 Lulu **2** "Some people are on the pitch … they think it's all over … IT IS NOW!" **3** To watch the Queen's coronation **4** The *Challenger* space shuttle **5** Charles, Prince of Wales and Lady Diana Spencer **6** The first men on the moon (Neil Armstrong and Buzz Aldrin descended to the lunar surface and spent 2.5 hours exploring, while Michael Collins orbited above) **7** Michael Portillo **8** Bill Grundy **9** "Fork handles – handles for forks!" **10** Michael Buerk's **11** *Boys from the Blackstuff* **12** Milly **13** He counters that it was simply to stop it escaping **14** Live Aid **15** "Don't tell him, Pike!" ***Tie-breaker*** *That's Life!*, Cyril Fletcher

History

QUIZ 43
PART 1
1 An earthquake **2** Harry Secombe **3** Kofi Anan, Secretary-General of the United Nations **4** *Pop Idol* **5** Deputy prime minister John Prescott; Craig Evans threw an egg at him **6** *Ocean's Eleven* **7** Secretary of State for Northern Ireland, Peter Mandelson **8** United Airlines and American Airlines **9** *The Lord of the Rings: The Fellowship of the Ring*; Peter Jackson **10** Venus Williams **11** Foot and mouth disease **12** *All Rise* **13** The Netherlands **14** *Harry Potter and the Philosopher's Stone* **15** June 7th
PART 2
1 England **2** Ariel Sharon **3** Wheatus **4** Jeffrey Archer; four years **5** Tom Cruise and Nicole Kidman **6** Slobodan Milosevic **7** *Gladiator* **8** Richard Reid; the Shoe Bomber **9** Sherpa Temba Tsheri; age 15 **10** Joey Ramone **11** The People's Republic of China and the Russian Federation **12** Douglas Adams **13** John Howard **14** (Genoa) Italy **15** The iPod; Windows XP
Tie-breaker *Moulin Rouge*

QUIZ 44
PART 1
1 1958 **2** 1964 **3** 1971 **4** 1977 **5** 1982 **6** 1987 **7** 1988 **8** 1991 **9** 1994 **10** 1998
PART 2
1 1985 **2** 1946 **3** 1979 **4** 2000 **5** 1956 **6** 1989 **7** 1986 **8** 1961 **9** 1968 **10** 1999
Tie-breaker 1890

QUIZ 45
PART 1
1 Herakles **2** Artemis **3** Narcissus **4** Theseus **5** The Golden Fleece **6** Orestes **7** Aphrodite **8** Pandora **9** Midas **10** Castor **11** Pan **12** Oedipus **13** Perseus **14** Pegasus **15** Andromeda
PART 2
1 Helen of Sparta **2** Priam **3** Myrmidons **4** Odysseus **5** Philoctetes **6** Hector **7** Patroclus **8** Cressida **9** Diomedes **10** Sean Bean **11** Sarpedon **12** His heel **13** Ajax **14** Neoptolemus **15** The Amazons ***Tie-breaker*** Agamemnon, Clytemnestra

QUIZ 46

PART 1

1 None **2** Knights Templar **3** Balaclava **4** Squadron Leader **5** Sweden **6** Lord Howard of Effingham **7** Julius Caesar **8** The Battle of Yom Kippur **9** Kursk **10** General Lee **11** Zulus **12** General Custer **13** Bosworth Field **14** Nicaragua **15** Culloden (Drumossie Moor is acceptable)

PART 2

1 H **2** F **3** E **4** J **5** A **6** I **7** B **8** C **9** G **10** D **Tie-breaker** (von) Blucher

QUIZ 47

PART 1

1 Salt Lake City, United States **2** President George W. Bush **3** Queen Elizabeth, The Queen Mother **4** 'Cry Me A River'; *Justified* **5** *Prestige* **6** *Star Wars Episode II: Attack of the Clones* **7** *Odyssey* **8** Goran Persson **9** Jimmy Carter **10** Germany; 2–0 **11** 'The Massacre of the Innocents'; (Peter Paul) Rubens **12** Irish football captain, Roy Keane **13** Estonia **14** The Queen's Golden Jubilee **15** The bombing of two nightclubs in Bali, which killed 202 and injured over 300 people

PART 2

1 *The Eminem Show* **2** *I'm A Celebrity, Get Me Out Of Here!*; Tony Blackburn; Tara Palmer-Tompkinson **3** Iran, Iraq, Cuba, Libya, North Korea, Sudan and Syria **4** *The Pianist* **5** Helen Clark **6** City Hall **7** President Jacques Chirac **8** Bulgaria, Estonia, Latvia, Lithuania, Romania, Slovakia and Slovenia **9** 'In Your Eyes'; *Fever* **10** Dudley Moore **11** *A Beautiful Mind* **12** John Entwistle; bass guitar **13** Switzerland **14** *Spin City* **15** Former president Jimmy Carter **Tie-breaker** Peter Ebdon beat Stephen Hendry 18–17

QUIZ 48

PART 1

1 1952 **2** Switzerland **3** *Sputnik 1* **4** 1957 (He then remained with Stoke City until the end of his playing career, appearing in his final game on February 6, 1965, just after his 50th birthday) **5** 1958 **6** Fidel Castro; 1959 **7** 1959 **8** Christopher Trace and Leila Williams; 1958 **9** The Warsaw Pact **10** Burt Lancaster, Montgomery Clift and Frank Sinatra **11** *The Bridge on the River Kwai* **12** The Algerian crisis; Charles De Gaulle **13** Chuck Berry **14** 1956 **15** 1954; William Golding

PART 2

1 Stalin **2** Marlon Brando; *On the Waterfront* **3** 1959 **4** Percival; New Zealand; Tenzing Norgay **5** 1950 **6** Patrick Troughton **7** Anthony Eden **8** *The Catcher in the Rye* **9** *Oxford; 1954* **10** *Panorama*; Richard Dimbleby **11** Britain, France and Israel **12** Coronation chicken; florist Constance Spry and chef Rosemary Hume **13** 1952 **14** European Economic Community **15** *To Catch a Thief* **Tie-breaker** Egypt and Syria

QUIZ 49

PART 1

1 192 **2** 'Mad World' by Gary Jules **3** SARS **4** Kieran Fallon **5** Governor of the Bank of England **6** The Shoe Bomber **7** Saddam Hussein **8** Concorde **9** Archbishop of Canterbury **10** Clare Short **11** His mobile phone rang **12** Walk to the North Pole **13** Roger Federer **14** Prince William **15** *Harry Potter and the Order of the Phoenix*

PART 2

1 The invasion of Iraq **2** Mother Teresa **3** Cheating on *Who Wants To Be A Millionaire?* **4** Ben Curtis **5** AC Milan and Juventus **6** *Columbia* **7** Andrew Gilligan **8** Anita Roddick **9** Phil Tufnell **10** He was the first black policeman to attain that rank **11** Hello! Magazine lost their court case against Douglas and Zeta-Jones **12** Arnold Schwarzenegger **13** Richard Attenborough **14** Congestion charge **15** Michael Jackson **Tie-breaker** Chris De Burgh, Beijing

QUIZ 50

PART 1

1 Cuba; Kruschchev **2** 4–2 **3** Georges Pompidou **4** Fitzgerald **5** Che Guevara **6** 1964 **7** Honey Ryder **8** Polio **9** (November 15th) 1969 **10** Alec Douglas-Home **11** Berlin Wall **12** 1969 **13** Belgium **14** Katharine Hepburn **15** 1966; Jacqueline Susann

PART 2

1 1963 **2** Carol White and Ray Brooks **3** 1963 **4** 1962 **5** 1960; William Hanna and Joseph Barbera **6** Adolf Eichmann **7** Cilla Black **8** *Who's Afraid of Virginia Woolf?* **9** *Magpie* **10** Caractacus Potts; 1964; Ian Fleming **11** Buzz Aldrin and Michael Collins (Armstrong and Aldrin became the first humans to set foot on the Moon, while Collins orbited above) **12** Cecil Day-Lewis **13** *I Know Why The Caged Bird Sings* **14** 1969 **15** *With the Beatles* **Tie-breaker** The Misfits; 1961

QUIZ 51

PART 1

1 Had to be over 30 **2** Nineteenth **3** New Zealand **4** Bertrand Russell **5** Emmeline Pankhurst **6** Birth control clinic **7** 1975 **8** MI5 (she was Director General 1992-1996) **9** Janis Joplin **10** First woman elected to Australian Parliament **11** Rudyard Kipling **12** Annie Beasant **13** 1869 **14** 'Sisters Are Doin' It For Themselves' **15** *The Vagina Monologues*

PART 2

1 P **2** G **3** N **4** K **5** J **6** A **7** D **8** I **9** H **10** M **11** E **12** C **13** F **14** B **15** L **Tie-breaker** Mary Wollstonecraft, Mary Shelley

Answers - History

QUIZ 52
PART 1
1 1776 **2** 1564 **3** 1215 **4** 1901 **5** 1649 **6** 1953 **7** 1620 **8** 1847 **9** 1815 **10** 1789 **11** 1588 **12** 1946 **13** 1872 **14** 1066 **15** 1877
PART 2
1 1959 **2** 1963 **3** 1986 **4** 1970 **5** 1992 **6** 1975 **7** 1981 **8** 1962 **9** 1957 **10** 1973
Tie-breaker Edward III, The Black Prince

QUIZ 53
PART 1
1 Romulus and Remus **2** Constantinople (or Byzantium) **3** Boudicca **4** Hannibal **5** Nephew **6** Sulla **7** Ireland **8** The great drain in Rome, built around 520 BC **9** Lucrece **10** Lucius Tarquinius Superbus (Tarquin The Proud) **11** Bath **12** Apollo, they use the same name **13** Fish **14** Caligula **15** Hadrian's Wall
PART 2
1 France **2** Martial **3** Cleopatra **4** Spartacus **5** Ovid **6** York **7** Mars **8** Carthage **9** Pontius Pilate **10** Siege of Troy *Tie-breaker* Cunobelinus, Cymbeline

QUIZ 54
PART 1
1 Blitzkrieg **2** Normandy **3** Barnes Wallis **4** Wehrmacht **5** It was the date of the attack on Pearl Harbor, which instigated US involvement in the war **6** Italy **7** The German invasion of Russia **8** Browning **9** Erwin Rommel **10** Operation Market Garden **11** Boeing B-29 Superfortress **12** Battle of the Bulge **13** Von Stauffenberg **14** Australia and New Zealand Army Corps **15** Germany's annexation of Austria
PART 2
1 VE (Victory in Europe) Day **2** Iwo Jima **3** Desert Rats **4** Operation Sealion **5** Sir Arthur "Bomber" Harris **6** Von Paulus **7** Montevideo, Uruguay **8** Patton **9** Kesselring **10** MacArthur **11** Crete **12** General De Gaulle **13** A tank **14** *Bismarck* **15** Phoney War
Tie-breaker Spitfire, Hawker Hurricane, and Messerchmitt (BME-109)

QUIZ 55
PART 1
1 (February 15th) 1971 **2** Gerald Ford **3** Michael Caine **4** Idi Amin **5** Farah Fawcett, Jaclyn Smith and Kate Jackson **6** Richard Adams; 1975 **7** Ceylon **8** Pope John Paul II **9** 6 times **10** James Callaghan **11** David Bowie; 'Suffragette City' **12** *The Towering Inferno* **13** June 7th **14** Tony Manero **15** Steve Biko
PART 2
1 Spain; Juan Carlos I **2** Ted Heath **3** *One Flew Over the Cuckoo's Nest* (this accomplishment was not repeated until 1991, with *The Silence of the Lambs*) **4** Zaire **5** *Wish You Were Here* **6** *Voyager I and Voyager II* **7** Soweto **8** Britain, Ireland and Denmark **9** Jack Warner; "Evening all!" **10** Canada **11** Derby **12** Khmer Rouge; Pol Pot **13** Nancy Spungen; New York **14** Alex Haley **15** (April 30th) 1975 ***Tie-breaker*** 1976

QUIZ 56
PART 1
1 60th anniversary of D-Day **2** Athens, Greece **3** Boscastle **4** *Friends* **5** Bird flu **6** Robert Kilroy-Silk **7** *Queen Mary 2* **8** Dr David Kelly (it ruled that he had committed suicide) **9** Sean Penn (in *Mystic River*) **10** Guantanamo Bay detainment camp; four **11** Purple; Fathers 4 Justice **12** Libya **13** Canada **14** *The Passion of the Christ* **15** Seven
PART 2
1 The Great Laxey Mine Railway **2** Eleven **3** Jean-Bertrand Aristide **4** Republic of Ireland **5** *Farenheit 9/11* **6** The withdrawal of Spain's 1300 troops in Iraq **7** Chechen (from Chechnya) **8** *American Idiot* **9** The Entente Cordiale (French for "friendly understanding") was a series of agreements signed on April 8, 1904, between the United Kingdom and France. (Beyond the immediate concerns of colonial expansion addressed by the agreement, the signing of the Entente Cordiale marked the end of centuries of intermittent conflict between the two nations, and the start of the peaceful co-existence that continues to the present day) **10** Ronald Reagan **11** *Harry Potter and the Prisoner of Azkaban* **12** Paris's Charles de Gaulle International Airport **13** Yasser Arafat **14** *Boston Red Sox* **15** John Peel ***Tie-breaker*** *Ramsay's Kitchen Nightmares*

QUIZ 57
PART 1
1 1939 **2** 2002 **3** 1957 **4** 1926 **5** 1840 **6** 1848 **7** 1984 **8** 1983 **9** 1810 **10** 1971 **11** 1759 **12** 1935 **13** 1955 **14** 1346 **15** 1963
PART 2
1 1997 **2** 1923 **3** 1984 **4** 1787 **5** 1948 **6** 1755 **7** 1905 **8** 1600 **9** 1990 **10** 1859 **11** 1972 **12** 1923 **13** 1864 **14** 1266 **15** 1901 ***Tie-breaker*** 1936, Stanley Baldwin

QUIZ 58

PART 1

1 Lady Godiva **2** Maid Marian **3** Locksley **4** Deirdre **5** Beowulf **6** Ray Winstone **7** The Morrigan **8** Taliesin **9** Cuchulain **10** Conor Mac Nessa **11** Connacht **12** Kevin Costner **13** Childe Rolande **14** Sir Guy of Gisborne **15** Brangwen

PART 2

1 Camelot **2** Gawain **3** Leodegraunce **4** Thomas Malory's *Morte d'Arthur* **5** Clive Owen **6** Igrayne of Cornwall **7** Elaine of Astalot **8** Morgana Le Fay **9** Helen Mirren **10** Joseph of Arimathea **11** The Green Knight **12** Lancelot **13** Vortigern **14** Kay **15** Bedevere *Tie-breaker* Bors de Ganis, Perceval

QUIZ 59

PART 1

1 Aztecs **2** Mycenae **3** Sumerian **4** Plato was the pupil **5** David **6** Babylon **7** Mexico **8** China **9** *Kama Sutra* **10** Hieroglyphs **11** Im-Hotep **12** Alexander The Great **13** Macchu Picchu **14** His dog, Argos **15** Assyrian

PART 2

1 True **2** Persia **3** Temple of Artemis **4** Philistines **5** Phoenicians **6** Persians **7** Egypt **8** Tutankhamun **9** Incas **10** Mount Vesuvius **11** Hannibal **12** Aztecs **13** Plato **14** Crete **15** Alexandria *Tie-breaker* Nebuchadnezzar II

QUIZ 60

PART 1

1 Ronald Reagan **2** 155 km **3** Seven; 1986 **4** Yuri Andropov **5** 1982 **6** The Grand Hotel **7** Phil Redmond; 1982 **8** Perestroika **9** 1988 **10** Jimmy Connors and Martina Navratilova **11** July 13th **12** *Rain Man* **13** *A Brief History of Time* **14** Romania **15** *Seven and the Ragged Tiger*

PART 2

1 *The Herald of Free Enterprise* **2** 1981 **3** Konstantin Chernenko **4** Ukraine; 1986 **5** Berkshire **6** 1989 **7** 'Geno' **8** *Out of Africa* **9** 1988; Pakistan **10** *Educating Rita* **11** Argentina beat West Germany 3-2 in Mexico **12** General Noriega; 1989 **13** Olof Palme **14** *Spycatcher;* Peter Wright **15** John Lennon *Tie-breaker* Alan Parker

QUIZ 61
PART 1
1 Hurricane Katrina **2** *Harry Potter and the Half-Blood Prince* **3** Its 50th birthday **4** 66
5 False: he is the 43rd president **6** Her Royal Highness and the Duchess of Cornwall **7** Ken
Barlow tied the knot with Deirdre Rachid (again) on Coronation Street **8** George Galloway, MP
9 It is a "superjumbo": the largest passenger airliner in the world (superseding the Boeing 747)
10 Greece (Elena Paparizou, with the song 'My Number One') **11** Aged 66 **12** Its Playstation 3
game console **13** *Star Wars Episode III: Revenge of the Sith* **14** Liverpool F.C.; 3–2
15 Michael Jackson
PART 2
1 Pope John Paul II; Pope Benedict XVI (Joseph Ratzinger) **2** 167 **3** The "Make Poverty History"
campaign **4** 1908 and 1948 **5** Four **6** It formally ordered an end to the armed campaign it has
pursued since 1969 and ordered all its units to dump their arms **7** Fenway Park (home of the
Boston Red Sox), Boston, USA **8** Since 1987; Michael Vaughan **9** Dave Allen **10** Another second
was added, 23:59:60, called a leap second (the last time this occurred was on June 30th, 1998)
11 The first parliamentary elections under Iraq's new constitution **12** The quality of school
dinners **13** Twisted Logic Tour; 127 **14** Docklands Light Railway **15** Hilary Swank (in *Million
Dollar Baby*) ***Tie-breaker*** Neighbours

QUIZ 62
PART 1
1 Victoria Cross **2** Ironsides **3** (Ottoman) Turks **4** The Dutch, in 1667 **5** Alamo **6** Boer War
7 *The Art of War* **8** Marathon **9** Spetsnaz **10** El Alamein **11** Cornwallis **12** Korean War
13 Cadiz **14** Longbow **15** Rorke's Drift
PART 2
1 F **2** H **3** I **4** A **5** B **6** J **7** E **8** C **9** D **10** G ***Tie-breaker*** Sandhurst, Dartmouth

QUIZ 63
PART 1
1 Poll Tax **2** Bayern Munich **3** Stepehn Lawrence **4** Tony Bullimore **5** Desert Storm
6 Madeleine Albright **7** Crystal Palace **8** F.W. de Klerk **9** US space station, *Mir* **10** James
Bulger **11** Kurds **12** New Zealand **13** South Africa **14** They joined the European Union
15 Pinochet of Chile
PART 2
1 Lance Armstrong **2** Aileen Wuornos **3** Oasis' *(What's The Story) Morning Glory* **4** Tonya
Harding **5** 1992 **6** Denmark won Euro '92; they only made the Finals after Yugoslavia were
expelled **7** Gianni Versace **8** Mike Tyson **9** Hyde Park, London **10** DVD **11** Osama Bin Laden
12 Paul Keating **13** Vaclav Havel **14** Norman Lamont **15** Michael Portillo ***Tie-breaker***
Rodney King

Answers - *History*

QUIZ 64

PART 1

1 Norse **2** Valkyries **3** Fire **4** H.P.Lovecraft **5** Anubis **6** Vishnu **7** A griffin, or gryphon
8 Valhalla **9** Persian **10** Tartarus **11** Androcles **12** Lugh (of the Long Spear) **13** Dragon
14 Aboriginal **15** Parsifal

PART 2

1 Germany **2** A horse **3** The Fates **4** Ragnarok **5** Iceland **6** Seal **7** The Minotaur **8** A swan
9 Rhiannon **10** Loki **11** Janus **12** Set **13** Ithaca **14** Winds (West and North respectively)
15 Iseult or Isolde ***Tie-breaker*** Scylla was a sea-monster with six heads, Charybdis was a
whirlpool

Music and culture

QUIZ 65
PART 1
1 Lonnie Donegan **2** Sonny and Cher **3** Spencer Davis Group **4** Marvin Gaye **5** Manfred Mann **6** Tom Jones **7** Elvis Presley **8** The Searchers **9** Gerry and The Pacemakers **10** Conway Twitty **11** The Rolling Stones **12** Moody Blues **13** Tremeloes **14** Cliff Richard **15** Connie Francis
PART 2
1 Jimmy Saville **2** False: he began wearing them after leaving his ordinary ones on a plane, and decided it looked cool. **3** Ken Dodd **4** Rolf Harris, 'Two Little Boys' **5** The Hollies **6** Diana Ross, The Supremes **7** Little Richard **8** Colonel Tom Parker **9** *Tommy* **10** 22 **11** Eric Clapton played guitar in all three bands **12** *The Jordanaires* **13** *The Righteous Brothers* **14** 'Fire' **15** Cliff Richard ***Tie-breaker*** Sandie Shaw with 'Puppet On A String', Cliff Richard, Lulu

QUIZ 66
PART 1
1 Japan **2** A sausage **3** Tea **4** Vindaloo **5** Sturgeon roe **6** A southern French fish stew **7** Marathon **8** Candied chestnuts **9** River Café **10** Hollandaise **11** Fine slicing, mainly of vegetables **12** Pancetta **13** On a skewer **14** Tapenade **15** Spiced ham
PART 2
1 Earl Grey **2** Aga **3** Battenburg cake **4** Teriyaki sauce **5** Grilled **6** Grape **7** Yoghourt **8** Kendal Mint Cake **9** Herring **10** Croque-Monsieur **11** Made from ewe's milk **12** Sour cream **13** A kind of bean **14** Brazil **15** Barbecue equipment ***Tie-breaker*** French Laundry, Per Se

QUIZ 67
PART 1
1 Michelangelo **2** Hermitage **3** Puccini **4** Montague and Capulet **5** All designed by Christopher Wren **6** Sisters **7** Action Painting **8** Venice **9** Spanish guitar **10** Hanging Gardens of Babylon **11** *The Spectator* **12** Porcelain **13** (Michel Eyquem de) Montaigne **14** Frank Lloyd Wright **15** They have all won the Turner Prize in recent years
PART 2
1 Prado **2** Kenneth Tynan **3** Australia, Mosman is a suburb of Sydney **4** Camden Town group **5** Giverny **6** Russian **7** *Madame Bovary* **8** Fakes **9** Cello **10** James McNeil Whistler **11** Henry David Thoreau **12** Chartres **13** London Bridge **14** Sculpture **15** William Morris ***Tie-breaker*** Das Rheingold (The Rhinegold), Die Walkure (The Valkyries), Siegfried, Der Gotterdammerung (Twilight of the Gods)

QUIZ 68

PART 1

1 'My Sweet Lord', twice **2** Apple **3** Pete Best **4** Charles Manson's **5** 'I Want To Hold Your Hand' **6** He murdered John Lennon **7** *Magical Mystery Tour* **8** Hamburg **9** Brian Epstein **10** *A Hard Day's Night* **11** Philippines (Imelda Marcos) **12** All are sung by Ringo **13** 'Yesterday' **14** 1969 (Their final live performance was on the rooftop of the Apple building at 3 Savile Row, on 30 January 1969) **15** George Martin

PART 2

1 *Sgt Pepper's Lonely Hearts Club Band* **2** *Please Please Me* **3** *Let It Be* **4** *Revolver* **5** *Help!* **6** *White Album* **7** *Rubber Soul* **8** *Anthology 1* **9** *Abbey Road* **10** *A Hard Day's Night* **Tie-breaker** 'Mull of Kintyre' (1977), 'Ebony and Ivory' (with Stevie Wonder, 1982) and 'Pipes of Peace' (1983)

QUIZ 69

PART 1

1 Rice **2** Shell-like **3** Pavlova **4** Haddock **5** Beetroot **6** Fish **7** A cheese sauce **8** Olive Oil **9** Gazpacho **10** Pectin **11** Choux **12** Onion **13** Baklava **14** Bubble and squeak **15** On a bed of ice

PART 2

1 Bread **2** Yorkshire Pudding **3** Basil Fawlty (John Cleese) in *Fawlty Towers* **4** Antipasti **5** Steak **6** Noodles **7** Spotted dick **8** Maize **9** Tahini (sesame puree) **10** Julienne **11** A small cake **12** Dried plums **13** Bain-marie **14** Croutons **15** Potato **Tie-breaker** *Superwoman*

QUIZ 70

PART 1

1 'My Ding-A-Ling' **2** Bob Dylan **3** Glen Matlock **4** 'Killer Queen' **5** Simon and Garfunkel **6** 'Teenage Kicks' by The Undertones **7** (Tony Orlando) and Dawn **8** Bread **9** Sweet **10** Flute **11** *Saturday Night Fever* **12** Alvin Stardust **13** Bangladesh **14** Barry White **15** Stevie Wonder

PART 2

1 *Bat Out Of Hell* (Meatloaf) **2** *Parallel Lines* (Blondie) **3** *Aladdin Sane* (David Bowie) **4** *Arrival* (Abba) **5** *Regatta de Blanc* (Police) **6** *Rumours* (Fleetwood Mac) **7** *Goodbye Yellow Brick Road* (Elton John) **8** *Led Zeppelin IV* (Led Zeppelin) **9** *Harvest* (Neil Young) **10** *Sticky Fingers* (The Rolling Stones) **Tie-breaker** The Commodores, Lionel Richie

QUIZ 71
PART 1
1 I **2** E **3** J **4** G **5** H **6** D **7** B **8** A **9** C **10** F
PART 2
1 *Beowulf* **2** Statue of Liberty **3** Cupola **4** St Hildegard of Bingen **5** Opera, she is a soprano
6 Japanese **7** Richard Rogers **8** Henrik Ibsen **9** Andoni Gaudi **10** *Pastoral* **11** Renoir
12 Muséée d'Orsay **13** King Arthur **14** Countertenor **15** Berthe Morisot ***Tie-breaker***
William Wordsworth and Samuel Taylor Coleridge

QUIZ 72
PART 1
1 Gladstone bag **2** On the feet **3** No 5 **4** A wig **5** Laura Ashley **6** Calvin Klein **7** Bolton
Wanderers (Reebok Stadium) **8** Luggage **9** Ruff **10** John Galliano **11** Hairstyling
12 Mini-skirt **13** Hot pants **14** Right arm **15** Teddy Tinling
PART 2
1 Cindy Crawford **2** Christian Dior **3** Asda **4** Baldric **5** Benetton **6** Naomi Campbell
7 Culottes **8** Kate Moss **9** On your head, it is a hat **10** Catherine Zeta-Jones **11** Yves Saint-
Laurent **12** Coco Chanel **13** Win Miss World **14** Pashmina **15** Panty hose ***Tie-breaker***
In bed, it is a long nightgown, usually made from chiffon.

QUIZ 73
PART 1
1 Bruce Springsteen **2** David Bowie **3** Genesis **4** Smashing Pumpkins **5** Eurythmics
6 *Rolling Stone* **7** They are all Canadian **8** Alan Freeman **9** The Byrds **10** Pink Floyd
11 Happy Mondays **12** The Pretenders **13** Phil Collins **14** *Old Grey Whistle Test*
15 Captain Beefheart
PART 2
1 Nirvana **2** Guns 'N'Roses **3** Joy Division **4** Led Zeppelin **5** Four Tops **6** Supergrass
7 Fun Lovin' Criminals **8** Ash **9** Thin Lizzy **10** The Stranglers **11** Erasure **12** Stone Roses
13 Rainbow **14** Rush **15** Slade ***Tie-breaker*** Style Council, Mick Talbot

QUIZ 74

PART 1

1 Glenfiddich **2** Apples **3** New Zealand **4** Bourbon whiskey **5** Black Velvet **6** Kir Royale
7 Tetley's bitter **8** Castlemaine **9** Sommelier **10** Sloe gin **11** India **12** Theakstons **13** Cider
14 Gin and Vermouth **15** CAMRA

PART 2

1 Portugal **2** Chile **3** Dry **4** Hungary **5** Chardonnay **6** Beaujolais **7** Italy **8** Cava
9 South Africa **10** England **11** They are allowed to rot on the vine before picking **12** Pinot Noir
13 Merlot **14** Bordeaux **15** Shiraz ***Tie-breaker*** Rheims and Epernay

QUIZ 75

PART 1

1 Take That **2** Bananarama **3** Bay City Rollers **4** Gareth Gates **5** Sugababes **6** Geri Halliwell
7 Paul Cattermole **8** David Sneddon **9** Delta Goodrem **10** *Starsky and Hutch* **11** *Popstars*
12 *The Partridge Family* **13** David Essex **14** 'Wannabe' **15** Backstreet Boys

PART 2

1 Atomic Kitten **2** B*witched **3** All Saints **4** S Club 7 **5** Monkees **6** Alex Parks **7** Girls Aloud
8 Justin Timberlake **9** *Whistle Down The Wind* **10** Marie Osmond **11** East 17 **12** Katie Price
(Jordan) **13** t.A.T.u. **14** Billie (Piper) **15** Kelly Osbourne ***Tie-breaker*** Stephen Gately and
Ronan Keating

QUIZ 76

PART 1

1 *Thriller* **2** 'Relax' **3** Cyndi Lauper **4** *Purple Rain* **5** Tracy Chapman **6** The Go-Go's
7 Tears For Fears **8** Run DMC **9** Bucks Fizz **10** Live Aid **11** Public Enemy **12** A CD player
13 *Brothers In Arms* **14** 'Tainted Love' **15** Celine Dion

PART 2

1 George Michael **2** Morrissey **3** Frankie Goes To Hollywood **4** The Jam **5** Wet Wet Wet
6 Police **7** Alison Moyet **8** Lionel Ritchie **9** U2 **10** Paul Simon **11** Human League
12 Def Leppard **13** Duran Duran **14** ABC **15** Marillion ***Tie-breaker*** 'Holiday', *Like A Virgin*

QUIZ 77

PART 1

1 Going out in the midday sun **2** Busby Berkeley **3** Cyd Charisse **4** Cole Porter **5** Eric Morley
6 Funny Face **7** Stephen Sondheim **8** Irene Cara **9** She's a welder. **10** *The Producers*
11 Poland **12** *Hair* **13** Hot Gossip **14** Bob Fosse **15** Rita Hayworth

PART 2

1 M **2** I **3** J **4** H **5** B **6** D **7** C **8** E **9** G **10** L **11** P **12** A **13** N **14** K **15** F
Tie-breaker Marni Nixon

QUIZ 78
PART 1

1 Arctic Monkeys, 'I'll Bet You Look Good On The Dancefloor' **2** Madonna, 'Like A Prayer' **3** Tears For Fears, 'Mad World' **4** Kaiser Chiefs, 'I Predict A Riot' **5** Girls Aloud, 'Sound of the Underground' **6** The Streets, Dry Your Eyes' **7** Spice Girls, 'Say You'll Be There' **8** Human League, 'Don't You Want Me' **9** Eminem, 'Lose Yourself' **10** The Beatles, 'A Day In The Life'

PART 2

1 Pink Floyd, 'Another Brick In The Wall' **2** Nirvana, Smells 'Like Teen Spirit' **3** Sinead O'Connor, 'Nothing Compares 2 U' (Written by Prince, but Sinead recorded it before he did his own version) **4** Pulp, 'Common People' **5** The Roilling Stones, 'Sympathy For The Devil' **6** David Bowie, 'Life On Mars?' **7** Led Zeppelin, 'Stairway To Heaven' **8** Green Day, 'American Idiot' **9** Queen, 'Killer Queen' **10** Joy Division, 'Love Will Tear Us Apart' ***Tie-breaker*** Oasis, 'Wonderwall'.

QUIZ 79
PART 1

1 Collage **2** Yves Klein **3** British Museum **4** Cubism **5** William Hogarth **6** A bell **7** Gustav Holst **8** John Nash **9** Ted Hughes **10** The Alhambra **11** Notre Dame (Cathedral) de Paris **12** The Tate **13** Sydney Opera House **14** William Blake **15** Harpsichord

PART 2

1 B **2** F **3** J **4** D **5** C **6** H **7** A **8** G **9** E **10** I ***Tie-breaker*** Jose Carrera, Luciano Pavarotti, Placido Domingo

QUIZ 80
PART 1

1 Jamie Oliver **2** Madhur Jaffrey **3** A.A.Gill **4** Fanny Craddock **5** Marco Pierre White **6** Ainsley Harriott **7** Heston Blumenthal **8** Waterside Inn **9** Claridge's **10** Ludlow **11** Le Manoir Aux Quatre Saisons **12** *(London) Evening Standard* **13** Nobu **14** Gary Rhodes **15** John Burton-Race

PART 2

1 M **2** C **3** J **4** F **5** K **6** G **7** P **8** L **9** B **10** I **11** E **12** H **13** N **14** D **15** A ***Tie-breaker*** Gordon Ramsay

Answers - Music and culture

QUIZ 81

PART 1

1 Destiny's Child **2** Madonna **3** True: July, 1996 in the UK and Jan '97 in the US **4** Tammy Wynette **5** Dr Dre **6** Hanson **7** Bryan Adams **8** No Doubt **9** Gary Barlow **10** Garth Brooks **11** Freddie Mercury **12** Fugees **13** R.E.M. **14** Cranberries **15** Britney Spears

PART 2

1 Robbie Williams **2** Prodigy **3** Green Day **4** En Vogue **5** Celine Dion **6** Smashing Pumpkins **7** Fat Boy Slim **8** Nirvana **9** Morrissey **10** Radiohead **11** Tori Amos **12** Madonna **13** Depeche Mode **14** Alanis Morissette **15** Chemical Brothers **Tie-breaker** Jarvis Cocker

QUIZ 82

PART 1

1 Marks and Spencer **2** Lindsay Lohan **3** Nina Ricci **4** Kilt **5** Stella McCartney **6** Vivienne Westwood **7** Shoes **8** Wonderbra **9** Philips Van Heusen **10** Yves St-Laurent **11** Burberry **12** Ralph Lauren **13** Hats **14** Florence **15** Twiggy

PART 2

1 Sari **2** Clark's **3** On your wrist, Tag Heuer make watches **4** Unbleached cotton fabric **5** Undergarments **6** Christian Dior **7** Low-cut at the neck **8** Dungarees **9** To get a haircut **10** Silk **11** Boa **12** Sophie Dahl **13** A hat **14** Harvey Nichols **15** Glass **Tie-breaker** Tattooing. They are removable henna tattoos.

QUIZ 83

PART 1

1 *Top Gun* **2** 'Up Where We Belong' **3** *Seven Brides for Seven Brothers* **4** Richard Gere **5** *Phantom of the Opera* **6** Sally Bowles (*Cabaret*) **7** 'Young Hearts Run Free' **8** *Chicago* **9** 'Time of My Life' **10** 'The Time Warp' (from *The Rocky Horror Picture Show*) **11** Renault Megane **12** Queen Latifah **13** James Cagney **14** Wayne Sleep **15** *Strictly Ballroom*

PART 2

1 Bruce Forsyth **2** Tess Daly **3** Natasha Kaplinsky **4** Claudia Winkleman **5** Erin Boag **6** Anton Du Beke **7** Zoe Ball **8** David Seaman **9** Graham Norton **10** Christopher Parker, Jill Halfpenny, Patsy Palmer **11** Arlene Phillips **12** Roger Black, Colin Jackson and Denise Lewis **13** Fiona Phillips **14** Darren Gough **15** Robbie Earle **Tie-breaker** Nathan Lane (Bialystock) and Matthew Broderick (Bloom)

QUIZ 84

PART 1

1 'All You Need Is Love' **2** *Tess of the d'Urbervilles* **3** Roxanne **4** Catherine Earnshaw **5** Paul Newman **6** Humphrey Bogart and Lauren Bacall **7** Pocahontas **8** Abelard **9** Robert Burns **10** Viola in *Twelfth Night* **11** Sonny and Cher **12** Thirty **13** Jeremy Irons **14** Liam Neeson **15** Charles Aznavour

PART 2

1 *Love Story* **2** Marlene Dietrich **3** Jane Eyre and Mr Rochester, in Charlotte Brontë's novel **4** Courtney Love **5** Laura **6** Richard Burton **7** Pattie Boyd, who was married first to Harrison and then to Clapton **8** Sealed With A Loving Kiss **9** Mr Bingley **10** Joy Division

Tie-breaker Leonardo DiCaprio and Claire Danes

QUIZ 85

PART 1

1 String instrument **2** Arts and Crafts Movement **3** Pieta **4** Rijksmuseum **5** John Tavener **6** (London) City Hall **7** Pre-Raphaelite Brotherhood **8** George Gershwin **9** (Maurice) Ravel **10** Bauhaus **11** Crystal Palace **12** Liverpool and St Ives, Cornwall **13** Georgia O'Keeffe **14** Medici **15** The Pentagon

PART 2

1 C **2** H **3** P **4** G **5** L **6** B **7** K **8** N **9** E **10** A **11** F **12** J **13** D **14** I **15** M

Tie-breaker Andrew Motion, Ted Hughes

QUIZ 86

PART 1

1 The Streets **2** Arctic Monkeys **3** Pink **4** Busted **5** Sugababes **6** Christina Aguilera **7** Will Young **8** Spiller **9** Eminem **10** Robbie Williams and Nicole Kidman **11** Nelly Furtado **12** Evanescence **13** Emma Bunton **14** McFly **15** Pussycat Dolls

PART 2

1 John Peel **2** Dido **3** The Killers **4** Joss Stone **5** *Back To Bedlam* **6** Linkin Park **7** Norah Jones *(Come Away With Me)* **8** Chemical Brothers **9** 50 Cent **10** Pete Doherty **11** Red Hot Chilli Peppers **12** Katie Melua **13** Scissor Sisters **14** *A New Day At Midnight* **15** Travis

Tie-breaker 1975

QUIZ 87

PART 1

1 Annie Nightingale **2** Humphrey Lyttelton **3** Andy Kershaw **4** Oxford(shire) **5** *Desert Island Discs* **6** Sue Lawley **7** Open University **8** Radio Luxembourg **9** *Book At Bedtime* **10** The time signal "pips" **11** 1951 **12** First song played on new Radio 1 **13** LBC **14** BBC Home Service **15** Jenni Murray

PART 2

1 Classic FM **2** Lionel Blue **3** *I'm Sorry, I'll Read That Again* **4** Tommy Vance **5** Manchester **6** *Not The Nine O'Clock News* **7** Brian Redhead **8** Libby Purves **9** 198M longwave **10** Terry Wogan **11** Jo Whiley **12** Tamsin Greig **13** *Brain of Britain* **14** *Loose Ends* **15** Jane Garvey **Tie-breaker** Zoe Ball and Sara Cox

People and places

QUIZ 88
PART 1
1 J **2** H **3** I **4** B **5** C **6** A **7** G **8** D **9** F **10** E
PART 2
1 1849 **2** Richard Burton and Elizabeth Taylor **3** 'Who's David' **4** Ten Pole Tudor **5** Who shot J.R. **6** *Who Framed Roger Rabbit?* **7** The Baha Men **8** Terry Nation **9** Bruce Wayne
10 The Penguin *Tie-breaker* Pete Townshend, Roger Daltrey, John Entwhistle, Keith Moon.

QUIZ 89
PART 1
1 Tintin **2** US Senate **3** Mark Thatcher **4** Keir Hardie **5** Martin Luther **6** Henley **7** Walk to the South Pole **8** Cecil Rhodes **9** Galileo **10** Elvis Presley **11** Westland Affair **12** League of Nations **13** Manchester City **14** Albania **15** Ranulph Fiennes
PART 2
1 Wayne Rooney **2** Schopenhauer **3** Lake Erie and Lake Ontario **4** George Villiers, Duke of Buckingham **5** Danzig **6** Izaak Walton **7** The Borgias **8** Queen Anne **9** Lord Kitchener
10 *The Winslow Boy* **11** The Pope **12** Rosa Luxemburg **13** Erenst Shackleton **14** Food
15 Abortion *Tie-breaker* Neil Hamilton

QUIZ 90
PART 1
1 March 1st **2** Snowdon **3** Rhodri Morgan **4** Pembrokeshire **5** River Dee **6** Menai Strait
7 Rhondda Valley **8** White and green **9** Full-back **10** Brecon Beacons **11** Owain Glyndwr
12 Neville Southall **13** Lampeter **14** Nicole Cooke **15** John Charles
PART 2
1 Glamorgan **2** True. **3** He was the first Secretary of State for Wales **4** Chepstow **5** (Royal National) Eisteddfod **6** Milford Haven **7** Aberfan **8** A waterfall **9** Plaid Cymru **10** River Taff
11 Gruffudd ap Llewellyn **12** Jonathan Davies **13** Arsenal, 1-0 **14** Llanelli RFC **15** Blaenau Gwent *Tie-breaker* Ynys Mon, Megan Lloyd George

Answers - *People and places*

QUIZ 91

PART 1

1 St Patrick's Day **2** Dana **3** David Trimble **4** 1991 **5** Liffey **6** Slieve Donard, Carrantuohill
7 Nelson **8** 1998 **9** Billy Bingham **10** Gerry Armstrong **11** Ian Paisley **12** Contraceptives
13 George Bernard Shaw **14** Mashed potato and cabbage **15** Limerick

PART 2

1 Pour the perfect pint of Guinness ('Good things come to those who wait' campaign). **2** The
Connemara town boasts the longest place name in Ireland **3** President of the International Olympic
Committee **4** Black and Tans **5** Bobby Sands **6** Bernadette Devlin **7** Roger Casement **8** May
1st **9** Eamon de Valera **10** Mick McCarthy **11** Shoemaking **12** Divorce **13** 1840s **14** West
Indies **15** Blarney Castle, Co. Cork ***Tie-breaker*** Robinson (1990–97) and McAleese (1997–)

QUIZ 92

PART 1

1 Dido **2** True: their shared birthday is July 31st. **3** He went down in the Titanic in 1912 **4** Edna
O'Brien **5** The Italian dictator, Benito Mussolini **6** Linford Christie **7** Paris, France **8** Winston
Churchill; Bladon, near Woodstock, not far from his birthplace at Blenheim Palace **9** She was
beheaded; nine days **10** Stephen Hawking **11** On the African island of Zanzibar **12** Sarah
Jessica Parker **13** (in a hotel room in) Sydney, Australia; 1968 **14** It was caused by anorexia
nervosa **15** Sir Alexander Fleming

PART 2

1 Rowan Atkinson **2** Jaqueline du Pré **3** Michael Hutchence **4** Orlando Bloom **5** Anne Boleyn
(second wife of Henry VIII) **6** Gwyneth Paltrow **7** "Am I my brother's keeper?" **8** An unsuccessful
eye operation **9** 1819; 1837 **10** He was murdered (stabbed) by Scottish noblemen in 1566, at the
instigation of Mary's husband, Lord Darnley **11** Goldie Hawn **12** Whitehall **13** Sylvia Plath
14 She commits hara-kiri **15** "Channel 5 is shit" ***Tie-breaker*** Joseph Stalin

QUIZ 93

PART 1

1 Margaret Thatcher **2** Dorothy Parker **3** Victoria Beckham **4** Samuel Johnson **5** Madonna
6 Mick Jagger **7** Dolly Parton **8** King Henry VIII **9** Dennis Healey **10** Richard Nixon **11** John
Wilmot, Earl of Rochester **12** Rod Stewart **13** Oscar Wilde **14** Jeffrey Archer **15** Jerry Springer

PART 2

1 Mark Twain **2** Nancy Astor **3** Timothy Leary **4** Lenin **5** David Lloyd George **6** Andy Warhol
7 Harold Macmillan **8** Soviet Union **9** Queen Elizabeth at Tilbury Docks as England awaited the
Spanish Armada **10** Benjamin Franklin **11** John F Kennedy **12** Thomas Carlyle **13** Girls who
wear glasses **14** Gertrude Stein **15** Napoleon Bonaparte ***Tie-breaker*** Abraham Lincoln

QUIZ 94

PART 1

1 Lake District **2** Brecon Hills or Beacons **3** New Forest **4** Cornwall **5** Hertfordshire **6** The Cotswolds **7** Lindisfarne Priory **8** Stonehenge **9** Powis Castle **10** Kew **11** Blenheim Palace **12** Hampton Court **13** Hever Castle is in Kent **14** Pembrokeshire **15** Yorkshire

PART 2

1 Sir Winston Churchill **2** King Arthur **3** Althorp **4** Chatsworth House **5** False. St. David's in Wales is the smallest city in the UK. **6** Bronte sisters **7** Vita Sackville-West **8** William Shakespeare **9** Blackpool **10** Tintern Abbey **11** Derbyshire **12** Snowdon Mountain Railway **13** (Stan) Laurel (and Hardy) **14** Alnwick **15** Manchester Ship Canal ***Tie-breaker*** Royal Leamington Spa

QUIZ 95

PART 1

1 Jennnifer Lopez **2** King Hussein **3** Chile **4** Romanovs **5** Matt Busby **6** Pathologist **7** Medicis **8** Denmark **9** Eton College **10** Thomas A Kempis **11** John F Kennedy **12** Nigel Lawson **13** Samaritans **14** Hans Blix **15** Panama

PART 2

1 Boy George **2** He cut it off himself **3** Charlie Chaplin **4** Boris Yeltsin **5** Alec Waugh **6** Knutsford **7** California and New Mexico **8** The Godwins **9** George Best **10** Brisbane ***Tie-breaker*** Ethiopia

QUIZ 96

PART 1

1 Freddie **2** Max Miller **3** Zinedine Zidane **4** Florence Nightingale **5** Dracula **6** Anne of Cleves **7** The Last of the Mohicans **8** Clara Bow **9** Warwick the Kingmaker **10** Louis Armstrong **11** Galloping Gourmet **12** Joel Garner **13** Ron Harris **14** Calamity Jane **15** Peter Sutcliffe

PART 2

1 J.K. **2** J.M. **3** J.R. **4** W.G. **5** B.B. **6** H.P. **7** J.P.R. **8** M.R. **9** P.D. **10** A.S. **11** W.B. **12** D.W. **13** W.C. **14** W.S. **15** K.T. ***Tie-breaker*** The Sun King

QUIZ 97

PART 1

1 Seven (She has been married eight times - twice to Richard Burton) **2** Madonna **3** Actress Mimi Rogers **4** Joe Scully **5** Jon Voight **6** Actor Rock Hudson (in 1985) **7** Matthew Perry **8** President John F. Kennedy and Senator Robert F. Kennedy **9** Footballer Dwight Yorke **10** They separated after Allen admitted to an affair with Soon-Yi Previn, Farrow's adopted daughter **11** Courtney Love **12** Sam Giancana **13** Singer Delta Goodrem **14** Seven **15** Paris Hilton and Nicole Richie

PART 2

1 Paul Merton **2** Three (to musicians Dan Donovan of Big Audio Dynamite, Jim Kerr of Simple Minds and Liam Gallagher of Oasis) **3** Elvis Presley's (Lisa-Marie Presley) **4** Anthony ('Tony') Booth **5** Caroline, Albert and Stephanie **6** The late quiz show host Hughie Green **7** David Furnish **8** Actor Hugh Grant **9** Twice **10** Pamela Anderson **11** Will Carling **12** Winona Ryder **13** Rebecca Loos **14** Cheryl Cole, nee Tweedy **15** Errol Flynn ***Tie-breaker*** He dressed as a German Nazi

QUIZ 98

PART 1

1 Leonardo Da Vinci **2** Dead Sea Scrolls **3** Miniatures **4** *Endeavour* **5** *Eva Braun* **6** Portugal **7** Gerard Manley Hopkins **8** The Pied Piper of Hamelin **9** Mary Queen of Scots **10** Bangladesh **11** William Laud **12** 455, when John Paul II was elected **13** George Washington **14** Lilith **15** Ron Atkinson

PART 2

1 Jack Straw **2** Gordon Brown **3** Boris Johnson **4** Rev Ian Paisley **5** William Hague **6** Dennis Skinner **7** Mark Oaten **8** Clare Short **9** Gerry Adams **10** Kate Hoey **11** George Galloway **12** John Prescott **13** Glenda Jackson **14** Kenneth Clarke **15** Austin Mitchell ***Tie-breaker*** Gerry Adams

QUIZ 99

PART 1

1 George VI (his younger brother) **2** Grandson **3** Edward The Confessor **4** True, 1936 **5** Henry VIII and Anne Boleyn **6** Queen Elizabeth II (in 1954) **7** Lily Langtry **8** King John **9** Canute **10** Edward I **11** John of Gaunt **12** Queen Anne **13** Queen Victoria **14** Henry (Bolingbroke) IV **15** Mary, William of Orange

PART 2

1 Louis XIV and XV **2** Napoleon **3** Poland **4** Wilhelmina **5** Empress Maria Theresa **6** House of Valois **7** Macbeth **8** Sweden **9** Charlemagne **10** Prussia ***Tie-breaker*** Edward VI, Mary, Elizabeth I

QUIZ 100

PART 1

1 *The Matrix* **2** The Monkees **3** Harvey Smith **4** Chris Read **5** Locomotive engineer
6 *Nineteen Eighty-Four*, by George Orwell **7** Steve Jones **8** *Hatful of Hollow* **9** Leeds United
10 Liverpool **11** Smithfield **12** Google **13** His refusal to play on Sundays would have ruled
him out of the quarter- and semi-finals **14** Smith and Wesson **15** Henry Fielding

PART 2

1 *The Snowman* **2** Parma **3** *Lock Stock and Two Smoking Barrels* **4** Washington DC
5 The Cure **6** James Earl Jones **7** *Not The Nine O'Clock News* **8** Cardiff City **9** James Stewart
10 Worcestershire **11** Plain old Tom Jones **12** Swindon **13** Bill Wyman **14** Inigo Jones
15 *The Fugitive* ***Tie-breaker*** Brad Pitt and Angelina Jolie

QUIZ 101

PART 1

1 Wallace **2** Mike Denness **3** Sandy Lyle and Paul Lawrie **4** Dorothy Dunnett **5** Kenny Dalglish
and Denis Law **6** Sir Walter Scott **7** Orkney Islands **8** Jack Vettriano **9** It was the plane that
crashed into Lockerbie in 1988 **10** None **11** Menzies Campbell **12** St Andrew **13** Whitsuntide
14 Curling **15** Ullapool

PART 2

1 Alex Ferguson **2** Six **3** Celtic's European Cup-winning team of 1967 **4** Sir Alec Douglas-Home
5 Church of Scotland **6** Battle of Bannockburn **7** A breed of cattle **8** Paul Le Guen **9** Marquis
of Montrose **10** Acts of Union **11** Roby Roy's wife **12** The Scottish Parliament **13** Dundee
and Perth **14** Flora Macdonald **15** Douglas Dunn ***Tie-breaker*** 1603, Queen Elizabeth I of
England

QUIZ 102

PART 1

1 Major James Hewitt **2** The Duchess of Kent **3** 1952 **4** St. Andrews, Scotland **5** A Nazi
uniform (swastika arm band) **6** Koo Stark **7** Princess Anne **8** Wallis Simpson **9** Princess
Michael of Kent **10** Mike Tindall **11** Royal Yacht, *Britannia* **12** (Commander) Tim Laurence
13 The last Queen Mother **14** Budgie, The Little Helicopter **15** Greece

PART 2

1 1969 **2** Caernarvon Castle **3** Louise (Louise Alice Elizabeth Mary Mountbatten Windsor)
4 Prince Andrew **5** Elizabeth and David Emmanuel **6** The Palace of Holyroodhouse (Holyrood
Palace). Balmoral is a private residence. **7** Saxe-Coburg-Gotha; in the anti-German climate of
World War I a German-sounding name was considered inappropriate. **8** Roddy Llewellyn
9 St Paul's Cathedral **10** Queen Mother ***Tie-breaker*** Sophie Rhys-Jones, Countess of
Wessex, Louise

Answers - People and places

QUIZ 103

PART 1

1 California **2** Florida **3** Alaska **4** Oahu **5** Arizona **6** Seattle **7** Nebraska **8** Ohio
9 San Francisco **10** Chicago **11** Wyoming **12** Texas **13** Michigan **14** Mason-Dixon Line
15 California

PART 2

1 G **2** C **3** H **4** J **5** E **6** B **7** F **8** D **9** A **10** I **Tie-breaker** Connecticut, Maine,
Massachussetts, New Hampshire, Rhode Island, Vermont

QUIZ 104

PART 1

1 'La Marseillaise' **2** La Manche **3** 1889 **4** Kepi **5** Jean Paul Marat **6** Napoleon **7** Moliere's
Miser **8** Charles The Fat **9** Dordogne **10** Cardinal Richelieu **11** Dauphin **12** The Royal
Standard **13** Les Frondes **14** Joan of Arc, La Pucelle means The Virgin **15** Agatha Christie

PART 2

1 65 million **2** Nantes **3** Francois Mitterand **4** Skiing **5** Guillotine **6** Jean-Paul Sartre
7 Auguste and Louis Lumiere **8** Yannick Noah **9** Grasse **10** Fontainebleau
11 Philippe Sella **12** Lot **13** Bourbon **14** Gascony **15** Blue **Tie-breaker** 1789

QUIZ 105

PART 1

1 Blue plaque **2** Soho **3** Bakerloo Line **4** St James' Park **5** *Brick Lane* **6** Fenchurch Street:
stations on a monopoly board **7** Leslie Grantham and Anita Dobson **8** Chelsea Bridge **9** The
Bank of England **10** Blackfriars Bridge **11** Crystal Palace **12** Islington **13** Teaching hospitals
14 University Boat Race **15** Lord's

PART 2

1 Samuel Pepys **2** Arsenal **3** Sadler's Wells **4** William The Conqueror **5** Vaughan Williams
6 Martin Amis **7** Spaniard's Inn **8** Cleopatra's Needle **9** Metropolitan **10** Sherlock Holmes
11 Hamley's **12** Peckham **13** *Me and My Girl* **14** Watford **15** Antiques **Tie-breaker**
1981, Gillette

QUIZ 106

PART 1

1 Daniella Westbrook **2** Velodrome **3** Leningrad **4** Dutch **5** Spanish Civil War **6** Sweden
7 The SDP **8** Sydney **9** On the roof of Abbey Road studios **10** Nelson's Column
11 Von Ribbentrop **12** Patty Hearst **13** Maoris **14** Switzerland **15** Joseph McCarthy

PART 2

1 Kate Bush **2** Golda Meir **3** *War and Peace*. Prokofiev's opera is based on Tolstoy's novel
4 The White House in Washington DC **5** Strategic Arms Limitation Talks **6** Thomas A Becket
7 Torino **8** Rhodesia **9** Sandy Lyle **10** Soweto **11** Watergate **12** Syria **13** False; they were
deported to Australia **14** Kenneth Wolstenholme **15** Hungary ***Tie-breaker*** Betty Boothroyd

QUIZ 107

PART 1

1 Dublin **2** Enya **3** Eamon de Valera **4** Fifteen **5** Limerick **6** Tara **7** Eddie Irvine **8** Norman
Whiteside **9** True; Dublin's two cathedrals, Christ Church and St. Patrick's, are both Church of
Ireland. **10** Garrett Fitzgerald **11** The Giant's Causeway **12** Phil Lynott **13** Shannon
14 False, of course – that would be plain silly! **15** Aran Isles

PART 2

1 Trinity College **2** Danny Blanchflower **3** Wicklow **4** Bob Geldof **5** Leinster from the old
five counties **6** Hurling **7** The Edge of U2 **8** Stephen Roche **9** James Joyce **10** Connemara
11 David Feherty **12** Airport at Knock (now Ireland West) **13** Rock of Cashel **14** Damien Rice
15 (Charles Stewart) Parnell ***Tie-breaker*** 1985

QUIZ 108

PART 1

1 (Condoleezza and Tim) Rice **2** (Steve and various) Redgrave **3** (Jackie and Patrick) Stewart
4 (Ashia and Alan) Hansen **5** (Tom and Cheryl) Baker **6** (Joan and Steve) Collins **7** (Robert and
Chet) Atkins **8** (Alan and Ray) Davies **9** (George and Sacha Baron) Cohen **10** (Ashley/Joe and
George) Cole **11** (Glenda and Jesse) Jackson **12** (Davis and Courtney) Love **13** (Barry and Keith)
Richards **14** (Eddie and Michael) Jordan **15** (Moira and Alan) Shearer

PART 2

1 E **2** I **3** H **4** A **5** B **6** J **7** C **8** G **9** F **10** D ***Tie-breaker*** Norma Jean Mortenson,
Baker

Answers - People and places

QUIZ 109
PART 1
1 Depp, Woods **2** Pitt, Graff **3** Spears, Johansson **4** Travolta, Peter Jackson **5** Jordan, Campbell **6** Prince, Cash **7** Lumley, Blair **8** Witherspoon, Williams **9** Archer, Jacklin **10** Pele, Barry Manilow
PART 2
1 1957 **2** 1982 **3** 1977 **4** 1976 **5** 1934 **6** 1966 **7** 1971 **8** 1985 **9** 1964 **10** 1973
Tie-breaker 1999

QUIZ 110
PART 1
1 Détente **2** Ayers Rock **3** Goran Ivanisevic **4** The eagle on the standard **5** Gibraltar **6** Paddy Ashdown **7** Martin Luther **8** Samuel Pepys **9** Nepal **10** Buckinghamshire **11** Norfolk **12** Malta **13** Last pitched battle on English soil **14** Oliver North **15** Bastille
PART 2
1 Stormont **2** John Redwood **3** Entebbe, Uganda **4** Leslie Ash **5** Arhcbishop of Canterbury **6** Latimer **7** Von Hindenburg **8** William Bligh **9** Gregorian calendar **10** Christine Keeler
Tie-breaker Jamie Theakston and Jayne Middlemiss

QUIZ 111
PART 1
1 Ipswich **2** Trent **3** Perth **4** York **5** Portsmouth **6** The Beatles – it was the venue for their early concerts **7** Edinburgh **8** Glasgow **9** Contemporary art **10** Exeter and Plymouth **11** Salisbury **12** St Albans **13** Southampton **14** Torquay **15** The Royal Yacht *Britannia*
PART 2
1 Brighton **2** Preston **3** Oxford **4** York **5** Bath **6** Cambridge **7** Hereford **8** Liverpool **9** Hull **10** Birmingham **11** Bath **12** Telford **13** Warwick (just checking if you're paying attention!) **14** Bradford **15** Edinburgh *Tie-breaker* Yorkshire (North Riding)

QUIZ 112
PART 1
1 Chris Evans **2** Charlotte Church **3** Arthur Miller. The others all married Elizabeth Taylor, he married Marilyn Monroe **4** Daniella Westbrook **5** Lisa-Marie Presley **6** Sean Penn **7** Will Carling **8** Aaliyah **9** Helena Bonham-Carter **10** Frank Sinatra **11** George Harrison **12** Nicole Kidman **13** Katie Holmes **14** Kevin Kline **15** Sinead Cusack
PART 2
1 E **2** P **3** M **4** K **5** H **6** L **7** I **8** N **9** J **10** C **11** B **12** D **13** A, **14** F **15** G.
Tie-breaker "You mean, other than my own?"

QUIZ 113

PART 1

1 David and Victoria Beckham **2** Mel Gibson **3** Prince Charles **4** George Michael **5** He threw a broken telephone at a hotel employee **6** Group Captain Peter Townsend **7** Ant (Anthony McPartlin) **8** Prince Andrew **9** Actress Kelly Preston **10** Michael Jackson's **11** Robert Downey, Jr. **12** Grant Bovey **13** Jane Fonda **14** Angus Deayton **15** The Rat Pack

PART 2

1 L **2** O **3** N **4** A **5** M **6** D **7** K **8** J **9** B **10** C **11** E **12** H **13** F **14** G **15** I

Tie-breaker Dwight Yorke, Dane Bowers

QUIZ 114

PART 1

1 Goldie Hawn **2** Diana Rigg **3** Debbie Reynolds **4** Liza Minnelli **5** Shirley MacLaine **6** Her father, Francis Ford Coppola, directed it **7** Charlie Sheen and Emilio Estevez **8** Clive Allen **9** Stuart Broad (Chris) **10** Joan Fontaine **11** Kirsty Gallagher (Bernard) **12** Jamie Lee Curtis **13** Stella McCartney **14** Paul Ince **15** Sajid Mahmood

PART 2

1 D **2** J **3** A **4** H **5** P **6** N **7** L **8** C **9** M **10** F **11** K **12** G **13** B **14** E **15** I

Tie-breaker Len Hutton (Richard) and Colin Cowdrey (Chris)

QUIZ 115

PART 1

1 18 **2** Boxer Rebellion **3** St Basil's Cathedral **4** Indonesia **5** Furniture **6** Rio de Janeiro **7** Granada **8** Ambrose Bierce **9** London Metropolitan Commissioner of Police **10** Cuba **11** New Zealand **12** (Black Hole of) Calcutta **13** Read the news **14** North invaded South **15** Isabel Peron

PART 2

1 Lord Palmerston **2** Earl of Beaconsfield **3** Edward Heath **4** George Canning **5** Hilda **6** Huyton **7** True: the last was Stanley Baldwin **8** Harold Wilson **9** Winston Churchill **10** Herbert Asquith **11** Abolition of slavery **12** Spencer Perceval **13** Andrew Bonar Law **14** Anthony Eden **15** Singer and actor, Tony Booth ***Tie-breaker*** He admitted his party lied to the electorate in order to win power.

QUIZ 116

PART 1

1 The McDonald's 'M' **2** Labour **3** Dingbat **4** Tottenham Hotspur **5** Swastika **6** College of Arms **7** Do not bleach **8** Do not tumble dry **9** By a red crescent. **10** Amnesty International **11** Site of a battlefield **12** The panda **13** Chanel **14** Aries **15** Lance Corporal

PART 2

1 Austria **2** Japan **3** Ireland **4** Italy **5** Poland **6** Canada **7** Finland **8** Sweden **9** Greece **10** Vietnam ***Tie-breaker*** Gold background with two horizontal black stripes.

QUIZ 117

PART 1

1 River Clyde **2** John Smith **3** Jim Baxter **4** Billy Connolly **5** 74: 1890 to 1964 **6** Just over 5 million **7** The Scottish flag **8** 37 **9** Ben Nevis **10** Murrayfield **11** Dunblane massacre **12** Stephen Hendry **13** Donald Dewar **14** Clydesdale Bank **15** National Trust For Scotland

PART 2

1 Aviemore **2** Andrew Murray **3** *Macbeth* **4** Adam Smith **5** Charles Kennedy **6** St Kilda **7** Ally McLeod **8** Sir William Wallace **9** Aberdeen **10** A cannon **11** Ayr **12** Fife **13** Sir Walter Scott **14** Crieff **15** Gavin and Scott Hastings ***Tie-breaker*** Allan Wells, the US sprinters did not compete due to a boycott

QUIZ 118

PART 1

1 Silvio Berlusconi **2** Copyright Act **3** Elba **4** Francois Duvalier **5** Outside the Libyan Embassy **6** Paul Revere **7** Salisbury **8** Nerve gas **9** Tanzania **10** Netherlands **11** Hellespont, Lord Byron **12** Simon De Montfort **13** Elton John **14** Liberace **15** Her skirts billowed and parachuted her to safety. She lived into her eighties.

PART 2

1 Stalin **2** The Duke of Edinburgh **3** Robert Dudley, Earl of Leicester **4** Rachel Hunter **5** The Bronte Sisters **6** Oliver Cromwell **7** Nehru **8** Duke Ellington **9** Sir Anthony Wedgwood-Benn (Tony Benn) **10** Colonel Qadaffi ***Tie-breaker*** Paris

QUIZ 119

PART 1

1 Liza Minnelli **2** Westminster Abbey **3** Timothy Dalton **4** Mark Twain **5** Sheriff Pat Garrett **6** River Ouse **7** Sir Alan Sugar **8** Sandra Rivett **9** India **10** They shot themselves **11** Peter (Mark Andrew) Phillips **12** Hamlet **13** Ralf Schumacher **14** John Cleese **15** She is stabbed by Don José

PART 2

1 Ewan McGregor **2** George Eastman **3** The Isle of Man (Douglas) **4** William Wordsworth **5** Suffolk **6** George Bernard Shaw **7** Boris Becker **8** 1924 **9** Malaga, Spain **10** Kylie Minogue **11** Tina Turner **12** Carol Vorderman **13** Lahore **14** Catherine Howard (Henry VIII's fifth wife) **15** Trier **Tie-breaker** Robbie Williams

QUIZ 120

PART 1

1 M4 **2** Settle **3** Thames Estuary **4** The Wash **5** Chilterns **6** M8 **7** Leeds and Manchester **8** Peterborough **9** False, the wall runs from Carlisle to Newcastle, the border from Gretna to Berwick **10** Dartford Tunnel **11** Severn Estuary **12** Medway **13** Anglesey **14** M6 **15** Scilly Isles

PART 2

1 Shetland Islands **2** Manchester **3** Lincoln **4** Winchester **5** Ipswich **6** Liverpool **7** Cambridge **8** Aberdeen **9** Jersey **10** Bristol **Tie-breaker** Sussex (West), Surrey, Berkshire, Wiltshire, Dorset

QUIZ 121

PART 1

1 The Gettysburg Address **2** Abraham Lincoln, on 19 November 1863 **3** Spiro Agnew **4** One from: Theodore Roosevelt (1906) or Woodrow Wilson (1919), Jimmy Carter (2002) **5** Lyndon B Johnson **6** John Adams and Thomas Jefferson **7** He was the only bachelor President **8** Thirty-five **9** John F Kennedy **10** First Lady **11** Richard Nixon **12** Old Hickory **13** Ronald Reagan; he was 69 when elected in 1981 **14** Thomas Jefferson (the Declaration was approved by the Continental Congress on 4th July 1776) **15** Walker

PART 2

1 F **2** C **3** P **4** A **5** J **6** I **7** H **8** G **9** K **10** D **11** N **12** M **13** B **14** L **15** E **Tie-breaker** November, every 4 years

QUIZ 122

PART 1

1 Yellow **2** Bronx **3** Rudolph Giuliani **4** *The Day After Tomorrow* **5** CBGB's **6** Statue of Liberty **7** *On The Town* **8** *Fame* **9** 'Fairytale of New York' (The Pogues and Kirsty MacColl) **10** *The Factory* **11** *Breakfast at Tiffany's* **12** *When Harry Met Sally* **13** Yankees and Mets **14** Manhattan **15** Times Square

PART 2

1 Wall Street **2** Coney Island **3** The Chrysler Building **4** Max's Kansas City **5** Freedom Tower **6** The Dutch; it was previously known as New Amsterdam. **7** John Carpenter **8** 381m (1250ft) **9** A flaming torch **10** *Bonfire Of The Vanities* ***Tie-breaker*** Forest Hills and Flushing Meadow

QUIZ 123

PART 1

1 Fred Trueman **2** A fish needs a bicycle **3** Margaret Thatcher **4** True: he held the title as Baron Tweedsmuir **5** Titus Oates **6** Sir Anthony Eden **7** Vladimir Putin **8** Russia **9** Slobodan Milosevic **10** Italy **11** Zulfiqar Ali Bhutto **12** Zimbabwe **13** Kuwait **14** British East India Company **15** Prince Philip, the Duke of Edinburgh

PART 2

1 Edmund Hillary **2** Mexico City **3** Anemones **4** Lincoln **5** William Hague **6** Lord Beaverbrook **7** Roald Amundsen **8** World Wildlife Fund **9** Nostradamus **10** Royal Academy **11** Hawaii **12** Wembley **13** Turkey **14** Poland **15** Denise Van Outen ***Tie-breaker*** Talleyrand

QUIZ 124

PART 1

1 Mayfair **2** When will you pay me? **3** Knightsbridge **4** Richard (Dick) Whittington **5** Treasures of Tutankhamun **6** Paddington **7** Somerset House on The Strand **8** Hyde Park **9** Edward The Confessor **10** Claude Monet **11** Imperial College **12** Canary Wharf Tower **13** Planetarium **14** Billingsgate **15** Law

PART 2

1 Ralph McTell **2** Green Park **3** Almeida **4** Regent Street **5** Berkeley Square **6** Inns of Court **7** St Pancras **8** Cambridge **9** The Clash **10** Southwark **11** Victoria Embankment **12** Vaughan Williams **13** Whitechapel **14** Lambeth Palace **15** Fulham ***Tie-breaker*** National Gallery, British Museum, London Eye, Tate Modern, Tower of London, Natural History Museum

Science and nature

QUIZ 125
PART 1
1 Brassica **2** A plant **3** Partridge **4** Hinny **5** Amaryllis **6** Marsupials **7** *Tales of the Riverbank* **8** Formic acid **9** Diane Fossey **10** Taxonomy **11** Otter **12** Pine **13** False. Many animals including cows, horses and dogs can also suffer from sunburn. **14** (Fruit) Bat **15** Stoat
PART 2
1 F **2** I **3** H **4** G **5** J **6** C **7** E **8** A **9** D **10** B ***Tie-breaker*** Albatross

QUIZ 126
PART 1
1 Potassium **2** 1982 **3** CO_2 **4** Sublimation **5** Alfred Nobel **6** Sodium Chloride, NaCl **7** Noble gases **8** Carbon **9** Humphry Davy **10** Polymers **11** Chlorine, Sodium **12** Potions, Severus Snape **13** Waterproof clothing **14** Deep Blue **15** Fahrenheit
PART 2
1 H_2S, Hydrogen Sulphide **2** Bauxite **3** Schrodinger's Cat **4** Mercury **5** Viscosity **6** Star groups **7** Kinetic **8** Hormones **9** Lower **10** False. That is an isotherm. An isobar connects points of equal pressure. ***Tie-breaker*** Anemometer, Beaufort scale

QUIZ 127
PART 1
1 Ostrich **2** Hedgehog **3** True. **4** Ruminant **5** It has webbed feet **6** Nightingale **7** Bill Oddie **8** Eucalyptus **9** A snake **10** Rodent **11** Deadly nightshade **12** Galapagos Islands **13** Birds **14** By rubbing together its back legs **15** Two
PART 2
1 A radish is a root vegetable, the others are herbs **2** A dingo is a wild dog, the others are species of antelope **3** Carbon is an element, the others are minerals **4** A lynx is a big cat, the others are birds **5** An alpaca is a mammal (similar to a llama), the others are fish **6** A gopher is a rodent, the others are all primates **7** Pine trees are evergreen, the others are deciduous **8** Fool's cap is a highly toxic mushroom, the others are edible **9** Turnip is a root vegetable, the others are all from the alium family **10** A gannet is a sea bird, the others are wading birds ***Tie-breaker*** Rosie's Larder

Answers - Science and nature

QUIZ 128
PART 1
1 Rhododendron **2** Container gardening **3** Topiary **4** Hydroponics **5** 1968 **6** Lancelot
7 *Gardeners' Question Time* **8** Chelsea Flower Show **9** Tomatoes **10** They are bell-shaped
11 Pergola **12** Honesty **13** Sissinghurst **14** It is the invasive plant also known as bindweed
15 Highly acidic
PART 2
1 Allotment **2** Henry David Thoreau **3** Lawnmower **4** Organic **5** Andrew Marvell **6** Peter
Seabrook (1976–1990) **7** Hidcote Manor **8** *Ground Force* **9** *Joseph Paxton* **10** *Percy Thrower*
Tie-breaker Gertrude Jekyll

QUIZ 129
PART 1
1 Prime number **2** Isaac Newton **3** Trigonometry **4** Pythagoras' Theorem **5** 22.5. **6** Calculus
7 Cone or pyramid **8** Probability **9** Perfect numbers **10** 11 (total = 96, divide by 6)
11 12 (lowest is 6, highest 30, split the difference) **12** 8 **13** Isosceles **14** Rhombus **15** X
PART 2
1 72 **2** 72 **3** 247 **4** 29 **5** 73 **6** 213 **7** 71 **8** 148 **9** 26 **10** 9 ***Tie-breaker*** 115

QUIZ 130
PART 1
1 206 **2** The aorta **3** False: it is of the intestines **4** Short-sightedness **5** The armpit
6 The humerus **7** Hydrochloric **8** Deltoid muscle **9** Epstein-Barr virus **10** The tongue
11 German measles **12** Canines, incisors and molars **13** Vitiligo **14** Blood vessels
15 Oestrogen and progesterone
PART 2
1 The liver **2** Maxilla (upper) and mandible (lower) **3** True: although smiling is more beneficial to
one's well-being, in fact, frowning uses more muscles **4** 10,000 million **5** The foot: the hallux is
the big toe **6** Femoral (upper thigh) and inguinal (groin) **7** Mouth diseases **8** Tooth enamel
9 Gluteus maximus **10** Magnetic resonance imaging **11** The pupil **12** A nose bleed
13 Hypotension **14** Rhinoplasty **15** The ulna ***Tie-breaker*** A hiccup

QUIZ 131

PART 1

1 Apollo 11 **2** John Glenn **3** Gemini **4** 2003, Lt Col Yang Li-wei **5** Alan Shepard **6** Carbon Dioxide **7** The stratosphere **8** Sirius, the Dog Star **9** *Challenger* **10** Jupiter **11** Jupiter and Mars **12** Astronomer Royal **13** A comet **14** Hubble Space Telescope **15** Nebula

PART 2

1 Pluto **2** Cosmology **3** *Mir* **4** *Apollo 13* **5** Yuri Gagarin **6** Canada **7** Paris **8** Cape Canaveral **9** Speed of light **10** Archer *Tie-breaker* Parsec

QUIZ 132

PART 1

1 C **2** H **3** I **4** J **5** E **6** B **7** F **8** A **9** G **10** D

PART 2

1 H **2** C **3** E **4** I **5** B **6** J **7** D **8** G **9** F **10** A *Tie-breaker* Woodpeckers

QUIZ 133

PART 1

1 Weather **2** 78% **3** Quark **4** Dry ice **5** True. **6** Mendeleyev **7** W **8** Joule **9** Two **10** Hydrogen, the others are all noble gases **11** Ullage **12** Marie Curie **13** Diffraction **14** Washing-up liquid or any detergent **15** The radius

PART 2

1 Copper **2** True. **3** Michael Faraday **4** Albert Einstein **5** False, hydrogen is the lightest element **6** Fire **7** Silica **8** Pressure **9** During sleep, it is eye movement of the "waking sleep" stage **10** Vitamin K *Tie-breaker* Coprolite

QUIZ 134

PART 1

1 *Friends* **2** *Blue Peter* **3** Wire fox terrier **4** The Egyptians **5** Hobbes (in Calvin and Hobbes) **6** Dr Samuel Johnson **7** Lassie **8** Macavity **9** Dodie Smith **10** *Alien* and *Aliens* **11** The tale of Dick Whittington **12** The dog licence scheme was abandoned **13** Desmond Morris **14** Great Dane **15** Garfield

PART 2

1 H **2** D **3** G **4** J **5** I **6** C **7** B **8** A **9** F **10** E *Tie-breaker* The Cheshire Cat and Alice's pet, Dinah

QUIZ 135
PART 1
1 Baltic Sea **2** Mount McKinley **3** Strait of Gibraltar **4** France and Switzerland **5** New Zealand **6** Mersey **7** Adriatic **8** Pangaea **9** Lancashire and Yorkshire **10** Sri Lanka **11** Mongolia **12** Emerald **13** Lake Victoria **14** Mediterranean **15** The Alps
PART 2
1 Italy **2** United Kingdom **3** Angola **4** Saudi Arabia **5** Japan **6** Corsica **7** Iran **8** India **9** China **10** Norway **11** Brisbane **12** Los Angeles **13** Amsterdam **14** Venice **15** Chicago
Tie-breaker Libya, (El Azizia, 58°C)

QUIZ 136
PART 1
1 Anthill **2** Herbs **3** Stamen **4** St Francis of Assisi **5** Wren **6** Hermit crab **7** Grasshoppers (specifically short-horned) **8** Pennyroyal **9** A duck **10** Fish (eel) **11** False. Male ducks also quack, but in a different and quieter tone. **12** Ross **13** Otter **14** A shark **15** Linseed oil
PART 2
1 Fawn **2** Elver **3** Squab **4** Leveret **5** Cub **6** Piglet **7** Lamb **8** Kitten **9** Calf **10** Duckling **11** Fry **12** Tadpole **13** Poult **14** Foal **15** Joey *Tie-breaker* molluscs

QUIZ 137
PART 1
1 Windows XP **2** X-Box **3** Apple Computers **4** Dell **5** Napster **6** Eight **7** InDesign **8** iTunes **9** Amazon.com **10** FORTRAN **11** Microsoft Access **12** Google **13** COBOL is a computer language, the others are operating systems **14** Ethernet **15** lastminute.com
PART 2
1 Internet Service Provider **2** Graphics Interchange Format **3** Internet Service Provider **4** Uniform Resource Locator **5** Digital Video Express **6** America OnLine **7** Integrated Services Digital Network **8** bits per second **9** Local Area Network **10** CD re-writable **11** Wireless Access Point **12** Short Message Service **13** Hewlett-Packard **14** Transmission Control Protocol **15** Structured Query Language *Tie-breaker* USB, Universal Serial Bus

QUIZ 138

PART 1

1 Badger **2** 1804 **3** Chitin **4** Newts **5** Dragonfly **6** Busy lizzie **7** *Daktari* **8** Mole
9 Gypsophila **10** The Americas **11** A girl **12** RSPB **13** Narwhal **14** Meerkats **15** Kestrel

PART 2

1 Italy **2** Pacific **3** Isle of Man **4** A dry African wind **5** Kent **6** Don **7** Khyber Pass **8** Lake
Superior **9** Bay of Bengal **10** Kilimanjaro **11** Lanzarote (Canary Islands) **12** Kalahari
13 Caribbean **14** Iceland **15** Chile *Tie-breaker* Beneath the earth, it is the boundary of
the mantle round the core of the earth

QUIZ 139

PART 1

1 Tin **2** 1834 **3** Hologram **4** Gabriel Fahrenheit **5** On the moon, they are craters
6 Technicolour **7** Frequency of sound **8** Newton's First Law of Motion **9** (Guglielmo) Marconi
10 Red **11** Refracting telescope **12** Samuel Crompton **13** Nitrous Oxide **14** Lysozyme
15 Charles Goodyear

PART 2

1 Nobel Prize **2** Electrical resistance or impedance **3** Benjamin Franklin **4** 14 **5** Thirty-five
6 Wheatstone Bridge **7** Second Law of Thermodynamics **8** Quicklime **9** See in the dark
10 A steam locomotive *Tie-breaker* The vacuum flask

QUIZ 140

PART 1

1 Hedwig **2** Professor McGonagall **3** Dorothy in *The Wizard of Oz* **4** E.T. **5** Their mittens
6 Cocker spaniel **7** Greyfriars Bobby **8** Antonio Banderas **9** *Call of the Wild* **10** Mogget
11 Figaro **12** Tobey Maguire **13** Hairy Maclary **14** Dr Johnson **15** Top Cat (or Boss Cat)

PART 2

1 K-9 **2** Deputy Dawg **3** Mr Jinx **4** Gobbolino **5** Doctor Dolittle **6** Copper **7** Humphrey
8 George **9** Obelix in the Asterix stories **10** Andrex toilet roll **11** Blofeld **12** Mrs Slocombe
('s pussy) **13** Denis The Menace **14** Spike **15** Speckled Jim *Tie-breaker* Green and Pink

QUIZ 141

PART 1

1 Loch Lomond **2** Yosemite **3** Seychelles **4** K2 **5** Turkey **6** Africa **7** Australia **8** Gale force **9** Canada **10** Hudson **11** Indonesia **12** Asia and North America **13** Greenland **14** The Caspian Sea in Russia **15** Loire

PART 2

1 ram or billie/doe or nannie **2** boar/sow **3** jack/jenny **4** buck/doe **5** drake/duck **6** cob/pen **7** ram/ewe **8** boomer/flyer **9** stallion/mare **10** reynard or dog or todd/vixen **11** dog/bitch **12** cock/hen **13** tiercel/falcon **14** boar/sow **15** tom/hen ***Tie-breaker*** FitzRoy

QUIZ 142

PART 1

1 Houseman **2** Pregnancy and birth **3** Dr Christiaan Barnard **4** Wetting the bed **5** German measles **6** Nose bleed **7** Tuberculosis **8** St John's Wort **9** A sexually transmitted disease **10** Epilepsy **11** Migraine **12** Hayfever **13** Ear, nose and throat **14** In a test tube **15** Ligature

PART 2

1 An anaesthetist **2** When he or she becomes a consultant **3** Cancer **4** Heel **5** Skin **6** High blood pressure **7** Short-sighted with a squint **8** Feet **9** Chicken pox **10** Ticks **11** Hippocratic **12** Fyes **13** Acupuncture **14** MRSA **15** Leukaemia ***Tie-breaker*** Gender change

QUIZ 143

PART 1

1 Sahara **2** Maize **3** Kiwi **4** Lurchers **5** Earthquakes **6** Butterflies **7** Chile **8** Grey squirrel **9** Cave **10** Condor **11** Nasturtium (Tropaeolum) **12** 8 **13** Minerals **14** 12th Century **15** Birds

PART 2

1 G **2** D **3** J **4** A **5** H **6** C **7** F **8** I **9** E **10** B ***Tie-breaker*** It attaches itself to floating driftwood, thus traversing the seas in the migratory manner of a goose.

Sports and pastimes

QUIZ 144

PART 1

1 Fifteen **2** Pasadena, California **3** Greg Lemond **4** Doncaster **5** Winter Olympics
6 Leon Spinks **7** Pippa Funnell **8** The reserve crews of Cambridge and Oxford rowing clubs
9 Larry Holmes **10** American Football **11** Uruguay **12** Harlem Globetrotters **13** Katy Sexton
14 Karate **15** Wasps

PART 2

1 G **2** I **3** D **4** H **5** A **6** B **7** J **8** E **9** F **10** C **Tie-breaker** Sir Stanley Rous,
Joao Havelange

QUIZ 145

PART 1

1 Ian Thorpe **2** Daley Thompson **3** Romania **4** Atlanta **5** Beijing, China **6** Al Oerter
7 True, through Lynn Davies and Mary Rand **8** Faster Higher Stronger **9** Tessa Sanderson
10 Emil Zatopek in 1952 **11** Stephanie Cook **12** Cassius Clay (Muhammad Ali scores one
point only) **13** Sailing **14** Mary Peters **15** Bettina Hoy

PART 2

1 Cycling **2** Equestrian, 3-Day Event (Team) **3** Boxing **4** Athletics, 4 x 100 metres relay **5** Lawn
Tennis **6** Hockey **7** Boxing **8** Cycling **9** Shooting **10** Swimming (200 metres breaststroke)
11 Athletics, 400 metres hurdles **12** Sailing **13** Cycling **14** Rowing **15** Boxing
Tie-breaker Kathy Freeman, 400 metres

QUIZ 146

PART 1

A John Arlott **B** Baseball Ground **C** Fabio Cannavaro **D** Dawn Run **E** Pat Eddery
F Feyenoord **G** Sally Gunnell **H** Naseem Hamed **I** Inzamam-ul-Haq **J** Colin Jackson
K Kingsholme **L** Lions **M** Lothar Matthaus **N** Jack Nicklaus **O** Jay-Jay Okocha **P** Nelson
Piquet **Q** Jason Queally **R** Brian Robson **S** David Speedie **T** Taekwon-do **U** Underwood
V Jean Van De Velde **W** Ian Woosnam **Y** York City **Z** Zaheer Abbas **Tie-breaker** Bradman,
Sobers, Hobbs, Warne, Richards

QUIZ 147
PART 1

1 Matthew Pinsent **2** Polo **3** Repechage **4** 1877 **5** First woman cox to steer a winning boat race crew **6** Muhammad Ali **7** Kentucky Derby **8** Tracy Edwards **9** False, it was his father, Julio **10** Foot and mouth disease **11** Kathy Cook **12** Jason Leonard **13** Arthur Ashe **14** Michael Lynagh **15** Guinness

PART 2

1 Sailing yacht **2** Bath **3** Steelers **4** Table tennis **5** No 7 **6** Squash **7** Augusta National **8** He became the first black champion **9** Croquet **10** Zara Phillips, Toytown ***Tie-breaker*** Ray Reardon, Terry Griffith, Mark Williams

QUIZ 148
PART 1

1 Pele **2** Luis Figo **3** Peter Schmeichel **4** Garrincha **5** Hugo Sanchez **6** Roberto Baggio **7** Gheorghe Hagi **8** Gabriel Batistuta **9** AC Milan **10** Lev Yashin **11** Dino Zoff **12** Brian and Michael Laudrup **13** Ruud Gullit **14** Diego Maradona **15** Franz Beckenbauer

PART 2

1 G **2** C **3** D **4** I **5** A **6** L **7** M **8** B **9** K **10** N **11** J **12** F **13** H **14** O **15** E ***Tie-breaker*** Carlos Alberto, 4-1

QUIZ 149
PART 1

1 Australia **2** Lake Coniston **3** On the M1 **4** Howard Hughes **5** Concorde jets, one from London, one from Paris **6** 1858 **7** Aeroflot **8** Fly non-stop round the world **9** Amy Johnson **10** Hot-air balloon **11** Louis Bleriot **12** Ladbroke Grove, just outside Paddington **13** Michael O'Leary **14** Preston **15** Heathrow Airport

PART 2

1 Emirates **2** Cherbourg in Brittany **3** Pullman **4** Donald Campbell **5** Blue Train **6** 1,523 **7** (HMHS) *Britannic* **8** GWR (Great Western Railways) **9** KLM **10** Glasgow ***Tie-breaker*** Moscow and Beijing

QUIZ 150

PART 1

1 Douglas Jardine **2** Len Hutton **3** Darren Gough **4** Bob Massie **5** Fred Spofforth **6** Ray Illingworth **7** John Snow **8** Jeff Thomson **9** Stan McCabe **10** Gilbert Jessop **11** David Gower **12** 19 **13** Chris Broad **14** Jim Laker **15** 13

PART 2

1 Kevin Pietersen **2** Glenn McGarth **3** Michael Kasprowicz **4** Brett Lee **5** Caught Jones, bowled Harmison **6** Michael Vaughan **7** Ricky Ponting **8** Simon Jones **9** Andrew Flintoff **10** Jason Gillespie **11** Gray Pratt **12** Andrew Strauss **13** Ashley Giles **14** Andrew Flintoff **15** Justin Langer ***Tie-breaker*** Forty

QUIZ 151

PART 1

1 Coca-Cola **2** Gillingham **3** Accrington Stanley **4** Colchester United **5** Nottingham Forest **6** Burnley **7** Port Vale **8** Leeds United (1992) **9** Hull City **10** Bristol Rovers **11** Barry Fry **12** Queens Park Rangers; Fulham shared their ground whilst Craven Cottage was upgraded **13** Cambridge United **14** Blackpool **15** Jim Magilton

PART 2

1 Brighton and Hove Albion **2** Mansfield Town **3** Blackpool **4** Grimsby Town **5** Sunderland **6** Brentford **7** Northampton Town **8** Oldham Athletic **9** Ipswich Town **10** Derby County **11** Huddersfield Town **12** Cardiff City **13** Luton Town **14** Norwich City **15** Bury ***Tie-breaker*** Bristol City have the badge, Swindon Town, Wrexham United

QUIZ 152

PART 1

1 Phil Mickelson **2** Harry Vardon **3** Nick Faldo **4** Bernhard Langer **5** Wentworth **6** Kiawah Island **7** Nick Price **8** Annika Sorenstam **9** Nick Faldo **10** Tony Jacklin **11** 9 **12** Lee Westwood **13** Laura Davies **14** Valderrama in 1997 **15** Paul McGinley

PART 2

1 Lee Trevino **2** Bobby Jones **3** Ernie Els **4** Bob Charles, of New Zealand, in 1963 **5** Walter Hagen **6** Ben Curtis **7** Hoylake **8** Muirfield **9** Justin Leonard **10** Mike Weir **11** Vijay Singh **12** True. He was in the 1999 team, but scarcely used **13** Peter Thomson **14** Tony Jacklin **15** Sam Torrance ***Tie-breaker*** Gary Player, Ernie Els, Retief Goosen

Answers - *Sports and pastimes*

QUIZ 153
PART 1
1 Polo **2** Pony **3** Martingale **4** A canter **5** Lungeing **6** Black and white mix **7** Mallenders
8 Point-To-Point **9** Chaps **10** Siena, Italy **11** Badminton Horse Trials **12** *Animal Farm*
(George Orwell) **13** Palomino **14** Pullein-Thompson **15** The Byrds
PART 2
1 D **2** G **3** B **4** I **5** F **6** A **7** J **8** E **9** H **10** C *Tie-breaker* Merrylegs and Ginger

QUIZ 154
PART 1
1 Italy **2** Miguel Indurain **3** Basketball **4** Decathlon **5** Fencing **6** Nine **7** Jack Brabham
8 Desert Orchid **9** Scotland **10** England and West Indies **11** Lennox Lewis **12** Greyhound
racing **13** Gold **14** Judo **15** Francois Pienaar
PART 2
1 E **2** I **3** J **4** G **5** F **6** H **7** D **8** B **9** C **10** A *Tie-breaker* *Freedom* and *Stars and
Stripes*

QUIZ 155
PART 1
1 Martin Peters **2** Graham Taylor in 1994 **3** Paolo Rossi **4** Senegal **5** Bulgaria **6** Gary Lineker,
in 1986 **7** Archie Gemmill **8** Italy, in 1994 **9** False; they made it in 1958, the only occasion all four
Home Nations appeared **10** Gerd Muller **11** Peter Shilton **12** South Korea **13** Peru
14 Argentina, in 1990 **15** Bryan Robson
PART 2
1 Montevideo, Uruguay **2** Mussolini **3** Pele **4** Italy and Chile **5** Just Fontaine **6** Grzegorz Lato
7 1958, Brazil 5 Sweden 2 **8** Jack Taylor **9** Berti Vogts **10** False. Fritz and Ottmar Walter played
for West Germany in 1954 **11** Turkey **12** Lothar Matthaus **13** Jack Charlton **14** David Platt
15 David Beckham *Tie-breaker* Laurent Blanc, Franck Leboeuf

QUIZ 156

PART 1

1 Greg Rusedski, US Open, 1997 **2** Betty Stove **3** True. She won the 1976 French Open **4** Helen Wills-Moody **5** Andre Agassi **6** French Open **7** Brazil **8** Sixteen **9** Billie Jean King **10** Justine Henin-Hardenne **11** Jana Novotna **12** Cedric Pioline **13** Steffi Graf **14** None of them won Wimbledon **15** Monica Seles

PART 2

1 Clive Woodward **2** American Football **3** Mary Decker **4** Edward Heath **5** It embraced professionalism **6** Excess alcohol! **7** Toronto Blue Jays **8** 'The Rumble In The Jungle' **9** Ellen MacArthur **10** Hank Aaron **11** Greyhound tracks **12** Steve Cauthen **13** Jan Ullrich **14** Australia **15** Best Mate ***Tie-breaker*** Mark Woodforde and Todd Woodbridge

QUIZ 157

PART 1

1 (Edmond) Hoyle **2** William Steinitz **3** Noughts and Crosses **4** Nigel Short **5** (Professor) Plum **6** The Crafty Cockney **7** Trivial Pursuit **8** Thirty six **9** Three **10** Spades **11** 144 **12** Cribbage **13** Marbles **14** Three of a kind **15** Thirty

PART 2

1 Sudoku **2** Automatic award when a player is dealt a hand with no picture cards. **3** Hungary **4** Bridge **5** Jelle Klaasen **6** Bobby Fischer **7** Boris Spassky **8** Anatoli Karpov **9** Risk **10** Ten **11** Hide-and-Seek **12** Quadrille **13** Cryptic **14** Poker **15** Tiddlywinks ***Tie-breaker*** $1 + 3 + 1 + 1 + 3 + 6 (2x3) + 1 + 1 = 17 \times 2 = 34 + 50$ for using all of your tiles $= 84$

QUIZ 158

PART 1

1 1984 **2** No it wasn't, it was Marc Rosset! **3** The US boycotted the Moscow Games, and the Soviets reciprocated in LA **4** Yachtsman Ben Ainslie **5** Vancouver, Canada **6** The Eight **7** Wrestling **8** Lennox Lewis **9** Gail Emms **10** Denise Lewis in the heptathlon **11** Bob Beamon **12** Carl Lewis **13** London **14** Richard Meade **15** Great Britain

PART 2

1 Ben Johnson **2** China **3** Taekwondo **4** Cook and Merry **5** Kate Howey **6** Alain Baxter **7** Venus and Serena Williams, Venus **8** Munich in 1972 **9** Dick Fosbury **10** David Hemery **11** Edwin Moses **12** Nigeria **13** Franz Klammer **14** Roger Black **15** Tennis ***Tie-breaker*** John Curry and Robin Cousins

Answers - *Sports and pastimes*

QUIZ 159
PART 1
1 The Oval **2** Dennis Lillee **3** Kapil Dev **4** Mahela Jayawardene and Kumar Sangakarra **5** 1971
6 Sunil Gavaskar **7** Greg Chappell **8** Allan Border in 1987 **9** Mike Gatting **10** Joel Garner
11 Cambridge **12** Antigua **13** Anil Kumble **14** Brian Close **15** Grant and Andy Flower
PART 2
1 Darryl Hair **2** Keith Miller **3** India **4** Ramadhin and Valentine **5** True, because he never
played against South Africa **6** Richie Benaud **7** Northamptonshire **8** Frank Tyson **9** Yousuf
Youhana **10** Kolkota (Calcutta), India **11** Alan Donald **12** Shakoor Rana **13** India, in 1983
14 Graeme Smith **15** Marcus Trescothick ***Tie-breaker*** Lance Klusener, Herschelle Gibbs

QUIZ 160
PART 1
1 Ferrari (replica Daytona then a Testarossa) **2** Bugatti Veyron **3** 14mph **4** Pontiac Trans-Am
5 Chrysler **6** Ferrari Daytona **7** Lamborghini **8** Pininfarina **9** Christine **10** Richard Burns
11 Jensen V8 Interceptor **12** Lola **13** Aston-Martin **14** Saleen **15** General Lee
PART 2
1 Detroit **2** In a plane crash (he was the pilot) **3** Grand Prix **4** Lotus Elan **5** John Surtees
6 Isle of Man **7** False: Juan Pablo Montoya won in 2000 **8** Miami Beach, Florida **9** Melbourne
10 Tom Kristensen ***Tie-breaker*** Ellen MacArthur

QUIZ 161
PART 1
1 Arsenal in 2003-04 **2** Brian Deane **3** Kevin Keegan **4** Fulham, Blackburn, Bolton
5 Manchester United **6** Charlton Athletic **7** George Burley of Ipswich Town **8** Andreas
Johansson **9** Alan Shearer and Chris Sutton **10** Seven **11** Robbie Fowler **12** West Bromwich
Albion **13** Swindon Town **14** Reading **15** 15
PART 2
1 H **2** E **3** G **4** J **5** I **6** L **7** C **8** O **9** D **10** F **11** M **12** N **13** K **14** B **15** A
Tie-breaker 11

QUIZ 162

PART 1

1 Steve Redgrave **2** Homer Simpson **3** Oscar Wilde **4** Harry Carpenter **5** John McEnroe
6 George Foreman **7** Pele **8** Maria Sharapova **9** Steve Ovett **10** Murray Walker
11 Tim Henman **12** Bill McLaren **13** Paula Radcliffe **14** Jack Nicklaus **15** Geoff Boycott

PART 2

1 Bill Shankly **2** Mark Lawrenson **3** Alf Ramsey at the end of full-time in the World Cup Final,
1966 **4** Paul Gascoigne **5** John Motson **6** Brian Clough **7** Eileen Drewery **8** Garth Crooks
9 Carlton Palmer **10** Roy Keane's autobiography **11** Ian Holloway, then of QPR **12** Kevin
Keegan **13** Eric Cantona **14** Tommy Smith **15** Gordon Strachan *Tie-breaker* There is
no town called Raith. Raith Rovers play in Kirkcaldy

QUIZ 163

PART 1

1 Gilles Villeneuve **2** Alfa Romeo **3** Tommi Makinen **4** Imola, San Martino **5** Juan Manuel
Fangio **6** Carl Fogarty **7** Benetton-Ford **8** 113 **9** Brands Hatch **10** Speedway GP **11** A top six
finish in a Formula One Grand Prix (Spain, 1975) **12** Barry Sheene **13** Michael Doohan
14 Valentino Rossi **15** Alain Prost

PART 2

1 Jonny Wilkinson **2** Man of the Match in the Superleague Final **3** False, it was his father, Julio
4 Luxembourg **5** Zara Phillips **6** Rowing (coxless pair) **7** Sean Fitzpatrick **8** Istabraq
9 Baseball **10** A.P. McCoy *Tie-breaker* Middleweight

QUIZ 164

PART 1

1 The Grand National **2** Frankie Dettori **3** Prix de L'Arc de Triomphe **4** Breeder's Cup
5 Shergar **6** Gordon Richards **7** Godolphin **8** Champion Hurdle **9** The Queen **10** York
11 Kieron Fallon **12** Cancelled after two false starts **13** Leopardstown **14** Eleven
15 Starting stalls

PART 2

1 E **2** N **3** J **4** H **5** L **6** F **7** M **8** D **9** P **10** K **11** C **12** I **13** B **14** A **15** G
Tie-breaker Epsom Oaks and 1,000 Guineas

QUIZ 165

PART 1

1 Real Madrid **2** Benfica **3** Chelsea **4** Jose Mourinho **5** Johann Cruyff **6** Valencia **7** Arsenal and Leeds United **8** Olympique Marseille **9** Wayne Bridge **10** Alfredo Di Stefano and Ferenc Puskas **11** Athens (Olympic Stadium) **12** Patrick Kluivert **13** Sol Campbell in 2006 **14** Bobby Charlton **15** SV Hamburg and Borussia Dortmund

PART 2

1 Tottenham Hotspur **2** Lazio **3** Gianfranco Zola **4** Galatasaray **5** CSKA Moscow **6** Henrik Larsson **7** Dundee United **8** Ipswich Town **9** Inter-Cities Fairs Cup **10** Wolves **11** Alex Ferguson **12** Middlesbrough **13** Dinamo Kiev **14** Rangers **15** Liverpool never won the Cup Winner's Cup **Tie-breaker** Liverpool, Nottingham Forest, Aston Villa

QUIZ 166

PART 1

1 Kelly Holmes **2** Jesse Owens **3** Mark Spitz **4** United States **5** None **6** Alpine skiing **7** Lasse Viren **8** Snowboarding **9** Shooting **10** Canada (Montreal) **11** Lillehammer, in 1994 **12** New Zealand **13** Cassius Clay **14** Ski Jump **15** German Democratic Republic (East Germany)

PART 2

1 M **2** E **3** K **4** F **5** A **6** I **7** B **8** L **9** H **10** P **11** D **12** N **13** C **14** J **15** G
Tie-breaker Riding, shooting, fencing, swimming, cross country (running)

QUIZ 167

PART 1

1 Alastair Cook **2** Jacques Kallis **3** Brian Lara **4** Nathan Astle **5** Sheffield Shield **6** Garfield Sobers **7** Derek Randall **8** Mark Waugh **9** Matthew Hoggard **10** Kerry Packer **11** Ian Botham **12** Heath Streak **13** Daniel Vettori **14** Fred Trueman **15** Alan Knott

PART 2

1 Hampshire **2** Nottinghamshire **3** Essex **4** Northamptonshire **5** Nottinghamshire **6** Kent **7** Gloucestershire **8** Middlesex **9** Surrey **10** Lancashire **11** Sussex **12** Warwickshire **13** Worcestershire **14** Hampshire **15** Leicestershire **Tie-breaker** Wasim Akram, Waqar Younis

Mixed bag

QUIZ 168

1 Neo **2** Jennifer Paterson and Clarissa Dickson-Wright **3** Goneril, Regan, Cordelia **4** Belgrade, Bratislava, Budapest, Vienna **5** Queens, Bronx, Manhattan, Brooklyn, Staten Island **6** Mansfield Park, Northanger Abbey, Emma, Pride and Prejudice, Sense and Sensibility, Persuasion **7** Pride, Envy, Wrath, Sloth, Avarice, Gluttony, Lust **8** Britain, US, Russia, France, Japan, Canada, Germany, France, Italy **9** Netherlands, Belgium, Luxembourg, France, Switzerland, Austria, Czech Republic, Poland, Denmark **10** Churchill, Brunel, Princess Diana, Darwin, Shakespeare, Isaac Newton, Queen Elizabeth I, John Lennon, Nelson, Cromwell **11** Alabama, Florida, Georgia, Louisiana, Mississippi, South Carolina, Texas; followed by Arkansas, North Carolina, Tennessee and Virginia **12** Snake, Horse, Sheep, Monkey, Rooster, Dog, Pig, Rat, Ox, Tiger, Rabbit, Dragon

QUIZ 169

1 Carl Lewis **2** Boris Becker, Michael Stich **3** Clyde Walcott, Frank Worrell, Everton Weekes **4** Arsenal, Liverpool, Manchester City, Bolton Wanderers, Chelsea **5** Kenny Dalglish, Jom Leighton, Alex McLeish, Pauyl McStay, Tom Boyd **6** Wally Hammond, Len Hutton, Ken Barrington, Denis Compton, Jack Hobbs, Herbert Sutcliffe **7** Alan Shearer, Andrew Cole, Thierry Henry, Robbie Fowler, Les ferdinand, Teddy Sheringham, Jimmy Floyd Hasselbaink **8** Mike Hawthorn, Graham Hill, Jim Clark, John Surtees, Jackie Stewart, James Hunt, Nigel Mansell, Damon Hill **9** Jason Gallian, John Crawley, Andrew Flintoff, Mike Watkinson, Warren Hegg, Chris Schofield, Saj Mahmood, James Anderson, Peter Martin **10** 100 metres; 400 metres; 1,500 metres; 110m hurdles; long jump; high jump; pole vault; discus; javelin; shot put **11** David Seaman, Gary Neville, Sol Campbell, Tony Adams, Graeme Le Saux, David Beckham, Paul Ince, Paul Scholes, Darren Anderton, Michael Owen, Alan Shearer **12** David Howell, Paul Casey, Luke Donald, Sergio Garcia, Colin Montgomerie, Henrik Stenson, Robert Karlsson, Padraig Harrington, Paul McGinley, Jose-Maria Olazabal, Darren Clarke, Lee Westwood

Answers - Mixed bag

QUIZ 170

1 Chesney Hawkes **2** Born on the 4th of July, Jerry Maguire, Magnolia **3** Bull Durham, Field of Dreams, For Love Of The Game **4** Reservoir Dogs, Pulp Fiction, Jackie Brown, Kill Bill, Kill Bill Volume 2, Death Proof **5** Tony Blackburn, Phil Tufnell, Kerry McFadden, Joe Pasquale, Carol Thatcher **6** Phoebe, Monica, Rachel, Joey, Ross, Chandler **7** The Magician's Nephew, The Lion, The Witch and The Wardrobe, Prince Caspian, The Voyage of The Dawn Treader, The Silver Chair, A Horse And His Boy, The Last Battle **8** Spencer Tracy, Fredric March, Gary Cooper, Marlon Brando, Dustin Hoffman, Tom Hanks, Jack Nicholson, Katharine Hepburn **9** Waterloo, Mamma Mia, Fernando, Dancing Queen, Knowing Me Knowing You, The Name of the Game, Take A Chance On Me, The Winner Takes It All, Super Trouper **10** Waltz, Quickstep, Ballroom Tango, Foxtrot, Viennese Waltz, Cha Cha Cha, Rumba, Jive, Paso Doble, Samba **11** The Man Who Sold The World, Ziggy Stardust, Hunky Dory, Aladdin Sane, Pin-Ups, Diamond Dogs, Young Americans, Station To Station, Low, Heroes, Lodger **12** *The Lord of the Rings, Pride and Prejudice, His Dark Materials, Hitch-hiker's Guide To The Galaxy, Harry Potter and the Goblet of Fire, To Kill A Mockingbird, Winnie-the-Pooh, Nineteen Eighty-four, The Lion The Witch and the Wardrobe, Jane Eyre, Catch-22, Wuthering Heights*

QUIZ 171

PART 1

1 Eighty **2** Sheree Murphy **3** Oxford Committee for Famine Relief **4** Knesset **5** Boxing Day **6** National Trust **7** Freemasons **8** Venice **9** Tennessee **10** Gordon Brown, the PM always holds this post **11** 'The Fly' **12** *Abba Gold* **13** Margaret Beckett **14** Carol Thatcher **15** Ashley Cole

PART 2

1 New Zealand **2** Lech Walesa **3** Peter Snow **4** False, he went to Harrow **5** Stars and Bars **6** The Labour landslide of 1945 **7** Hay-on-Wye **8** Four **9** One hundred **10** Amsterdam **11** English villages **12** David Bowie **13** Algeria **14** Mafia **15** False; he scored, but for Real Madrid ***Tie-breaker*** ballroom

QUIZ 172

PART 1

A Arachnida **B** Bucharest **C** The Clones Cyclone **D** Raoul Dufy **E** Esperanto **F** Lucien Freud **G** Gamete **H** Hickory **I** Intermezzo **J** Jerome K Jerome **K** Karachi **L** Leadbelly **M** Maelstrom **N** Nova Scotia **O** Milton Obote **P** Kevin Pietersen **Q** Niall Quinn **R** Anderson Montgomery Everto Roberts **S** Sayonara **T** Tenko **U** Derek Underwood **V** Virginal (music) **W** John Wesley **Y** Yale **Z** Zealots (historically) ***Tie-breaker*** Mike Wilks

QUIZ 173

PART 1

1 *Rocky Horror Picture Show* **2** Taurus **3** Northampton **4** Editor of The Sun **5** Bloody Sunday **6** Mali **7** Josip Broz (Marshal Tito) **8** Liquorice Allsorts **9** Denmark **10** Garibaldi **11** Iran **12** Paul Gauguin **13** Georgia **14** Florida **15** All appear on £20 notes

PART 2

1 J **2** E **3** H **4** A **5** L **6** D **7** G **8** K **9** M **10** P **11** I **12** C **13** N **14** B **15** F

Tie-breaker Cher, *Moonstruck*

QUIZ 174

PART 1

1 A butterfly **2** *Gone With The Wind* **3** China **4** Scaffold **5** Louisiana **6** The Scarlet Pimpernel **7** Aldo Moro **8** Central Line **9** Purple **10** Wales **11** Scarlet Fever **12** Gay Pride **13** Bordeaux **14** Nena **15** Red Hot Chili Peppers

PART 2

1 Raspberry **2** Leeds United **3** International Red Cross **4** Mick Hucknall **5** *The Red Badge of Courage* **6** UB 40 **7** Red sky in the morning **8** Jack Ruby **9** Scarlett Johansson **10** Hampshire **11** Lady Marmalade **12** Robin Hood **13** Ferrari **14** Gules **15** Joanna Lumley

Tie-breaker Red Marauder, ridden by Richard Guest, in 2001

QUIZ 175

PART 1

1 Digital Versatile (or Video) Disc **2** NASA (National Aeronautics and Space Administration) **3** Special Air Service **4** Ministry for Agriculture, Fisheries and Food **5** Digital Audio Broadcasting **6** Teaching (English as a Foreign Language) **7** That they have a science degree (Batchelor of Science) **8** Personal Equity Plan **9** Women's Royal Naval Service **10** GCHQ **11** European Monetary System **12** John Lewis Partnership **13** University of California Los Angeles **14** A vet (Fellow of the Royal College of Veterinary Surgeons) **15** A journalist (National Union of ......)

PART 2

1 BBC **2** Children's Welfare **3** Be a farmer **4** Drive a heavy goods vehicle **5** Internet Service (provider) **6** District Attorney **7** Social Democratic Party **8** A musician (London Symphony Orchestra) **9** Repetitive Stress (or Strain) Injury **10** Grievous Bodily Harm **11** e.g. (exempla gratia) **12** ANC (African National Congress) **13** Point-of-Sale **14** Statutory Sick Pay **15** Trade and Industry *Tie-breaker* A Member of the Order of the British Empire

Answers - *Mixed bag*

QUIZ 176
PART 1
1 The Moors Murders **2** Carl Bridgewater **3** Peter Sutcliffe **4** Harold Shipman **5** Dr Hawley Crippen **6** He reprieved all 167 inmates on Death Row in Illinois prisons **7** Soham **8** Charles Manson **9** 10, Rillington Place **10** Son of Sam **11** Gary Gilmore, the following year **12** Ronnie and Reggie **13** Charlie Richardson **14** Fred West **15** Jeffrey Dahmer
PART 2
1 Slade **2** 307 **3** Broadmoor **4** Manchester **5** Derek Bentley **6** Jeffrey Archer **7** True, he got three months **8** First conviction using DNA **9** Duncan Ferguson **10** Long Kesh
Tie-breaker Hare testified against his partner in crime, who was executed.

QUIZ 177
PART 1
1 Black Monday **2** Bill Gates **3** Walmart **4** *Wall Street Journal* **5** Checking account **6** Bundesbank **7** Cameras **8** Lire **9** Dilbert **10** True **11** His Master's Voice, the company's original slogan **12** The Guardian **13** One pound and one shilling **14** Easy-jet **15** Lloyd-George
PART 2
1 Income tax **2** Barings **3** Confederation of British Industry **4** 1891 **5** Fort Knox in Kentucky **6** Enron **7** Lend-Lease **8** Wall Street Crash **9** 1966 **10** Midland Bank ***Tie-breaker*** Nikkei and Hang Seng

QUIZ 178
PART 1
1 William V **2** Mason-Dixon line **3** Patsy Cline **4** Korea **5** Edinburgh **6** Indira Gandhi **7** Thomas More **8** York **9** The Sermon On The Mount **10** Jarvis Cocker **11** Lanzarote **12** Francis Ford Coppola **13** Basketball **14** Marmalade **15** Gene Hackman
PART 2
1 April 1st **2** 23 **3** King James' Bible **4** A nautical mile **5** Longleat **6** Robert Kilroy-Silk **7** Veritas **8** John Constable **9** Colombo **10** Martin Luther King **11** Attorney General **12** Nylon stockings **13** Sarah Brightman **14** Farthing **15** Robin Knox-Johnston
Tie-breaker Opal Fruits, Starburst

QUIZ 179

PART 1

1 Matthew Kelly **2** Yellow **3** Jamie Oliver **4** Orlando **5** Edward Elgar **6** Jeffrey Archer **7** Singapore **8** Eamon de Valera **9** Ayatollah Khomeini **10** 1979 **11** The Avengers **12** 1649, on the execution of Charles I **13** Hara kiri **14** Volga, Caspian **15** Agnetha Faltskog

PART 2

1 Brian Clough **2** Learie Constantine **3** Tasmania **4** A hat **5** Ibrox, home of Glasgow Rangers **6** Peter Sissons **7** Palace of Westminster **8** The Chiltern Hundreds **9** Peter Pears **10** Thursday **11** (Candido) Jacuzzi **12** A child that is born on the Sabbath day **13** *Tomorrow's World* **14** Donald Woods **15** Tony Booth ***Tie-breaker*** Sir James Goldsmith, David Mellor

QUIZ 180

PART 1

A African National Congress **B** Botswana **C** Chiton **D** Duma **E** Eros **F** C.S.Forester **G** GI (health) **H** Lord Haw-Haw **I** IVF **J** Jarrow Marches **K** Akira Kurosawa **L** Sophia Loren **M** Mossad **N** Natation **O** Georgia O'Keeffe **P** Port Salut **Q** Quetzal **R** Reflexology **S** Monica Seles **T** TGWU **U** Under Milk Wood **V** Valium **W** Whippoorwill **Y** YWCA **Z** Warren Zevon ***Tie-breaker*** Seventh century BC

QUIZ 181

PART 1

1 Richard Branson **2** Alan Sugar **3** Twentieth Century Fox **4** F.W. Woolworth **5** Sunday Times **6** Tobacco **7** As the lady dragon on *Dragon's Den* **8** John Harvey-Jones **9** Land's End **10** Nottingham **11** Lloyd's of London **12** Harold Macmillan **13** Donald Trump **14** Exchange Rate Mechanism **15** Marks and Spencer

PART 2

1 G **2** F **3** I **4** E **5** B **6** C **7** A **8** D **9** J **10** H ***Tie-breaker*** NASDAQ

Answers - Mixed bag

QUIZ 182

PART 1

1 Idi Amin **2** HMS *Belfast* **3** Stamford Bridge **4** Venice **5** (Samuel) Colt **6** Wine **7** Alaska **8** John Stonehouse **9** Solheim Cup **10** Mecca **11** Sierra Nevada **12** Seventeenth **13** Carl Orff **14** Ulrike Meinhof **15** Honeydukes

PART 2

1 Kilimanjaro - the others are all active **2** Ronnie Corbett (the others were all Goons) **3** Portia; the others are King Lear's daughters **4** *The Glass In the Smoke*, the others are the three parts of Phillip Pullman's *His Dark Materials* trilogy **5** Moldova; the others are former Soviet states, now Republics, on the Baltic coast. **6** Ricky Gervais; the others were all regulars on *The Fast Show* **7** Callaghan; the others led the Labour Party but never served as Prime Minister **8** Stelios; the others are the Three Musketeers, Stelios plays for Bolton Wanderers! **9** Misery; the others, along with War, are the Four Horsemen of the Apocalyse **10** Joe Strummer; the others are the members of The Jam - Strummer was singer with The Clash ***Tie-breaker*** Rugby League, Wigan

QUIZ 183

PART 1

1 Che Guevara **2** Simone De Beauvoir **3** Salvation Army **4** Footlights **5** *1812 Overture* **6** Tasmania **7** Kirov Ballet **8** Mont Blanc **9** Anthony Wedgwood-Benn (Tony Benn) **10** John and Charles Wesley **11** The Long March **12** Islas Malvinas **13** The Algarve **14** Shirley Williams **15** White

PART 2

1 Forty **2** Insulin **3** Wales **4** Kent **5** John Smith **6** Rome **7** 'The Eve of St Agnes', which falls on that day **8** Tehran **9** Australia, it is Australia Day, when the first colony was officially founded in 1788 **10** Florida **11** Sally Clark **12** Labor Day **13** Passover (Pesach) **14** All made cities as part of the Golden Jubilee **15** *Amoco Cadiz* ***Tie-breaker*** *Madama Butterfly*, Milan

QUIZ 184

PART 1

1 Twenty-one **2** Gleneagles **3** Seraphim **4** On the moon **5** Serpent **6** Order of the Garter **7** Liver **8** Cherries **9** London School of Economics **10** Thomas Hardy **11** Uffington **12** F-Plan **13** False: The FBI is internal, the CIA looks after foreign affairs **14** Sinn Fein **15** Canada Day

PART 2

1 Pennyroyal **2** 99 **3** Coca-Cola **4** Mount Rushmore - they are the four presidents carved into the rock **5** Potatoes **6** Bay of Pigs **7** Miranda Richardson **8** Timothy McVeigh **9** Algonquin **10** Good Friday **11** Sir Charles Barry **12** Ottoman Empire **13** Sinn Fein **14** Mormons **15** Exxon Valdez ***Tie-breaker*** Eiger

QUIZ 185
PART 1
1 J **2** N **3** E **4** F **5** M **6** L **7** I **8** P **9** B **10** D **11** H **12** K **13** A, **14** G **15** C
PART 2
1 I **2** A **3** E **4** M **5** J **6** H **7** C **8** B **9** N **10** K **11** O **12** F **13** D **14** L **15** G
Tie-breaker Canberra. It has its own Capital State (the Australia Capital Territory), to preserve neutrality

QUIZ 186
PART 1
1 Hindu **2** Geneva **3** Sikhism **4** Ron L Hubbard **5** Buddhism **6** Islam **7** Months in the Jewish calendar **8** Jehovah's Witnesses **9** Qu'ran **10** Kosher **11** Zoroastrianism **12** All Saint's Day **13** To Mecca **14** Gautama Siddhartha **15** John Wycliffe
PART 2
1 Roman Catholicism **2** Shahadah **3** Buddhism **4** Qu'ran **5** The skullcap worn by Jewish males **6** An earlier prophet **7** 1st Muharram, Year 1 – the first year of the Muslim calendar **8** Sikhism **9** Abu-Bakr **10** Nirvana **11** Palm Sunday **12** His daughter **13** Jainism **14** Ganges **15** Salvation Army ***Tie-breaker*** Twelfth Night

QUIZ 187
PART 1
A Armadillo **B** Bhutan **C** Joseph Conrad **D** D'Artagnan **E** Exoskeleton **F** Frank Finlay **G** Gallowgate **H** Hiawatha **I** Impeachment **J** Mick Jagger **K** Gustav Klimt **L** *Lusitania* **M** Monte Carlo **N** David Niven **O** Oregano **P** Pomegranate **Q** Quakers **R** Christopher Reeve **S** Soda (or Sodium Carbonate) **T** Titania **U** Ulster Unionist Party **V** Vasectomy **W** Wise Men **Y** *Young Ones* **Z** Zico ***Tie-breaker*** Exeter City, The Grecians

QUIZ 188
PART 1
1 Edinburgh **2** Stanley Matthews **3** Taffeta **4** Paul Lawrie **5** Black and white **6** Botany Bay **7** Andrew Murray **8** Elizabeth I **9** Coventry **10** Sunflower **11** Martin Peters **12** Coffee **13** They were invaded by the US **14** Adam Smith **15** Charles De Gaulle
PART 2
1 Hampshire **2** Staffordshire **3** Lincolnshire **4** Lancashire **5** Buckinghamshire **6** East Sussex **7** Wiltshire **8** Yorkshire **9** Cornwall **10** Cumbria **11** Essex **12** West Glamorgan **13** Warwickshire **14** Nottinghamshire **15** Tyne and Wear ***Tie-breaker*** Elizabeth Barrett Browning

Answers - *Mixed bag*

QUIZ 189

PART 1

1 Beowulf **2** Thirteen and three quarters **3** Fine Young Cannibals **4** Menelaus **5** Glencoe **6** Charles Lindbergh **7** Herbert Asquith and David Lloyd George **8** Red Rum **9** Globe **10** Chuck Yeager **11** Montgolfier Brothers **12** General Franco **13** Albus **14** Friedrich Engels **15** John Terry

PART 2

1 Whipsnade **2** Playing cards **3** Israel **4** Father's Day **5** Luxembourg **6** Mineworkers' Union **7** Los Angeles **8** Hallée **9** New Orleans **10** Cheltenham (Ladies College) **11** Great Ormond Street **12** Syria **13** 90 **14** The Women's Institute **15** Big Ben ***Tie-breaker*** Kenneth Clarke

QUIZ 190

PART 1

1 Hallowe'en, 31st October **2** China **3** 1969 **4** Diwali **5** Rosh Hashanah **6** Oktoberfest **7** Columbus Day **8** Gandhi **9** Thanksgiving **10** *Babette's Feast* **11** Wassail Cup **12** Hannukah **13** Hootenanny **14** Bachelor Party **15** Ramadan, the month of fasting

PART 2

1 Epiphany **2** Best Man **3** Kool and The Gang **4** A birthday **5** Bat or Bar (B'nai) Mitzvah **6** Love Parade **7** Passover **8** July **9** Masks **10** New York ***Tie-breaker*** Dave Stewart and Barbara Gaskin

QUIZ 191

PART 1

1 A legion **2** Katarina Witt **3** Modesty Blaise **4** Arteries, aorta **5** Biggles **6** Pig **7** Buckingham Palace **8** Bathsheba **9** Scheherezade **10** Brendan Behan **11** Hiawatha **12** Bats **13** Robbie Williams **14** A.S.Byatt **15** Thomas Gainsborough

PART 2

1 Botticelli **2** Sunderland **3** Munchausen's Syndrome **4** Airey Neave and Lord Mountbatten **5** Clive Ponting **6** 1948 **7** Andy Warhol **8** Herbert Chapman **9** Kofi Annan **10** Caribou **11** Hanse Cronje **12** *Today* **13** Jesuits **14** Boer Wars **15** Lewis Carroll ***Tie-breaker*** Thomas Arne

QUIZ 192
PART 1

1 James Brown **2** Tea **3** Sweetcorn **4** Brownshirts **5** Netherlands **6** 'Yellow' **7** Roald Dahl's *Charlie and The Chocolate Factory* **8** Joni Mitchell **9** John Brown **10** London **11** *Final Fantasy (VI)* **12** Indigo Girls **13** Yellow Pages **14** Green Day **15** Rodgers and Hart

PART 2

1 Peter Sellers **2** Robert Green **3** Deep Purple **4** South Africa **5** Green room **6** Seville **7** Woody Allen **8** Claret and Blue **9** Pink **10** Khaki ***Tie-breaker*** Dulux

QUIZ 193
PART 1

1 Last Monday in May **2** *Goon Show* **3** Photography **4** 58 dead Chinese people **5** Familiar or famulus **6** Kenneth Williams **7** Bosun **8** Barrels **9** Velvet Revolution **10** Pony Express **11** The Sky At Night **12** 1938 **13** Parliament **14** The first Oxford English Dictionary **15** Greece

PART 2

1 Subpoena **2** Loire, Bay of Biscay **3** Chicago **4** Nikolai Ceaucescu **5** Torvill and Dean **6** Foxhunting **7** Uruguay, Montevideo **8** Cheeses **9** Bangladesh **10** Thomas Cranmer **11** The World Cup **12** Coliseum **13** Senegal **14** Bosphorus **15** Bertrand Russell ***Tie-breaker*** Surrey Quarry

QUIZ 194
PART 1

1 'Rule Britannia' **2** Alzheimer's disease **3** Dry for most of the year **4** Lady Jane Grey **5** Bali **6** Rupert the Bear **7** Legendary racing greyhound **8** 1990 **9** Cherie Blair **10** Cyprus **11** 1666 **12** Colorado **13** Salt (sodium chloride) **14** Eye **15** Rand

PART 2

1 J **2** I **3** G **4** K **5** L **6** M **7** H **8** N **9** D **10** B **11** P **12** C **13** F **14** E **15** A ***Tie-breaker*** Nancy Barbato, Ava Gardner, Mia Farrow, Barbara Marx

Answers - Mixed bag

QUIZ 195

PART 1

1 President Sadat of Egypt **2** Moonies **3** Roger Bannister **4** Mike Flowers Pops **5** Alexander Solzhenitsyn **6** Ceylon (now Sri Lanka) **7** Alf Garnett (in *'Til Death Us Do Part*) **8** Herald of Free Enterprise **9** La Scala **10** David Walliams **11** Charles Darwin **12** Treaty of Rome **13** Chechens **14** Gilbert and Sullivan **15** First player to be sent off in an FA Cup Final

PART 2

1 Tracey Emin **2** DNA **3** Be elected Pope **4** Tiffany's **5** Emmett's Peachy; the others are apples **6** Jesse James **7** Bob Dylan **8** Moscow and Vladivostok **9** Jeroboam **10** Magna Carta **11** Lord Chamberlain **12** She became the first Briton in space **13** Saigon **14** Kilt **15** Allende *Tie-breaker* Groovy Greeks and Vicious Vikings

QUIZ 196

PART 1

1 Sirius Black **2** Black Rod **3** Black Flag **4** Black September **5** Black Dahlia **6** Black Widow **7** Black and Tans **8** Black Caps **9** Jack Black **10** Black-Eyed Peas **11** Black-Eyed Susan **12** Black Russian **13** *The Woman In Black* **14** *Black Hawk Down* **15** 'Black Coffee'

PART 2

1 White Stripes **2** Jimmy White **3** Mont Blanc **4** Craig White **5** Raymond Blanc **6** *White Men Can't Jump* **7** *White Fang* **8** Barry White **9** Michael Caine **10** *Snow White* **11** *Charlotte's Web* **12** White Paper **13** Laurent Blanc **14** 'White Wedding' **15** The White Peacock
Tie-breaker Juventus, Notts County

QUIZ 197

PART 1

A Battle of Austerlitz **B** Charles Baudelaire **C** Cambrian age **D** Gottlieb Daimler **E** Etymology **F** Fauvism **G** Geiger Counter **H** Hansard **I** Innsbruck **J** Lionel Jospin **K** Klondike **L** Lorraine **M** Madonna **N** Henri Nestle **O** Martin O'Neill **P** Plantagenets **Q** Vidkun Quisling **R** Theodore Roosevelt **S** Senegal **T** Shirley Temple **U** Uzbekistan **V** Vandals **W** Wounded Knee **Y** Yugoslavia **Z** Franco Zeffirelli *Tie-breaker* Cyrillic

QUIZ 198

PART 1

1 Queen's Christmas message **2** King's College, Cambridge **3** Site of the UK's first atom bomb test **4** Four: The three Christmas ghosts and the ghost of his former work partner Jacob Marley. **5** 'White Christmas' **6** 'Mary's Boy Child' **7** Russia **8** 1998 **9** Kriss Kringle **10** Norway

PART 2

1 E **2** C **3** I **4** P **5** M **6** L **7** F **8** D **9** N **10** A **11** B **12** H **13** J **14** K **15** G
Tie-breaker Holiday Inn (1942), Irving Berlin

QUIZ 199

PART 1

1 Shergar **2** Loretta Lynn **3** Gutenberg Bible **4** Emma, Lady Hamilton **5** Ulrika Jonsson **6** Dinner jacket **7** Thorax **8** Barbados **9** Jeremy Paxman **10** Uma Thurman **11** Los Angeles to Amsterdam **12** Spain **13** Zeus **14** France **15** Perestroika

PART 2

1 *The Belgariad* was written by David Eddings, the others are all by Tolkien **2** Khalid Boulahrouz; the others left Chelsea in Summer, 2006, he joined **3** Hoover; the other three were assassinated **4** Jodie Marsh – the others were all in Celebrity Big Brother in 2006 **5** David Steel was not a member of the Gang of Four who started the SDP **6** Desmond Tutu, others were all Secretary-General of the UN **7** GOCAL is just rubbish, the others are computer languages **8** Lisa Tarbuck, the others were all members of *Smack The Pony* **9** Colin Jackson; the others won Olympic Gold medals **10** Owen Hargreaves; the others all missed their penalties against Portugal in the 2006 World Cup **Tie-breaker** Romania and Bulgaria

QUIZ 200

PART 1

1 Christina Aguilera **2** Batman **3** Evonne Goolagong-Cawley in 1980 **4** Butler to Diana, Princess of Wales **5** Old Uncle Tom Cobbleigh **6** Darlington **7** Gary Speed **8** Lake Geneva **9** He is the narrator **10** Black Sea **11** Darwin **12** Milan **13** Sam Allardyce **14** Bounty **15** Thutmose II

PART 2

1 CO_2 **2** *The Beggar's Opera* **3** Anglesey **4** Straits of Gibraltar **5** Virginia Wade **6** Al Qaeda **7** Louis Pasteur **8** Salad **9** Escudo **10** King Arthur **11** Watergate **12** Witney **13** The Spanish Inquisition **14** Anna Friel **15** Kieran Fallon **Tie-breaker** Lithuania, Belarus, Ukraine

QUIZ 201

PART 1

A Asuncion **B** Roger Bannister **C** Monica Coghlan **D** Doge's Palace **E** ETA **F** Federico Fellini **G** Ginkgo **H** Hary Houdini **I** IMF **J** Juvenal **K** Kremlin **L** Lotte Lehmann **M** Mosquito Coast **N** Nicosia **O** Omnivore **P** Joan Plowright **Q** Carlos Queiroz **R** Sonny Rollins **S** Seoul **T** Tempura **U** Ulan Bator **V** Eddie Van Halen **W** Karol Wojtyla **Y** Yakuza **Z** ZZ Top **Tie-breaker** 1244

QUIZ 202
PART 1
1 Yasser Arafat 2 Ashford 3 Blackhead 4 Wat Tyler 5 Libya 6 Haggis 7 Habitat 8 Alf Common (Middlesbrough) 9 Sudetenland 10 Hungary 11 Francis Chichester 12 Jacob 13 Anders Celsius 14 The goat 15 Paris

PART 2
1 John Fashanu 2 George Dawes (Matt Lucas of *Little Britain* fame) 3 John Thomson 4 *The Likely Lads* 5 Kenny Everett 6 Patricia Routledge 7 Sweep 8 Peter Firth 9 *Up Pompeii! (actually Further Up Pompeii!)* 10 Victoria Wood ***Tie-breaker*** Abbey, Liz, Ellie, Zoey

QUIZ 203
PART 1
1 Qantas 2 Sister-in-law 3 California 4 Ross and Norris McWhirter 5 Page 3 girls 6 Rouen 7 Women got the vote 8 It's an insect 9 Wicklow 10 With the tip of an umbrella 11 Kuwait 12 Mary Queen of Scots 13 Orient Express 14 Tim Rice 15 Davy Lamps

PART 2
1 Sir Frank Whittle 2 Sepoys 3 Mary Robinson 4 Cheshire Cat; he isn't present at the Mad Hatter's Tea Party 5 Charles Clarke 6 Istanbul 7 Terry Waite 8 Paris 9 Chernobyl 10 Christoper (Kit) Marlowe 11 Albatross 12 Hilaire Belloc 13 Sydney 14 Cape Town 15 Bertholt Brecht ***Tie-breaker*** Winter of Discontent

QUIZ 204
PART 1
1 David Mellor 2 Cecil Parkinson 3 *News of the World* 4 *Moulin Rouge* 5 A fletcher makes arrows 6 Gary Larson 7 *The Domesday Book* 8 BNP 9 Malta 10 In a theatre 11 Mary Westmacott 12 Mother Teresa 13 Figaro, he reappears in *The Marriage of Figaro* 14 Finland 15 Grenada

PART 2
1 Florence Nightingale 2 Winston Churchill 3 Andre Agassi 4 Ramadan 5 Suez Canal 6 Temperature 7 Oswald Moseley 8 Doppelganger 9 Mongolia 10 ££1.05 11 Pop Art 12 Vichy 13 St Augustine 14 Lot 15 Charles II ***Tie-breaker*** November

QUIZ 205
PART 1
A Asgard B Bobolink C Caerdydd D Dawes Plan E Existentialism F Flemish G Giotto H Oscar Hammerstein II I Iroquois J Jacobins K DeForest Kelley L Anders Limpar M Mangonel N Lough Neagh O Peter Ooterhuis P Peristalsis Q Dan Quayle R Retiarius S Streptococcus T Tamil Tigers U Uterus V VHF W Victoria Woodhull Y Yaounde Z Andoni Zubizaretta ***Tie-breaker*** 1930s

QUIZ 206

PART 1

1 Book of Revelations **2** Terminus **3** Graham Greene **4** The final whistle **5** 35 **6** *Edwin Drood*
7 *Armageddon* **8** Epilogue **9** River Phoenix **10** Andre Agassi **11** Douglas Adams
12 Gary Lineker **13** Samuel Beckett **14** 25 **15** Charlton Heston

PART 2

1 C **2** G **3** H **4** B **5** F **6** J **7** D **8** I **9** A **10** E ***Tie-breaker*** "I think this is the
beginning of a beautiful friendship."

QUIZ 207

PART 1

1 Marc Bolan **2** Michael Hutchence (lead singer of INXS) **3** Sassoon. Owen was killed in action a
week before the armistice; Brooke died of septicaemia in 1915. **4** She threw herself under the King's
horse (at the 1913 Epsom Derby). **5** Canterbury Cathedral **6** Ben Hollioake **7** Mark Chapman
8 Grand Hotel, Brighton **9** In his bath. **10** She gassed herself (using the oven in her kitchen).
11 Kurt Cobain's **12** Karen Carpenter **13** Billy the Kid (aka Henry McCarty; William H Bonney)
14 Brian Jones **15** Marc-Vivien Foe

PART 2

1 K **2** H **3** D **4** M **5** L **6** B **7** G **8** P **9** F **10** I **11** E **12** N **13** J **14** C **15** A
Tie-breaker Buddy Holly, Richie Valens and the Big Bopper